Problems and Solutions for Federal Income Taxation

Problems and Solutions for Federal Income Taxation

John A. Miller
WELDON SCHIMKE DISTINGUISHED PROFESSOR OF LAW
UNIVERSITY OF IDAHO COLLEGE OF LAW

Jeffrey A. Maine
MAINE LAW FOUNDATION PROFESSOR OF LAW
UNIVERSITY OF MAINE SCHOOL OF LAW

CAROLINA ACADEMIC PRESS
Durham, North Carolina

ISBN: 978-1-61163-063-3

Carolina Academic Press, LLC
700 Kent Street
Durham, North Carolina 27701
Telephone (919) 489-7486
Fax (919) 493-5668
www.cap-press.com
Printed in the United States of America

Contents

Foreword

The problems and solutions in this book can be used with any regular tax textbook to assist the student in learning federal tax law. This is because, in addition to a word index and a table of contents, this book contains tables that allow a student to access the appropriate problems and solutions by code section number, case name, treasury regulation or administrative pronouncement. Thus, for example, if you are studying like kind exchanges addressed by code section 1031, you need only look in the code section table to locate the problem set in this book that addresses that topic (Chapter 24). Similarly, if you are studying the assignment of income doctrine addressed by *Lucas v. Earl*, you need only look it up in the case table to find where that topic is addressed (Chapter 30). The chapter structure in this book correlates precisely to the chapters in our own casebook, THE FUNDAMENTALS OF FEDERAL TAXATION: PROBLEMS AND MATERIALS, but you do not need to use our casebook in order to fully utilize this book.

At the beginning of each problem set we include an overview of the material addressed in the set. We also list the primary authorities relevant to the topic. The student who wishes to test her or his abilities could use those primary materials to attempt to solve the problems before looking at our answers.

Problems and Solutions for Federal Income Taxation

Chapter 1

Introduction

Overview

In the United States, the federal government derives the bulk of its revenue from an income tax. A taxpayer's federal income tax liability for any given year is determined by applying the appropriate tax rates to the appropriate tax base. The tax base for all taxpayers (individuals, corporations, estates, and trusts) is *taxable income*, which is defined loosely as *gross income* minus allowable *deductions*. IRC § 63. Once a taxpayer's taxable income is calculated, the appropriate tax rates are applied. Section 1 provides the schedule of tax rates for all individuals as well as estates and trusts. Section 11 provides a different schedule of rates for corporations. Certain privately-held corporations (S corporations), partnerships, and other unincorporated entities (such as limited liability companies) are generally not subject to an entity tax as these business forms are flow-through entities. That is, their income and deductions flow through to the owners of the entities and are reported on their individual tax returns. If the owner is an individual, estate, or trust, section 1 tax rates apply; if the owner is a corporation section 11 tax rates apply. Once the applicable tax rates are applied to the taxpayer's taxable income, *credits* may be available to reduce the amount of tax due. In the table below, we offer a federal income tax computation overview.

Computational Overview of the Income Tax

  Pre-exclusions Gross Income
− Exclusions
  Gross Income
− Above-the-Line Deductions
  Adjusted Gross Income
− Standard Deduction or Itemized Deductions
− Personal Exemptions
  Taxable Income
× Tax Rates
  Gross Tax Liability
− Tax Credits
Net Tax Liability (or Refund)

Congress' power to levy taxes emanates from Article I, section 8, clause 1 of the United States Constitution (the "tax clause"). Certain technical complexities made it necessary to amend the constitution in order to impose a federal income tax. Thus, the modern income tax only came into existence after the enactment of the 16th Amendment in 1913. We have had a recent illustration of the breadth of the tax power in National Federation of Independent Business v. Sebelius, 132 S. Ct. 2566 (2012). There the Supreme Court relied on the tax clause to uphold the mandate in the Patient Protection and Affordable Care Act of 2010 that individuals must buy health insurance or make a payment to the Treasury in lieu of doing so.

The primary source of federal tax law is the Internal Revenue Code (the "Code"). The "section" is the basic unit in the Code. Sections are numbered sequentially, with breaks in sequence to provide room for new Code provisions to be added. Sections are divided into subsections. Subsections are divided into paragraphs. Paragraphs are divided into subparagraphs. Subparagraphs are divided into clauses and even subclauses.

The treasury regulations are the most important administrative interpretation of the Code, and should be part of any tax research. Congress granted general authority to the Treasury Department to promulgate regulations to interpret and give meaning to the Code. *See* IRC § 7805(a). Congress also delegated specific rule-making authority to the Treasury Department in certain Code sections. *See, e.g.*, IRC § 25A. As a result of the congressional grant of power, treasury regulations generally have the force and effect of law. But still they may not overrule the Code. In Mayo Foundation v. United States, 131 S. Ct. 704 (2011), the Supreme Court clarified the level of deference that courts should grant treasury regulations when they interpret an ambiguous Code provision. *Mayo Foundation* also clarified how general principles of administrative law may apply in the tax context by considering the application of Chevron, U.S.A., Inc. v. Natural Resources Defense Council, Inc., 467 U.S. 837 (1984).

The Internal Revenue Service (hereinafter "IRS" or "Service") issues interpretative pronouncements, called Revenue Rulings, which indicate the Service's official position regarding the application of tax law to a certain set of facts. Revenue Rulings are official interpretations published by the Service for information and guidance to taxpayers. Revenue Rulings are not as authoritative as regulations. Nevertheless, a Revenue Ruling can be relied upon by any taxpayer whose circumstances are substantially the same as those described in the ruling. The Service also issues Revenue Procedures, which typically are statements of its internal practices and procedures.

Three trial courts have original jurisdiction over tax cases: (1) the U.S. District Court; (2) the U.S. Claims Court; and (3) the U.S. Tax Court. The United States Tax Court is the only forum in which a taxpayer may litigate a disputed tax claim without first having to pay the asserted deficiency.

Primary Authority

Code: § 7805(a).

Regulations: None.

Cases: Chevron, U.S.A., Inc. v. Natural Resources Defense Council, Inc., 467 U.S. 837 (1984); Mayo Foundation v. United States, 131 S. Ct. 704 (2011); United States v. Home Concrete & Supply, LLC., 132 S. Ct.

1836 (2012). See also National Federation of Independent Business v. Sebelius, 132 S. Ct. 2566 (2012).

Rulings: None.

Problems

1.1 Flagship University employs many pre-doctoral fellows as full-time employees to teach freshman level classes and to do basic research in its laboratories. These pre-doctoral fellows are also students working on their Ph.D.'s in one of several disciplines including, biology, chemistry, engineering, and physics. Their compensation for their teaching and research activities includes tuition waivers for their doctoral studies. Federal law exempts "students" and their employers from paying certain payroll taxes (FICA). The statute does not define students. Recently, the Treasury Department issued a regulation categorically providing that anyone who is a full-time employee cannot qualify as a "student" for purposes of the payroll tax exemption.

> **(a) Flagship has come to you for advice on whether to contest the validity of the new regulation. What do you think of Flagship's chances to get a court to strike down the regulation?**

On the whole, the chances are not very good in light of the Supreme Court's decision in *Mayo Foundation v. United States.* On facts similar to these, the Court applied its analysis in *Chevron U.S.A., Inc. v. Natural Resources Defense Council, Inc.* to uphold the regulation. It began its analysis with the first step of the two-part framework announced in *Chevron,* and asked whether Congress has "directly addressed the precise question at issue" and found that it had not. The Court said "[t]he statute does not define the term 'student,' and does not otherwise attend to the precise question whether medical residents are subject to FICA. *See* 26 U.S.C. § 3121(b)(10)."

The Court then went on to reject Mayo's argument that the regulation must be struck down because it conflicted with the plain and ordinary meaning of the word "student." It proceeded to step two of *Chevron* "under which we may not disturb an agency rule unless it is 'arbitrary or capricious in substance, or manifestly contrary to the statute.'" The Court concluded "that the full-time employee rule easily satisfies the second step of *Chevron,* which asks whether the Department's rule is a 'reasonable interpretation' of the enacted text."

> **(b) Would it make any difference if the new regulation contradicts an earlier repealed but longstanding regulation that allowed exempt status to students who were also full-time employees?**

It seems doubtful. The Court down played the importance of past agency inconsistency in *Mayo* when it rejected applying the multi-factor analysis it had used to review a tax regulation in National Muffler Dealers Assn., Inc. v. United States, 440 U.S. 472 (1979). The Court came close to saying that *Chevron* supersedes *National Muffler.*

(c) Would it make any difference in (a) if the new regulation contradicts the legislative history of the statute in question?

Now we are in uncertain territory. In *United States v. Home Concrete & Supply, LLC*, a divided Supreme Court invalidated a regulation interpreting an admittedly ambiguous statute. The central ground for striking down the regulation was a plurality view that the legislative history was unambiguously counter to the regulation. However, the regulation in question sought to overrule a pre-*Chevron* Supreme Court decision and this factor was of key importance to the concurrence by Justice Scalia. There was no majority opinion in *Home Concrete*. The IRS appears to interpret *Home Concrete* to mean that pre-*Chevron* Supreme Court holdings cannot be overruled by regulation but that post-*Chevron* holdings can be overruled by regulation where the court's opinion indicates the statute is ambiguous. *See* Wilkins, *Butler Give Their Take in Home Concrete*, 135 Tax Notes 974 (May 21, 2012). The impact of legislative history that contradicts an otherwise valid tax regulation remains unsettled.

Chapter 2

Gross Income

Overview

The starting point for computing a taxpayer's tax liability is determining what is included in *gross income*. Section 61 of the Code defines gross income broadly as "all *income* from whatever source derived," and then lists types of receipts that are included in gross income. The list is extensive and includes common items, such as compensation for services. However, the list is not exhaustive, and it is necessarily preceded and supplemented by a catch-all clause that includes non-listed items that may be properly defined as *income*. There are other Code provisions that address particular items by including them or excluding them from gross income. There are also many regulations, cases, and rulings relevant to this topic. The problem set below illustrates many of the key principles that have emerged over time.

Case law has played a key role in our understanding of what constitutes gross income. In Eisner v. Macomber, 252 U.S. 189, 207 (1920), the Supreme Court first attempted to define income: "Income may be defined as the gain derived from capital, from labor, or from both combined." This definition of income clearly encompasses receipts derived from personal services and capital investments, but what about items not traceable to labor or to capital, such as windfalls (e.g., prizes, scholarships, or cash found in a taxi)? Should such receipts not be included within the scope of income merely because they are traceable to good fortune and not to labor or capital? In other words, should the source of receipts be relevant? The Supreme Court answered these questions and formulated a different concept of income for tax purposes in Commissioner v. Glenshaw Glass Co., 348 U.S. 426 (1955). In *Glenshaw Glass*, the Supreme Court defined income as "undeniable accessions to wealth, clearly realized, and over which taxpayers have complete dominion." As can be seen, the *Glenshaw Glass* definition of income is much broader than the *Macomber* definition. Although the statutory concept of gross income resembles the concept of economic income, the two are not always the same. *Realization* is generally a prerequisite to income for tax purposes. Moreover, for various policy reasons, there are statutory rules of exclusion as well as judicial and administrative exceptions that place further limits on the meaning of gross income.

Primary Authority

Code: § 61. Skim §§ 74-109.

Regulations: § 1.61-1, -2(a)(1), -2(d)(1), -2(d)(2)(i), -8(a)-(b), -14(a).

Cases: Cesarini v. United States, 296 F. Supp. 3 (N.D. Ohio 1969); Commissioner v. Glenshaw Glass Co., 348 U.S. 426 (1955); Old Colony Trust Co. v. Commissioner, 279 U.S. 716 (1929). See also Commissioner v. Daehler, 281 F.2d 823 (5th Cir. 1960); Eisner v. Macomber, 252 U.S. 189, 207 (1920); Gilbert v. Commissioner, 552 F.2d 478 (2d Cir. 1977); James v. United States, 366 U.S. 213 (1961).

Rulings: Rev. Rul. 65-254, 1965-2 C.B. 50; Rev. Rul. 75-271, 1975-2 C.B. 23; Rev. Rul. 79-24, 1979-1 C.B. 60; Notice 2012-75, 2012- 51 I.R.B. 1; Announcement 2002-18, 2002-1 C.B. 621.

Problems

2.1. **Bela Lugosi is a successful sales agent at a well-known stock brokerage firm. Which, if any, of the following items must Bela report as gross income?**

(a) **Bela received $100,000 in commissions. As an added bonus for his excellent performance, Bela also received from his employer an all-expenses paid trip to Miami for both he and his domestic partner worth $5,000.**

The $100,000 is included in Bela's gross income. Section 61(a)(1) specifically includes in gross income "compensation for services."

The bonus trip is also included in Bela's gross income. Treas. Reg. § 1.61-2(a) specifically lists bonuses as compensation income. Section 61 does not distinguish between cash and non-cash benefits. Indeed, the regulations under section 61 provide that gross income may be realized in any form, whether in money, property, or services. Treas. Reg. § 1.61-1(a). When non-cash benefits are involved, the fair market value of the benefits is the amount to be included. Treas. Reg. § 1.61-2(d)(1).

(b) **Bela was stranded on the highway during a hurricane and afterwards the National Guard evacuated him to safety by helicopter at a cost of $5,000. He was not billed for the service.**

This is an accession to wealth that is likely excluded from gross income under the general welfare exception set out in Rev. Rul. 75-271. "To qualify under the general welfare exclusion, the payments must (1) be made pursuant to a governmental program, (2) be for the promotion of the general welfare (that is, based on need), and (3) not represent compensation for services." Notice 2012-75.

(c) **Bela borrowed $5,000 from a local bank to repair his underinsured car after it was damaged in an accident. Shortly thereafter, Bela's employer paid off the loan because Bela was working at the time the car was damaged.**

Bela experienced no accession to wealth when he borrowed $5,000 because tax law recognizes his obligation to repay; thus, he had no income within the meaning of section 61 at the time of borrowing. Bela did, however, experience an accession to wealth when his employer paid off the loan and he realized $5,000 gross income at that time (compensation income within the meaning of section 61(a)(1)). *See Old Colony Trust Co. v. Commissioner. Old Colony*, which involved the payment of an employee's taxes by his employer, illustrates that gross income does not have to be received directly by the taxpayer.

> **(d) Bela bought a block of closely held stock from the estate of an unrelated third party for $75,000, which was its appraised value. In fact, the stock was worth $100,000 at the time of purchase. Because Bela acted as his own broker, he ultimately received a $5,000 commission from the seller.**

Bela seemingly experienced a $25,000 accession to wealth when he purchased the stock. Under a long-standing administrative exception, however, Bela will not have to report the benefit of the bargain at the time of purchase assuming the seller was not his employer. [Note: If he purchased the stock from his employer and there was a compensation element in the bargain, then Bela would have gross income. *See* Treas. Reg. § 1.61-2(d)(2).] The bargain element will be taxed when Bela later sells the stock (a realization event).

The $5,000 commission is included in Bela's gross income. IRC § 61(a)(1). Could Bela successfully argue that the commission is not income, but, instead, is a reduction in purchase price–part of the bargain purchase (i.e., he paid only $70,000, in effect, for the stock worth $75,000)? Such arguments have not met with success. *See, e.g., Commissioner v. Daehler.*

> **(e) Bela bought a small parcel of land. Shortly after the purchase, Bela discovered an antique diamond ring in the hollow of a tree on the property. The ring was worth $20,000. In addition, Bela had the land rezoned for multiple family dwellings which increased its value by $100,000.**

The diamond ring is considered treasure trove, included in gross income when reduced to undisputed possession. *See* Treas. Reg. § 1.61-14 and *Cesarini v. United States.* For an interesting article arguing that the treasure trove regulation is of doubtful validity, and that the finding of valuable property should not be a taxable event but rather should be treated as one kind of imputed income, see Lawrence A. Zelenak & Martin J. McMahon, Jr., *Taxing Baseballs and Other Found Property*, 84 TAX NOTES 1299 (August 30, 1999).

When the land increased in value by $100,000 as a result of rezoning, Bela had no gross income. He will have gross income when he experiences a realization event (i.e., he sells or otherwise disposes of the land for its value). *Glenshaw Glass.*

> **(f) Bela negotiated a business purchase for his lawyer in exchange for the lawyer's work on the rezoning project in (e). Each party's services were worth $5,000.**

This is a taxable barter transaction. The amount of gross income realized is the market value of the services ($5,000). Rev. Rul. 79-24.

(g) Bela painted his own home and increased its value by $10,000.

This economic gain, called imputed income, represents an accession to wealth and, under *Glenshaw Glass*, seemingly would be required to be included in gross income. The government, however, has never sought to tax imputed income for various reasons including the administrative challenges such taxation would impose on both the government and the taxpayer. This example of imputed income is akin to mere appreciation in value. Thus, one might argue that it does not constitute *realized* income under *Eisner v. Macomber*. Another justification for non-taxation of imputed income is the difficulty of valuation that may often arise (and was assumed away in the facts of this problem).

(h) Bela harvested some blackberries on his new lot and sold them for $100 at the local farmer's market.

Bela realizes gross income when he sells the blackberries. The amount of gross income realized is the $100 cash received, minus the costs, if any, of harvesting.

2.2. **Michael Begay is a successful lawyer with a far-flung client base. His law firm pays for his business travel and permits him to keep the frequent flyer miles earned on those trips. What are the tax consequences to Michael in the following circumstances?**

(a) This year Michael earned 100,000 frequent flyer miles (worth $1,000) while travelling on behalf of his clients.

Though this appears to be income under the *Glenshaw Glass* analysis, the IRS does not seek to enforce such an interpretation of its holding. *See* IRS Announcement 2002-18.

(b) Late in the year Michael used 50,000 of those miles (worth $500) to fly to Miami for a vacation.

The announcement cited above makes clear that personal use of the miles is not treated as reportable income.

(c) Late in the year Michael gave 50,000 of those miles (worth $500) to his sister so she could fly to Miami for a vacation.

Since the transfer of the miles was for no consideration Michael still has no income.

(d) Late in the year Michael used 50,000 of those miles to acquire a plane ticket for his brother to fly to Miami for a vacation. His brother paid Michael $400 for the ticket.

Now Michael has converted the miles into cash. This is outside of the scope of the income carve out of IRS Announcement 2002-18. Michael has $400 of gross income. The next chapter addresses gains and losses from sales of property. At this point we might simply note that Michael paid nothing for the frequent flyer miles. Thus, their sale is pure income.

2.3. Sam Roberts is the bookkeeper for a major casino. Last year he forged his boss's signature on a casino check that he made out to himself in the amount of $10,000 in order to make the down payment on a new car. At the end of this year, he received a bonus that he used to pay back the "borrowed" funds in January of the following year. After his employer discovered the forged check, Sam was fired.

One might question whether the $10,000 constitutes, in the current year, borrowed funds (excludable from gross income) or illegal funds (includable in gross income per *James v. United States*). This situation is most likely different from that in *Gilbert v. Commissioner*, in which the Second Circuit held that unauthorized withdrawals of corporate funds were not illegal receipts, but were in the nature of a loan, because (1) the taxpayer intended to, and was reasonably believed to have the ability to, repay the funds, (2) the taxpayer thought the corporation would approve the withdrawals, and (3) the taxpayer made an assignment of assets as security. If the withdrawn funds constitute illegal receipts, Sam would include $10,000 in gross income in the current year. When he restored the funds in the following year, he would be entitled to a $10,000 deduction. *See* Rev. Rul. 65-254 (holding repayment of embezzled funds is a loss deductible under section 165).

Chapter 3

Gains and Losses from Dealings in Property

Overview

Section 61(a)(3) states that gross income includes *gains derived from dealings in property*. To understand this phrase, we turn to section 1001. Section 1001(a) provides that gain from the *sale or other disposition of property* is the excess of *amount realized* over *adjusted basis*. Conversely, loss from the sale or other disposition of property is the excess of *adjusted basis* over *amount realized*. The Code defines *amount realized* from a sale or other disposition of property as the sum of any money received plus the fair market value of property (other than money) received in the transaction. IRC § 1001(b). Section 1011(a) provides that the *adjusted basis* of property is the *basis* as determined under section 1012 (or other applicable Code section), *adjusted* as provided in section 1016. Basis is determined when a taxpayer initially acquires property. Generally, basis is the amount a taxpayer has invested in a "tax sense" in the property. Section 1012 prescribes that the basis of property is equal to its *cost*. In this context cost means the fair market value of the property received in a taxable transaction. Philadelphia Amusement Co. v. Commissioner, 126 F. Supp. 184 (Ct. Cl. 1954). The Supreme Court has established that borrowed funds used to acquire property are part of a taxpayer's cost and thus are included in the taxpayer's basis; in addition, relief of outstanding debt on a later sale or disposition of property is included in amount realized. Crane v. Commissioner, 331 U.S. 1 (1947).

Increases and decreases in the value of property are not taken into account for tax purposes as they accrue, but only when they are *realized* by a taxable event. Realization usually does not occur until there has been a dealing in property (to use section 61(a)(3)'s phrase) or a sale or other disposition of property (to use section 1001(a)'s phrase). A gift of property is not a realization event within the meaning of section 1001(a). On the other hand, a transfer of property in satisfaction of a debt is a realization event (i.e., functionally equivalent to a sale of the property for cash followed by use of the proceeds to pay the debt). The phrase *sale or other disposition* is broad and includes most transactions producing a quid pro quo for the taxpayer. *See* Treas. Reg. § 1.1001-1(a).

Once a taxpayer has calculated the gain or loss *realized* on a sale or other disposition, the taxpayer must determine whether the gain or loss is *recognized* (i.e., reportable on the tax return for the year of disposition). As a general rule, the entire gain or loss realized on a sale or other disposition of property is recognized for tax purposes, unless an exception is provided in the Code. IRC § 1001(c). The Code provides a number of exceptions commonly referred to as non- recognition provisions. These non- recognition provisions, which are often narrowly defined, are based on the rationale that the taxpayer's economic position has not really changed. We examine several of these non-recognition provisions in later problem sets.

Primary Authority

Code: §§ 61(a)(3); 109; 1001(a)-(c); 1011(a); 1012; 1016(a)(1)-(2); 7701(g). Skim §§ 165(a), (c); 351(a); 721(a); 1014(a); 1015(a); 1031(a); 1041.

Regulations: §§ 1.61-6(a); 1.1001-1(a), -2(a)-(b); 1.1012-1(c)(1).

Cases: Crane v. Commissioner, 331 U.S. 1 (1947); Philadelphia Park Amusement Co. v. United States, 126 F. Supp. 184 (Ct. Cl. 1954); Commissioner v. Tufts, 461 U.S. 300 (1983). See also United States v. Davis, 370 U.S. 65 (1962); Estate of Franklin v. Commissioner, 544 F.2d 1045 (9th Cir. 19765); Haverly v. United States, 513 F.2d 224 (7th Cir. 1975); Pleasant Summit Land Corp. v. Commissioner, 863 F.2d 263 (3d Cir. 1988).

Rulings: Rev. Rul. 70-498, 1970-2 C.B. 6.

Problems

3.1. Celebrity lawyer Mark Bellows, who typically bills $500 per hour, provides legal services worth $10,000 for his celebrity client, Winona Cosby, in exchange for Winona's diamond ring that is worth $10,000 (but that cost Winona only $2,000). Mark doesn't understand why he has income in this transaction since he had to spend 20 hours of his valuable time on the case. Winona doesn't understand why she has income in this transaction because she is giving up property worth $10,000 in exchange for the legal services worth $10,000. What is your response to Mark and Winona?

Mark provided services to Winona and received property worth $10,000 in return. As we learned in Chapter 2, gross income may be realized in any form, whether in money, property, or services. Treas. Reg. § 1.61-1(a). If property is included in gross income, the fair market value of the property received is the amount of income reported. One might argue that Mark should be able to recover or "back out" the value of his time, which is $10,000 here (20 hours × his typical hourly rate of $500), and which would negate any income. But one does not have basis in his or her time. Thus, Mark must report $10,000 in gross income. At best, Mark will be able to deduct ordinary business expenses in rendering legal services to Winona. Section 162 is the subject of Chapter 8.

Winona will have income as well. The transfer of appreciated property to satisfy an obligation owed to a third party is a realization event within the meaning of section 1001 (a "sale or other disposition"). The amount realized from the disposition is the amount of liabilities from which Winona is discharged as a result of the disposition, or $10,000. With an adjusted basis of $2,000, Winona's gain realized is $8,000. The gain realized is recognized per section 1001(c). Note that this is the same result as if Winona sold the diamond ring for $10,000 in cash to an unrelated third party and then used the sales proceeds to satisfy the obligation to Mark.

3.2. **Christopher Langdell, a law professor who teaches non-tax courses, acquired a number of different assets during the current year. What is the professor's adjusted basis in each of the following assets?**

   (a) **The professor purchased a car on Craigslist for $30,000 in cash. The seller was asking $40,000 for the car, and the Kelley Blue Book value was $35,000. The professor uses the car solely for personal purposes.**

The professor's initial "basis" in the car is $30,000—its cost. IRC § 1012. The original list price and KBB value are irrelevant in a transaction between unrelated third parties. Because the professor made no subsequent improvements and because a personal-use car is not property subject to the allowance for tax depreciation, the professor's "adjusted basis" in the car is also $30,000. IRC §§ 167, 1016. Why is "adjusted basis" relevant in this case? After all, most personal-use cars do not appreciate in value, so it is unlikely that the professor will have a gain realized on any later sale. Most personal-use cars decline in value, but any personal loss realized on a later sale would not be deductible. IRC § 165(a) (noting that only three types of losses are deductible: business, investment, and personal casualty losses). Adjusted basis might be relevant if the car were ever stolen or destroyed in a casualty. IRC § 165(c)(3), (h); Treas. Reg. § 1.165-7(b) (noting the amount of the casualty loss is the lesser of the decline in value of the property due to the casualty or the adjusted basis of the property). Personal casualty losses are the subject of Chapter 10.

   (b) **Same as (a), above, except that he put $5,000 cash down and took out a $25,000 loan to buy the car.**

Same as (a) above. The borrowed funds are treated like cash and included in basis. *Crane v. Commissioner.*

   (c) **Same as (a), above, except that the professor purchased the car for $25,000 from a car dealership. The professor was able to purchase the car for $5,000 less than its true value because the professor recently performed consulting services for the car dealership.**

The difference between the amount paid for the car ($25,000) and the amount of its fair market value at time of transfer ($30,000) is considered compensation for services and included in the professor's gross income. The professor's basis would be $30,000—i.e., the amount paid for the car plus the amount included in gross income. Treas. Reg. § 1.61-2(d)(2).

(d) The professor received a new computer worth $1,000 from his school for being named "Teacher of the Year."

The professor must include the value of the computer ($1,000) in gross income. IRC § 74(a). [The computer does not qualify as an "employee achievement award" excludable under section 74(c), as the award was not for safety achievement or length of service. *See* IRC § 274(j). Likewise, the computer does not qualify as an excludable gift (see IRC § 102(c)) or de minimis fringe benefit (see IRC § 132(e)).] As a result, the professor has a $1,000 "tax cost" basis in the computer. *See Philadelphia Park Amusement Co. v. United States.*

(e) The professor found a Rolex watch worth $5,000 in the school parking lot. Under state law, it is his to keep.

The professor must include the value of the watch ($5,000) in gross income in the year it is reduced to undisputed possession. *See* Treas. Reg. § 1.61-14(a); *Cesarini v. United States*, discussed in Chapter 2. As a result, the professor has a $5,000 "tax cost" basis in the watch. *See Philadelphia Park Amusement Co. v. United States.*

(f) The professor exchanged a parcel of land (that he purchased several years ago for $50,000 but that was worth $100,000 at the time of the exchange) for a colleague's yacht (that was worth $100,000 at the time of the exchange).

This exchange is a realization event. The professor's gain realized is $50,000 because his amount realized is $100,000, the fair market value of the yacht received, and his adjusted basis in the land exchanged is $50,000. IRC § 1001(a), (b). The gain realized is recognized per section 1001(c), since the section 1031 non-recognition rule does not apply (the land and the yacht are not considered "like-kind" properties as will be covered in a later chapter). The professor's basis in the yacht will be $100,000, the fair market value of the yacht at the time of the exchange. *See Philadelphia Park Amusement Co. v. United States*, which held that the basis of property received in a *taxable exchange* is the fair market value of the property *received* at the time of exchange.

(g) The professor received a free examination copy of a casebook from a publishing company. The publisher sent the book, which was worth $125, to encourage the professor to review and adopt it for classroom use.

The professor's basis in the free examination copy depends upon whether the value of the book is includable in his gross income or not. If it is, then he will have a $125 "tax cost" basis in the book. If it is not, then he will have a $0 basis. As we will learn in Chapter 6, with respect to free samples such as the examination copy, the IRS seems to accept that no income need be reported as long as the recipient does not seek a charitable gift deduction for any subsequent transfer of the property received. *See* Rev. Rul. 70-498. Thus, the professor would have no income unless he sought a charitable deduction for a subsequent gift of the book to a charity such as a library. *But see Haverly v. United States*. And, his initial basis would be $0.

One might try to argue that the free examination copy is a "gift" from the publisher excludable under section 102, and that the professor's basis is the same as the publisher's basis under section 1015. However, this would not likely be considered a gift within the meaning of section 102, as the book was not given out the publisher's detached and disinterested generosity. Gifts are the subject of Chapter 4.

(h) The professor accepted a motorcycle (with a value of $10,000) from a colleague in full satisfaction of a $10,000 loan the professor had previously made to the colleague.

The professor's basis in the motorcycle is $10,000, its value at the time of receipt. There are a couple ways to look at this transaction. The easiest is to throw cash into the transaction—i.e., if the professor received $10,000 cash from his colleague in full payment of the loan and then used the cash to purchase the motorcycle, the professor would have a $10,000 cost basis in the motorcycle. Another approach is to recall that the professor had a $10,000 basis in the cash he loaned out (cash always has a basis equal to its face value). When the professor loaned the $10,000 to his colleague, the professor then had a $10,000 basis in the loan. The $10,000 basis in the loan assures that the professor will not have tax consequences when he collects $10,000 cash or receives property worth $10,000 from his colleague in satisfaction of the loan (as he's merely recovering his initial investment in the loan). The $10,000 basis in the motorcycle thus assures that the professor will not have taxable income if he decides to sell it for $10,000 cash, which would put him in his original position. One might also again think of the *Philadelphia Park Amusement* principle that one's basis in property received in a taxable exchange is its fair market value. Interest paid on the loan is a separate matter and is gross income to the professor. IRC § 61(a)(4)

3.3. Five years ago, Anne purchased a vacation home in Colorado for $200,000 cash. Three years ago, Anne borrowed on a recourse basis $50,000 from a bank using the vacation home as security for the loan, and used the $50,000 to make permanent improvements to the vacation home. What are the federal income tax consequences, if any, to Anne in each of the following separate situations?

As a preliminary matter, Anne's *initial basis* in the vacation home was $200,000. IRC § 1012 (cost basis). Two years after purchasing the home, Anne borrowed $50,000. Because she used all of the borrowed funds to make improvements to the vacation home, her basis was *adjusted upwards* to $250,000 to reflect the additional investment. IRC § 1016 (adjusted basis). It should be noted that any principal payments made on the loan would not increase basis as she already received a basis credit earlier. Likewise, interest payments made on the loan would not impact basis, but will be treated separately under the tax law (perhaps deductible under section 163).

The questions that follow require us to focus on a later transfer of the vacation home. We should address whether any of the following are realization events and, if so, the amount of gain or loss realized.

(a) **This year, after having paid $10,000 on the loan, Anne sold the vacation home to an unrelated buyer for $300,000 (with the buyer paying $260,000 and assuming the $40,000 remaining principal balance of the loan).**

Over the years, Anne's property has increased in value. Increases in the value of property, however, are not taken into account for tax purposes as they accrue. We wait until there has been a *realization event*. Here, the sale is clearly a realization event. *See* Treas. Reg. § 1.1001-1(a) ("Except as otherwise provided in subtitle A of the Code, the gain or loss realized from the *conversion of property into cash, or from the exchange of property for other property differing materially either in kind or in extent*, is treated as income or as loss sustained.").

Anne's gain realized on the sale is $50,000 ("amount realized" minus "adjusted basis"). IRC § 1001(a). Amount realized is $300,000 ($260,000 money received plus $40,000 debt relieved). IRC § 1001(b). [Note: Any real estate commissions, advertising, and fix-up expenses reduce amount realized. *See* Treas. Reg. § 1.263(a)-1(e)(1).] Adjusted basis in the vacation home is $250,000 as noted above ($200,000 cost basis under section 1012 plus $50,000 adjustments under section 1016). IRC §§ 1001(a); 1011(a); 1012; 1016. [Note: Vacation homes are generally not subject to the allowance for tax depreciation unless they are rented, so there are no downward adjustments to basis per section 1016(a)(2).]

The $50,000 gain realized is recognized (reportable) per section 1001(c).

(b) **Same as (a) except that Anne sold the vacation home for only $200,000 (with the buyer paying $160,000 cash and assuming the $40,000 remaining principal balance of the loan).**

Here, Anne would realize a loss of $50,000 ($250,000 adjusted basis minus $200,000 amount realized). An interesting issue is whether Anne may deduct the loss. Deductions are a matter of legislative grace. Section 165(a) allows a deduction for "any loss sustained during the taxable year and not compensated for by insurance or otherwise." Section 165(c), however, limits losses in the case of individuals to: (1) losses incurred in a trade or business; (2) losses incurred in a transaction entered into for profit; and (3) casualty losses. Is this loss a "loss incurred in a transaction entered into for profit"? We would need more information as to Anne's use of the vacation home.

(c) **Same as (a) except that, instead of selling the vacation home, Anne pays off the $40,000 balance due on the loan and then gives the vacation home to her son for the love and affection he has always shown her. (Would it make a difference if her son assumed the $40,000 loan encumbering the gifted property?)**

The gift is not a realization event and, therefore, is without federal income tax consequences to Anne. Anne did not, for example, convert the property into cash, exchange the property for other property, or satisfy an obligation owing to her son. *See, e.g.,* Treas. Reg. § 1.1001-1(a). Anne may have to pay a gift tax on the transfer. The federal gift tax is considered in Chapter 41. The tax consequences, if any, to Anne's son will be considered in the next chapter.

If Anne's son assumed the $40,000 loan encumbering the gifted property, then Anne would experience a realization event, with the debt relief treated as her amount realized. However, this would be viewed as a part-sale, part-gift and the regulations provide that no loss is sustained if the amount realized ($40,000) is less than the adjusted basis ($250,000). Treas. Reg. § 1.1001-1(e). For Anne, the transaction would have no tax consequences. Her son's basis would be determined under Treas. Reg. § 1.1015-4, which is addressed in the next chapter dealing with gifts.

> **(d) Same as (a) except that, instead of selling the vacation home, Anne pays off the $40,000 balance due on the loan and then transfers the vacation home to Plaintiff in full satisfaction of a $300,000 court judgment.**

Although Anne is not converting the property into cash or exchanging it for different property, she is using the property to satisfy a $300,000 judgment. This is a realization event within the meaning of section 1001(a) ("sale or other disposition"). The amount realized from the disposition is the amount of liabilities from which Anne is discharged as a result of the disposition, or $300,000. With an adjusted basis of $250,000, Anne's gain realized is $50,000. The gain realized is recognized per section 1001(c). Note that this is the same result as if Anne had sold the property for $300,000 to an unrelated third party and then used the sales proceeds to satisfy the court judgment.

> **(e) Same as (a) except that, instead of selling the vacation home, Anne pays off the $40,000 balance due on the loan and then transfers the vacation home to her spouse pursuant to a separation agreement in which he agrees to release all of his claims and marital rights against Anne's property. *But see* IRC § 1041(a).**

In *United States v. Davis,* the Supreme Court held that such a transfer was a realization event producing taxable gain for the transferor. The *Davis* result is consistent with the principle noted in part (d) above, i.e., that a transfer of appreciated property to satisfy a legal obligation is a realization event. In 1984, Congress legislatively reversed *Davis* by enacting section 1041. Section 1041(a) prevents recognition of gain or loss on property transfers between spouses or incident to divorce. Section 1041(b)(1) provides that the transferee has no income by specifying that the transfer is treated as a gift. In sum, Anne recognizes no gain on the transfer. Section 1041 is the subject of Chapter 32.

3.4. **Fred borrowed $300,000 from Bank on a nonrecourse basis and invested $10,000 of his own money to purchase an apartment building for $310,000 (its fair market value). Unable to make any payments on the loan, Fred transferred the building to Neil who took the property subject to the nonrecourse liability. At the time of this transaction, the building had a value of $220,000 and Fred's adjusted basis in the building was $200,000 (as a result of claiming a total of $110,000 in depreciation during the time he held the property).**

(a) **What is the amount of gain or loss Fred realizes on the transaction with Neil, and what is Neil's basis in the building?**

Fred realizes and recognizes a gain of $100,000 ($300,000 amount realized per *Commissioner v. Tufts,* minus $200,000 adjusted basis). *Tufts* resolved footnote 37 of the *Crane* case, and held that the entire amount of nonrecourse debt must be included in amount realized even though it exceeded the fair market value of the property. No part of the nonrecourse debt is considered discharge of indebtedness income.

What is Neil's basis in the building (e.g., for depreciation purposes)? Is it the amount of the nonrecourse mortgage ($300,000), which substantially exceeds the building's fair market value ($220,000)? Under *Estate of Franklin v. Commissioner,* Neil would get no basis until the amount of the debt is equal to or less than the value of the property. Under *Pleasant Summit Land Corp. v. Commissioner,* Neil would get a basis of only $220,000–the property's fair market value. The latter approach is consistent with *Philadelphia Park Amusement Co.*

You might wonder what would happen if the $300,000 debt were recourse debt as opposed to nonrecourse debt (i.e., Neil assumed the recourse debt and agreed to be personally liable, *and Bank agreed to hold Fred harmless from repayment*). Fred's transfer would be treated as a sale or other disposition only to the extent of the fair market value of the building transferred, and Fred would realize income from the discharge of indebtedness to the extent the amount of the debt ($300,000) exceeds the fair market value of the building ($220,000). As a result, Fred would have $20,000 of *gain derived from dealing in property* under section 61(a)(3) ($220,000 AR minus $200,000 AB), and $80,000 of *income from discharge of indebtedness* under section 61(a)(12). Does bifurcating the transaction into two categories of gross income—section 61(a)(3) and section 61(a)(12)—make any difference? After all, Fred still reports a total of $100,000 of gross income as if the debt were nonrecourse. It does. As discussed in later chapters, the $80,000 income from discharge of indebtedness is potentially excludable from gross income under section 108. If the discharge of indebtedness income is not excludable under section 108, it is treated as ordinary income subject to the regular tax rates of section 1(a), whereas the $20,000 of gain from dealing in property is subject to reduced capital gains rates of section 1(h). If Neil assumed a $300,000 recourse debt, his basis in the building would be $300,000. Why are the approaches for nonrecourse and recourse debt different? With nonrecourse debt, Bank is not forfeiting the right to collect (the debt is merely transferred to Neil), and thus there is no discharge of indebtedness. With recourse debt, Bank is forfeiting its right to collect from Fred (Neil assumed the debt and Bank agreed to hold Fred harmless from repayment), and thus Fred has some discharge of indebtedness income.

(b) **Would the answer to (a) change if Fred transferred the building by means of a quitclaim deed to Bank, and Bank released Fred from all liability?**

The results to Fred would be the same as above. The identity of the transferee is irrelevant from his perspective.

Chapter 4

Gifts and Inheritance

Overview

Although gross income is a very broad concept, there are limitations on its meaning. Indeed, Congress decided to exclude (or partially exclude) certain types of receipts or benefits from the income tax base. Skim IRC §§ 101–140. Each statutory exclusion addresses some particular congressional concern or achieves some particular goal. This problem set will address section 102, the longstanding exclusion rule for gifts and inheritances and will consider the correlative basis rules that apply when property is acquired by devise or gift. *See* IRC §§ 1014, 1015.

Section 102(a) specifically excludes the value of property "acquired by gift" from gross income. Although the Code does not define "gift" for income tax purposes, the Supreme Court established criteria for determining whether a particular transfer is a gift in Commissioner v. Duberstein, 363 U.S. 278 (1960) (providing that a gift proceeds from the "donor's detached and disinterested generosity," "out of affection, respect, admiration, charity or like impulses"). Section 102(a) also provides that the value of property acquired by "bequest, devise, or inheritance" is excludable. The phrase "bequest, devise, or inheritance" refers to property "received under a will or under statutes of descent and distribution." Treas. Reg. § 1.102-1(a). The Supreme Court has held that the exclusion also applies to a settlement obtained in a will contest action. Lyeth v. Hoey, 305 U.S. 188 (1938). However, not everything received under a will is excludable. As illustrated in Wolder v. Commissioner, 493 F.2d 608 (2d Cir. 1974), section 102(b) also places some important limits on the exclusion.

When section 102(a) applies, we are also then obliged to consider the recipient's basis in the property. Section 1014 and 1015 are the key authorities here. In the case of property acquired by gift, the donee's basis is generally the same basis the donor had in the property (this is called "transferred basis"). IRC §§ 1015(a), 7701(a)(43). Having a donee of gifted property take the donor's basis results in any gain that accrued while the donor held the property being shifted to the donee, and such gain being realized by the donee on a later disposition of the property. Although Congress is willing to shift accrued gain from a donor to a donee through the concept of transferred basis, Congress is unwilling to shift accrued losses from a donor to a donee. F*or purposes of determining loss* by the donee on a later sale, the donee's basis is the lesser of the donor's basis or date of gift fair market value of the property (if the value was less than the donor's basis at the time of gift).

Death is the last great tax loophole. The basis of property acquired from a decedent is not the decedent's basis as one might expect. Instead, it is generally the fair market value of the property on the date of decedent's death. *See* IRC § 1014(a) (providing that the basis of property in the hands of a person to whom the property *passed* from a decedent shall be the fair market value of the property at the date of the decedent's death). *See also* IRC § 1014(b)(1) (providing that property shall be considered to have *passed* from the decedent if the property was acquired by bequest, devise, or inheritance). It should be noted that under section 1014(a), only the portion of property that "passes" from the decedent receives a stepped-up basis. In *common-law* states, property jointly owned by a husband and wife is treated as half-owned by each. Therefore, a surviving spouse is entitled to a stepped-up basis only in the decedent spouse's half of the property that passes to the surviving spouse. *See* IRC §§ 1014(b)(9) & 2040(b)(1). The basis of the surviving spouse's one-half share is not stepped up. In *community property* states, each spouse is also treated as owning one-half of community property. However, under section 1014(b)(6), the basis of a surviving spouse's one-half share of community property is stepped up to fair market value on the date of the decedent's death if at least one-half of the community property is included in the decedent's gross estate for estate tax purposes. As a result, if a decedent transfers his half of community property to his surviving spouse, the surviving spouse will have a stepped-up basis in both halves of the community property even though only one-half of the property actually passed and was included in the decedent's estate for estate tax purposes.

Primary Authorities

Code: §§ 102; 1014(a), (b)(1), (b)(6), (b)(9), (e); 1015(a). Skim: §§ 74(c); 274(b)(1).

Regulations: §§ 1.102-1(a)-(c); 1.1001-1(e); 1.1014-2(a)(5); 1.1015-1, -4; Prop. Treas. Reg. § 1.102-1(f).

Cases: Commissioner v. Duberstein, 363 U.S. 278 (1960); Wolder v. Commissioner, 493 F.2d 608 (2d Cir. 1974). See also Lyeth v. Hoey, 305 U.S. 188 (1938); Peebles v. Commissioner, T.C. Summary Opinion 2006-61; Roberts v. Commissioner, 10 T.C. 581 (1948).

Rulings: Rev. Rul. 87-98, 1987-2 C.B. 206.

Problems

4.1. To what extent can the recipients in the following situations exclude amounts received from income? (Indicate, if necessary, any additional information that might be helpful.)

(a) In Year 1, Billy Ray Clayton deeded his apartment building to his daughter Miley. In Year 2, Miley collects $10,000 in rents from the property.

The value of the building is excludable from Miley's gross income, provided the dominant reason for the transfer (Billy Ray's intention) was "out of affection, respect, admiration, charity or like impulses," or from Bill Ray's "detached and disinterested generosity." *See* IRC § 102(a); *Commissioner v. Duberstein.*

The $10,000 in rents is not excludable from Miley's gross income, since the gift exclusion does not apply to income from property received by gift. IRC § 102(b)(1).

> **(b) Same as (a) except that pursuant to an irrevocable trust he created, Billy transferred title to his apartment building to Ted, the trustee. The trust agreement instructed Ted to pay the rental income from the building to Miley, for Miley's life. Ted paid $10,000 in rents to Miley.**

Ted is only receiving title as trustee and thus has no accession to wealth/gross income. Miley, the income beneficiary, has no gross income at the time the trust is created. However, she has $10,000 of gross income when the rent is paid to her. The gift exclusion does not apply where the gift is one of income from property. IRC § 102(b)(2).

> **(c) Charles discovered that his wife Diana and their neighbor Dr. James Wilberforce were having an affair. Charles confronted James with evidence of the affair and threatened to sue him for $150,000 and report him to the state's medical board. James told Charles that he didn't have $150,000, but he did have $25,000. When James gave the $25,000 to Charles, James apologized and said that he regretted the affair and hoped the money would help Charles and Diana. Charles then stated: "Now James, this isn't blackmail money," to which James replied: "No, I hope it helps you, both of you."**

This fact pattern was based on an actual Tax Court case. *See* Peebles v. Commissioner, T.C. Summary Opinion 2006-61. The Tax Court believed that the doctor thought the taxpayer wanted a payment because of the affair, and that the doctor offered the payment not because of detached generosity, but rather as a way to close the matter and avoid being sued by the taxpayer. The court concluded: "[T]he $25,000 payment by [the doctor] was not the result of detached and disinterested generosity or paid out of affection, respect, admiration, or charity. Instead it was paid to avoid a lawsuit, to avoid public and professional embarrassment, and to assuage his own feelings of guilt or moral application. Therefore, the $25,000 payment . . . is not a gift and is includable in petitioners' gross income . . . ." *Id.*

> **(d) Clarence Darrow, who is a full-time tax associate at a law firm, writes a daily Internet blog on tax law. To his surprise, he receives small donations (about $20,000 per year) through an on-line tip jar administered by Paypal, for which he sends donors a "thank you" email.**

Tips are included in gross income unless excluded by law. Treas. Reg. § 1.61-2(a). You should ask whether the donors gave out of detached and disinterested generosity in deciding whether Clarence is eligible for the gift exclusion under section 102(a). Additional facts would be helpful. For example, are donors required to read the website? Does Clarence offer any explicit quid pro quo, such as offering donors some type of advertising? Do some donors hope for increased access to Clarence or give with the hopes of receiving free legal advice later?

(e) Lesley is employed as a full-time waitress at a small restaurant owned by her parents. In addition to her regular tips, Lesley received the following: (1) $500 from a customer who wanted to honor his late brother's wish "to leave an awesome tip for a waiter or waitress"; (2) a $100 check and plaque in recognition of her length of service; (3) with all other employees, a $25 gift card redeemable at a local grocery-retail store for a holiday ham; and (4) from her parents, a $1,000 TV under the tree on Christmas day.

Lesley's regular tips are included in gross income. Treas. Reg. § 1.61-2(a) (stating tips are included in income unless excluded by law). Lesley may attempt to argue, however, that the $500 special tip is an excludable gift under section 102(a)/*Duberstein*. [In general, tips usually involve an element of compulsion (e.g., patrons expect to tip waiters and waiters expect to be tipped). As a result, tips usually don't satisfy the "gift" standard. *See Roberts v. Commissioner* (stating "the milk of human kindness has little to do with the matter of tipping"). To enforce the reporting of tips, which often are paid in cash, Congress has enacted stringent reporting requirements. *See, e.g.,* IRC § 6053 (requiring certain employers to establish that a certain percentage of the business' gross receipts are reported on the employees' W-2s). *See also* Publication 531 ("Reporting Tip Income"); Publication 1244 ("Employee's Daily Record of Tips and Report to Employer").]

Lesley also received from her employer $100 and a plaque in recognition of her length of service. Section 102(c) provides an exception to the broad exclusionary rule of section 102(a) and should thus be the starting point. Section 102(c) denies "gift" classification to all transfers by employers to employees. There are limited exceptions to the section 102(c) inclusion rule (i.e., specific statutory rules of exclusion that override the broader rule of inclusion), none of which seem to apply here. The $100 is not an employee achievement award excludable under section 74(c), since cash is not an "item of tangible personal property." *See* IRC § 274(j)(3). The $100 is not a de minimis fringe benefit excludable under section 132. *See* IRC § 132(e); Treas. Reg. § 1.132-6(c) (providing that, except for occasional meal money or local transportation fare, "the provision of any cash fringe benefit is never excludable under section 132(a) as a de minimis fringe benefit"). In sum, Lesley has $100 of income under section 102(c); we never get to the section 102(a)/*Duberstein* analysis. The fringe benefit exclusions are the subject of Chapter 6.

The gift card (transferred from an employer to an employee) is included in gross income per section 102(c) unless a specific statutory rule of exclusion applies. Because the $25 gift card is redeemable only for a ham, it should be excludable from Lesley's gross income as a de minimis fringe benefit under section 132. Note that if the gift card could be converted into cash, then it would not constitute an excludable de minimis fringe benefit. *See* Treas. Reg. § 1.132-6(c) (providing that a cash equivalent fringe benefit (such as a fringe benefit provided to an employee through the use of a gift certificate) is generally not excludable under section 132(a)).

The $1,000 TV appears taxable since section 102(c) denies "gift" classification to ALL transfers by employers to employees. There is a limited exception to the section 102(c) inclusion rule in Prop. Treas. Reg. § 1.102-1(f)(2). If this extraordinary transfer was made because of the family relationship and not in recognition of Lesley's employment, Lesley could exclude it. It would be nice to know whether other employees received a TV. Here, section 102(a) and not section 102(c) most likely applies to exclude the gift.

> **(f) Paul, a long-time employee and football coach at State University, received a check for $10,000 at a testimonial dinner in honor of his retirement. The funds were given by various persons (current and past players, faculty, and assistant coaches) as well as various local business organizations.**

A preliminary issue is whether section 102(c) applies given that Paul has been a long-time employee at State University. If so, the $10,000 check could not be classified as a gift, and would be income for Paul. Arguments can be made that section 102(c) does not apply. First, Paul has retired and he is no longer an employee. Second, even if he still is an employee at State University at the time of the testimonial dinner, the check may not be drawn on a State University account. Even if it is a State University check, the university is merely a conduit for funds contributed by players, faculty, and assistant coaches.

Assuming section 102(c) is inapplicable, further analysis is necessary to establish the applicability of the gift exclusion under section 102(a). Did the $10,000 gift proceed from the donors' detached and disinterested generosity? Here different groups—players, faculty, and assistant coaches—whose motivations might have differed, gave the funds. What if the players gave funds out of respect, but the faculty felt pressured by the university to contribute? What if the assistant coaches experienced peer pressure from fellow assistant coaches and players to contribute? Certainly most (if not all) gave out of pure generosity and, thus, the bulk (if not all) of the funds should be excludable.

> **(g) Mother dies and her will provides for the following: (1) $10,000 to Son A; and (2) $20,000 to Son B, executor of her estate, "in lieu of all compensation or commissions to which he would otherwise be entitled as executor." Mother's will did not leave anything to Daughter, but Daughter later received $10,000 in settlement of a contest she brought against the estate of Mother; Daughter claimed that she was left out of Mother's will because of fraud by Son A and Son B.**

Section 102(a) provides that a bequest, devise, or inheritance is excludable from gross income. The phrase "bequest, devise, or inheritance" refers to property "received under a will or under statutes of descent and distribution." Treas. Reg. § 1.102-1(a). However, not all amounts received pursuant to a will are excludable. *Wolder v. Commissioner* illustrates that *Duberstein* (decedent's intent) must be taken into account.

The $10,000 gift to Son A is probably an excludable gift because it was given out of Mother's detached and disinterested generosity.

The $20,000 to Son B is a bit tricky. Son B would likely argue that he has gross income only to the extent of the amount he could have claimed for his services as executor, and the amount in excess is an excludable gift. The Service would likely argue that the entire amount is compensation income (i.e., the excess over what he could have claimed for services as executor is merely additional compensation). Of course, we need more facts. What is reasonable or statutorily prescribed compensation for services as personal representative? Did all of Mother's children receive some form of gift?

The $10,000 received by Daughter is probably excludable. The Supreme Court has held that the section 102 exclusion applies to a settlement obtained in a will contest action. *See Lyeth v. Hoey.*

4.2. Judy Dolittle deeded unimproved land to her daughter, Liza, as a gift. At the time of gift, Judy's basis was $60,000 and the land was worth $100,000.

   (a) A year later, Liza sold the land to a third party for $110,000. What are the tax consequences to Liza upon receipt and subsequent sale of the land?

Liza has no gross income upon receipt of the land from Judy. IRC § 102(a). Liza's basis in the land is $60,000–that is, Judy's adjusted basis at the time of gift. IRC §§ 1015(a), 7701(a)(43). [Assume no gross up for gift tax paid by Judy. IRC § 1015(d).] When Liza subsequently sells the land, she has a gain realized of $50,000—$110,000 amount realized, minus $60,000 adjusted basis (assuming no adjustments to basis per section 1016). Notice that the transferred basis rule results in some gain that accrued while Judy held the land being shifted to Liza. While this seems unfair, the alternative, taxing Judy at the time of gift on gain that accrued in her hands, would involve obvious valuation problems and perhaps discourage the gift. In addition, Liza may be in a more liquid position than Judy when she later disposes of the land for cash.

   (b) Same as (a) except that the land was worth only $50,000 at the time Liza received it. What are the tax consequences to Liza upon receipt and subsequent sale of the land for $110,000? For $40,000? For $55,000?

The exception to the general transferred basis rule applies because the value of the land at the time of gift ($50,000) was less than Judy's basis in the land ($60,000). The exception produces the following results:

If Liza later sells the land for $110,000, Liza's basis *for purposes of determining the gain* would be $60,000 (the general rule). She would realize a gain of $50,000.

If Liza later sells the land for $40,000, Liza's basis *for purposes of determining the loss* would be $50,000 (the exception). She would realize a loss of $10,000. Note the effect of this exception is to limit Liza's loss to only the loss that accrued in her hands. While Congress is willing to shift accrued gain from a donor to a donee through the concept of transferred basis (as in part (a) above), Congress is unwilling to shift accrued loss from a donor to a donee.

If Liza later sells the land for $55,000, Liza will have neither gain nor loss. The basis for determining gain is $60,000; therefore, there is no gain. The basis for determining loss is $50,000; therefore, there is no loss. *See* Treas. Reg. § 1.1015-1(a)(2), Example.

> **(c) Same as (a) except that instead of giving the land to Liza, Judy sold it to Liza for $80,000 and, a year later, Liza sold the land to a third party for $110,000. What are the tax consequences to Judy and Liza.**

This was a part-sale, part-gift to Liza. Judy's gain realized was $20,000 ($80,000 amount realized, minus $60,000 adjusted basis). Note that Judy could recover the full $60,000 basis in the land even though the amount realized was only 80% of the land's fair market value. Treas. Reg. § 1.1001-1(e).

Liza had no income as a result of the gift (the gift was the excess of the land's fair market value over what Liza paid). IRC § 102(a). Liza's basis in the land was $80,000—the greater of the amount she paid ($80,000) or Judy's adjusted basis at the time of the transfer ($60,000). Treas. Reg. § 1.1015-4. When Liza sold the land to a third party for $110,000, she had a gain realized of $30,000 ($110,000 amount realized minus $80,000 adjusted basis).

> **(d) Same as (a) except that the land gifted to Liza was subject to an $80,000 mortgage which Liza assumed. What are the tax consequences to Judy and Liza?**

This may not look like a part-sale, part gift, but it is. Although Liza is not paying $80,000 in cash, as in part (c) above, she is relieving Judy from an $80,000 liability. Review the *Crane* case from Chapter 3. Judy realizes gain of $20,000 on the gift of the encumbered property ($80,000 amount realized, minus $60,000 adjusted basis). Liza has no income as result of the gift portion of the transfer. IRC § 102(a). Liza's basis in the property is $80,000. In sum, the results are the same as in part (c) above.

> **4.3. Husband and Wife live in Maine, a non-community property state. Several years ago, they purchased property for $100,000. This year, Husband dies when the property is worth $500,000. His interest is included in his gross estate.**

> **(a) What will Wife's basis be in the "tenancy in common" property if husband leaves his interest to Wife in his will?**

$300,000. Wife takes a stepped-up basis in Husband's half interest in the property. Note that under section 1014(a), only the portion of the property that "passes" from a decedent receives a stepped-up basis. *See* IRC § 1014(a) (providing that the basis of property in the hands of a person to whom the property passed from a decedent shall be the fair market value of the property at the date of the decedent's death). *See also* IRC § 1014(b)(1) (providing that property shall be considered to have passed from the decedent if the property was acquired by bequest, devise, or inheritance).

> **(b) Same as (a) except that Husband and Wife live in Idaho, a community property state, and Husband left his one-half share of the community property to Wife.**

$500,000. In community property states, each spouse is treated as owning one-half of community property. Accordingly, it would appear here that only the decedent's one-half share (all that the decedent can pass) is stepped up to fair market value on the date of his death under sections 1014(a) & (b)(1). Section 1014(b)(6), however, provides that the surviving spouse's one-half share is also deemed to pass from the decedent. Thus, the basis of the surviving spouse's one-half share of community property is also stepped up to fair market value (provided at least one-half of the community property is included in the decedent's gross estate for estate tax purposes). Here, if Husband transfers his half of the community property to Wife, Wife will have a stepped-up basis in both halves of the community property even though only one-half actually passed and was included in Husband's gross estate for estate tax purposes.

> **(c) Same as (b) except that Husband left his one-half share of the community property to his child from a prior marriage.**

$250,000. Section 1014(b)(6) confers a stepped-up basis on Wife's one-half share of the community property if the other half was includable in Husband's gross estate for estate tax purposes. This result is the same result that would occur if Husband and Wife lived in a common law state, Husband owned all the property, and Husband transferred half to his child and half to Wife—Wife would get a stepped-up basis in the half passing to her. Note the same result would not occur if they lived in a common law state and owned the property as tenants in common, Husband owned only half of the property before death, and he transferred his half to his child from a prior marriage—Wife would not get a stepped up basis. In light of the latter scenario, section 1014(b)(6) is quite kind to spouses in community property states. Some say . . . quite anomalous.

> **(d) Same as (b) except that this is joint tenancy property and Wife gets Husband's one-half by operation of law.**

$300,000. The property is non-probate property (i.e., it is not passed by bequest, devise, or inheritance, but rather it is acquired by operation of law). Under section 1014(b)(9), Wife, the surviving joint tenant, gets a stepped-up basis in one-half of the joint property (the portion of the property previously owned by Husband, the deceased joint tenant), or $250,000. She had a $50,000 basis in her half. As a result, her basis will be $300,000 in entire the property. Planning Note: To ensure a full stepped-up basis, parties should pay attention as to how property is titled. Property intended to be characterized as community property should be titled as community property and not as joint tenancy property. *See* Rev. Rul. 87-98 (holding that property purchased with community funds in a community property state but titled as "joint tenants with rights of survivorship" nevertheless obtained a complete basis step-up since the husband and wife expressly stated in joint wills that the property was intended to be a "community" asset).

Chapter 5

Discharge of Indebtedness

Overview

Borrowed funds are not included in gross income because the borrower has assumed an obligation to repay the debt in full at some point in the future. Since any increase in assets is offset by an increase in liabilities of an equal amount, any accession to wealth is negated. Suppose, however, that the borrower does not pay back the loan, in whole or in part, or the lender subsequently forgives the debt. Is it not fair to say that the borrower has experienced, *at that time*, an accession to wealth that should be taxed? In United States v. Kirby Lumber Co., 284 U.S. 1 (1931), the Supreme Court held that the repayment of a debt at less than its face amount constituted income to the debtor. This concept was later codified in section 61(a)(12), which expressly includes in gross income the amount of a taxpayer's "discharge of indebtedness."

Different theories have been set forth to rationalize the concept of discharge-of-indebtedness income. Under the *Kirby Lumber* "balance sheet" theory, taxation is appropriate since the taxpayer has an increase in net worth due to the cancellation of an established liability for less than its face amount. Under another theory, discharge of indebtedness is income at the time of discharge since the debtor went untaxed at the time of the borrowing. In other words, borrowed funds were not included in income because of the obligation to repay, and the discharge of the obligation to repay removes the justification for the original borrowing exclusion.

A number of judicial and statutory exceptions (see IRC § 108) to the discharge-of-indebtedness inclusion rule exist. These exceptions address questions such as: Is taxation appropriate if a debtor disputes the enforceability of a debt and subsequently settles the dispute for an amount less than the original debt? *See* Preslar v. Commissioner, 167 F.3d 1323 (10th Cir. 1999). Is taxation appropriate if the cancellation of indebtedness is a gift to the debtor? Is taxation appropriate if at the time of discharge the debtor has no assets or wherewithal to pay tax on the discharge-of-indebtedness income?

Primary Authority

Code: §§ 61(a)(12); 108(a), (b)(1)-(2), (b)(5), (c), (d)(1)-(3), (e)(1)-(2), (e)(4)-(5), (f), (g); 1017(a), (b)(1)-(3). Skim § 166.

Regulations: §§ 1.61-12(a); 1.1001-2(a), 2(c) ex. 8; 1.1017-1. Skim §§ 1.166-1(c), -2(a)–(b).

Cases: United States v. Kirby Lumber Co., 284 U.S. 1 (1931); Preslar v. Commissioner, 167 F.3d 1323 (10th Cir. 1999). See also Gehl v. Commissioner, 50 F.3d 12 (8th Cir. 1995); Merkel v. Commissioner, 192 F.3d 844 (9th Cir. 1999); Zarin v. Commissioner, 916 F.2d 110 (3d Cir. 1990).

Rulings: Rev. Rul 84-176, 1984-2 C.B. 34; IRS Memorandum 200039037.

Problems

5.1.   Will Robert have any income in the following events? Assume Robert is technically *solvent* at all times and all loans are recourse unless stated otherwise.

    (a)   Robert borrowed $10,000 from a local bank to help pay for his law school tuition. After repaying $8,000, Robert was unable to make further payments on the loan. So, the bank forgave the balance of the loan.

Robert has $2,000 of discharge of indebtedness income. IRC § 61(a)(12). He does not qualify for any of the exclusions in section 108.

    (b)   Same as (a) except that Robert borrowed the $10,000 from his grandmother, who forgave the $2,000 balance of the loan.

It would appear that Robert, again, has $2,000 of discharge of indebtedness income under section 61(a)(12), since he is satisfying a $10,000 debt with an $8,000 payment. However, the discharge of indebtedness may be treated as a gift and excluded from gross income under section 102. "[D]ebt discharge that is only a medium for some other form of payment, such as a gift or salary, is treated as that form of payment rather than under the debt discharge rules." Rev. Rul 84-176 (citing S. Rep. No. 1035, 96th Cong., 2d Sess. 8 n.6 (1980)). Here, the intent of Don's grandmother must be considered before the forgiveness is characterized as a gift.

    (c)   Same as (a) except that Robert borrowed the $10,000 from his employer, who forgave the $2,000 balance of the loan.

If Robert's employer forgave $2,000 of the loan because the employer owed Robert compensation for services, then Robert has gross income under section 61(a)(1), not section 61(a)(12). Again, "debt discharge that is only a medium for some other form of payment, such as a gift or salary, is treated as that form of payment rather than under the debt discharge rules." Rev. Rul 84-176 (citing S. Rep. No. 1035, 96th Cong., 2d Sess. 8 n.6 (1980)). It does not matter here whether Robert has income under section 61(a)(1) or section 61(a)(12), but it would if he were insolvent. The reason is that section 108 grants an exclusion to insolvent taxpayers as to section 61(a)(12) income; it does not grant an exclusion to insolvent taxpayers as to other types of income. *See Gehl v. Commissioner.*

    (d)   Same as (a) except that Robert borrowed the $10,000 from his wholly-owned corporation, which forgave the $2,000 balance of the loan.

Most likely, Robert would be viewed as receiving a $2,000 disguised dividend from his controlled corporation. Dividends are specifically included in gross income under section 61(a)(7). The applicable tax rate on dividends is addressed in Chapter 17.

(e) **Same as (a) except that Robert was granted $10,000 credit by Office Depot (an office supply store) to purchase $10,000 of office supplies for his business. After purchasing, receiving, and using the supplies, Robert repaid $8,000 and Office Depot forgave the $2,000 balance.**

Robert has no discharge of indebtedness income. Section 108(e)(2) provides that gross income does not include the discharge of a liability if payment of that liability would have been deductible had it been paid. Payments of accounts payable are generally deductible under section 162.

(f) **Same as (a) except that Robert purchased a small tract of swampland in Okeechobee, Florida, for $15,000. Robert had difficulty qualifying for a conventional loan, so the seller financed the real estate transaction, accepting a $5,000 cash payment from Robert and taking back a $10,000 mortgage. Robert repaid $8,000 and the seller forgave the $2,000 balance.**

Robert has no discharge of indebtedness income. Section 108(e)(5) provides that a so-called "purchase money" debt reduction does not create discharge-of-indebtedness income. Rather, the reduction in debt is treated as a purchase price adjustment and the buyer's basis in the property is decreased by the amount of the reduction. Robert's basis will be $13,000, rather than $15,000.

5.2. **James Hickock, better known as Wild Bill, is an avid gambler who makes frequent visits to Oxserver Casino. Does Wild Bill, who is *solvent*, have income in the following events?**

(a) **Wild Bill signs a marker (a debt instrument with the casino) and receives chips equal to $5,000, the face amount of the marker. Wild Bill lost it all, and the casino attempted to collect the full amount of the marker. Wild Bill disputed the debt on the basis that it was unenforceable under state law. Wild Bill and the casino later agreed to settle the dispute for $2,000. Wild Bill ultimately paid only $1,000 to the casino and the casino never sought to collect the rest of the debt.**

Wild Bill has discharge of indebtedness income of either $4,000 or $1,000, depending on whether the "contested liability" doctrine applies. Review *Preslar v. Commissioner.* Under the contested liability doctrine, if a taxpayer disputes the original amount of a debt in good faith and later settles that dispute, the settled amount is treated as the amount of recognizable debt for tax purposes (i.e., the excess of the amount the lender originally said was owed over the settled amount may be disregarded and payment of the settled amount does not generate discharge of indebtedness income).

In *Preslar*, the Tenth Circuit held that the contested liability doctrine applies only if the original amount of the debt is unliquidated (i.e., the amount of the debt must be disputed before the doctrine is triggered). Here, enforceability of the debt, and not the amount of the debt, is in dispute. Under *Preslar*, therefore, the contested liability doctrine seemingly would not apply, and Will Bill would have $4,000 of income. Note that in *Zarin v. Commissioner*, discussed in *Preslar*, the Third Circuit treated liquidated and unliquidated debts alike. In *Zarin*, enforceability of the debt, not the amount of the debt owed, was in dispute. The Third Circuit emphasized that when a debt is unenforceable the amount of the debt is in dispute. Under a *Zarin* analysis, the contested liability doctrine would apply and Wild Bill would have only $1,000 of income.

> (b) **Same as (a) except that Wild Bill bargained for and received a marker discount at which he may settle his marker for 10% less if he loses it all by the end of the visit. (If he wins, the full amount of the marker is required to be paid.) The terms of the discount were set before signing of the marker and the agreement was informally noted in the casino's records. Wild Bill received $5,000 worth of chips, lost them all, and paid the casino $4,500 as a result of the prearranged discount.**

The prearranged discount on a gaming customer's marker should be treated as a purchase price adjustment. *See* IRS Memorandum 200039037 (Sept. 29, 2000), which stated:

> Purchase price adjustment treatment is appropriate in this case because the facts in this situation indicate that the intent and purpose of the parties was to effect a discount to the cost of the gambling services and entertainment, i.e., the customer's wagering losses. Among the salient facts so indicating are that the discount was negotiated prior to the customer's visit to the casino for the purpose of inducing the customer's visit to the casino, and was noted in writing in the casino's books prior to the signing of the marker.

The IRS did not rest its conclusion upon the application of section 108(e)(5), because section 108(e)(5), by its terms, applies only to a reduction of debt for the purchase of "property." A casino is in the business of providing entertainment and gambling services, and a customer's wager may be likened to the purchase of such services. However, although the purchase price discount authorities deal mostly with adjustments to the purchase price of "property," the theory is likewise applicable to the purchase of "services." *Id.* (citing Alan Gunn, *Another Look at the Zarin Case*, 50 TAX NOTES 893 (Feb. 25, 1991)).

5.3. Charles borrowed $500,000 from First Bank. Later, when Charles was *insolvent*, First Bank accepted a parcel of unencumbered land (with a value of $400,000 and an adjusted basis of $100,000) from Charles in full satisfaction of the recourse debt. Prior to the transfer, Charles' assets consisted of the parcel of land and some household effects with a total value of $75,000.

Charles' liabilities included the $500,000 debt to First Bank and $50,000 indebtedness to another bank. In addition, Charles has personally guaranteed a $25,000 bank loan that his daughter took out and there is a "50/50 chance" he will have to pay it.

(a) **How much income, if any, must Charles report as a result of the settlement of the debt owed to First Bank?**

First Bank is accepting land worth $400,000 in satisfaction of a $500,000 debt. As a result, Charles has $100,000 discharge of indebtedness income. IRC § 61(a)(12). Because it appears that Charles may be insolvent at the time of discharge, some or all of this income may be excludable under section 108.

Section 108(a)(1)(B) provides that gross income does not include discharge of indebtedness income if the discharge occurs when the taxpayer is insolvent. The maximum amount excluded, however, cannot exceed the amount by which the debtor is insolvent. IRC § 108(a)(3). A taxpayer is insolvent to the extent his liabilities exceed the fair market value of his assets determined on the basis of assets and liabilities immediately before the discharge. IRC § 108(d)(3).

Let's determine the extent to which Charles was insolvent before satisfaction of the debt. Before satisfaction of the debt, Charles had assets worth $475,000 (land worth $400,000 and household effects worth $75,000), and liabilities of $550,000 ($500,000 to First Bank and $50,000 to another bank). Note that Charles has guaranteed a $25,000 bank loan that his daughter took out. He cannot, however, include the guarantee in the amount of his liabilities for purposes of determining the extent to which he is insolvent, since it is *not* more probable than not that he will be called upon to pay that obligation. *See Merkel v. Commissioner.* Accordingly, at the time of Charles' settlement of his debt to First Bank, Charles was insolvent to the tune of $75,000. Therefore, he can only exclude $75,000 of the $100,000 of discharge of indebtedness income. [Note that Charles has discharge of indebtedness income under section 61(a)(12) to the extent the discharge made him solvent ($25,000). After satisfaction of the debt, he had assets worth $75,000 and liabilities of $50,000.]

Because Charles gets to exclude $75,000 of discharge of indebtedness income under section 108(a)(1)(B), he must adjust certain tax attributes by $75,000. The tax attributes that must be reduced, and the order in which they must be reduced, are provided in section 108(b). Note that as an alternative to this ordering of attribute reduction, Charles may first elect to reduce the adjusted basis of property by the amount excluded. IRC § 108(b)(5). Section 1017 and the regulations thereunder provide special rules for making the basis adjustment under section 108(b). *See* IRC § 1017(b)(1)-(2); Treas. Reg. § 1.1017-1.

In addition to realizing $75,000 of section 61(a)(12) income, does Charles realize any section 61(a)(3) income (gain derived from dealing in property)? Charles is using appreciated property to satisfy $400,000 of a $500,000 obligation. This is a realization event. His gain realized is $300,000 ($400,000 amount realized, minus $100,000 adjusted basis). An interesting issue is whether Charles can exclude any of this gain under section 108 due to his insolvency? In *Gehl v. Commissioner*, the Eight Circuit held that while section 108 grants an exclusion to insolvent taxpayers as to section 61(a)(12) income, it does not grant an exclusion to insolvent taxpayers as to section 61(a)(3) income. Charles will have to report the $300,000 of gain.

> **(b) What are the tax consequences to First Bank upon acceptance of the land in satisfaction of the debt? Specifically, is First Bank entitled to any deductions, and what is First Bank's basis in the land?** *See* **IRC § 166(a).**

First Bank will have a $400,000 basis in the land (same basis the bank would have if Charles gave the bank $400,000 cash in satisfaction of the debt, and the bank used the $400,000 to purchase Charles' land). First Bank will be entitled to a $100,000 business bad debt deduction under section 166(a). This was a bona fide debt. Treas. Reg. § 1.166-1(c). Moreover, the debt became worthless within this tax year. Treas. Reg. § 1.166-2(a)-(b).

Chapter 6

Fringe Benefits

Overview

Non-salary employee perquisites ("perks") are commonly called fringe benefits. Typical examples include employer subsidized health and life insurance, retirement benefits, travel expense reimbursements, and education benefits. In theory anything one receives from one's employer as compensation for work performed should be included in gross income. Indeed, as we saw in Chapter 4, even a gift from the employer is income to the employee. IRC § 102(c). Moreover it should not matter whether the payment is in cash or in some other form. It should not matter whether the payment is made directly to the employee or to another person in relief of the employee's obligation to that third party. It is still an accession to wealth that should constitute gross income. Treas. Reg. § 1.61-1(a). But Congress has seen fit to exclude a number of fringe benefits from the employee's gross income while continuing to permit the employer to deduct the costs of those benefits. The continued deductibility of payment by the employer is a crucial aspect of the benefit. Both the deduction for the employer and the exclusion for the employee may serve as opportunities for tax planning.

Section 132 deals with many, but not all, excluded fringe benefits of employment, and is the main focus of this chapter. It establishes seven categories of excludable fringes but we will focus on four: (1) no-additional-cost-services; (2) qualified employee discounts; (3) working condition fringes; and (4) de minimis fringes. As we delve into this topic it is important to remember that if a fringe benefit is not specifically excluded by the Code, it is gross income under section 61(a)(1). *See* Commissioner v. Smith, 324 U.S. 177 (1945). The amount of gross income is determined by reference to the fair market value of the service or property received. Treas. Reg. §§ 1.61-2(d)(1), -21(b)(3).

Section 119 excludes from an employee's gross income the value of employer provided meals and lodging when those benefits are provided as a condition of employment for the convenience of the employer. IRC § 119(a). The classic case where this exclusion applies is with respect to firefighters residing at the firehouse in order to be ready to fight fires at a moment's notice. But there are a number of other types of employees to which the exclusion can apply, including funeral home directors, casino workers, hotel managers, ranch workers, and security personnel. Where the exclusion applies it covers the spouse and dependents of the employee as well. The exclusion under section 119 is only available for meals if they are furnished on the business premises of the employer. IRC § 119(a)(1). It is worth mentioning that high-tech firms and professional sports teams and other businesses are exploiting sections 119 and 132 in circumstances that may end up being tested by the IRS.

Primary Authority

Code: §§ 119(a); 132(a), (b), (c), (d), (e), (h), (j)(1).

Regulations: §§ 1.61-1(a), -2(d)(1), -21(b)(3); 1.132-2(a)(3), -3(a)(4),-4(a)(1).

Cases: Charley v. Commissioner, 91 F.3d 72 (9th Cir. 1996); J. Grant Farms, Inc. v. Commissioner, 49 T.C.M. (CCH) 1197 (U.S. Tax Court 1985); Commissioner v. Smith, 324 U.S. 177 (1945).

Rulings: None.

Problems

6.1. **Ursula Burns works for Xanadu, a major electric automobile manufacturer and appliance maker, as the chief executive officer. Xanadu's aggregate sales for cars are $500,000,000 for a representative period. Its aggregate cost of cars is $400,000,000 for that same period. Coincidentally its aggregate sales and costs for appliance sales are the same as for cars. Determine whether and to what extent the following fringe benefits are excludable from Ursula's gross income.**

  (a) **Ursula buys a Xanadu car for personal use. The car normally costs $50,000 at retail but Ursula receives an employee discount of $10,000 (available to all employees) and so only pays $40,000.**

Ursula is entitled to exclude the entire $10,000 discount under section 132(a)(2), as a qualified employee discount, since she works in the line of business (§ 132(c)(4)) and the discount does not exceed the 20% gross profit percentage for the line of business. IRC § 132(c)(2). The gross profit percentage is determined by subtracting the $400,000,000 aggregate costs from the $500,000,000 aggregate sales to derive a gross profit of $100,000,000 and dividing it by the $500,000,000 of aggregate sales. IRC § 132(c)(2)(B). Note that there is no discrimination permitted in the availability of discounts in favor of highly compensated employees. *See* IRC § 132(j)(1).

[What is Ursula's basis in the car? One argument is that Ursula's basis in the car is $50,000 under the *Philadelphia Park Amusement* case principle that basis is the fair market value of the property acquired in a taxable exchange. If Ursula's basis were her actual cost of $40,000 and she then sold the car for $50,0000 she would have $10,000 of taxable gain and the exclusion would have only served as a deferral provision. In other words, to give a $40,000 basis would be to treat this as a non-recognition transaction (taxation deferred) rather than as an exclusion (taxation forgiven). *Philadelphia Park* is highlighted in Chapter 3. The counter-argument is that a $50,000 basis creates an opportunity for cash transfers to escape taxation through sales of property received by employees to third parties for full price.

Ursula's basis in the car is debatable. We think the more likely outcome is a fair market value basis.]

(b) Same as (a) except that Ursula initially pays full price and the discount is received in the form of a $10,000 rebate check mailed from the home office.

The exclusion still applies. Treas. Reg. § 1.132-2(a)(3)-(4).

(c) Same as (a) except Ursula buys a Xanadu dishwasher that retails for $2,500 but Ursula only pays $2,000.

She still gets the exclusion since she is deemed to work in both lines of business. Treas. Reg. § 1.132-4(a)(1)(iii).

(d) Same as (c) except that Ursula is the division head of Xanadu Auto.

No exclusion is permitted since Ursula does not work in the line of business that produces the discount item; thus the dishwasher is not "qualified property" under section 132(c)(4). *See also* Treas. Reg. § 1.132-4(a)(1).

(e) Same as (a) except that the discount is not available to non-executive personnel.

No exclusion is permitted since this discount is discriminatory (presumably she is highly compensated). IRC § 132(j)(1).

One could note that if a smaller discount was available to all employees even the smaller discount would not be available to Ursula. *See* Treas. Reg. § 1.132-8(a)(2) (disallowing any apportionment).

(f) Same as (a) except that the car is bought by Ursula's son, Tesla.

The exclusion is still available since the purchase by Tesla is deemed to be made by Ursula. IRC § 132(h)(2)(A).

6.2. Paris Lincoln works for the Four Seasons Hotel chain as a concierge in Santa Barbara. Determine whether and to what extent the following fringe benefits are excludable from Paris's gross income.

(a) Paris is permitted to stay for free at a half-full Four Seasons Hotel in Las Vegas for a vacation.

This is excluded as a no-additional-cost service. IRC § 132(a)(1), (b).

(b) Same as (a) except that Paris is given a reserved room and the hotel is full. A paying customer is turned away so that Paris can stay in Las Vegas.

No exclusion is permitted as a no-additional-cost service since foregone revenue is considered a cost. IRC § 132(b)(2) parenthetical. *See* Treas. Reg. § 1.132-2(c) example.

However, arguably the 20% qualified employee discount for services is still available under section 132(a)(2). *See* IRC § 132(c)(1)(B); Treas. Reg. § 1.132-2(a)(2).

(c) Same as (b) except the trip to Las Vegas is for hotel business purposes.

This is excludable as a working condition fringe. IRC § 132(a)(3), (d).

(d) Same as (a) except that the room occupant is Paris's fifteen-year-old son, Beau.

This is still excluded from Paris's and Beau's incomes under the special rule for family members of employees in section 132(h)(2)(A). This assumes that Beau is a "dependent child." *See* IRC §§ 132(h)(2)(B), 152(f)(1).

6.3. Joe Black is a National Basketball Association referee. Joe is given a first class air travel ticket in order to fly from game to game. Joe routinely cashes in his first class ticket, buys a coach class ticket and pockets the difference. Joe also keeps the frequent flyer miles he earns on these trips.

(a) Assuming the first class ticket would otherwise qualify as an excludable working condition fringe benefit, what is the tax consequence of Joe's approach?

Joe should have income to the extent of the excess of his allowance over his actual cost since his net worth is increased by that amount. *Glenshaw Glass*. This principle is also embodied in the section 162 regulations, where it is made plain that a reimbursement in excess of actual expenses is income. *See* Treas. Reg. § 1.162-17(b)(2). These regulations have been partially superseded by regulation § 1.62-2 but not in this respect.

(b) What if Joe cashed in the first class ticket, bought himself a cheaper coach class ticket, and then upgraded the ticket to first class with frequent flyer miles?

No change. Joes has still experienced an accession to wealth in the form of the excess money he obtained by cashing in the first class ticket. One might even argue that he has converted the frequent flyer miles to cash.

The IRS has said it will not seek to tax frequent flyer miles as income unless a taxpayer seeks to convert them to cash. Announcement 2002-18. By analogy to the *Charley v. Commissioner* case, one could argue that this is what Joe is doing here.

In *Charley*, a taxpayer billed clients through a controlled corporation for first class travel and had his travel agent purchase coach class tickets. Then he upgraded those tickets to first class with frequent flyer miles. The court held that the reimbursement in excess of actual cost of the coach tickets was income to the taxpayer.

6.4. Bronco Chavez owns all of the preferred stock of the Four C's Ranch, Inc. This cattle ranch covers thousands of acres in west Texas. Bronco is also the

foreman of the ranch. His duties as foreman include overseeing the ranch hands, buying and selling livestock, seeing to the repair and maintenance of the ranch buildings and equipment, and being available for emergencies. His employment contract with the company requires that he live in the main hacienda on the ranch so that he can be available to address his duties as they arise. He is also obliged to eat his meals on the ranch during his regular working hours. He normally works ten hours a day, five days a week. Bronco is on call 24 hours a day for emergencies. What exclusions, if any, apply to Bronco in the following circumstances?

(a) Bronco is unmarried.

The lodging qualifies for exclusion under section 119(a) since it is a condition of employment, it is on the premises of the employer, and it is for the employer's convenience. The meals eaten during working hours are also excluded. This scenario illustrates the tax planning opportunities of section 119 that are exemplified by the *J. Grant Farms, Inc. v. Commissioner* case. There are potential down sides to such arrangements. In *Grant Farms*, for example, where the family home was deeded to a farming corporation, the Grants would have been obliged to take the rental value of the housing into income had they ceased to manage the farm. Had they turned the running of the farm over to their children this could have become a problem. They also lost the potential benefit of the section 121 exclusion for the sale of a residence with respect to the farmhouse. Section 121 is addressed in Chapter 22.

(b) Same as (a) except that Bronco's family resides with him in the hacienda.

The exclusion applies to his family members as well. IRC § 119(a) first sentence.

(c) Same as (a) except that Bronco has assistant foremen who actually handle all the matters that are nominally Bronco's responsibilities except for Bronco's supervision of the assistants.

Arguably, the third prong of the section 119 test is not met since Bronco is not living on the premises for the convenience of the employer. Now the residential arrangement looks more like a tax dodge than a legitimate business necessity.

Chapter 7

Business and Investment Expense Deductions

Overview

The income tax only attempts to tax net income. That is, it only attempts to tax the net increase in wealth generated by money-making activities. This implies that we should be entitled to deduct the money we spend from the money we make before we apply the tax rates to the remainder. In general this is what the tax rules try to do. Thus, for example, a business that is conducted through the activities of its employees is entitled to deduct the reasonable salaries of those employees from its gross income in determining its taxable income. IRC § 162(a)(1). For the most part, the rules for deducting expenses arising from money-making efforts are straightforward. But there are some interesting complexities in reaching a fair result with respect to business and investment deductions. In this chapter we will examine the general deduction rules and some of the difficulties associated with applying them.

The rich complexity of this area is inherent in its nature, but the key rules addressing deductions are short and, seemingly, simple. The two primary Code provisions in question are sections 162 and 212. Section 162 addresses trade or business deductions. Section 212 addresses expenses related to investment activities and expenses related to obtaining tax advice. The need for a separate provision addressing investment activities arose from an early Supreme Court decision in which the Court ruled that buying and selling stocks and other investment activities did not constitute a trade or business and, thus, what is now section 162 did not apply to the expenses arising from those activities. Higgins v. Commissioner, 312 U.S. 212 (1941). Congress responded by enacting what is now section 212 in order to allow for the deduction of those expenses. Both sections authorize the deductions if the expenses are "ordinary and necessary." Section 162(a)(2) specifically authorizes deduction of "traveling expenses . . . while away from home in pursuit of a trade or business." The IRS takes the position that a taxpayer has only one tax home and that home is located at his or her principal place of business. Rev. Rul. 75-432, 1975-2 C.B. 60. The courts generally accede to this position. It has been established for many years that commuting expenses are not business travel. Commissioner v. Flowers, 326 U.S. 465 (1946).

Because business meals have an element of personal consumption the code limits the deduction to 50% of the meal's cost. IRC § 274(n)(1). However, employees who are reimbursed by their employer for an otherwise deductible meal can normally ignore both the expense and the reimbursement. The employer would remain subject to the 50% limit.

Primary Authority

Code: §§ 161; 162(a); 212; 274(n)(1). Skim §§ 195(a)-(c); 262(a); 274(n)(2); 280A(a).

Regulations: §§ 1.162-1(a), -2(e), -3, -4, -5, -17(b); 1.212-1(a)-(h), -1(l); 1.263(a)-2(e).

Cases: Henderson v. Commissioner, 143 F.3d 497 (9th Cir. 1998); Commissioner v. Flowers, 326 U.S. 465 (1946); Jenkins v. Commissioner; T.C. Memo 1983-667; Welch v. Helvering, 290 U.S. 111 (1933). See also United States v. Correll, 389 U.S. 299 (1967); Moss v. Commissioner, 758 F.2d 211 (7th Cir. 1985); Pevsner v. Commissioner, 628 F.2d 467 (5th Cir. 1980); Rosenspan v. United States, 438 F.2d 905 (2d Cir. 1971); Smith v. Commissioner, 40 BTA 1038 (1939), *aff'd per curiam* 113 F.2d 114 (2d Cir 1940); Trebilcock v. Commissioner, 64 T.C. 852 (1975).

Rulings: Rev. Rul. 54-147, 1954-1 C.B. 51; Rev. Rul. 55-109, 1955 C.B. 261; Rev. Rul. 75-432, 1975-2 C.B. 60; Rev. Rul. 99-7, 1999-1 C.B. 361.

Problems

7.1   **Ally Tran is a lawyer with a solo practice in Boston specializing in estate planning and tax litigation. Ally owns the building in which she practices and rents out space to an accountant, Rick Morales. Which of the following expenditures may Ally deduct under section 162?**

(a) Utility costs for the building;

Yes, this is an ordinary and necessary expense.

(b) Letterhead stationary;

Yes. This is ordinary and necessary as a form of office supplies. Note, the timing of some deductions for supplies can vary between time of purchase and time of consumption. *See* Treas. Reg. § 1.162-3.

(c) The modest salary paid to her administrative assistant;

Yes. This is ordinary and necessary. IRC § 162(a)(1). The provision does limit the deduction to salaries that are "reasonable."

(d) Subscription to *People* magazine for the waiting room;

Yes. This is ordinary and necessary. This is a customary practice in many service-based businesses.

(e) Subscription to online legal databases for legal research;

Yes. These are ordinary and necessary tools of the trade.

(f) Elder care payments for her eighty-four-year-old father, who lives with Ally;

Under the logic applicable to childcare, this is a personal expenditure. *Smith v. Commissioner.* We should note that there is a dependent care tax credit available under section 21. In order to qualify her father would need to be her dependent within the meaning of section 152. The dependency exemption is addressed in Chapter 12.

(g) Suits designed by Georgio Armani and matching shoes that she only wears on days when she is going to court;

Since these clothes could be worn for general use, their costs are not deductible. *Pevsner v. Commissioner.* Clothes that can only be worn for work such as police uniforms and the costumes worn by ballet dancers are deductible.

(h) A high end Apple Macintosh computer used exclusively in her work;

This is a business expenditure but it is not deductible under section 162 since it is a capital expenditure. The cost may be recovered through depreciation, which is addressed in Chapter 9. Note, however, that section 179 could permit a current deduction. Section 179 is also addressed in Chapter 9.

(i) A roundtrip ticket to New York City to take a deposition, departing and returning on the same day. Ally also spent $50 for lunch on her own on that trip;

The plane fare is deductible. But the meal expense is a non-deductible personal expense since it was not taken with a client. IRC § 262; *see United States v. Correll* (holding that meal expenses covered by section 162(a)(2) are those involving a lengthy period of rest or an overnight stay away from home); *but see Moss v. Commissioner* (providing that business meals involving clients or customers may be separately deductible under the main rule of section 162(a) as an ordinary and necessary business expense).

(j) A roundtrip ticket to New York City to take a deposition returning on the following day. Ally spent $100 for dinner on her own on that trip.

The plane fare is deductible. Fifty percent of the meal expense (IRC § 274(n)(2)) is now deductible as a business travel expense since she stayed overnight. IRC § 162(a)(2); *Correll*. It is worth noting that if Ally were an employee and was reimbursed by her employer, she could treat the reimbursement and the expense as a wash (Treas. Reg. § 1.162-17(b)) and her employer would take a full deduction for the plane fare and a 50% deduction for the meal expense. *See* IRC § 274(e)(3), (n)(2)(A).

7.2. Rick Morales, Ally's accountant tenant, also rents office space in Lexington, Massachusetts, fifteen miles from Boston. Rick works three days a week in Boston and two days a week in Lexington. By having offices in both towns

he is able to attract clients from both places. He has one assistant and one receptionist in each office. Eighty percent of his revenue is generated out of his Boston office. Rick maintains his personal residence with his wife and children in Lexington. Consider the deductibility of his expenses in the following circumstances.

(a) Rick drives directly from his home to whichever office he is working in that day. He has lunch brought in and does paperwork while eating. He drives directly home from whichever office he is working in that day. Can he deduct his transportation expense or the cost of his meals? His office rent at both locations?

The travel is commuting and is not deductible under *Commissioner v. Flowers* and Treas. Reg. § 1.162-2(e). The meals are not deductible under section 162(a)(2) (as interpreted under *Correll)* because he is not traveling away from home in a fashion that requires sleep or rest. Nor are the meals deductible under the general rule of section 162(a) since there is no business client involved. *Moss.* The office rent at both locations is deductible since the expense is incurred to do business in two locations with different clienteles. It seems ordinary and necessary under the *Welch* analysis.

(b) Rick sometimes drives between the two offices during the day in order to see clients at both locations and in order to meet with his staff. He also meets with his spiritual adviser occasionally over lunch, his only free time during the day. At these lunches he pays for both meals as well as the cost of the advice. Are his transportation expenses between offices deductible? The costs of his luncheon meetings with his adviser?

The transportation expense is deductible as a regular section 162(a) expense since it arises from business necessity. This principle has been long accepted by the Service. *See* Rev. Rul. 55-109. *See also* Rev. Rul. 99-7. Mileage rates are set each year and published by the IRS in the Internal Revenue Bulletin. The luncheon meeting costs are not deductible under section 162(a) because they are personal in nature. IRC § 262. Even if the spiritual advice related to the business of accounting it would still likely be deemed personal in nature. *See Trebilcock v. Commissioner.*

(c) The facts are the same as in the original scenario except that Boston and Lexington are 100 miles apart and Rick spends two nights a week in Boston in a small apartment he rents for the sole purpose of having a place to stay when he is working in Boston. May he deduct the costs of traveling to Boston and living there two days a week?

Under the Service's view that his tax home is his principal place of business (*see* Rev. Rul. 75-432), Rick's home is Boston. His meals (subject to IRC § 274(n)(1)) and lodging expenses associated with doing business in Lexington should be deductible under section 162(a)(2). This may or may not include his travel expenses from Lexington to Boston if he drives directly from his home in Lexington to his office in Boston. *See* Rev. Rul. 99-7 (holding that transportation costs for travel from one's home to a temporary work location outside the metropolitan area of one's principal place of business are deductible). The question is whether the travel to Boston should be treated as a commuting expense personal in nature or as a business expense. The better view seems to be that the expenses should be deductible since the problem could not be cured by Rick moving to Boston because he would then have to rent an apartment in Lexington and travel to Lexington. His transportation costs arise from business necessity not personal choice about where to live. In the view of some courts, his home in Lexington is his tax home because it is his principal place of residence (*see, e.g., Rosenspan v. United States*). Thus, his Boston housing costs would be the deductible expenses.

> **(d) Same as (c) except that Rick's personal residence where his wife and children reside is in Boston. He rents an apartment in Lexington and lives there three days a week. May he deduct the cost of one of his dwellings? If so, which one?**

Now it appears that his principal place of business and his principal place of residence are in the same location, Boston. Thus, he is away from home when he is in Lexington and his Lexington expenses would be deductible under section 162(a)(2). *See* Rev. Rul. 54-147 (providing home is where the greatest amount of the taxpayer's earnings arise). Under the common sense view that home is where one's family is, Boston is home and the Lexington expenses should be deductible.

7.3 Bruce Chung is a popular rock musician who decided to launch an online music provider to compete with iTunes. He called it Chungtunes. He persuaded some of his musician friends to invest $1,000,000 each in the new enterprise. In order to attract additional outside investors Bruce decided to clear his family's good name by paying $1,000,000 to the creditors of his bankrupt father. Ultimately Chungtunes failed to make a profit and was dissolved. Bruce decided that he should pay back his friends who had invested in Chungtunes in order to protect his reputation in the music business. Are the payments to his father's creditors and to his friends tax deductible?

One might observe that the payments to his father's creditors resemble the facts of *Welch v. Helvering* where deduction under section 162 was denied, and the payments to his friends resemble the facts of *Jenkins v. Commissioner* where the payments were deductible. This frames the question of whether the two cases are really distinguishable. One way to distinguish them is to note that in *Welch* the payments were made in order to prepare the ground for a new business while in *Jenkins* the payments were made in order to protect an ongoing business. Arguably, this makes the payments in *Welch* more like capital expenditures (governed by section 263) than the payments in *Jenkins*. Capital expenditures are not currently deductible and are addressed in the next chapter.

Chapter 8

Capital Expenditures

Overview

There are a number of overriding Code provisions that prevent the current deductibility of otherwise allowable items. *See* IRC § 261 (warning that no deduction shall be allowed "in any case" with respect to certain items specified in Part IX of the Code). Thus, what may seem to be a deductible expense under one provision (e.g., § 162) may be classified as non-deductible under another separate overriding provision. Two overriding provisions are section 263(a) and section 263A(a), which are the subject of this chapter.

Section 263(a) disallows the immediate deduction of "capital expenditures." This provision is less than clear in its full impact and depends on the regulations, administrative rulings, and case law for much amplification and clarification. Capital expenditures are generally those amounts paid to create, acquire, or improve long-lived assets. The reason such costs are not currently deductible is that the property produced, acquired, or improved is not consumed or used up within the year, but rather it continues to contribute to income over a period of years. Classic examples of capital expenditures related to *tangible property* include amounts paid to: (1) acquire tangible property (other than materials or supplies); (2) construct tangible property; (3) sell tangible property; (4) defend title to tangible property; and (5) improve tangible property (i.e., expenditures for betterments of property, expenditures for restorations of property, or expenditures that adapt property to a new or different use). Treas. Reg. § 1.263(a)-1, -2, -3. Examples of capital expenditures related to *intangible property* include amounts paid to acquire or create intangible property, although, under the "12-month rule," a taxpayer is not required to capitalize amounts that provide benefits only for a relatively brief duration. Treas. Reg. § 1.263(a)-4.

Section 263A(a) requires the capitalization of all direct and indirect costs allocable to construction or production of real property or tangible personal property. [It also applies to taxpayers who acquire or hold inventory property for resale.] IRC § 263A(a), (b), (f), (g). An important exemption exists in the case of freelance writers, photographers, and artists. IRC § 263A(h).

If expenditures are not deductible when paid or incurred, they are capitalized, that is, they are added to the taxpayer's basis in the property to which the expenditures relate. Although they are not immediately deductible, these capitalized costs may be eligible to be deducted over time through an appropriate depreciation or amortization allowance under a separate Code provision. If not, such capitalized costs will be recovered when the property is disposed of (recall that gain realized on the disposition of property is the excess of amount realized over the property's adjusted basis).

Primary Authority

Code: §§ 161; 263(a); 263A(a), (b), (g), (h). Skim § 195.

Regulations: §§ 1.162-3, -4, -6; 1.212-1(k); 1.263(a)-1(e)(1), (f), -2(d)(1), (e), (f)(1)-(2), (4), ex. 8, -3(a)(1)-(2), (c)(1), (d), (e)(1)-(4), (6), ex. 8, (g)(2), (i)(1), (j)(1), (j)(3), ex. 12, (k)(1), (7), ex. 6, (l)(1), (3), ex. 12.

Cases: Nabisco, Inc. v. Commissioner, 76 T.C.M. (CCH) 71.

Rulings: Rev. Rul. 92-80, 1992-2 C.B. 57; Technical Advice Memorandum 9643003 (Oct. 25, 1996).

Problems

8.1. X Corporation manufactures and sells widgets. Discuss whether each expenditure below is currently deductible as an expense under section 162 or constitutes a nondeductible capital expenditure.

(a) $1,000,000 to buy land and an old manufacturing building.

The $1 million cost of purchasing the land and building is a nondeductible capital expenditure. IRC § 263(a); Treas. Reg. § 1.263(a)-2(d)(1) (requiring capitalization of amounts paid to acquire "a unit of real or personal property"). A building is usually a unit of property. Treas. Reg. § 1.263(a)-3(e)(2).

It should be noted that any related acquisition costs, such as appraisal fees, commissions, and legal fees, would also have to be capitalized and added to the bases of the purchased assets. Treas. Reg. § 1.263(a)-2(f)(1) (requiring capitalization of amounts paid to facilitate the acquisition of real or personal property), -2(f)(2)(ii) (providing a list of inherently facilitative costs that generally must be capitalized as transaction costs), -2(f)(4), ex. 8 (providing an exception for certain costs incurred in investigating real property purchases).

(b) $15,000 to remove asbestos-containing insulation from the building and replace it with new insulation that is safer to employees; $100,000 to bring the building into the high-quality condition for which X's other facilities are known (repainting, replacing windows and doors, repairing and replacing roofing materials); and $200,000 to convert part of the manufacturing building into a showroom.

The issue here is whether these amounts are considered deductible repairs or capital improvements to the building. Amounts paid for repairs and maintenance to tangible property are deductible unless they are required to be capitalized. Treas. Reg. § 1.162-4(a). A taxpayer must generally capitalize expenditures that result in an "improvement" to a unit of property. The regulations provide that a unit of property is deemed to be improved in three situations—(1) betterments, (2) restorations, and (3) adaptations to new or different uses. Treas. Reg. § 1.263(a)-3(d).

The $15,000 to remove asbestos-containing insulation and replace it with new, safer insulation is likely deductible. According to Treas. Reg. § 1.263(a)-3(j)(3), example. 2, the $15,000 paid to remove and replace the asbestos insulation is *not* for a *betterment* to the building structure or an improvement to the building. Although the asbestos is determined to be unsafe under certain circumstances, the presence of asbestos insulation in a building, by itself, is not a preexisting material condition or defect of the building structure under Treas. Reg. § 1.263(a)-3(j)(1)(i). In addition, the removal and replacement of the asbestos is not for a material addition to the building structure or a material increase in the capacity of the building structured under Treas. Reg. § 1.263(a)-3(j)(1)(ii), (iv). Similarly, the removal and replacement of asbestos is not reasonably expected to materially increase the productivity, efficiency, strength, quality, or output of the building structure per Treas. Reg. § 1.263(a)-3(j)(1)(iii), (iv).

In contrast to the cost of removing and replacing asbestos, the $100,000 paid to bring the building into the high-quality condition for which X Corporation's facilities are known comprises a *betterment* to the building under Treas. Reg. § 1.263(a)-3(j)(1)(i) because the amount ameliorates material conditions that existed prior to X Corporation's acquisition of the building. Therefore, X must treat the amount paid for the betterment to the building as an improvement to the building and must capitalize the amount under Treas. Reg. § 1.263(a)-(d)(1) and (j).

The $200,000 paid to convert the manufacturing building into a showroom *adapts* the building structure to a *new and different use*. *See* Treas. Reg. § 1.263(a)-(l)(3), example 1. Therefore, X Corporation must capitalize the amount as an improvement under Treas. Reg. § 1.263(a)-3(d)(3) and (l).

> **(c) $18,000 to buy a new widget-making machine, $2,000 to install the machine; and $500 for the first-year's maintenance on the machine (cleaning and oiling of the machine, inspection of parts for defects; and the replacement of springs, bearings, and seals).**

The $18,000 cost of the new machine must be capitalized (the machine is a unit of property as determined under Treas. Reg. § 1.263(a)-3(e) and is not a material or supply under Treas. Reg. § 1.162-3). *See* Treas. Reg. § 1.263(a)-2(d)(1). The $2,000 installation cost is part of the acquisition cost of the machine and must also be capitalized.

The $500 for the first-year's maintenance is not required to be capitalized as an improvement under the *safe harbor for routine maintenance*. Treas. Reg. § 1.263(a)-3(i). This is an amount paid for recurring activities X Corporation is expected to perform to keep the machine in its ordinarily efficient operating condition, and X Corporation reasonably expects at the time the machine is placed in service to perform the maintenance more than once during the class life of the machine. Treas.

Reg. § 1.263(a)-3(i)(1)(ii). Note that even if the $500 doesn't meet all of the require-
ments for the routine maintenance safe harbor, X Corporation might still be able to
deduct the amount if it is not for an improvement under a facts and circumstances
analysis.

> **(d) $50,000 to purchase a competitor's patent on a special manufacturing
> process ($40,000 for the patent and $10,000 in legal fees to facilitate the
> acquisition).**

The $40,000 paid to acquire the patent must be capitalized. Treas. Reg.
§ 1.263(a)-4(b)(1)(i), -4(c). Likewise, the $10,000 paid to lawyers to facilitate the
patent acquisition must be capitalized. Treas. Reg. § 1.263(a)-4(b)(1)(v), -4(e)(1)(i).
Note that a taxpayer is not required to capitalize employee compensation related to
the acquisition of an intangible. Thus, if X Corporation utilized in-house counsel
to facilitate the patent acquisition, the in-house counsel's salary would remain deductible.

> **(e) $300,000 in salary to the company's president. The president spent two
> thirds of his time running the day-to-day affairs of the business, and
> one third of his time negotiating the acquisition of the machine in (c)
> and the patent in (d) above.**

Based on what we learned in the last chapter, X Corporation should be able to
deduct the $300,000 president's salary, provided it is reasonable. IRC § 162(a)(1).
Based on what we have learned in this chapter, however, should X Corporation be
required to capitalize $100,000 of this amount since the president spent one-third
of his time negotiating the acquisition of a machine and a patent?

The regulations under section 263 (governing both tangible property and intangible property) require the capitalization of an amount paid to facilitate the taxpayer's acquisition of property (tangible or intangible). Treas. Reg. § 1.263(a)-2(f)(1)
(tangible property); Treas. Reg. § 1.263(a)-4(b)(1)(v), -4(e)(1)(i) (intangible property).
Fortunately, there is an important exception. A taxpayer is not required to capitalize
employee compensation related to the acquisition of an asset. Treas. Reg. § 1.263(a)-
2(f)(1)(iv) (tangible property); Treas. Reg. § 1.263(a)-4(e)(4)(i) (intangible property).
This simplifying convention was designed to resolve controversy and to eliminate
the burden on taxpayers of allocating certain transaction costs among various assets.
In sum, X Corporation may deduct $300,000.

> **(f) $40,000 to develop an advertising campaign (including costs to develop
> a package design for its newest widget product) and $10,000 to execute
> the advertising campaign (including costs of using social media, pur-
> chasing keywords, placing ads in the newspaper, and bundling inserts
> of ad pages with newspapers).**

The $40,000 to develop the campaign is deductible. The regulations under sec-
tion 263 require capitalization of amounts paid to create "separate and distinct
intangible assets." Treas. Reg. § 1.263(a)-4(b)(1)(iii), -4(b)(3)(i). Interestingly, the

regulations provide that an amount paid to create a package design is not treated as an amount that creates a separate and distinct intangible asset. Treas. Reg. § 1.263(a)-4(b)(3)(v). [Note: Before the regulations were issued in 2004, the costs of creating a package design were held to be capitalized because package designs do not have ascertainable useful lives. *See* Rev. Proc. 2002-9, 2002-3 I.R.B. 327 (app. § 3.01); Rev. Proc. 97-35, 1997-2 C.B. 48 (§ 5); Rev. Rul. 89-23, 1989-1 C.B. 85. Now, under the regulations, the costs of creating a package design are deductible because a package design is not considered a separate and distinct intangible asset.] It should be noted that although a taxpayer can deduct the costs of developing a package design, the taxpayer must capitalize the costs of obtaining trademarks and copyrights on elements of the package design, since these are rights granted by a governmental agency. Treas. Reg. § 1.263(a)-4(d)(5). The regulations provide an example right on point. *See* Treas. Reg. § 1.263(a)-4(l), example 9.

The $10,000 paid to execute the campaign is also deductible under Rev. Rul. 92-80. It should be noted that expenditures for tangible assets associated with advertising, such as billboards, must be capitalized.

Nabisco, Inc. v. Commissioner held that both advertising *campaign* and execution *expenditures* are deductible under Rev. Rul. 92-80. In *Nabsico*, the government argued that advertising campaign expenditures provide long-term benefits, whereas advertising execution expenditures give rise to short-term benefits; thus the former should be capitalized, while the latter may be expensed. But the court did not accept the long-term, short-term distinction, and instead found that trade dress is a product of both advertising campaign and execution expenditures. The court then concluded that the long-term benefit associated with trade dress must be a benefit traditionally associated with ordinary business advertising and cannot serve as a basis to require capitalization of advertising campaign expenditures. The government apparently conceded the issue with the regulations issued in 2004.

(g) **$85,000 paid to a web design and development firm to build a custom e-commerce website with a content management system and customer database; and a $2,400 annual fee for dedicated hosting for the period from October 1 of this year to September 30 of next year.**

The fee paid to the web design and development firm could be classified as an "advertising" expense, deductible under Rev. Rul. 92-80. Alternatively, the fee could be viewed as a "software development" expense, deductible under Rev. Proc. 2000-50, which is discussed in Chapter 28.

What about the $2,400 annual fee for web hosting? As a general rule, a taxpayer must capitalize prepaid expenses (*see* Treas. Reg. § 1.263(a)-4(d)(3)) and amounts paid for certain contract rights (*see* Treas. Reg. § 1.263(a)-4(d)(6)). There is an important exception, termed the 12-month rule, applicable to most created intangibles. Under the 12-month rule, a taxpayer is not required to capitalize amounts if the amounts do not create any right or benefit for the taxpayer that extends beyond the earlier of (1) 12 months after the first date on which the taxpayer realizes the right or benefit, or (2) the end of the taxable year following the taxable year in which the payment is made. Treas. Reg. § 1.263(a)-4(f)(1). The 12-month rule applies to the $2,400 payment because the right or benefit attributable to the payment neither extends more than 12 months beyond October 1 of the current year (the first date the benefit is realized by X Corporation) nor beyond the end of the taxable year following the taxable year in which the payment is made. Accordingly, X Corporation is not required to capitalize the $3,000 payment. *See* Treas. Reg. § 1.263(a)-4(f)(8), example 2.

(h) $3,000 for the annual premium for general liability insurance covering from February 1 of next year to January 31 of the year after.

The amount paid by X Corporation is a prepaid expense. Because the right or benefit attributable to the $3,000 payment extends beyond the end of the taxable year following the taxable year in which the payment is made, the 12-month rule does not apply. Treas. Reg. § 1.263(a)-4(f)(1). X Corporation must capitalize the $3,000 payment.

8.2. Ira Gertrude is a full-time music teacher at a local high school. For the past three years, Ira has also written a number of musical compositions and performed at a number of local venues. This year, Ira spent $1,500 (costs of pens, paper, and a one-day writing camp for songwriters) to write a song, and he spent $5,000 to record the song on a rough-cut "demo" tape (cost of renting a recording studio and hiring a recording engineer) hoping that he would find a record company to produce and distribute his music. Are these amounts currently deductible?

$1,500 to write a song:

The costs paid by Ira to create a musical composition are most likely deductible. This is because (1) such costs are section 263A(h) "qualified creative expenses" and, hence, are exempt from the general capitalization rule of section 263A(a), and (2) such costs are section 162 "ordinary and necessary" expenses paid "in carrying on" Ira's song writing "trade or business."

Section 263A(h)(1) provides an exception from the general rule of section 263A(a) for any qualified creative expense. Section 263A(h)(2) provides the term "qualified creative expense" means any expense which is paid or incurred by an individual in the trade or business of such individual of being a writer, photographer, or artist, and which without regard to section 263A would be allowable as a deduction for the taxable year. Section 263A(h)(3)(A) provides the term "writer" means any individual if the personal efforts of such individual create (or may reasonably be expected to create) a literary manuscript, *musical composition (including any accompanying words)*, or a dance score.

Clearly, Ira is a "writer" as defined in section 263(h)(3)(A). That is not enough, however, for the exemption provision of section 263A(h) to apply. First, under section 263(h)(2), Ira's activities must rise to the level of a trade or business within the meaning of the Code. It could be concluded on these facts that Ira's song writing activities do rise to the level of a trade or business. Second, under section 263(h)(2) (flush language), the $1,500 must not relate to printing, photographic plates, motion picture films, video tapes, or similar items. Because the $1,500 paid to create a song is not an expense related to printing, photographic plates, motion picture films, video tapes, or similar items, it is a section 263A(h) qualified creative expense exempt from the general rule of section 263A.

$5,000 to record the song on a rough-cut demo tape

Here, the first issue is whether the $5,000 paid by Ira in producing a demo tape of his song is subject to the general rule of section 263A(a). Section 263A(a) provides in the case of property to which section 263A applies, the direct costs of the property, and such property's proper share of part or all of those indirect costs that are allocable to such property, shall be capitalized. Section 263A(b)(1) provides that section 263A applies to "tangible personal property" produced by the taxpayer. Section 263A(b)(1) (flush language) additionally provides that the term "tangible personal property" shall include a film, a *sound recording*, video tape, book, or similar property. Accordingly, the rough-cut demo tape is tangible personal property, and is subject to capitalization unless otherwise excepted by the Code.

Does section 263A(h) permit a deduction of the $5,000 cost to create and produce the demo tape? The Code specifically provides that a qualified creative expense does not include "any expense related to printing, photographic plates, motion picture films, video tapes, or *similar items*." IRC § 263A(h)(2) (flush language). In Technical Advice Memorandum 9643003 (Oct. 25, 1996), the IRS concluded that a demo tape is a "similar item," and the cost of producing the tape is expressly excluded from the definition of a qualified creative expense. Thus, the $5,000 paid to create and produce the sound recording is not a qualified creative expense.

In sum, if Ira creates a song, the cost of writing the song is a qualified creative expense. If he then creates a sound recording (demo tape) of the song, the cost of producing the tape is not a qualified creative expenses. The deduction is limited to the written creation, and is not available for the expression of that creation.

Chapter 9

Depreciation and Amortization

Overview

In an economic sense, depreciation is the decline in value of an asset due to wear and tear and obsolescence. In the tax sense, depreciation is a deduction from gross income to permit the taxpayer to recover the capitalized cost of that asset over a certain period of time. Indeed, tax depreciation methods are sometimes called cost recovery systems.

The depreciation deduction for *tangible property* is authorized in section 167 and is limited to property used in a trade or business or property held for production of income. IRC § 167(a). Among other things this excludes inventory and personal use property, such as a personal residence. Rules for *computing* the depreciation deductions for tangible property are found in section 168. Enacted to simplify computation rules and stimulate the economy, it provides that depreciation deductions for tangible property shall be determined using: (1) the applicable depreciation method; (2) the applicable recovery period; and (3) the applicable convention. IRC § 168(a)-(e). These rules generally allow a taxpayer to recover the capitalized cost of tangible property well before it ceases to be useful in her business or income-producing activity. The IRS has issued Rev. Proc. 87-57, 1987-2 C.B. 687, to help compute the proper depreciation allowances. It sets forth tables that incorporate the various depreciation methods, recovery periods, and conventions provided in section 168.

There is a significant bonus depreciation rule, section 179, which Congress recently made *permanent*. It allows one to elect to write off (immediately expense) the cost of depreciable, tangible, personal property (as opposed to real property) purchased for the active conduct of a trade or business. IRC § 179(a), (d). Certain qualified leasehold improvements also qualify. There is a limit on the maximum amount that can be expensed in any given year ($500,000), and this dollar limitation is reduced/phased out if the cost of qualifying property placed in service during the year exceeds an investment threshold ($2,000,000). IRC § 179(b)(1)-(2). Both amounts are indexed for inflation beginning in 2016. In addition, the amount eligible to be expensed cannot exceed the taxpayer's taxable income; any disallowed deductions due to this limitation are permitted to be carried forward. IRC § 179(b)(3). [Note that Congress has also enacted section 168(k), a *temporary* provision that provides an extra, up-front depreciation deduction for qualified property (i.e., new, depreciable tangible personal property). It is subject to a phase-down schedule through

2019: 50% for 2015–2017; 40% in 2018; and 30% in 2019. This additional first-year depreciation is computed after applying section 179 (if it was elected) and before the regular depreciation deduction is calculated for the year.]

The amortization deduction for intangible property is generally found in section 197. It provides an arbitrary 15-year recovery period for many types of intangible property. IRC § 197(a). It generally applies only to purchased rather than self-generated section 197 intangibles. IRC § 197(c)(2). Section 197 intangible property includes goodwill, customer lists, patents, copyrights, covenants not to compete, franchises, trademarks, trade names, and a few other intangibles. IRC § 197(d)(1). If section 197 does not apply to an intangible asset (i.e., the asset is not listed as a section 197 intangible or is specifically excluded from the definition), amortization continues to be governed by pre-section 197 law. Treas. Reg. § 1.167(a)-14. It should be noted that there is no bonus depreciation rule for intangible property other than off-the-shelf software.

Primary Authority

Code:	§§ 167(a)-(c), (i)(2); 168(a)-(e); 179(a), (b)(1)-(3)(A), (b)(5), (d)(1); 197(a)-(d)(1); 1016(a)(2).
Regulations:	§§ 1.167(a)-3, -14(a); 1.167(b)-1(a), -2(a); 1.167(g)-1.
Cases:	Simon v. Commissioner, 68 F.3d 41 (2d Cir. 1995), non-acq. 1996-2 C.B. 2.
Rulings:	Rev. Rul. 68-232, 1968-1 C.B. 79; Rev. Proc. 87-56, 1987-2 C.B. 674; Rev. Proc. 87-57, 1987-2 C.B. 687.

Problems

9.1. Marketing materials from a major U.S corporation that designs, develops, and sells personal computers state: "Buy our computers by December 31 and you may be able to deduct them from your current year's business income." Is this statement true or false? Why?

The statement is "true." We learned in the previous chapter that the cost of acquiring a computer is a capital expenditure. IRC § 263; Treas. Reg. § 1.263(a)-2(d)(1) (requiring a taxpayer to capitalize amounts paid to acquire a unit of real or personal property). Section 179, however, allows one to elect to write off the cost of acquisition of section 179 property as an expense "not chargeable to a capital account." IRC § 179(a). A computer used in active business is section 179 property—i.e., depreciable, tangible, personal property purchased for the active conduct of a trade or business. IRC § 179(d)(1).

It is appropriate for the marketing materials to qualify the statement, i.e., "you *may* be able to deduct" the computers, because the maximum allowable deduction for *all* qualifying property placed in service during a year is $500,000 (adjusted for inflation). IRC § 179(b)(1). This amount is reduced dollar-for-dollar (but not below zero) by the amount by which the cost of qualifying proper placed in service during the year exceeds $2 million (also adjusted for inflation). IRC § 179(b)(2). In addition, the amount eligible to be expensed cannot exceed the taxable income derived by the taxpayer from the active conduct of any trade or business. Thus, a large business that has purchased a lot of equipment during the year, may not be able to deduct the computers from its current year's income. Likewise, a small business with little to no taxable income also may be precluded from writing off the computers.

9.2. **Charles, who is a real estate developer, owns a number of assets. Which of the following assets are of a character that is subject to the allowance for depreciation or amortization? And which of the following assets are eligible for a bonus depreciation election under section 179?**

(a) **Three lots from a tract of land that Charles has subdivided for sale.**

The regulations under section 167 explicitly state that the allowance for tax depreciation does not apply to land (apart from improvements of physical development added to it). Treas. Reg. § 1.167(a)-2 (noting also that the depreciation allowance does not apply to natural resources which are subject to the allowance for depletion provided in section 611). The reasoning is that land is not subject to wear and tear, to decay or decline from natural causes, to exhaustion or obsolescence.

Section 179 does not apply to unimproved, vacant land. IRC § 179(d).

(b) **A residence used by Charles as his principal residence.**

The regulations under section 167 provide that no deduction for depreciation is allowed on a building used by the taxpayer solely as his residence. Treas. Reg. § 1.167(a)-2.

Section 179 does not apply to personal use property. IRC § 179(d).

(c) **Same as (b) except that one of the bedrooms in the residence is used exclusively by Charles as a home office for his real estate business.**

If Charles' home office qualifies as his principal place of business, a partial depreciation deduction may be allowed with respect to the building structure (not the land). IRC § 280A(c). The depreciation allowance would be based on the percentage of the home used for business. A common method to determine the percentage of a home used for business is to divide the square footage of the home office by the square footage of the total home. For example, if Charles' spare bedroom used as an office is 240 square feet and the total square footage of his home is 1,200 feet, then 20% (240/1,200) of a full year's depreciation allowance would be allowed. There is an important income limitation in IRC § 280A(c)(5). Home office deductions are explored more fully in Chapter 22, which is devoted to the tax treatment of residential real estate.

Section 179 would not apply as the building, although partially depreciable, is not section 1245 property, i.e., depreciable tangible *personal property.*

> **(d) A small one-family house that Charles inherited from his mother five years ago and that has been rented out to the same tenant since her death.**

The building (not the land) is subject to wear and tear and held for production of income. Thus it is subject to a depreciation allowance. IRC § 167(a)(2).

Section 179 generally applies to section 1245 property and not to buildings. (Note that the exception for qualified leasehold improvements does not apply to residential buildings.)

> **(e) A computer, sofa, and antique desk that are located in Charles' business office and used solely in his real estate business. Although the computer and sofa have declined in value every year, the antique desk has increased in value every year since it was made over a century ago.**

The office furniture (computer, sofa, and antique desk) are subject to wear and tear and are used in Charles' real estate trade or business. Therefore, they are depreciable assets. IRC § 167(a)(1); Treas. Reg. § 1.167(a)-2 (stating that properties used exclusively in business may be depreciated).

All three assets are considered section 179 properties—i.e., depreciable, tangible, personal properties acquired by purchase and used in an active business.

You may question why the antique desk is depreciable since it has increased in value every year since it was made over a century ago. Under the *Simon v. Commissioner* court's analysis, the antique desk need not have a determinable useful life in order to be depreciable. The ACRS rules establish arbitrary recovery periods that do not mirror actual useful lives. However, under *Simon* the property must be subject to exhaustion, wear and tear, or obsolescence in order to be depreciable. Under the dissent's analysis no deduction would be permitted since the antique desk has no determinable useful life. This approach rests on the implicit requirement of determinable useful life found in Treas. Reg. § 1.167(a)-1(b). Keep in mind that the IRS has not acquiesced to *Simon*.

> **(f) A portrait of Charles' father that Charles' mother painted and gave to Charles as a gift. The portrait hangs on the wall in Charles' office.**

Although the painting is hanging in Charles' office, it is not subject to wear and tear and, therefore, is not depreciable. Some students may suggest that the painting is arguably subject to wear and tear because of damage caused by sunlight, humidity, etc. But the IRS has long held that works of art are not depreciable. *See* Rev. Rul. 68-232.

Section 179 does not apply, since the painting is not of a character subject to the allowance for depreciation. IRC § 179(d).

> **(g) Computer software that Charles purchased for use in his real estate development business.**

Computer software used in business is depreciable due to its obsolescence. Treas. Reg. § 167(a)-2, -9. The difficulty with purchased software is determining the appropriate cost recovery period.

If the computer software purchased by Charles is *off-the-shelf software* (i.e., readily available for purchase by the general public, subject to a nonexclusive license, and not substantially modified), then Charles can make a section 179 election to expense currently the purchase costs. IRC § 179(d)(1)(A)(ii). If an election is not made, then the off-the-shelf software costs are depreciated over three years using the straight-line method. IRC § 167(f)(1).

If the computer software is *custom software*, then the appropriate cost recovery deductions depend on how the custom software was acquired. If the custom software was acquired in a transaction involving the acquisition of assets constituting a trade or business or substantial portion thereof, then the purchase costs are amortized over fifteen years using the straight line method. IRC § 197. But if the custom software was acquired separately, then the purchase costs are depreciated over three years using the straight-line method. IRC § 167(f)(1); Treas. Reg. § 1.167(a)-14(b)(1).

It should be noted that the above rules do not apply to bundled software. In other words, if the computer software is included, without being separately stated, in the cost of any hardware or other tangible property purchased, then the bundled software costs are depreciated under the rules for the associated hardware or other tangible property. Treas. Reg. § 1.167(a)-14(b)(2). Recall that computers have a five-year applicable recovery period. IRC § 168.

(h) Shares of stock in a closely-held company that has operated a family farm business for years.

Shares of stock in a company, although perhaps held for production of income, are not subject to wear and tear, and, therefore, are not depreciable under IRC §§ 167, 168. Further, stock is specifically excluded from section 197 amortization. IRC § 197(e)(1)(A).

9.3. **In the first quarter of the current year, Yao purchased three pieces of equipment for use in her business for a total cost of $300,000. One of these business assets was a small pick-up truck that cost $30,000. The truck has a 6-year class life and is 5-year property under section 168(e). Compute Yao's depreciation deductions in each year and the adjusted basis of the truck under the following circumstances.**

(a) Yao elects to employ the straight-line method under section 168(b) (5) and makes no bonus depreciation elections under section 179 or 168(k).

We begin by determining what convention applies. In this case, the half-year convention applies. IRC § 168(d)(4)(A).

We must also determine the straight-line percentage; in this case, it is 20% (100/5 = 20).

Year	Depreciation rate		Amount of depreciation	§1016(a)(2) AB
1	.20 × ½ × 30,000	=	3,000	27,000
2	.20 × 30,000	=	6,000	21,000
3	.20 × 30,000	=	6,000	15,000
4	.20 × 30,000	=	6,000	9,000
5	.20 × 30,000	=	6,000	3,000
6	.20 × ½ × 30,000	=	3,000	0

We take the last half year in Year 6. *See* Rev. Proc. 87-57 (which shows an allowance in Year 6 for an asset with an applicable recovery period of five years.). Salvage value is zero. IRC § 168(b)(4).

> **(b) What if Yao does not make the election under section 168(b)(5) and instead employs the regular ACRS method? Again, assume that Yao makes no section 179 election and that section 168(k) does not apply.**

Again we use a 5-year applicable recovery period under section 168(c) with a zero salvage value under section 168(b)(4). We use the 200% declining balance method under section 168(b)(1). This yields a 40% deduction each year (100/5 × 2 = 40). We again use the half-year convention under section 168(d)(1). We switch to straight line in Year 5 when that deduction is greater. IRC § 168(b)(1)(B). *See* Rev. Proc. 87-57.

Year	Depreciation rate		Amount of depreciation	§1016(a)(2) AB
1	.40 × ½ × 30,000	=	6,000	24,000
2	.40 × 24,000	=	9,600	14,400
3	.40 × 14,400	=	5,760	8,640
4	.40 × 8,640	=	3,456	5,184
5	.66 (SL) × 5,184	=	3,456	1,728
6	.66 (SL) × ½ × 5,184	=	1,728	0

In Year 5, we switch because .40 × 5,184 = 2,073 as opposed to .666 × 5,184 = 3,456. We might note that we need to switch methods because DDB method never gets to zero. Again we take the last half year of depreciation in Year 6.

> **(c) Same as (b) except that Yao sells the equipment on November 1, Year 4, for $10,000.**

The half-year convention applies in Year 4. IRC § 168(d)(4)(A).

Year	Depreciation rate		Amount of depreciation	§1016(a)(2) AB
1	.40 × ½ × 30,000	=	6,000	24,000
2	.40 × 24,000	=	9,600	14,400
3	.40 × 14,400	=	5,760	8,640
4	.40 × ½ × 8,640	=	1,728	6,912

Thus, on the sale Yao has a gain of $3,088 ($10,000 − $6,912 = $3,088) under section 1001. The gain would be ordinary under section 1245, as explained more fully in

Chapter 19. Note that the half-year convention does no harm since it causes Yao's basis to be higher for gain measurement purposes thereby reducing Yao's recognized gain.

(d) Same as (c) except that Yao gives the equipment to Daughter.

The half-year convention applies to any "disposition" so the result is the same for Yao as in (c) with respect to the amount of depreciation deductions allowed. Of course there is no gain recognition. In Chapter 19, we will consider the operation of section 1245(b)(3) and the effect of section 1245 on Daughter. As a reminder, don't forget the operation of sections 102(a) and 1015(a), which were considered in Chapter 4.

(e) What if in (b) Yao elects section 179, which has an expensing limit of $500,000 and a $2 million overall investment limit before phase out under section 179(b)(2)? You may assume that the income limit under section 179(b)(3) does not apply and that section 168(k) also does not apply.

Under section 179, the maximum dollar amount ($500,000) is reduced dollar-for-dollar (but not below zero) by the amount by which the cost of qualifying property placed in service during the tax year exceeds $2,000,000. IRC § 179(b)(2). Because Yao bought $300,000 of section 179 property this year, which is well below the $2,000,000 investment limit, she is eligible to expense the cost of the pick-up truck. This would reduce the adjusted basis in the truck to $0, leaving nothing to recover under regular ACRS.

What would happen if the cost of all three pieces of equipment for use in her business were $2,100,000 ($100,000 more than the investment limit)? In such case, she could elect to expense only $400,000 of the cost of the three pieces of equipment; she would have to pick and choose which assets she wants subject to section 179 and the amount. IRC § 179(c). Basis would be reduced by the expensed amount before applying regular depreciation rules (i.e., the double declining balance method).

What would happen if the cost of all three pieces of equipment for use in her business were $2,500,000 ($500,000 more than the investment limit)? In such case, she would get no section 179 deduction because of the dollar and investment limitations.

9.4. Best Cleaners, Inc. will purchase all of the assets of an existing dry cleaning business from Comet Cleaners, Inc., including the following intangible assets: (1) Comet's customer list; (2) a patent obtained by Comet on a dry cleaning chemical that does not dissolve buttons; (3) Comet's website including all the copyrighted contents; (4) Comet's registered trademark "Where Buttons Don't Dissolve"; (5) the domain name "cometcleaners.com" that is registered by Comet.

(a) What are the tax consequences to Best Cleaners upon the acquisition of these intangible assets?

Best Cleaners must capitalize the costs of acquiring these intangible assets. IRC § 263(a); Treas. Reg. § 1.263(a)-4(b)(1) (requiring a taxpayer to capitalize amounts paid to another party to acquire an intangible from that party in a purchase or similar transaction). Best Cleaners must also capitalize any amounts paid to facilitate the acquisition of the assets that constitute a trade or business. Treas. Reg. § 1.263(a)-5.

These acquired intangibles are all "section 197 intangibles." *See* IRC § 197(d)(1) (C)(ii) (customer lists), 197(d)(1)(C)(iii) (patents and copyrights), 197(d)(1)(F) (trademarks and domains name that functions as a trademark). If the total consideration paid by Best Cleaners exceeded the fair market values of the acquired assets, the excess would be considered goodwill, which is also a section 197 intangible. IRC § 197(d)(1)(A). Best Cleaners must amortize the capitalized cost of these intangibles ratably over a fifteen-year period. IRC § 197(a). The fifteen-year period begins on the first day of the month in which these intangibles are acquired and held in connection with a trade or business (within the meaning of section 162). Treas. Reg. § 1.197-2(f)(1)(i)(A).

(b) Would Best Cleaners be better off, from a tax standpoint, if it allocates more of the purchase price to Comet Cleaners' tangible assets instead of the intangible assets? Would such allocation necessarily be respected by the IRS?

As noted in (a), these intangibles have a fifteen-year recovery period under section 197. Most tangible assets, other than buildings, have much shorter recovery periods (e.g., 3, 5, or 7 years) under section 168. Best Cleaners could achieve larger cost recovery deductions now if the purchase agreement allocated more of the purchase price to tangible assets with shorter recovery periods. But, the Service would not necessarily have to respect purchase price allocations made by the parties.

(c) Would Best Cleaners be better off, from a tax standpoint, if it purchases all the stock of Comet Cleaners, Inc., instead of its assets?

No. The capitalized costs of purchasing stock are not amortizable under section 197 because stock in a corporation is not a "section 197 intangible." IRC § 197(e)(1). Further, corporate stock is not property subject to the allowance for depreciation in sections 167/168. [Note, however, if the requirements of section 338 are satisfied and if a proper election is made under section 338, a "qualified stock purchase" will be treated as a transaction involving the acquisition of assets constituting a trade or business (deemed asset purchase) if the direct acquisition of the assets of the corporation would have been treated as the acquisition of assets constituting a trade or business. Treas. Reg. § 1.197-2(e)(5). There is a quid pro quo for obtaining a cost basis in the underlying assets and fifteen-year amortization. *See* IRC § 338. Section 338 is beyond the scope of this chapter.]

Chapter 10

Deductible Personal Expenses: Casualty and Theft Losses

Overview

This chapter is about losses. Specifically, it focuses on a narrow category of personal losses known as personal casualty losses. When we speak of a loss we are usually referring to property dispositions. Section 1001 tells us that a loss is realized when the adjusted basis of the property disposed of exceeds the amount realized on the disposition. The amount of the loss is the difference between the adjusted basis and the amount realized. The deductibility of uncompensated losses is governed, in major part, by section 165. This provision authorizes deductions for losses arising from business and investment activities. IRC § 165(c)(1) & (2). Generally speaking, taxpayers are not allowed to deduct losses or expenses that arise from personal concerns. Thus, if your personal use car is damaged your loss is non-deductible, and your costs to repair it are also non-deductible. *See* IRC §§ 165(a), (c), & 262. (As Chapter 9 illustrates, you also get no depreciation deduction for its gradual decline in value.) The rationale for disallowing all but a few personal losses is that those losses are deemed to arise from personal consumption. As we have already seen from our study of sections 162 and 262, personal expenditures are non-deductible.

A potential point of ambiguity inherent to this area is distinguishing between investment property and personal use property. For example, most people might contend that their purchase of a home had a substantial investment component. It is well settled, however, that personal residences are not treated as investment property for tax loss purposes. Gevirtz v. Commissioner, 123 F.2d 707 (2d Cir. 1941). A personal residence may be converted to investment property by renting it out. But in such cases any loss recognition will be limited to losses that arose after the residence was converted. Treas. Reg. § 1.165-9(b)(2).

The law provides limited relief for a category of personal losses known as casualty losses. We will consider this deduction in some detail in this chapter. In the next chapter we will look at a variety of other personal expenses that are also deductible. Section 165(c)(3) authorizes the deduction of personal losses "if such losses arise from fire, storm, shipwreck, or other *casualty*, or from theft." Casualty losses arise when there is damage or destruction of property by sudden, unexpected, or unusual events. Ruecker v. Commissioner, 41 T.C.M. 1587, 1588 (1981). Losses from casualties to personal use property are subject to two main limitations: a $100 threshold, and a ten percent of adjusted gross income threshold. IRC § 165(h).

Primary Authority

Code: § 165(a), (b), (c), (h).

Regulations: § 1.165-1(c)(4), -1(d)(1)-(2)(i), -7(b)(1), -7(b)(2)(ii), -9(b)(2).

Cases: Blackman v. Commissioner, 88 T.C. 677 (1987); Chamales v. Commissioner, T.C. Memo 2000-33; Finkbohner v. Commissioner, 788 F.2d. 723 (11th Cir. 1986); Gevirtz v. Commissioner, 123 F.2d 707 (2d Cir. 1941); Ruecker v. Commissioner, 41 T.C.M. 1587, 1588 (1981).

Rulings: None.

Problems

10.1. Gwyneth Taylor's adjusted gross income in the current year is $1,000,000. What is the amount of her casualty loss deduction, if any, arising from the various events described below?

(a) Her uninsured personal use motor home was destroyed by a tidal wave at a time when it was worth $300,100 and her basis was $350,000.

This is a casualty loss since it arises from a sudden event similar to a fire, storm, or other casualty. The loss is deductible under section 165(c)(3) but is limited by the provisions of section 165(h). The initial amount of her deductible loss is $300,100, the fair market value of the motor home. Treas. Reg. § 1.165-7(b)(1). This appears to conflict with the language of section 165(b). However, it is consistent with the disallowance of the depreciation deduction on her personal use property. *See* IRC § 167(a).

The deduction is reduced by $100 pursuant to section 165(h)(1). It is further reduced by $100,000 (10% of her $1,000,000 AGI) under section 165(h)(2)(A). Thus the actual deduction amount is $200,000. Though perhaps premature to bring it up at this point, Gwyneth will have to itemize in order to claim the deduction. *See* IRC § 63 which is addressed in detail in Chapter 12.

$300,100	Initial FMV
− 100	Deductible 165(h)(1)
− 100,000	Deductible 165(h)(2)(A)
$200,000	Deduction under 165

(b) Assume that instead of her motor home it is Gwyneth's guest cottage that was damaged by the tidal wave. She had the cottage constructed on the property after she bought her beach home. Her basis in the cottage was $300,000 and its fair market value before the tidal wave was $500,000. The decline in value of the cottage as a result of the tidal wave was $400,000. Her aggregate basis in her home (including the cottage) was $1,100,000. The fair market value of her home (including the cot-

tage) before the tidal wave was $2,000,000. The fair market value of her home after the tidal wave was $1,600,000.

This is a casualty loss since it arises from a sudden event similar to a fire, storm, or other casualty. The loss is deductible under section 165(c)(3) but is limited by the provisions of section 165(h). The initial amount of her deductible loss is $400,000, the decline in the fair market value of the cottage. This is because where property is only damaged but not rendered worthless, the difference between its fair market value before the disaster and its fair market value after the disaster is the appropriate measure of the loss unless that amount exceeds the taxpayer's basis in the property. Treas. Reg. § 1.165-7(b)(1)(i). Improvements to real property such as the cottage are regarded as integral components of the real property and have no separate basis for purposes of computing the loss. Treas. Reg. § 1.165-7(b)(2)(ii). Thus, Gwyneth's separate basis in the cottage of $300,000 does not limit her loss deduction.

The deduction is reduced by $100 pursuant to section 165(h)(1). It is further reduced by $100,000 (10% of her $1,000,000 AGI) under section 165(h)(2)(A). Thus the actual deduction amount is $299,900.

$2,000,000	Initial FMV of home
− 1,600,000	Post casualty FMV of home
$400,000	Loss
− 100	Deductible 165(h)(1)
− 100,000	Deductible 165(h)(2)(A)
$299,900	Deduction under 165

(c) Same as (b) except that Gwyneth's insurance company reimbursed her for $100,000 of her loss.

The reimbursement reduces her deductible loss to $199,900. Treas. Reg. § 1.165-1(c)(4).

(d) Assume that under the combined facts of (b) and (c), Gwyneth spends $250,000 to restore her cottage to its original condition. What is her ending integrated basis in her home including the cottage?

This problem reminds us of the adjustments to basis that occur as a result of her reinvestment, her insurance reimbursement, and of her tax deduction. Gwyneth's pre-casualty basis in her residence, including the cottage, is $1,100,000. She spends $250,000 restoring her cottage. She receives $100,000 reimbursement for the loss from her insurance company, and she is allowed a $199,900 casualty loss deduction after the application of the $100 and 10% of A.G.I. thresholds. Her basis in her residence after all these events is $1,050,100, calculated as follows:

Pre-casualty basis	$1,100,000	
Cost of repair	+ 250,000	§ 1016(a)(1)
Insurance payment	− 100,000	§ 1016(a)(1)
Loss deduction	− 199,900	§ 1016(a)(1)
Post-casualty basis	$1,050,100	

10.2. Jimmy Jones likes fast cars and enjoys dirt track racing in vintage sports cars on the weekends. He keeps a 1965 Austin Healey 3000 Mark III in his home's attached garage and does all of the maintenance and repairs on it himself. He tows the Healey to and from the races behind his Dodge RAM pickup. Late last Sunday Jimmy returned home from racing and parked his Healey in the garage. During the night fuel dripped out of the Healey from a leak in a fuel line and caught fire when the fumes came into contact with a nearby space heater that Jimmy used for warmth while working under the car. Though no one was injured, Jimmy's home and everything in it was destroyed. Assuming that his loss is uncompensated and that the ten percent threshold is exceeded, consider whether Jimmy has a deductible loss in the following circumstances.

    (a) Before going to bed, Jimmy noticed some liquid dripping from beneath the Healey and assumed it was an oil leak that could be addressed on Monday rather than fuel that might pose a serious risk of fire. He also did not notice that the space heater was on.

Is Jimmy merely negligent here? If so, the loss is deductible since it arises from mere negligence. But if he was grossly negligent or guilty of intentional wrongdoing allowing the deduction would violate public policy by rewarding such conduct. *Blackman v. Commissioner.*

    (b) Same as (a) except that last week Jimmy purchased a new fuel additive called Nitro-gas for his Healey that is supposed to bump its speed by a few miles per hour. Nitro-gas is much more combustible than regular gasoline. He used it for the first time last weekend and was winning his race until the engine blew a gasket and he was forced to withdraw. Jimmy towed the Healey home without making a close inspection of its condition and went to bed.

Now Jimmy's behavior might rise to the level of gross negligence. If so, his casualty loss is disallowed on the policy grounds described in *Blackman.*

    (c) Same as (b) except that using Nitro-gas was in violation of the racing league's rules. Jimmy was charged with violating the rules and rather than contest the charge agreed to pay a stiff fine.

The question becomes whether the violation of the racing league's rules automatically causes Jimmy to lose his casualty loss deduction under the public policy rule. As *Blackman* notes, a conviction is not essential to disallowance of the loss deduction. But the facts here are certainly less extreme than in *Blackman* where the taxpayer intentionally started a fire in his home by burning his unfaithful wife's clothes on the stove.

10.3. Roberta owns a cooperative apartment on the fifth floor of the Dakota Apartment building overlooking Central Park in New York City. Earlier this year a neighboring apartment building, The Bramford, was bombed by terrorists using a truck full of ammonia based fertilizer. The resulting explosion not only severely damaged The Bramford, it also damaged the Dakota. The intended victim of the attack was a wealthy oil magnate who is a leading advocate for "fracking" for natural gas. He was uninjured and continues to live at The Bramford. The only physical damages to Roberta's co-op were some broken windows and some discoloration of an outside wall. These damages were quickly repaired at a modest cost. But the Dakota's side entrance was seriously damaged and took several weeks to be repaired at a cost of $500,000. Roberta's share of that cost was $10,000. This year two local Realtors told Roberta that her property is now worth $1,000,000 less than it was before the bombing because of fears of repeat bombings. Roberta's adjusted gross income is $1,000,000. Is Roberta's loss deductible under the following circumstances?

(a) The oil magnate, who is forty years old, plans to live at the The Bramford for many more years and to continue to lobby for liberal policies toward fracking.

The explosion was certainly a casualty for tax purposes for the owners of The Bramford. It was also a casualty with respect to the physical damage done to the Dakota. But is the diminution in value to Roberta's apartment a deductible casualty loss? The Tax Court in the *Chamales v. Commissioner* case follows the rule that a casualty for tax purposes must involve physical harm to the property and that the deduction is limited to the decline in value caused by that physical damage. This is the rule in the Ninth Circuit. The Eleventh Circuit case, *Finkbohner v. Commissioner*, stands for the proposition that the damages to the residence do not need to be physical in character as long as the harm is sudden and long-term. *Finkbohner* involved a physical casualty to nearby property. Here we have very limited physical harm to Roberta's home but there is the real potential for actual physical harm in the future and for long-term reduction in market value because of the continued presence of the controversial figure at The Bramford next door. The threat could be long term since the controversial oil magnate plans to remain in the neighborhood for years. Is this situation more like a market fluctuation or more like a casualty? Probably the Ninth Circuit would find no casualty. In the Eleventh Circuit and others it may come down to how convincing the testimony of the experts is as to the duration of the harm.

(b) After the bombing the oil magnate moved out of The Bramford.

Since the harm seems temporary, even the Eleventh Circuit would be unlikely to find a casualty.

Chapter 11

Other Deductible Personal Expenses: Taxes, Interest, Charitable Gifts, Moving Expenses, and Medical Expenses

Overview

As discussed in the last chapter, section 262 prohibits the deduction of personal, living or family expenses from income. As we saw, however, personal casualty losses are an exception to that general rule. In this chapter, we look at several other personal expenses that can be deducted from gross income. These deductible personal expenses include home mortgage interest (§ 163), state and local taxes (§ 164), charitable gifts (§ 170), addressed in more detail in Chapter 20), moving expenses (§ 217), and medical expenses (§ 213). Most of these deductions are *itemized deductions*. This means that their deductibility is limited in the manner described in the next chapter. Despite the limitations, they are important tools used by millions of Americans to minimize their federal income tax liability.

It is important to note that businesses can also deduct expenses such as interest and taxes. Indeed, just as in the case of losses, business deductions for these items are granted more freely than personal ones. *See, e.g.,* IRC §§ 163(a), (h)(1), (h)(2)(A); 164(a). However, there are special rules for the deduction of investment interest. Basically investment interest may only be deducted to the extent of "net investment income." IRC § 163(d)(1). The excess investment interest expense carries over to later years. IRC § 163(d)(2). The definition of investment income excludes net capital gains from the disposition of investment property and qualified dividend income unless the taxpayer agrees to have them taxed at ordinary income rates. IRC §§ 1(h)(3); 163(d)(4).

Primary Authority

Code: §§ 163(a), (h); 164(a), (b)(5), (d)(1); 170(a)(1), (b)(1)(A)-(B), (G), (d)(1)(A); 213(a), (d)(1), (9); 217(a)-(c); 280A(d)(1)(A); 461(g). Skim § 163(d).

Regulations: § 1.213-1(e)(1)(iii).

Cases: Cathcart v. Commissioner, 36 T.C.M. 1321 (1977); Ferris v. Commissioner, 582 F.2d 1112 (7th Cir. 1978); Voss v. Commissioner, 796 F. 3rd 1051(9th Cir. 2015).

Rulings: Revenue Ruling 87-106, 1987-2 C.B. 67; Revenue Ruling 2003-57, 2003-1 C.B. 959; Rev. Rul. 2010-25, 2010-44 I.R.B. 571.

Problems

11.1 Ellen and Portia, a married couple, purchase a home in Year 1 and use it as a principal residence. In the problems below, unless otherwise advised, assume that the loans involved are secured by the real property described. Consider the deductibility of the loan interest in the various circumstances described.

> **(a) The home cost $1,000,000 and they borrow $400,000 from a bank to help pay for the home and pay market rate interest along with 3 points. The points are paid from their personal savings.**

The interest is deductible under section 163(h)(2)(D) since the residence is a qualified residence under section 163(h)(3)(B) and the loan is acquisition indebtedness under section 163(h)(3)(A)(i). The points are currently deductible under section 461(g)(2) since they are paid from personal funds and not simply withheld from the loan. *Cathcart v. Commissioner.*

> **(b) Same as (a) except that by Year 5 they have paid down the mortgage to $300,000 and the house is now worth $1,200,000. They take out a second mortgage for $400,000 and use $200,000 of the proceeds to build an addition to their home and the other $200,000 to buy new cars and a boat.**

The first mortgage interest is still deductible under section 163(h)(2)(D) since the residence is a qualified residence under section 163(h)(3)(B) and the first mortgage is acquisition indebtedness under section 163(h)(3)(A)(i).

The $200,000 used for the addition qualifies as acquisition indebtedness since it is used for a home improvement. IRC § 163(h)(3)(B).

The interest on $100,000 of the $200,000 used for cars and a boat is deductible as interest on home equity indebtedness. IRC § 163(h)(3)(C)(i). The excess $100,000 cannot qualify as home equity indebtedness because of the cap under IRC § 163(h)(3)(C)(ii).

> **(c) Same as (a) except that in Year 10 the mortgage is paid down to $200,000 and the house is worth $1,500,000. In Year 10 they borrow $300,000 secured by the home. They use the funds to pay off the mortgage and buy themselves new cars.**

The first $200,000 of the new mortgage qualifies as acquisition indebtedness since it is used to pay off the old mortgage. *See* IRC § 163(h)(3)(B) flush. The $100,000 of the new mortgage in excess of the principal amount of the first mortgage qualifies as home equity indebtedness. IRC § 163(h)(3)(C)(i). Thus, interest on the entire $300,000 debt can be deducted.

(d) **Same as (a) except that they also buy a condominium on the beach in Kauai. The total cost of acquisition is $1,400,000 and they finance $800,000 of the cost. They live in the condo for eight weeks in the winter and elect to treat it as a qualified residence. They do not rent the condo when they are away.**

The second home qualifies as a residence under IRC § 163(h)(4)(A), which references IRC § 280A. Section 280A(d)(1) requires that in order to be a residence it must be used by the taxpayer for the greater of 14 days or 10% of the number of the days the home is rented out. Here that is met since the condo is not rented out.

Note, however, that here total acquisition indebtedness on the two homes is $1,200,000. This exceeds the cap under section 163(h)(3)(B)(ii) of $1,000,000. The legislative history tells us that when the cap is exceeded the limit will apply to the last debt incurred (here the $800,000 loan). However, $100,000 of the loan that exceeds the cap will qualify as home equity indebtedness. Rev. Rul. 2010-25. So $1,100,000 of debt is within the deductibility rules. The interest on the excess $100,000 is not deductible.

An interesting question is whether the section 163(h)(3) limitations on the deductibility of mortgage interest ($1 million of acquisition indebtedness plus $100,000 of home equity indebtedness) are applied on a per-residence basis (for a total of $1.1 million of debt) or on a per-taxpayer basis (for a total of $2.2 million of debt). The Ninth Circuit recently reversed the Tax Court and held, contrary to the Service's position, that the limitations are applied on a per-taxpayer basis. *Voss v. Commissioner.* Do you think the decision, which allows unmarried taxpayers who buy an expensive residence together to deduct twice the amount of interest spouses would be allowed to deduct, comports with the language of the statute?

11.2. Alicia Kane gains new employment and moves to a new residence. Her former residence is 15 miles from her former place of employment. Her new place of employment is 70 miles from her former residence. Assuming the other requirements of section 217 are met, may Alicia deduct her moving expenses?

Yes. The distance requirement specifies that the new job must be at least 50 miles farther from the taxpayer's former residence than the distance between the former residence and the former place of work. IRC § 217(c)(1). Thus, Alicia's new job must be at least 65 miles from her former residence. Since under the facts it is 70 miles from her former residence, the requirement is satisfied.

11.3. Lou Gehrig, age 50, was diagnosed with a serious ailment affecting the central nervous system and the sense of balance. Pursuant to doctor's directions, in the current year Lou expended $25,000 to modify his home to accommodate his disability. These modifications included entrance ramps, wider doorways, lower kitchen cabinets, and bathroom rails. In addition, Lou installed an indoor pool his doctor recommended to combat his disease.

Chapter 12

The Deduction Hierarchy: Adjusted Gross Income, Taxable Income, the Standard Deduction, and the Personal Exemptions

Overview

The Code establishes a deduction hierarchy for the various deductions. This hierarchy primarily arises from the operation of sections 62 and 63. Section 62 authorizes certain deductions to be deducted from gross income to arrive at "adjusted gross income." These are often referred to as "above the line" deductions. Section 63 authorizes other deductions to be taken from adjusted gross income to arrive at taxable income. These are referred to as "below the line" deductions. Below the line deductions are also known as "itemized" deductions. IRC § 63(b) & (d). It is important to understand that section 62 does not create any tax deductions. Instead it merely establishes the point in the tax calculation process at which deductions authorized by other Code sections may be taken. Section 63 has a similar traffic cop function, but it also authorizes a deduction, the standard deduction discussed below.

Adjusted gross income (or AGI for short) is often a reference point for limitations on deductions. For example, in the previous chapter we saw that the medical care expense deduction under section 213(a) is limited to those otherwise deductible medical expenses that exceed 10% of AGI. We have seen similar limitations on casualty loss deductions and charitable deductions. But there is another critical reason for the distinction between above the line deductions and itemized deductions; itemized deductions must be taken in lieu of what is known as "the standard deduction." *See* IRC § 63(b) & (d). This is a distinct disadvantage if the taxpayer would otherwise have taken the standard deduction. The standard deduction, like the personal exemptions, is indexed for inflation. (*See* IRC § 63(c)(2) & (7) to see the peculiar method by which the standard deduction is calculated). It is available to every taxpayer without having to prove any deductible expenses. Since a taxpayer must choose between itemizing and taking the standard deduction, this means that a taxpayer's itemized deductions must exceed the standard before the taxpayer will receive any tax benefit from those deductions. Persons over age 64 and blind persons are entitled to an extra standard deduction of $600 (indexed for inflation). IRC § 63(f)(1).

Section 62 authorizes above the line deductions for most trade or business expenses, many investment expenses, business and investment losses, depreciation expenses, alimony, moving expenses, certain expenses associated with attending college, and a few other expenses beyond the scope of our study. *See* IRC § 62(a). Itemized deductions are all deductions other than those addressed by section 62 and other than the personal exemptions, which will be discussed below. *See* IRC § 63(d). The itemized deductions include interest (§ 163), property and state income taxes (§ 164), casualty losses (§ 165), medical expenses (§ 213), and the charitable deduction (§ 170).

Some itemized deductions, known as the "miscellaneous itemized deductions," are not only below the line deductions but are also subject to a further disability known as the 2% threshold. As such, they are deductible only to the extent that they exceed 2% of the taxpayer's adjusted gross income. IRC § 67(a). For example, if a taxpayer, whose adjusted gross income is $100,000, incurs $3,000 in miscellaneous itemized deductions, the first $2,000 is not deductible, but the remaining $1,000 can be deducted. The most prominent miscellaneous itemized deduction is the deduction under section 162 for un-reimbursed employee business expenses. *See* IRC §§ 62(a)(1) &(2)(A); 67(b).

The final step in reaching taxable income involves taking the personal exemptions to which the taxpayer may be entitled. The personal exemptions are the same for taxpayers whether they itemize their deductions or claim the standard deduction. *See* IRC §§ 151, 152. Each taxpayer gets a personal exemption for him or her self and also for each dependent. Determining who is a dependent involves close reading of section 152.

Primary Authority

Code: §§ 62; 63; 67(a)-(b); 151; 152. Skim § 68.

Regulations: §§ 1.62-2(c)(4); 1.152-4(b).

Cases: Gevirtz v. Commissioner, 123 F.2d 707 (2d Cir. 1941).

Rulings: None.

Problems

12.1. Are the following expenses deductible? If so, are they deductible above the line or below the line? If they are deductible below the line, are they itemized deductions or miscellaneous itemized deductions?

(a) A homeowner's payment to the city for trash pickup at her personal residence.

This is a non-deductible personal expense. IRC § 262. Some might suggest that the home is investment property making this deductible below the line under section 212. This view has been rejected. *Gevirtz v. Commissioner.*

(b) An apartment building owner's payment to the city for trash pickup at one of her rental properties.

This is deductible above the line under IRC §§ 162 or 212(2) and 62(a)(4). Remember section 62 does not create any deductions. Instead it merely tells where in the tax calculation process they are taken.

(c) A homeowner's payment of mortgage interest and property taxes relating to her personal residence.

These are deductible below the line. IRC §§ 163(a), (h) (2)(D); 164; 63. These are itemized deductions under 63(d) since they are not allowed under section 62(a). They are not miscellaneous itemized deductions since they are listed under sections 67(b)(1) & (2).

(d) An apartment building owner's payments of mortgage interest and property taxes with respect to one of her rental properties. Assume that section 163(d) has no application.

These are deductible above the line. IRC §§ 163(a); 164; 62(a)(4).

(e) The unreimbursed payment of state bar dues by an associate in a law firm

This is a below the line deduction. It is a business expense deductible under section 162. But it is also an un-reimbursed employee business expense within the meaning of section 62(a)(1). It is an itemized deduction under section 63(d) since it is not allowed under section 62(a). The taxpayer must elect to itemize under section 63(e). An unreimbursed employee business expense is also a miscellaneous itemized deduction subject to the 2% of AGI threshold imposed by section 67(a) since it is not listed in section 67(b).

(f) What if the associate in (e) is reimbursed by her firm and reports the reimbursement as income?

Now we have an above the line deduction. *See* IRC § 62(a)(2)(A). If the employer has an accountable plan the employee can choose not to report the reimbursement as income. *See* Treas. Reg. § 1.62-2(c)(4). No deduction would then be taken either. *Cf.* Treas. Reg. § 1.162-17(b) (which is superseded by the section 62(c) regulations pursuant to Treas. Reg. § 1.162-17(e)(3)) (but not in this respect).

(g) A doctor employed by a hospital pays interest on student loans incurred while in medical school. *See* IRC § 221.

This is an above the line deduction under sections 221 and 62(a)(17).

(h) Taxpayer pays a former spouse $5,000 in alimony. *See* IRC § 215(a); *compare with* IRC § 71(a).

This is an above the line deduction. IRC §§ 215(a); 62(a)(10). It might be noted that the above the line treatment of this deduction (which seems personal in nature) is justified by the fact that the payee is obliged to report the payment as income under section 71(a).

12.2. **Consider whether Kanye is entitled to a dependency exemption assuming, unless stated otherwise, that Kanye provided over one half of the support for the particular person involved. Assume further that the potential dependent did not earn more than the exemption amount and that no one else is entitled to the dependency exemption.**

    (a) **The potential dependent, who is away at college, is Zoe, Kanye's 21-year-old orphaned stepsister and ward. Zoe lives with Kanye when she is not in school.**

Yes, she is a qualifying child. IRC § 152(c)(1). Note that the statute lists "stepsister" as one of the relationships that can qualify. *See* IRC § 152(c)(2)(B). She may also meet the definition of a qualifying relative but in cases of overlap the person is treated as a qualifying child. IRC § 152(d)(1)(D). The fact that she does not live with Kanye while she's in school probably does not matter assuming that Treas. Reg. § 1.152-1(b) is still good law. [The important distinction between the qualifying child and the qualifying relative is that the latter cannot have gross income in excess of the exemption amount. *See* IRC § 152(d)(1)(B). This is a stricter standard that could be problematic since many children work during college and are likely to earn more than the exemption amount. It is worth pointing out that scholarships of a taxpayer's child are disregarded for the section 152(c)(1) support test. *See* IRC § 152(f)(5).]

    (b) **Same as (a) except Zoe was adopted by Kanye's stepmother.**

Yes, she is a dependent (as a stepsister) since adopted children are treated the same as children by blood. IRC § 152(f)(1)(B).

    (c) **The potential dependent is Lucia, Kanye's mother-in-law, who lives next door. Lucia has no gross income.**

Yes, she is a dependent as a qualifying relative. *See* IRC § 152(d)(2)(G).

    (d) **Same as (c) except that Lucia is the daughter of Kanye's aunt.**

No, she is not a dependent since cousins are not a relationship specified in section 152(d)(2) and she does not live with Kanye. Aunts and uncles are included under section 152(d)(2)(F), but not their descendants.

    (e) **Same as (d) except that Lucia lives with Kanye.**

Yes, she is a dependent. IRC § 152(d)(2)(H). No blood relationship is required when the potential dependent lives with the taxpayer and is a member of the taxpayer's household. But take note of section 152(f)(3) which specifies that relationships that are illegal under local law will prevent the person from being a member of the taxpayer's household. Thus, for example, an illegal alien might be prevented from being a dependent.

    (f) The potential dependent is Zoe again, but who now is Kanye's minor daughter residing with Kanye's former spouse's ex-husband, Liam (who legally adopted Zoe). Liam has custody of Zoe.

Normally the parent with custody for the greater part of the year is entitled to claim the child as a dependent. IRC § 152(c)(4)(B)(i). This is Liam.

When two or more persons are entitled to claim a person as a qualifying child there are various tie-breaking rules that come into play to prevent more than one person from claiming the child as a dependent. The first tie breaker is parentage. IRC § 152(c)(4)(A)(i). If neither person is the parent, the one with the higher adjusted gross income gets the exemption. IRC § 152(c)(4)(A)(ii). If both claimants are parents, the one with whom the child resided for the longer period during the year gets the exemption. IRC § 152(c)(4)(B)(i). If the period of residence with each parent was equal, the parent with the higher adjusted gross income gets the exemption. IRC § 152(c)(4)(B)(ii). But note also that there are rules that permit the custodial parent to release the exemption to the non-custodial parent by written release. IRC § 152(e)(2).

12.3. Miley and Liam, married taxpayers in their thirties with one infant child, file a joint return in the current year. They have the following items of income and expense: combined salaries of $80,000, $10,000 of royalty income on a song Miley wrote, $13,000 of interest expense on their education loans, $14,000 alimony expense paid to a former spouse of Liam, $4,000 of interest paid on their personal residence mortgage, $1,000 of property taxes on their personal residence, $2,000 in state income taxes, $2,000 of un-reimbursed employee travel expenses, and a $1,000 charitable expense.

    (a) *Ignoring any of the statutorily authorized inflation adjustments*, what are Miley and Liam's adjusted gross income and taxable income? Will they elect to itemize?

Adjusted gross income is $63,000, determined as follows:

$90,000	gross income
− 13,000	education interest expense IRC §§ 221; 62(a)(17)
− 14,000	alimony expense IRC §§ 215(a); 62(a)(10)
$63,000	adjusted gross income

Taxable income is $49,260 if they elect to itemize and $57,000 if they take the standard deduction. Presumably, they will elect to itemize.

Itemizing yields the following results:

$63,000	adjusted gross income
− 4,000	personal residence interest IRC §§ 163(a), (h)(2)(D); 63(d) & (e).
− 1,000	personal residence property taxes IRC §§ 164(a)(1); 63(d) & (e).

–	2,000	state income taxes IRC §§ 164(a)(3); 63(d) & (e).
–	740	unreim. employee travel expenses* IRC §§162(a); 63(d) & (e); 67(a).
	$55,260	
–	6,000	personal exemptions IRC §§ 63(d)(2); 151(a)-(d)(1); 152(a)(1).
	$49,260	taxable income

*Miscellaneous itemized deductions subject to the 2% of AGI reduction. ($63,000 × .02 = $1,260 disallowed per section 67(a). $2,000 – $1,260 = $740)

Using the standard deduction yields the following results:

	$63,000	adjusted gross income
–	6,000	standard deduction IRC §§ 63(c)(1); (c)(2)(A).
	$57,000	
–	6,000	personal exemptions IRC §§ 63(d)(2); 151(a)-(d)(1); 152(a)(1).
	$51,000	taxable income

It should be noted that the standard deduction and the personal exemption amounts adjust for inflation. *See* IRC § 63(c)(4). The 2016 amounts are set out in Rev. Proc. 2015-53.

(b) Same as (a) except that both Miley and Liam are over age 65.

Miley & Liam are each entitled to an extra $600 standard deduction under section 63(f)(1)(A). Using the basic and extra standard deductions would yield a taxable income of $49,800. Itemizing would yield the same results above (taxable income of $49,260).

Chapter 13

Timing Rules and Related Principles

Overview

The income tax is imposed on an annual basis, the tax year. Thus, it is necessary to establish rules concerning *when* an item of income is included and *when* an item of expense is deducted. That is this chapter's topic. As one considers the topic of timing of income and deductions it is important to keep in mind where the "pressure" is. Taxpayers will nearly always be economically advantaged by the deferral of taxable income. Also, there is often advantage in the acceleration of tax deductions. Both of these advantages will reduce the taxpayer's current tax liability thereby leaving him with the use of his money for a while longer. Since money makes money, the use of money has value. We call this "the time value of money." The government has an interest in the acceleration of income reporting and deferral of deduction reporting since that will increase the government's current tax revenues. An evenhanded set of rules should impartially navigate between these competing interests of taxpayer and government.

The primary determinant of the timing of income and deductions is the taxpayer's accounting method. There are two main methods: the cash method and the accrual method. IRC § 446(c). Both methods employ some version of the "matching" principle. This means they seek to match expenses to the income they produce so that we get a fair and accurate picture of net income. The cash method is less effective at matching. But it is also more simple and intuitive. It is the method that most individuals employ.

An individual taxpayer can generally choose his tax accounting method; however, big businesses are obliged to use the accrual method. *See* IRC § 448. The accrual method is in accordance with "Generally Accepted Accounting Principles" or GAAP. These are the principles that have been adopted by the Financial Accounting Standards Board. The cash method is not always in accordance with GAAP. Furthermore, the GAAP rules were developed for financial accounting rather than tax accounting purposes. Tax accounting under the accrual method is not identical to financial accounting under the accrual method.

One must recognize that the timing rules do not establish that an item is income or that one has the right to deduct an expenditure. The timing rules just tell us *when* to report or to deduct it. We still need to refer to the various applicable sections of the Code such as section 61 or section 162 to see if an item is includable or deductible.

Primary Authority

Code: §§ 446; 451(a), (h)(1)-(2); 461(a), (g), (h)(1)-(2). Skim §§ 111; 1341.

Regulations: §§ 1.170A-1(b); 1.446-1(a)(4)(i), -1(c)(1)(i) & (ii)(A), -1(c)(2)(i); 1.451-1(a), -2(a); 1.461-1(a)(1)-(2)(i).

Cases: Ames v. Commissioner; 112 T.C. 304 (1999); 372 U.S. 128 (1963); Bliss Dairy, Inc. v. United States, 460 U.S. 370 91983); Estate of Stranahan v. Commissioner, 472 F.2d 867 (6th Cir. 1973); International Freighting Corporation, Inc. v. Commissioner, 135 F.2d 310 (2nd Cir. 1943); James v. United States, 366 U.S. 213 (1961); Kahler v. Commissioner, 18 T.C. 31 (1952); North American Oil Consolidated v. Burnet, 286 U.S. 417 (1932); Schlude v. Commissioner, 372 U.S. 128 (1963).

Rulings: None.

Problems

13.1. Hubert, a professional inventor, recently invented the *Smelliscope*, a patented device that can detect odors from thousands of miles away. In Year 1, Hubert agreed to assign to Wolfgang, an entrepreneur, all of his right, title, and interest in the invention and patent for a lump sum payment of $100,000. Assuming Hubert is an accrual method taxpayer and Wolfgang is also an accrual method taxpayer, in what year does Hubert have income and in what year does Wolfgang have a deduction under the following circumstances?

(a) Hubert executes the assignment and delivers the device and patent to Wolfgang on December 27th. Wolfgang cuts a check on December 28th and mails it to Hubert's home. Hubert receives the check on December 31st and cashes the check on January 2nd of Year 2.

Note that the tax treatment of sales and licensing of intellectual property is addressed in detail in Chapters 28 and 29. Chapter 28 focuses on the treatment of the buyer and Chapter 29 on the seller. In this chapter we are only concerned with timing of income and deduction and not the nuances of characterization or amortization.

Under the accrual method Hubert has income in Year 1 since it has been earned by the end of the year. Treas. Reg. § 1.446-1(c)(1)(ii)(A). This answer is reinforced by the fact of receipt of payment. *Schlude v. Commissioner.*

Wolfgang has his deduction in Year 1 as well since all events have occurred fixing his liability and economic performance has occurred. Under the accrual method deductions are taken in the year in which all events have occurred establishing the fact of liability and the amount of liability and in which economic performance has occurred with respect to the liability. Treas. Reg. § 1.461-1(a)(2)(i). Economic performance occurs when the person to whom the liability is owed performs his end of the bargain. *See* IRC § 461(h)(1) & (2).

(b) Same as (a) except Hubert is out of town on December 31st.

No change for either party. Receipt is irrelevant for Hubert under the accrual method.

(c) Same as (a) except that the check arrives at Hubert's home on January 2nd of Year 2.

No change for either party. Receipt is irrelevant for Hubert under the accrual method.

(d) Same as (a) except that Hubert executes the assignment and delivers the device to Wolfgang on January 2nd of Year 2.

Hubert probably has income in Year 1 even though he does not perform until Year 2 since he has received payment. *Schlude.* Under a pure accrual system he would not have income until Year 2 when the all events test is satisfied. *See* Treas. Reg. § 1.446-1(c)(1)(ii)(A).

Wolfgang would have his deduction in Year 2 even though he paid in Year 1. This is because all events fixing his liability and economic performance have occurred in Year 2. Under the accrual method deductions are taken in the year in which all events have occurred establishing the fact of liability and the amount of liability and in which economic performance has occurred with respect to the liability. Treas. Reg. § 1.461-1(a)(2)(i). Economic performance occurs when the person to whom the liability is owed performs his end of the bargain. *See* IRC § 461(h) (1) & (2).

(e) Same as (a) except that Fred filed suit against Hubert on December 30th of Year 1, alleging that before Year 1 Fred had been granted a patent on the device and asking that a decree be entered declaring that Fred is the rightful owner of the patent and the rightful owner of all funds from any sale. Hubert vigorously denies Fred's claim.

As in (a) above under the accrual method Hubert has income in Year 1 since it has been earned by the end of the year. Treas. Reg. § 1.446-1(c)(1)(ii)(A). This answer is reinforced by the fact of receipt of payment. *Schlude.* Despite the lawsuit Hubert still has income in Year 1 since he holds the $100,000 under claim of right. *North American Consolidated v. Burnet.* If he is forced to pay the proceeds in a later year he will get tax relief in that year under section 1341.

(f) Same as (a) except that Wolfgang pays Hubert with Google stock worth $100,000 in which Wolfgang had a basis of $60,000.

No change except that Wolfgang has $40,000 of taxable gain in Year 1 from the sale of the stock in exchange for the license rights. IRC § 1001. *See, e.g., International*

Freighting Corporation, Inc. v. Commissioner. Hubert will take a cost basis in the stock of $100,000. IRC § 1012.

13.2. How would your answers with respect to Hubert change in 13.1 (a) through (e) if he were a cash method taxpayer?

(a) **Hubert executes the assignment and delivers the devise and patent to Wolfgang on December 27th. Wolfgang cuts a check on December 28th and mails it to Hubert's home. Hubert receives the check on December 31st and cashes the check on January 2nd of Year 2.**

Hubert has income on December 31, Year 1 since the check is a cash equivalent and he has actual receipt of it in Year 1. Treas. Reg. § 1.451-1(a); *Kahler v. Commissioner.*

(b) **Same as (a) except Hubert is out of town on December 31st.**

No change. Arguably Hubert had actual receipt of the check at his home, but he certainly had constructive receipt. An item is constructively received when it is credited to the taxpayer's account or set aside for him and there are no substantial restrictions on his control. Treas. Reg. § 1.451-2(a).

(c) **Same as (a) except that the check arrives at Hubert's home on January 2nd of Year 2.**

Hubert has income in Year 2. Treas. Reg. § 1.451-1(a). If it were shown that Hubert asked Wolfgang to delay mailing the check so that it would arrive after the first of the year, an argument could be made for applying constructive receipt principles.

(d) **Same as (a) except that Hubert executes the assignment and delivers the device and patent to Wolfgang on January 2nd of Year 2.**

Hubert still has income in Year 1 since that is when the cash equivalent was received.

(e) **Same as (a) except that Fred filed suit against Hubert on December 30th of Year 1, alleging that before Year 1 Fred had been granted a patent on the device and asking that a decree be entered declaring that Fred is the rightful owner of the patent and the rightful owner of all funds from any sale. Hubert vigorously denies Fred's claim.**

No change. Hubert holds the $100,000 under claim of right. *North American Consolidated.* If he is forced to pay the proceeds in a later year he will be entitled to tax relief (e.g., a tax deduction) pursuant to section 1341.

13.3. Trader Jack is an accrual method taxpayer who sells bottles of wine throughout the State of California. He is duly licensed by the state to engage in this business. He uses the first in-first out (FIFO) method of inventory accounting. In the current year, Trader Jack's beginning inventory was 5,000 bottles of wine which cost him $6 per bottle. In May, Trader Jack purchased 4,000

additional bottles for $7 per bottle. In October, he purchased 6,000 bottles for $8 per bottle. During the year, Trader Jack sold 10,000 bottles of wine for gross revenues of $136,000.

(a) What was Trader Jack's cost of goods sold and gross profit for the year?

Under FIFO, Trader Jack's cost of goods sold would be $66,000 (the sum of the beginning inventory costs of $30,000 ($6 × 5,000 = $30,000), the May costs of $28,000 ($7 × 4,000 = $28,000), and $8,000 (the cost of 1,000 bottles from October ($8 × 1,000 = $8,000).

Therefore under FIFO, Trader Jack will have a gross profit from wine sales of $70,000 for the year.

Gross Sales	$136,000
Cost of Goods sold	− $66,000
Gross Profit (FIFO)	$70,000

(b) Would Trader Jack be obliged to report his income if he conducted his business in violation of state alcohol licensing laws and, thus, was not entitled to keep any of the proceeds of his selling activities?

Yes, he still is obliged to report his income. *See James v. United States. James*, in effect, extended the claim of right doctrine to illegal earnings. *James* was a case of embezzlement and so involved the question whether an embezzlement was subject to the same rules as for a loan. The court held that it was not because the embezzler had not recognized an obligation to repay the funds and the person from whom the funds were taken had not agreed to the transfer.

13.4. Christian is a highly successful fashion designer with offices in New York and Los Angeles. He is a cash method taxpayer. Many of Christian's clients are slow to pay. As a consequence, Christian eases his cash flow problems by selling his accounts receivable to a Los Angeles bank at a 10% discount from face value. In Year 1, Christian generated $10,000,000 of accounts receivable which he sold in Year 2 for $9,000,000. What was Christian's basis in those accounts receivable and what is the tax consequence of the sale of the receivables? What difference would it make if Christian were an accrual method taxpayer?

As a cash method taxpayer, Christian would not have reported any income on the receivables in Year 1. Thus, his basis in them is zero. The sale would produce $9,000,000 of ordinary income in Year 2 under section 1001. *See, e.g., Estate of Stranahan v. Commissioner.*

The accrual version of this problem illustrates the principle that tax liability generates tax cost basis. Basis, after all, is a mechanism for avoiding taxing the same income twice in the hands of the same taxpayer. As an accrual method taxpayer, Christian would have been obliged to report the $10,000,000 of accounts receivable in income in Year 1 when they were earned. As a consequence, his basis in the receivables was $10,000,000. Thus, when he sold them in Year 2 he would have a $1,000,000 loss under section 1001. Over two years the net effect is $9,000,000 of income. It might be noted that both the income and the loss are ordinary (as opposed to capital). IRC § 1221(a)(4), considered in Chapter 17.

13.5. Elsa, an accrual method taxpayer, sells ice cream through retail outlets. In Year 1, Elsa loaned $100,000 to one of her suppliers, Anna, so that Anna could expand her dairy operation. In Year 2, Anna's business failed to pay the debt when it was due and Elsa deducted the $100,000 as a bad debt. The tax deduction reduced her income taxes for that year. In Year 6, Anna's business turned around and she was able to pay Elsa the full $100,000 debt plus interest. How must Elsa treat the debt repayment?

Under the tax benefit rule, Elsa must report the debt repayment as income. *Bliss Dairy, Inc. v. United States.*

There is a significant statutory qualification to what has just been said. Section 111 provides that gross income does not include income from the recovery of a prior year's deduction to the extent that the prior year's deduction did not reduce the taxpayer's tax liability. Thus, the recovery of a deduction will not create income for a taxpayer unless there was a "tax benefit" in taking the deduction in the first place. Here the facts state that a tax benefit was received.

One might wonder why in the foregoing circumstance the taxpayer would not be obliged to file an amended return to correct the erroneous deduction rather than apply the tax benefit rule to the current year's recovery. First, a taxpayer has no obligation to file an amended return if the original return was filed in good faith. Second, the return was correct when filed. In this limited sense the taxable year stands alone and hindsight is irrelevant. Finally, the statute of limitations may have run on the original return. Thus, if the government could not oblige the taxpayer to report the current year recovery in income, it would have no redress.

Chapter 14

Ordinary Tax Rates and Taxpayer Classification

Overview

There are two rate structures specified in section 1 of the Code: the ordinary income rate structure and the capital gains rate structure. In this chapter we are only concerned with the ordinary income rate structure. Capital gains, the gains that arise from the sale or exchange of capital assets, will be addressed in a later chapter. The basic tax rates for individuals are set out in subsections 1(a) through (d), as adjusted by subsection (i). These subsections currently establish seven tax rates: 10%, 15%, 25%, 28%, 33%, 35%, and 39.6%. Each rate applies to a different segment of income known as a tax bracket. It is the combined effect of the tax rates and the tax brackets that creates the rate structure. The rates rise with the tax brackets. Thus, the 10% rate applies to the lowest tax bracket and the 39.6% rate applies to the highest tax bracket. The percentage of one's total income that one pays in taxes is termed the person's *effective tax rate*. The tax brackets change slightly every year due to the fact that they have been indexed for inflation. *See* IRC § 1(f)(1)-(2). The IRS publishes new brackets each year in a revenue procedure. There are various other complexities in the rate structure due to transition rules and sunset clauses.

The rate and bracket structure for the federal income tax is progressive, that is, the rate rises with income. Two points about the present rate of progressivity are worth noting. First, over the past forty years or so, payroll taxes (e.g., Social Security and Medicare) have risen significantly, especially for the lower and middle classes. These regressive taxes have rendered the overall federal tax structure even less progressive than appears to be the case when only the income tax rate structure is considered. Second, as we will address later, the tax rates on capital gains and dividends are generally lower than the tax rates on ordinary income. Most capital gains and dividends are realized by wealthier individuals. These two facts taken together tend to further reduce the overall progressivity of the federal tax system.

Today we have four classes of individuals for rate structure purposes: married persons filing jointly (including surviving spouses), heads of households, unmarried persons, and married persons filing separately. The tax rates are the same for all four classes but the brackets are different. The higher tax brackets take effect sooner for the various categories of taxpayers in the following order: married persons filing separately, unmarried persons, heads of household, and married persons filing jointly. Thus, married persons will almost always find it advantageous to file jointly rather than separately. Marital status is determined in part by federal tax law rather than simply by reference to state law. Moreover, the terms *surviving spouse* and *head of household* have specific tax meanings that are delineated by statute.

Normally marital status for tax purposes is determined at year's end. *See* IRC § 7703(a)(1). *See also* IRC § 6013. Marriage is a legal union recognized by state law. Under federal tax law, however, a person who is legally separated from her spouse under a decree of divorce or separate maintenance is not considered married for federal tax purposes. IRC § 2(b)(2)(A). Nor is a person considered married for tax purposes if the person's spouse is a non-resident alien. IRC § 2(b)(2)(B). In addition, sometimes if a married couple lives apart for an extended period, they are treated as unmarried for tax purposes. IRC § 7703(b). On the other hand, a person whose spouse died during the tax year is treated as married for tax purposes for that tax year. IRC § 2(b)(2)(C). Thus, if one's spouse dies during the tax year, it is permissible for such person to file a joint return with the decedent spouse in the year of death. IRC § 7703(a)(1).

Primary Authority

Code: §§ 1(a)-(d); 2. Skim §§ 1(f), (i); 55(b)(2); 56; 57; 58; 6013(a); 7703(a).

Regulations: None.

Cases: Poe v. Seaborn, 282 U.S. 101 (1930).

Rulings: Rev. Proc. 2015-53, 2015-44 I.R.B. 615.

Problems

14.1. Tim is a calendar-year taxpayer. In each subpart below, compute Tim's tax liability for Year 1 before credits. Assume, unless otherwise directed, that he and anyone else filing with him have $600,000 of taxable earned income. Use the rate tables in Revenue Procedure 2015-53, which can be found in the Appendix.

   (a) On December 31, Year 1, Tim is unmarried and has no children or dependents.

$193,769.95.

The table for section 1(c) applies. The tax is $120,579.75 plus $73,240.20 (39.6% of $184,950 which is the excess of $600,000 over $415,050 which is the point when the top bracket begins).

   (b) On March 1, Year 1, Tim marries Faith but they divorce on November 1, Year 1.

Same as above since marital status is determined at the end of the year. IRC § 7703(a)(1).

(c) Same as (b) except that Tim and Faith remain married through the remainder of Year 1 and file jointly.

$183,266.30.

The table for section 1(a) applies. The tax is $130,578.50 plus $52,687.80 (39.6% of $133,050 which is the excess of $600,000 over $466,950 which is the point when the top bracket begins).

(d) Same as (c) except that Tim and Faith file separately and reside in a non-community property state. Tim's taxable income is $600,000.

$210,433.15.

The table for section 1(d) applies. The tax is $65,289.25 plus $145,143.90 (39.6% of $366,525 which is the excess of $600,000 over $233,475 which is the point when the top bracket begins).

(e) Same as (d) except that Tim and Faith live in a community property state. Their total taxable income of $600,000 is all earned income. Tim earned $200,000 and Faith earned $400,000.

Tim will report $300,000, half their total earned income. Faith will report the other half. *Poe v. Seaborn.*

Each will owe $91,633.15. In the aggregate they will owe $183,266.30, which is the same as if they had filed jointly.

The table for section 1(d) applies. The tax for each is $65,289.25 plus $26,343.90 (39.6% of $66,525 which is the excess of $300,000 over $233,475 which is the point when the top bracket begins). This equals $91,633.15 each.

(f) Same as (c) except that Faith died on October 1, Year 1.

The answer is the same as in (c), above. In the year of Faith's death, Tim is treated as married. *See* IRC § 7703(a)(1) exception clause. Faith's executor should sign the return. IRC § 6013(a)(3). If no executor has been appointed and no return is filed for Faith, Tim may sign the joint return for her. *Id.* If an executor is later appointed, the executor has one year from the due date for the return to dis-affirm the joint return and file separately.

(g) What if Tim and Faith had married the year prior to Year 1, had a child in that year, and Faith died in that year?

Again the tax is $183,266.30. Tim is a surviving spouse under section 2(a) and can use the married rates in table 1(a).

Surviving spouse requirements are:

1. Spouse died in one of the two immediately preceding years. IRC § 2(a)(1)(A).
2. Taxpayer maintains household providing over half the cost of maintenance. IRC § 2(a)(1) last sentence.

3. Taxpayer's household constitutes the principal place of abode for section 151 dependents of Taxpayer who are children of Taxpayer. The children must be qualified dependents of Taxpayer under section 152(a)(1) for whom Taxpayer can claim deductions under section 151(c)(1). IRC § 2(a)(1)(B)(i) & (ii).
4. And it is assumed that none of the section 2(a)(2) limitations are violated.

(h) Same as (g) except that all events occurred three years prior to Year 1.

The table for section 1(b) applies. The tax is $125,936 plus $62,964 (39.6% of $159,000 which is the excess of $600,000 over $441,000 which is the point when the top bracket begins).

Requirements for head of household status are:

1. Taxpayer is not married at close of year. IRC § 2(b)(1).
2. Taxpayer is not a surviving spouse. IRC § 2(a)(1)(A).
3. Taxpayer maintains a household and provides over half the cost of maintenance. IRC § 2(b)(1) last sentence.
4. Taxpayer maintains as the taxpayer's home a household that is the principal place of abode for the taxpayer's children for over half the year. IRC § 2(b)(1)(A)(i).
5. Taxpayer does not fall within the section 2(b)(3) limitations.

Chapter 15

Tax Credits

Overview

In this chapter, we consider only a few of the many available credits found in the Code. The difference between a deduction and a credit rests upon their different places in the calculation of final tax liability. A deduction reduces income before the tax rate is applied to arrive at a tax liability. A credit reduces tax liability dollar for dollar. That being so, a credit is worth more than a deduction of the same dollar amount since the deduction only reduces tax liability in proportion to the taxpayer's top marginal tax rate. For example, while a $100 credit saves $100 in taxes, a $100 deduction for a taxpayer in the 35% bracket saves only $35 in taxes. This points the way to another notable difference between credits and deductions. While deductions are more valuable as one's marginal tax rate rises, credits are equally valuable to everyone who is able to utilize them. In our example above, if the taxpayer's marginal rate was 15%, the $100 deduction would only save $15 of taxes. The equality aspect of the credit makes it particularly appropriate for use in providing tax subsidies and incentives.

It should be noted that some credits are non-refundable credits and others are refundable credits. A non-refundable credit can reduce one's tax liability no lower than zero. A refundable credit can trigger a payment from the government to the taxpayer if the credit exceeds her tax liability. Non-refundable credits are taken ahead of refundable credits, which is a taxpayer favorable result.

Primary Authority

Code: §§ 21(a)-(c), (d)(1); 24(a)-(c); 25A(a)-(g)(2); 31; 32(a)-(b).

Regulations: None.

Cases: None.

Rulings: None.

Problems

15.1. **Feist is a full-time student at Indypop University, an eligible education institution within the meaning of section 25A(f)(2). Feist is married to Melissa a local rock performer. Melissa supports Feist on her earnings. Consider how section 25A applies to them if they file a joint return. In doing so, ignore the inflation adjustments called for by section 25A(h).**

(a) Their modified adjusted gross income is $60,000, and Feist pays $24,000 of tuition to Indypop U as a third-year student.

Because Feist is within the first four years of post-secondary education, Feist is entitled to the American Opportunity Tax Credit, which is an enhanced version of the former Hope Scholarship Credit that was recently made permanent. IRC § 25A(i). The credit is $2,500. Note the increased phase out rules applicable to the American Opportunity Tax Credit ($80,000 for single taxpayers and $160,000 for joint filers) do not apply at their income level.

(b) Same as (a) except that Feist is in graduate school.

The American Opportunity Tax Credit does not apply since Feist is not in the first four years of college. IRC § 25A(i). The Lifetime Learning Credit, however, applies and would be $2,000. IRC § 25A(c)(1). There is no problem with phase out under section 25A(d).

(c) Same as (b) except that the tuition is paid from a gift from Feist's parents.

No change. The fact that the payment is traceable from a gift seems not to matter. *Cf* the parenthetical language in IRC § 25A(g)(2)(C).

(d) Same as (b) except that Feist receives a $16,000 tuition waiver as compensation for her work as a research assistant for her major professor. The waiver is included in her gross income.

No change from (b). The tuition waiver is not a qualified scholarship under section 117 since it is not excludable from gross income. *See* IRC § 25A(g)(2)(A). If it were excludable under section 117, the credit amount would be reduced to 20% of $8,000, or $1,600. IRC § 25A(c)(1).

(e) Same as (b) except that Melissa is also a half-time student working on an advanced degree in music. She pays $5,000 tuition.

Only one Lifetime Learning Credit is available to the couple since there is only one credit allowed per taxpayer. IRC § 25A(c)(1). Filing separately would not help because of section 25A(g)(6), which denies the credit in such cases. Their expenses can be aggregated (IRC § 25A(f)(1)), but this doesn't help either since they are able to get the maximum credit from Feist's expenses alone. Though only one tax credit is available to Feist and Melissa, they can take the section 222 deduction with respect to her tuition expenses (before 2017). The deduction is limited to $4,000. The coordination provisions of section 25A and 222 do not address this particular scenario. *See* IRC §§ 25A(g)(5), 222(c)(2)(A). Note that although section 222 is scheduled to expire in 2017, Congress has extended the life of this provision on more than one occasion.

(f) Same as (b) except that they have modified adjusted gross income of $95,000.

The amount of the Lifetime Learning Credit otherwise allowed is partially phased out at this AGI level (the phase out begins at $80,000 for a joint return). The amount of the reduction equals the credit otherwise allowed without regard to the phase out ($2,000) multiplied by a fraction, the numerator of which is the excess modified AGI over $80,000 (here $15,000) and the denominator of which is $20,000. Thus, the credit is partially phased out to $500 [$2,000 × ($15,000/$20,000) = $1,500; $2,000 − $1,500 = $500.]. IRC § 25A(d)(1) & (2).

15.2. Kate is unmarried and has two young sons. Kate qualifies as a head of household for tax purposes. Her sons are her tax dependents. Kate has $20,000 of earned income and has no other income. Income tax of $700 was withheld from her wages by her employer. Assuming no inflation adjustments (other than the tax rate adjustments in Rev. Proc. 2015-53), what is Kate's total tax refund (including her earned income tax credit) for the current year? In making this calculation, assume that Kate does not itemize deductions and that no tax credits apply other than the credits under sections 24 (child tax credit), 31 (tax withheld on wages), and 32 (earned income tax credit). To calculate her initial tax liability, use the tables from Revenue Procedure 2015-53, which can be found in the Appendix.

$20,000.00	Gross income
(4,400.00)	Standard deduction as head of household § 63(c)(2)(B)
(6,000.00)	3 personal exemptions §§ 151(a), (c), (d)(1); 152(a)(1) & (c)
$9,600.00	Taxable income
960.00	Tax liability under Rev. Proc. 2015-53 Table 2 Head of Household (10% of $9,600)
(960.00)	Child tax credit § 24(a)(2) ($960.00 allowed against tax; $1,040.00 would be refundable under § 24(d))
00000.00	**Post non-refundable credit tax liability**
$1,040.00	Child tax credit § 24(d) (refundable) (see calculation below)
700.00	Withholding tax credit § 31(a) (refundable)
1,789.00	Earned income credit § 32 (refundable) (see calculation below)
$3,529.00	**Total refund**

Child Tax Credit Computation: As a non-refundable credit, it would appear that $960.00 of the $2,000 is allowed to Kate, as $960.00 is the amount of Kate's tax liability using the tables from Revenue Procedure 2015-53. However, the credit can be partially refundable in limited cases. *See* IRC § 24(d).

Here, the refundable portion of the child tax credit is equal to $1,040.00—the lesser of either (1) the unclaimed portion of the total credit amount ($1,040.00), or

(2) $2,550 (15% of $17,000). This latter number is her earned income in excess of $3,000 ($20,000 − $3,000 = $17,000).

Earned Income Credit Computation: The initial credit is determined by multiplying the credit percentage in section 32(b)(1)(A) (here 40%) times the earned income amount in section 32(b)(2)(A) (here $8,890). This figure is then reduced by the phase out percentage in section 32(b)(1)(A) (here 21.06%) multiplied times $8,390, the excess of the taxpayer's earned income (here given as $20,000) over the phase out amount in section 32(b)(2)(A) (the phase out amount here is $11,610).

$3,556	Initial credit (40% × $8,890) §§ 32(a)(2), (b)(1) and (2)
(1,767)	Phase out reduction (21.06% × $8,390) § 32(b)(1)(A), (b)(2)
	$20,000 − $11,610 = $8,390 Income above phase out amount § 32(b)(2)(A)
$1,789	**Earned income credit**

Chapter 16

First Review Problem

The following problem is designed to review what has been addressed in the preceding chapters and to help integrate what has been learned. The problem simulates many aspects of a typical middle to upper-middle class married couple's tax return. In doing this problem, assume that Taxpayers file a joint return for the year. To calculate their tax liability, please use the rate structure set out in Revenue Procedure 2015-53, which is provided in the Appendix. You may assume the standard deduction for a married couple filing jointly is $12,600 and the personal and dependency exemption amount is $4,050.

Taxpayers, Isabella and Tommy, a married couple, have two children, Jude and Sienna, ages 6 and 12. In August of the year in question, Tommy's father, Harvey, moves in with Tommy and Isabella. They provided over half of his support for the year. Harvey's gross income for the year is $1,500. Prior to living with Tommy and Isabella, Harvey lived on his own in a rented apartment.

Tommy and Isabella are cash method taxpayers. Tommy is a musician who generated $90,000 of cash receipts in the current year as a performer. He has various expenses relating to his business considered below. Isabella is a physical therapist who has a $100,000 annual salary with a local hospital.

Part 16.1. Gross Income: Determine Taxpayers' gross income, if, in addition to the amounts above, the following items, services or amounts are received during the year:

Taxpayers' gross income is $233,000, determined as follows:

Both Tommy's business and Isabella's salary income, $190,000, are included in gross income. IRC § 61(a)(1)-(2).

(a) **Tommy performed at his accountant's wedding in exchange for the accountant's bookkeeping services for the year. Tommy's normal fee for wedding performances is $5,000.**

Tommy has gross income of $5,000. This is an in-kind bartered exchange. *See* Rev. Rul. 79-24, 1979-1 C.B. 60, considered in Chapter 2. Note that under the principles of *Philadelphia Amusement* we can assume that the bookkeeping service is worth the music service.

(b) **Tommy and Isabella recover $15,000 from their insurance company when their car, used solely for personal purposes, is totaled by a falling**

tree during a thunderstorm. They paid $22,000 for the car two years ago. Before the storm its fair market value was $15,000.

There is no gross income here since the amount of reimbursement is less than their basis. Instead, this is a casualty loss since it arises from a storm. The loss is potentially deductible under section 165(c)(3) but is limited by the provisions of section 165(h). The initial amount of their deductible loss is $15,000, the fair market value of the car. Treas. Reg. § 1.165-7(b)(1). This appears to conflict with the language of section 165(b). However, it is consistent with the disallowance of the depreciation deduction on their personal use property. *See* IRC § 167(a). The reimbursement reduces their potentially deductible loss to zero. Treas. Reg. § 1.165-1(c)(4).

If there were a deductible loss, the deduction is reduced by $100 pursuant to IRC § 165(h)(1). It is further reduced by 10% of their adjusted gross income (determined below in part 16.2 of this problem) under IRC § 165(h)(2)(A).

(c) Isabella buys a painting at a garage sale for $100. Later she learns it is an early work of Edward Hopper and is worth $1,000,000.

The painting is not income since there has been no realization event with respect to it. *Glenshaw Glass.* Assuming the purchase was at arm's length, Isabella has simply made a bargain purchase. *See* Pellar v. Commissioner, 25 T.C. 299 (1955), acq. 1956-2 C.B. 7. Some may see this as a windfall similar to *Cesarini v. United States*, where money was found in a piano. However, all she ever had in this scenario is a painting. Unlike *Cesarini*, there was no separate item of property for her to realize after she acquired it.

(d) Tommy receives a patent worth $50,000 as a gift from his mother.

Tommy's gift is excluded from gross income by section 102(a), assuming his mother gave the patent out of detached and disinterested generosity. *Commissioner v. Duberstein.*

(e) Tommy receives a royalty check for $1,000 on the patent for royalties earned after the date of gift.

The $1,000 of royalties generated by the patent is included in gross income under section 61(a)(6). The gift exclusion does not apply to income from a gift. *See* IRC § 102(b)(1).

(f) Tommy performs music for various clients during the year for which he has not yet been paid. At year's end, these accounts receivable amount to $30,000.

Since he is a cash method taxpayer, these accounts receivables are not income until they are collected. Treas. Reg. § 1.451-1(a).

(g) In order to improve his cash flow situation, Tommy sells $9,000 of his accounts receivable to his bank for $8,000.

As a cash method taxpayer, Tommy will not have reported any income on the receivables when they are earned. Thus, his basis in them is zero. The sale would produce $8,000 of ordinary income under section 1001. *See, e.g., Estate of Stranahan v. Commissioner.*

> **(h) Isabella won a car worth $25,001 at a nearby tribal casino on a $1 instant lottery ticket. This was her only gambling experience of the year.**

This is $25,000 of income to Isabella (the $1 she invested represents a cost basis in the ticket). IRC §§ 61(a), 74(a); *Cesarini.* The fact that her winnings are not in the form of cash does not change the outcome. Treas. Reg. § 1.61-1(a). Since this is her only gaming experience for the year, the possible application of §165(d) is eliminated.

> **(i) Tommy performed at a benefit concert for Isabella's hospital in order to raise money for a new children's wing. In exchange he was given free use of the hospital grounds and facilities for two days while shooting a music video. The hospital normally charges $4,000 for such access.**

This is gross income. Payment in a form other than cash is irrelevant. *See* IRC § 61(a)(1); Treas. Reg. § 1.61-1(a), -2(d); *see also Glenshaw Glass.* The value is determined by reference to fair market value. Presumably the prior rentals establish that at $4,000. *See* Treas. Reg. § 20.2031-1(b).

> **(j) Isabella has back surgery at the hospital where she works. Since she works in the same line of business, the hospital discounts her bill by $5,000. This is 20% of the amount of the hospital's usual charge for the surgery. *See* IRC IRC § 132(a) & (c).**

The $5,000 discount is excluded from income as a qualified employee discount under sections 132(a)(2) & (c)(1)(B). The facts eliminate any line of business issue.

Gross Income Summary:

$100,000	Salary
90,000	Gross receipts
5,000	bartered accounting services
1,000	royalties
8,000	Sale of AR
25,000	Lottery winnings
4,000	Bartered services for use of grounds
$233,000	**Gross Income**

Part 16.2. Adjusted Gross Income (AGI): Determine Taxpayers' AGI assuming they make the expenditures listed below. (Though more than one approach is rational, we recommend that you first determine which expenditures are potentially deductible and then segregate deductible items into above the line (IRC § 62) and below the line (IRC § 63) deductions. Do not forget to apply the rules of section 67 where applicable.

(a) **Tommy incurs the following expenses in his music business: (1) $20,000 cost of roadies; (2) $17,000 of studio rent; and (3) $30,000 of management fees.**

Tommy's $67,000 of expenses are all deductible as ordinary and necessary business expenses under section 162(a).

(b) **Tommy purchases new musical equipment at a cost of $10,000. The equipment has a 5-year class life. However, Tommy properly elects to expense the entire amount under section 179.**

Tommy's equipment qualifies for $10,000 of deductions under section 179. None of the section 179 limits are exceeded. Thus, no depreciation deduction calculation need be done.

(c) **Isabella incurs $3,400 of expenses to attend the annual meeting of the American Physical Therapy Association. She spent $400 for meals and the rest went to pay for plane fare, registration fees and lodging. She is not reimbursed by her employer.**

Isabella's $3,400 of business expenses are ordinary and necessary expenses incurred by an employee deductible under section 162(a). But the meals are deductible at 50% under section 274(n)(1). So the deduction is limited to $3,200. But note the expenses will be treated further under section 67.

(d) **Tommy spends $2,000 for chain festooned neon yellow leather pants that he only wears when he is performing.**

A deduction should be permitted as an ordinary and necessary business expense under section 162 since the pants are not suitable for wear outside of work. *See Pevsner v. Commissioner.* This could be debated. *Pevsner* sets out a three-part test: (1) the clothes are required as a condition of employment, (2) they are not suitable for street wear, (3) and they are not so used. *Pevsner* (citing Donnelly v. Commissioner, 262 F.2d 411, 412 (2d Cir. 1959)). It may be that the first part is not satisfied. We would argue that this is a theatrical costume and should be deemed required by the employment as a rock musician. According to the IRS "[m]usicians and entertainers can deduct the cost of theatrical clothing and accessories that are not suitable for everyday wear." IRS Publication No. 17.

(e) **Isabella pays $300 in dues to the American Physical Therapy Association.**

Isabella's dues are deductible as ordinary and necessary business expenses under section 162(a). But note they will be treated further under section 67.

(f) **Tommy pays $1,000 in dues to the American Federation of Musicians Local 47.**

Tommy's dues are deductible as ordinary and necessary business expenses under section 162(a). *See* Treas. Reg. § 1.162-15(d).

(g) Taxpayers pay $9,000 of interest on the mortgage of their residence, $1,000 of interest on their personal credit cards, and $4,000 of property taxes.

Taxpayers' $9,000 of mortgage interest is deductible under sections 163(a) & (h)(2)(D) and the $4,000 of property taxes are deductible under section 164(a)(1). The credit card interest is not deductible since it is personal interest. IRC § 163(h)(1).

(h) Taxpayers give $8,000 of cash to various public charities.

Taxpayers' $8,000 cash gifts to charities are deductible under section 170.

(i) Taxpayers pay $7,000 in state income taxes and $3,000 in state sales taxes.

The state income taxes are deductible under section 164(a)(3). Note that taxpayers have the option of deducting state and local sales taxes in lieu of state and local income taxes. The sales taxes are deductible if the taxpayers elect not to deduct the state income taxes. IRC § 164(b)(5). Here, Taxpayers would have elected to deduct the income taxes since the amount is greater than the sales taxes.

(j) Taxpayers incur $4,000 in medical expenses.

Taxpayers' medical expenses are nondeductible because they do not exceed 10.0% of Taxpayers' $153,000 adjusted gross income. IRC § 213(a). (Adjusted gross income is determined below.)

(k) Taxpayers spend $25,000 to remodel the kitchen of their residence.

Taxpayers' renovation of their home is a nondeductible capital personal expenditure. IRC §§ 262; 263. Their basis in the home is increased by $25,000. IRC § 1016(a)(1).

Above the Line Deductions

Having determined the extent to which the above items are deductible, the next step is to determine which items are deductible above-the-line under section 62:

Tommy's $67,000 of business expenses under section 62(a)(1).

Tommy's $10,000 section 179 expenses under section 62(a)(1).

Tommy's $2,000 section 162 expenses for the yellow leather pants under section 62(a)(1).

Tommy's $1,000 professional dues under section 62(a)(1). (The contrast with the treatment of Isabella's professional dues as miscellaneous itemized deductions highlights the advantages of self-employment with respect to such expenses.)

Thus, total above the line deductions are $80,000. [Note that answer ignores the fact that one-half of the self-employment tax owed on Tommy's self-employment income (net profit from schedule C) is also an above the line deduction. *See* Form 1040, line 27.]

All other deductible items are not listed under section 62 and so they are itemized deductions.

Taxpayers' Adjusted Gross Income is:

$233,000	Gross income
− 80,000	Above the line deductions
$153,000	Adjusted gross income

Part 16.3. Taxable Income: Determine Taxpayers' taxable income. Do not forget the personal and dependency exemptions.

(a) Itemized Deductions

The next step is to determine the amount of Taxpayers' itemized deductions. Those deductions include:

Isabella's seminar expenses	$3,200	not listed in IRC § 67(b)
Isabella's dues	300	not listed in IRC § 67(b)
Mortgage interest	9,000	IRC § 67(b)(1)
Property taxes	4,000	IRC § 67(b)(2)
Charitable deductions	8,000	IRC § 67(b)(4)
State income taxes	7,000	IRC § 67(b)(2)
Pre-§67 item. Deductions	$31,500	
Apply § 67	− 3,060	reducing I's $3,500 employee expenses
Allowed Item. Deds.	$28,440	

Section 67 imposes a 2% floor on "miscellaneous" itemized deductions, which are itemized deductions other than those listed under section 67(b). Isabella's unreimbursed employee business expenses are not listed under section 67(b). They total $3,500 and they do exceed 2% of adjusted gross income ($3,060) by $440. **Thus, total itemized deductions are $28,440.** Since the total itemized deductions exceed the $12,600 standard deduction allowed to married taxpayers filing a joint return (*See* Rev. Proc. 2015-53), Taxpayers would deduct their $28,440 of itemized deductions. IRC § 63.

Under section 68, the amount of otherwise allowable itemized deductions will be reduced if AGI exceeds a threshold amount (adjusted annually for inflation). The applicable threshold amount for married taxpayers filing a joint return in 2016 was $311,300. Therefore, the phase out will not apply to the taxpayers in this problem.

Reminder: The medical expenses were disallowed because they did not exceed the appropriate AGI threshold. There was no casualty loss because of the insurance reimbursement.

(b) Personal and Dependency Exemptions

Taxpayers filing a joint return are allowed two personal exemptions (IRC §§ 151(a) & (c); Treas. Reg. § 1.151-1(b)) and two dependency exemptions for their "qualifying children" (IRC § 152(c)). Harvey is also a dependent (i.e., qualifying relative) since

Tommy and Isabella provided over half of his support for the year. *See* IRC § 152(d)(1)(C). He is a qualified relative because he is Tommy's father. *See* IRC § 152(d)(2)(C). The fact that he did not live with them for the entire year is irrelevant since we are not relying on IRC § 152(d)(1)(H). Thus, their five personal exemptions total $20,250. See Rev. Proc. 2015-53 for the amount of exemptions. As a result Taxpayers have $104,310 of taxable income, determined as follows:

AGI	$153,000
Itemized Deductions	− 28,440
Exemptions	− 20,250
Taxable Income	$104,310

Part 16.4. Pre-Credit Tax Liability: Using Rev. Proc. 2015-53, which can be found in the Appendix, determine Taxpayers' pre-credit tax liability under section 1(a), which applies to taxpayers who file a joint return.

Employing the section 1(a) tax rates as implemented by Rev. Proc. 2015-53 (which makes adjustments under sections 1((f) and (i)) applicable to Taxpayers filing a joint return, Taxpayers have $17,620 of pre-credit tax liability computed as follows:

$10,367.50 plus $7,252.50, i.e., 25% of $29,010 ($104,310 minus $75,300 = $29,010). *See* Rev. Proc. 2015-53 in the Appendix.

Part 16.5. Final Tax Liability: Determine Taxpayers' post-credit tax liability and the amount of any further payment they must make or refund they will receive if Isabella's employer withheld $10,000 in federal income taxes and Tommy paid $6,000 in estimated taxes. *See* IRC §§ 24, 31.

$17,620.00	Pre-credit liability
− 000.00	§ 24 credit (see below)
− 16,000.00	§ 31 credit (see below)
$ 1,620.00	TAX OWED

The section 24 child tax credit starts at $2,000 ($1,000 for each child), then declines by $2,000, i.e., $50 for each $1,000 by which adjusted gross income ($153,000) exceeds the threshold amount ($110,000). IRC § 24(b)(1) & (b)(2)(A). Because the couple has two kids, the total phase out would occur at $150,000 of adjusted gross income. Here their AGI is 153,000. Thus, their child tax credit is entirely phased out.

As a result of the withholding and estimated taxes of $16,000, Taxpayers have a section 31 credit of $16,000 and will owe an additional $1,620 for the year.

Note: Sections 35 or 36 treat excess estimated tax as an "overpayment." Section 6401 says which credits are refundable by saying which are "overpayments." Section 6402 authorizes refunds of "overpayments."

Chapter 17

Capital Gains and Losses

Overview

After determining whether a gain is included in gross income or whether a loss is deductible from gross income, the character of the gain or loss must be determined. A recognized gain or deductible loss is characterized either as *capital* or *ordinary* depending on a number of factors. Individual taxpayers generally prefer gains to be classified as capital gains rather than ordinary income because certain capital gains (in particular, "long-term capital gains") are afforded preferential tax treatment. Presently, the maximum rate at which most long-term capital gains are taxed is 15% (0% for taxpayers in the bottom two ordinary income tax brackets and 20% for taxpayers in the top ordinary income tax bracket). In contrast to gains, taxpayers tend to prefer that their losses be characterized as ordinary losses because of a statutory limitation on capital loss deductions. More specifically, in the case of individuals, capital losses can only be used to offset capital gains plus $3,000 of ordinary income. IRC § 1211(b). Unused capital losses are carried forward and can be deducted in future years subject to the same limitation on deductibility. IRC § 1212(b).

A taxpayer's interest in property must be terminated in a special way—a *sale or exchange*—in order to qualify for capital gain or loss treatment. If property is stolen or destroyed in a casualty transaction and the taxpayer is reimbursed by insurance or otherwise, the involuntary conversion is not a sale or exchange and, thus, it produces ordinary gain or loss unless otherwise provided by another Code provision.

In addition, a sale or exchange transaction must involve a *capital asset* in order to qualify for capital gain or loss treatment. Section 1221(a) defines the term capital asset as all property held by the taxpayer (whether or not connected with a trade or business), subject to some important exceptions. Exceptions include inventory and inventory-like property (§ 1221(a)(1)), trade or business property (§ 1221(a)(2)), self-created literary, musical, or artistic compositions and similar property (§ 1221(a)(3)), accounts receivable (§ 1221(a)(4)), supplies used in a business (§ 1221(a)(8)), and a few other types of property. Special rate treatment applies to sales/exchanges of capital assets provided the capital assets were held for more than one year.

If a transaction is missing one or more of the requirements for capital gain or loss treatment, it gives rise to ordinary income or loss unless a special characterization provision applies. There are several special characterization provisions that supply one or more of the requirements to a transaction. For example, under section 1231 considered in the next chapter, property excluded from the definition of capital asset (trade or business property) may nevertheless be accorded capital asset status, and involuntary conversions which are not considered sales or exchanges may be accorded sale or exchange status. Not all special characterization provisions are pro-taxpayer. Section 1245, for example, mandates that gain on the disposition of certain property be treated as ordinary income to the extent of the depreciation or amortization deductions taken with respect to the property.

It should be noted that qualified dividends (dividends with respect to stock held for at least 61 days during a prescribed period) are taxed at capital gains rates. § 1(h)(11). Although taxed at preferential rates, they are not characterized as capital gains for other purposes and, therefore, cannot be used to offset capital losses.

Primary Authority

Code: §§ 1211(a)-(b); 1212(a)-(b); 1221; 1222; 1223(1)-(2), (10). Skim §§ 1(h); 165(c), (f), (g)(1)-(2); 408(m); 1060, 1202(a)-(e); 1235; 1236; 1237; 1241; 1271.

Regulations: § 1.1221-1(a)-(d). Skim § 1.1060-1(c).

Cases: Bynum v. Commissioner, 46 T.C. 295 (1966); Cameron v. Commissioner, T.C. Memo. 2007-260; Mayer v. Commissioner, T.C. Memo. 1994-209; Moller v. United States, 721 F.2d 810 (Fed. Cir. 1983); Olstein v. Commissioner, T.C. Memo 1999-290; Williams v. McGowan, 152 F.2d 570 (2d Cir. 1945).

Rulings: None.

Problems

17.1. Are your house, car, furniture, clothing, and laptop computer considered capital assets? Why does it matter?

Yes, all of the personal-use assets mentioned are capital assets under section 1221 as none of the eight exceptions apply. IRC § 1221.

It may not matter in the case of a *sale* of these assets. Your car, furniture, clothing, and computer typically do not appreciate in value so there will never be capital gain realized on their sale. These assets typically decline in value, but personal losses from their sale are not deductible. IRC § 165(c). Your house may appreciate, but section 121 (addressed in Chapter 22) excludes up to $250,000 ($500,000 in the case of certain joint filers) of gain on the sale of a principal residence.

Characterization of these assets might matter, however, in the case of a *casualty* transaction. *See* IRC § 165(c)(3), addressed in Chapter 10, permitting a personal casualty loss deduction. *See also* IRC § 165(h)(2)(B).

17.2. Frank, a self-employed architect, recently decided to sell his architectural business and move to the Caribbean. Gensler, Inc. agrees to pay Frank $1 million for the following assets: (1) drafting supplies and drafting equipment;

(2) building and land Frank uses in the business; (3) a valuable antique rug on the floor in the lobby; (4) architectural plans created by Frank; (5) accounts receivable; and (6) goodwill of the business.

(a) Which of the above are capital assets?

Drafting supplies and drafting equipment: The drafting supplies are not capital assets. IRC § 1221(a)(8). Likewise, the drafting equipment is not a capital asset because it is depreciable property used in Frank's business. IRC § 1221(a)(2). [As will be addressed in the next chapter, the equipment is considered "section 1231 property" (quasi-capital asset) provided Frank has owned it more than a year. IRC § 1231(b). Therefore, even though the equipment is not a capital asset within the meaning section 1221, it may nevertheless qualify for capital gain treatment.]

Building and land Frank uses in the business: The building and the land used in business are not capital assets. IRC § 1221(a)(2). [They are "section 1231 property" as addressed in the next chapter.]

Valuable antique rug on the floor in the lobby: Whether the antique rug is a capital asset or not depends on whether it is depreciable property. If the rug is not depreciable, then it is a capital asset. If, however, the rug is depreciable, then it is not a capital asset. IRC § 1221(a)(2). You might review *Simon v. Commissioner*, discussed in Chapter 9, to determine whether the rug is property of a character subject to the allowance for depreciation.

Architectural plans created by Frank: The architectural plans are not capital assets. IRC § 1221(a)(3); Treas. Reg. § 1.1221-1(c). The purpose of treating such property as noncapital in the hands of its creator is consistent with taxing wages and salaries as ordinary income. *See* S. Rep. No. 91-522 (1969), reprinted in 1969-3 C.B. 423, 549 (describing reasons for the copyright exclusion). Gains from personal efforts should be taxed as ordinary income just as wages and salaries are taxed as ordinary income.

Accounts receivable: The accounts receivable are not capital assets. IRC § 1221(a)(4).

Goodwill: Self-created goodwill is a capital asset, as none of the exceptions in section 1221(a)(1)-(8) apply. Some may wonder whether self-generated goodwill is depreciable under section 167 or amortizable under section 197, and, thus, excluded under section 1221(a)(2). (Any amortizable section 197 intangible is treated as property that is of a character subject to the allowance for depreciation provided in section 167. IRC § 197(f)(7)). First, self-created goodwill is specifically excluded from section 197 per section 197(c)(2). Second, self-created goodwill is not subject to the allowance for depreciation under section 167 per Treas. Reg. § 1.167(a)-3(a). ("No deduction for depreciation is allowable with respect to goodwill.") Thus, the exception in section 1221(a)(2) does not apply. So, self-created goodwill is a capital asset. [Note that, in contrast, purchased goodwill is a section 197 intangible and thus is excluded from the capital asset definition. Purchased goodwill, however, is section 1231 property eligible for capital gain treatment nevertheless.]

(b) In general, how will the tax consequences of the sale be determined? *See Williams v. McGowan. See also* **IRC § 1060; Treas. Reg. § 1.1060-1(c).**

Frank is selling his entire business, which includes all the tangible and intangible assets listed above—some of which are capital assets (or quasi capital assets under section 1231) and some of which are not. How should the tax consequences of the sale of the business be determined? As the sale of a unified asset (his sole proprietorship)? As the separate sale of each business asset? In *Williams v. McGowan*, the Second Circuit required the latter approach. In other words, the sale of Frank's business must be fragmented, and the tax consequences of each asset sold must be determined separately. We have already determined the character (capital asset or non-capital asset) of each asset sold. We now need to determine the amount of gain or loss realized with respect to each asset [gain realized = amount realized – adjusted basis; loss realized = adjusted basis – amount realized]. We can easily ascertain Frank's adjusted basis in each asset. To determine the amount realized with respect to each asset sold, we must allocate the total purchase price to each asset sold.

Purchase price allocations can be tricky due to competing incentives of buyers and sellers. For example, Frank will want to allocate a large portion of the total purchase price to capital assets sold, such as goodwill, to maximize the amount of gain taxed at preferential capital gains rates. The buyer, however, will want to allocate a large portion of the total purchase price to depreciable tangible assets with short recovery periods, such as the equipment. (The costs allocable to the equipment might be depreciable over five years under section 168, whereas costs allocable to purchased goodwill are amortizable over fifteen years under section 197.) Purchase price allocations are generally respected by the Service provided they are the result of adversarial, arm's-length negotiations. The Service is not bound by allocations or valuations of assets established by the parties, and may challenge such allocations and valuation determinations.

[Note: If a trade or business is acquired in an "applicable asset acquisition" under section 1060, the total amount paid for the trade or business must be allocated among the various acquired assets in accordance with the rules of section 1060. *See* IRC § 1060(c) (defining "applicable asset acquisition"). Regulations under section 1060 require that the seller and purchaser allocate the total consideration among seven classes of assets specified in Treas. Reg. § 1.338-6. Treas. Reg. § 1.1060-1(c). Note the seventh class is "goodwill and going concern value," and the amount of consideration allocable to goodwill and going concern value is the excess of the total consideration over the amounts allocable to all other tangible and intangible assets listed in the first six classes (this is known as the "residual method" in valuing goodwill and going concern value). The seller and buyer are bound by their written allocations or valuations of assets. IRC § 1060(a). The Service, of course, is free to challenge the parties' valuation determinations.]

(c) Assume that Frank did not operate the architecture business as a sole proprietorship, but instead was the sole shareholder and president of

> **FLW, Inc., which owned and operated the business. Assuming he has held the stock for two years and he has an adjusted basis in his stock of $300,000, what are the tax consequences to Frank if he sells all of his stock in FLW, Inc. to Gensler, Inc. for $1 million?**

The sale of stock is the sale of a single asset. Frank will have a gain of $700,000 ($1,000,000 amount realized, minus $300,000 adjusted basis in the stock). IRC § 1001(a), (c). The entire gain will be treated as a long-term capital gain, taxed at preferential rates. IRC §§ 1(h); 1221; 1222(3). Note that because Frank held the stock for only two years, it does not qualify for gain exclusion under section 1202. The 100% exclusion allowed for gain on the sale of "qualified small business stock" held for more than five years by non-corporate taxpayers was recently made permanent by Congress.

[Although the problem does not call for it, you may want to consider the tax consequences to Gensler, Inc. Gensler, Inc. will have a $1 million cost basis in the stock (which is not amortizable), and it will not get a basis step-up in FLW's assets for increased depreciation/amortization allowances. Note, however, that section 338 allows a purchaser to elect to treat certain stock purchases as asset purchases (which provides the purchaser a cost basis in the assets of the target company). The quid pro quo for obtaining a cost basis in the assets is that the acquired company will be deemed to have sold its assets, which may result in taxable gain. How would this work here? If Gensler, Inc. makes a qualified stock purchase and follows up with a timely section 338 election, FLW, Inc. is deemed to have engaged in two significant transactions. First, FLW, Inc. is treated as having sold all its assets at the close of the acquisition date at fair market value in a single transaction (deemed sale), which triggers gain or loss to FLW, Inc. IRC § 338(a)(1). Second, FLW, Inc. is treated as a new corporation that purchased (reacquired) all the assets on the following day (deemed purchase). IRC § 338(a)(2). This deemed purchase of assets effectively provides Gensler, Inc. with a cost basis in FLW, Inc.'s assets. Query: When would it make sense to elect to pay tax currently in order to step up asset bases and avoid tax later? Perhaps where the target company has large net operating losses that would be available to offset the gain recognized on the deemed asset sale.]

17.3. Determine whether the following taxpayers should report the transactions as capital or ordinary. What additional information might be helpful?

> **(a) Developer Dan acquired a tract of land and subdivided it into 133 lots. Single-family homes were constructed on 77 lots and sold to individual homebuyers. The homeowners became dissatisfied with the workmanship of the homes and filed suit against Dan. Dan's reputation became tarnished, and the city subsequently withheld approval for development of the remaining 56 lots. Dan sold the 56 lots in three blocks to another developer, Denise.**

The 77 lots sold to individual homebuyers were clearly inventory with gains taxed as ordinary income. But what about the 56 lots later sold in three blocks to a developer? In *Olstein v. Commissioner*, the Tax Court held that under similar facts the three blocks were considered capital assets rather than inventory, and the resulting gains were capital gains. Although the developer originally acquired the lots to develop and sell individually to homebuyers, the developer abandoned the development plans and instead sought to sell the 56 undeveloped lots to a single buyer. His intent *at the time of sale* was inconsistent with the purpose of holding lots for sale to customers. The decision, which found that the developer's purpose for holding the lots changed from a dealer to a non-dealer, seems generous to the taxpayer.

Note that section 1237 renders section 1221(a)(1) determinations unnecessary for certain landowners who subdivide realty and sell it off piece-meal (i.e., it assures certain landowners that their efforts will not place them in the dealer category). Section 1237 is of limited application, however, and would not apply to Developer Dan. The land in question must never have been held primarily for sale to customers and must not have been the subject of substantial improvements, requirements that dilute the effectiveness of the statute. Note that section 1237 is not exclusive; even if Dan does not qualify for its benefits, he may still argue that he is an investor in order to classify his gains as capital gains. Treas. Reg. § 1.1237-1(a)(4).

(b) Day trader David, who is collecting unemployment compensation as a result of losing his job, opened a brokerage account with TD Ameritrade to enable him to execute stock trades quickly. Last year, he made 46 purchases and 14 sales. This year, he made 109 purchases and 103 sales.

In *Cameron v. Commissioner*, the Tax Court held that a day trader who engaged in 46 purchases and 14 sales in one year, and 109 purchases and 103 sales in the following year, was an "investor" and was not a "trader" engaged in the securities business because the numbers of stock purchases were not "substantial." The court also noted that the taxpayer's collecting unemployment compensation further undermined his argument that he was engaged in a trade or business. *See also Moller v. United States* (holding 83 purchases and 41 sales in one year, and 76 purchases and 30 sales in the following year, were not substantial). *But see Mayer v. Commissioner* (finding 1,100 sales and purchases were substantial).

(c) Ivy, an Ivy League college student, accepted $50,000 for donating her eggs to an infertile couple.

Some may argue that Ivy has earned $50,000 of ordinary income for her services. IRC § 61(a)(1). Others may argue that Ivy has realized gain from the sale of a capital asset. IRC §§ 61(a)(3), 1221, 1222. The latter will need to consider whether section 1221(a)(1) applies and the holding period for Ivy's eggs? If the holding period were the issue, might she have the eggs frozen and stored for a year before selling them? Another question that naturally arises if this were the sale of a capital asset is what is her basis in the eggs? If you think we are just making this up take a look at Christopher Weeg, *How Do You Want Your Eggs: Taxed or Nontaxed?*, Tax Notes (October 6, 2014). In Perez v. Commissioner, 144 T.C. No. 4 (Jan. 22, 2015), the Tax Court ruled that egg donor fees were taxable (and not excludable under section 104(a)(2)). But the case leaves many issues undecided.

17.4. During the current year, Grace had salary income of $100,000 and engaged in only two property transactions: On December 30th, she sold stock held for investment for $5,000, which she bought eight months before for $7,000. On December 31st, she sold different stock held for investment for $5,000, which she bought eight years before for $12,000.

(a) To what extent are the losses from the property transactions deductible in the *current year*?

On the December 30th sale, Grace realizes and recognizes a $2,000 loss ($7,000 adjusted basis minus $5,000 amount realized). The loss is a deductible loss per section 165(c)(2). The character of the loss is *short term capital loss* (loss from the sale or exchange of a capital asset held for eight months).

On the December 31st sale, Grace realizes and recognizes a $7,000 loss ($12,000 adjusted basis minus $5,000 amount realized). The loss is a deductible loss per section 165(c)(2). The character of the loss is *long term capital loss* (loss from the sale or exchange of a capital asset held for eight years).

Although Grace's losses are the types of deductible losses allowed under section 165(c), section 165(f) provides that the deduction of capital losses is restricted by section 1211 and 1212. Under section 1211(b), capital losses (whether short term or long term) may be deducted to the extent of capital gains (whether short term or long term). To the extent capital losses exceed capital gains in a given tax year, up to $3,000 of the excess can be used to offset ordinary income in that year. Here, Grace may deduct in the current year only $3,000, i.e., lower of $3,000 or $9,000 (excess of capital losses over capital gains).

(b) To what extent will the net capital loss carryover be deductible *next year*? Do you need more information?

What happens to the $6,000 ($9,000-$3,000) that exceeds the section 1211(b) limitation? As a general rule, losses not allowed in the current year carry over into subsequent years and are treated as short term or long term capital losses depending on their original character. The problem here is that Grace had both short term and long term capital losses. So which type of loss pays for the $3,000 deduction from ordinary income and what losses remain to be carried forward? Should the $2,000 short term loss be used first in the current year to offset ordinary income, or should the $7,000 long term loss be used first in the current year to pay for the deduction from ordinary income? The answer is found in section 1212(b).

Before determining the character of the carry over losses under section 1212(b)(1), we must first complete the section 1212(b)(2) computation. Section 1212(b)(2) generates a constructive short term capital gain of $3,000. Now we can apply section 1212(b)(1)(A) & (B):

1212(b)(1)(A):	NSTCL	–	NLTCG	=	STCL c/o
	(STCL – STCG)		(LTCG – LTCL)		($0)
	($2,000 – $3,000)		($0 – $7,000)		
	($0)		($0)		
1212(b)(1)(B):	NLTCL	–	NSTCG	=	LTCL c/o
	(LTCL – LTCG)		(STCG – STCL)		($6,000)
	($7,000 – $0)		($3,000 – $2,000)		
	($7,000)		($1,000)		

In sum, the character of the $6,000 capital loss carry over is long term. The effect of this provision was to use the $2,000 short term capital loss first in paying for the $3,000 deduction from ordinary income. Of the $7,000 long term capital loss, $1,000 was used to pay for the $3,000 and $6,000 is carried forward.

17.5. During the current year, Janice, a single taxpayer, had salary income of $200,000 and incurred the following transactions:

- **Janice sold stock in ABC, Inc. for $20,000. Janice bought the stock three years before for $12,000.**
- **Janice sold stock in XYZ, Inc. for $3,000. Janice bought the stock seven months before for $1,000.**
- **Janice sold a collection of 1880s music boxes for $6,000. Janice bought the music boxes as an investment six years before for $2,000.**

(a) What is Janice's "net capital gain"?

To determine Janice's net capital gain, we must analyze each transaction.

Sale of ABC stock: On the sale of ABC stock, Janice realizes and recognizes $8,000 of gain ($20,000 amount realized, minus $12,000 adjusted basis). Section 1202 does not apply to exclude the gain. The gain is characterized as a long-term capital gain (gain from the sale of a capital asset held for more than one year). IRC § 1222(3).

Sale of XYZ stock: On the sale of XYZ stock, Janice realizes and recognizes $2,000 of gain ($3,000 amount realized, minus $1,000 adjusted basis). Section 1202 does not apply to exclude the gain. The gain is characterized as a short-term capital gain (gain from the sale of a capital asset held for one year or less). IRC § 1222(1).

Sale of antique music boxes: On the sale of the 1880s music boxes, Janice realizes and recognizes $4,000 of gain ($6,000 amount realized, minus $2,000 adjusted basis). The gain is characterized as long-term capital gain (gain from the sale of a capital asset held for more than one year). IRC § 1222(3).

Although Janice has recognized $14,000 of capital gains, she has a "net capital gain" of only $12,000 (the amount by which the net long-term capital gain ($12,000) exceeds the net short-term capital loss ($0)). IRC § 1222(11) (defining net capital gain), 1222(7) (defining net long-term capital gain), 1222(6) (defining net short-term capital loss). Only the $12,000 of net capital gain will be entitled to preferential rate treatment under section 1(h). The $2,000 of short-term capital gain is not eligible for preferential rate treatment and will be taxed as ordinary income.

Although not required by the question, you might be interested in considering the special rate(s) at which that net capital gain is taxed. That will depend on Janice's marginal tax rate on ordinary income. Janice has $200,000 of ordinary salary income and a $2,000 short-term capital gain, which is taxed as ordinary income. Assuming no other income and no deductions, the last dollar of ordinary income is taxed at 33% (for 2016, the ceiling of the 33% bracket for single filers was $413,350). Now we can layer on the net capital gain to determine the proper capital gains rates. Section 1(h) stacks the components of net capital gain in the following order: (1) 28% rate gains (e.g., collectibles gains); (2) unrecaptured section 1250 gains; and (3) adjusted net capital gain.

$4,000 of the net capital gain is considered "28-percent rate gain" (i.e., gain from the sale of a collectible). IRC §§ 1(h)(5); 408(m). This $4,000 is taxed at a rate of 28% since Janice's last dollar of ordinary income is taxed at a rate of 33%.

$0 of her net capital gain is considered "unrecaptured section 1250 gain" (i.e., gain attributable to depreciation allowed with respect to depreciable real estate held for more than one year). IRC § 1(h)(6).

$8,000 of the net capital gain is considered "adjusted net capital gain." IRC § 1(h)(3). This $8,000 is taxed at 15% since she is in the 33% ordinary rate bracket.

(b) Same as (a) except that Janice also sold a parcel of land for $150,000. Janice purchased the land eight months ago for $156,000 and held it for investment.

On the sale of the land, Janice would realize and recognize a loss of $6,000 ($156,000 adjusted basis, minus $150,000 amount realized). IRC § 1001(a), (c). The loss is a deductible-type loss under section 165. *See* IRC § 165(a), (c)(2). But to what extent is the loss deductible in the current year? Section 165(f) provides that the deduction of capital losses is restricted by sections 1211 and 1212. Section 1211(b) provides that capital losses may be deducted to the extent of capital gains. To the extent capital losses exceed capital gains in a given tax year, up to $3,000 of the excess can be used to offset ordinary income in that year. The $6,000 loss is characterized as a short-term capital loss (a deductible loss from the sale of a capital asset held for not more than one year). IRC § 1222(2). Because Janice has $14,000 of capital gains, the full $6,000 capital loss is deductible this year, and no amount need be carried over to next year.

Because some of Janice's capital gains absorbed the capital loss, Janice's "net capital gain" has changed:

NCG	=	NLTCG	–	NSTCL
$8,000	=	LTCG – LTCL	–	STCL – STCG
		$12,000 – $0	–	$6,000 – $2,000
		$12,000	–	$4,000

Notice that Janice has a net short-term capital loss of $4,000 that is netted against the $12,000 of net long-term capital gain to produce an $8,000 net capital gain. Even though she had $12,000 of long-term capital gains, she's only going to enjoy preferential rates on $8,000.

You may wish to consider what rates apply to the $8,000 of net capital gain. How much of the $8,000 net capital gain is made up of 28-percent rate gain (taxed at 28%) and how much of it is made up of adjusted net capital gain (taxed at 15%)? This depends on whether the $4,000 net short-term capital loss is applied to reduce gain taxed at 28% ($4,000) or gain taxed at 15% ($8,000)? Fortunately, the Code takes a pro-taxpayer approach.

The short-term capital loss ($6,000) is first applied to reduce short-term capital gains ($2,000). The excess (net short-term capital loss of $4,000) is then applied to reduce the long-term capital gains in a particular order: first to reduce 28-percent rate gain ($4,000), then unrecaptured section 1250 gain ($0), and then adjusted net capital gain ($8,000). As a result, $0 of the net capital gain (28-percent rate gain) will be taxed at 28%, and all $8,000 of the net capital gain (adjusted net capital gain) will be taxed at 15%.

(c) Same as (b) except that Janice purchased the land eighteen months ago.

The $6,000 loss is now characterized as a long-term capital loss. IRC § 1222(4). Because Janice has $14,000 of capital gains, the full $6,000 capital loss is deductible this year, and no amount need be carried over to next year.

Janice's net capital gain is $6,000, determined as follows:

NCG	=	NLTCG	–	NSTCL
$6,000	=	LTCG – LTCL	–	STCL – STCG
		$12,000 – $6,000	–	$0 – $2,000
		$6,000	–	$0 (no excess)

Consider the manner in which the long-term capital loss is allocated. In contrast to the allocation of short-term capital losses, long-term capital losses are allocated to their related category of long-term capital gain. For example, long-term capital losses from the sale of collectibles are applied to reduce any 28-percent rate gain (gain from the sale of collectibles). IRC § 1(h)(4). Here, the $6,000 long-term capital loss did not result from the sale of collectibles and will not be applied against the 28-percent rate gain. Instead, it will be applied against the $8,000 long-term capital gain from the sale of ABC stock. In sum, $4,000 of the net capital gain (28-percent rate gain) will be taxed at 28%, and $2,000 of the net capital gain (adjusted net capital gain) will be taxed at 15%.

Chapter 18

Quasi-Capital Assets

Overview

Section 1231 is a special characterization provision that operates on certain transactions that are not already characterized under the general characterization provisions discussed in the previous chapter. It is a pro-taxpayer provision in that certain property excluded from the definition of capital asset (i.e., trade or business property) may be accorded capital asset status. Likewise, certain dispositions that do not rise to the level of sale or exchange (i.e., thefts and casualties of property) may be accorded sale or exchange status.

Section 1231 applies to only two types of transactions. The first transaction to which section 1231 applies is the sale or exchange of property used in a trade or business. IRC § 1231(a)(3)(A)(i). The term "property used in the trade or business" means depreciable or real property used in trade or business that has been held more than one year, and specifically excludes (1) inventory or property held primarily for sale to customers in the ordinary course of trade or business and (2) self-created works if held by the creator or a taxpayer with a basis carried over from the creator. IRC § 1231(b)(1)(A)-(C). It should be clear that by referring to trade or business property, section 1231 embraces property that is not considered a capital asset under section 1221(a)(2). The second transaction to which section 1231 applies is the involuntary or compulsory conversion of (1) property used in a trade or business held for more than one year or (2) capital assets held for more than one year in connection with a trade or business or a transaction entered for profit. IRC § 1231(a)(3)(A)(ii). As a result, if property is not disposed of through a sale or exchange (e.g., involuntary casualty transaction), capital gain or loss treatment may, nevertheless, be available.

The operation of section 1231 requires a taxpayer to place in an imaginary basket all "section 1231 gains" and "section 1231 losses" that occur during the year and to net those gains and losses to determine their character. If the taxpayer's "section 1231 gains" exceed "section 1231 losses," all gains and losses are treated as long-term capital gains and losses. IRC § 1231(a)(1). On the other hand, if the taxpayer's "section 1231 losses" equal or exceed "section 1231 gains," then all such gains and losses are ordinary. IRC § 1231(a)(2). This treatment gives the taxpayer the best of both worlds. Gains may be characterized as capital gains and losses may remain characterized as ordinary losses. It should be noted that a special rule provides that gains and losses from involuntary conversions (e.g., fire and storm losses) are not subject to section 1231 if the total involuntary losses exceed the involuntary gains. IRC

§ 1231(a)(4)(C). As shown in the problems below, this too is a pro-taxpayer rule permitting casualty losses to remain characterized as ordinary losses while permitting section 1231 gains in the same year to be characterized as capital gains.

Primary Authority

Code: § 1231. Skim §§ 1(h); 165(a)-(c); 1211(b); 1221(a)(2); 1222.

Regulations: § 1.1231-1(d).

Cases: Grier v. United States, 120 F. Supp. 395 (D. Conn. 1954), *aff'd*, 218 F.2d 603 (2d Cir. 1955); Leland Hazard, 7 T.C. 372 91946); Wasnok v. Commissioner, 30 T.C.M. (CCH) 39 (1971).

Rulings: None.

Problems

18.1. John owns and operates a small ski resort business as a sole proprietor. In the current year, John sold a parcel of land used in his business for $110,000; he paid $100,000 for the land four years ago. John also sustained an uninsured loss as a result of the theft of his SnowCat (snow grooming equipment) that he used in his business for three years; at the time of theft, the SnowCat had an adjusted basis of $5,000 and a value of $10,000.

(a) What are the tax consequences of the land sale and equipment theft?

Sale of land: John realized a gain of $10,000 on the land sale ($110,000 amount realized, minus $100,000 adjusted basis). IRC § 1001(a). The realized gain is recognized. IRC § 1001(c). What is the character of the gain? John would like the gain to be characterized as long-term capital gain to receive preferential rate treatment. A long-term capital gain is defined as gain from the sale or exchange of a capital asset held for more than one year. IRC § 1222(3). The land is not a capital asset within the meaning of section 1221, because it is real property used in his trade or business. IRC § 1221(a)(2). It appears then that the $10,000 gain is characterized as ordinary income. But wait! Section 1231 may add to the characterization issue. Is the gain considered section 1231 gain? Section 1231 gain is defined as recognized gain on the sale or exchange of property used in the trade or business. IRC § 1231(a)(3)(A) (i). The term "property used in the trade or business" includes non-inventory real property used in the trade or business held for more than one year. IRC § 1231(b) (1). The land is section 1231 property, and the gain is section 1231 gain to be placed in the section 1231 principal hotchpot to be netted with other section 1231 gains and losses to determine the gain's ultimate character. Before we do any netting, let's analyze the theft of the snow grooming equipment.

Theft of SnowCat: John has a deductible loss of $5,000 on the theft of the snow grooming equipment. *See* IRC § 165(a), (b), (c)(1). *See also* Treas. Reg. § 1.165-7, -8. What is the character of the loss? John would prefer the loss to be characterized as an ordinary loss to avoid the capital loss limitation rules of section 1211 and 1212. A long-term capital loss is defined as a deductible loss from the sale or exchange of a capital asset held for more than one year. IRC § 1222(4). It looks like the loss is ordinary because two elements for capital loss classification (sale or exchange and capital asset) are not met. But wait! The loss is a section 1231 loss as defined in section 1231(a)(3)(B) (recognized loss from the involuntary conversion (as a result of theft) of section 1231 property). [The SnowCat is section 1231 property because it is property used in the trade or business, of a character which is subject to the allowance for depreciation, held for more than one year. IRC § 1231(b)(1).] Because the loss resulted from theft, we must place it in the preliminary hotchpot to be netted with other involuntary gains and losses.

Netting of preliminary hotchpot: Assuming no other property transactions during the year, we must net the preliminary hotchpot first. Because involuntary losses ($5,000) exceed involuntary gains ($0) for the year, the involuntary loss is not subject to section 1231 (i.e., does not drop into the principal hotchpot for netting with the $10,000 section 1231 gain that resulted from the sale of land) and is characterized as ordinary loss under general tax principles (the theft is not a sale or exchange, and the SnowCat was not a capital asset). IRC § 1231(a)(4)(C).

Netting of principal hotchpot: We can then net the principal hotchpot to determine the character of the $10,000 section 1231 gain that resulted from the sale of land. Because the section 1231 gains ($10,000) exceed the section 1231 losses ($0) for the year, the section 1231 gain will be characterized as a long-term capital gain. IRC § 1231(a)(1).

In sum, John got what he wanted. Under section 1231, the $5,000 theft loss is treated as ordinary loss and is deductible in full, and the $10,000 gain from the land sale is treated as long-term capital gain and is taxed at a preferential capital gains rate.

> **(b) Same as (a) except that, in addition to the land sale and equipment theft, John had a $15,000 gain as a result of collecting insurance proceeds when his building, used for several years in his business to serve food and drinks, was destroyed in a fire.**

The $15,000 gain is a section 1231 gain (recognized gain from the involuntary conversion into money of property used in the trade or business). IRC § 1231(a)(3) (A)(ii)(I), (b). Because the gain resulted from fire, we must place it in the preliminary hotchpot to be netted with the loss from the SnowCat theft.

Netting of preliminary hotchpot: Because involuntary losses ($5,000) do not exceed involuntary gains ($15,000) for the year, both the theft loss and the fire gain drop down to the principal hotchpot for netting with the section 1231 gain from the land sale. IRC § 1231(a)(4)(C).

Netting of principal hotchpot: Because the section 1231 gains ($25,000) exceed the section 1231 loss ($5,000), the section 1231 gains are characterized a long-term capital gains and the section 1231 loss is characterized as a long-term capital loss. IRC § 1231(a)(1).

In sum, John has $10,000 long-term capital gain from the land sale, $5,000 long-term capital loss from the equipment theft, and $15,000 long-term capital gain from the building fire.

(c) Same as (a) except that, in addition to the land sale and equipment theft, John had a $15,000 loss as a result of the condemnation of his building, used for several years in his business to serve food and drinks.

The $15,000 condemnation loss is a section 1231 loss (recognized loss from the compulsory conversion of property used in the trade or business). IRC § 1231(a)(3)(B), (b). Because the loss resulted from condemnation, it is placed in the principal hotchpot (and not the preliminary hotchpot) for netting with other section 1231 gains and losses for the year.

Netting of preliminary hotchpot: Assuming no other transactions, we net the preliminary hotchpot first. Because involuntary losses ($5,000 from theft of the Snow-Cat) exceed involuntary gains ($0) for the year, the involuntary loss is not subject to section 1231 (i.e., it does not drop down into the principal hotchpot for netting), and is characterized as ordinary loss under general tax principles. IRC § 1231(a)(4)(C).

Netting of principal hotchpot: We then can net the principal hotchpot to determine the character of the $10,000 section 1231 gain from the land sale and the $15,000 loss from the building condemnation. Because the section 1231 gain does not exceed the section 1231 loss, both are characterized as ordinary.

In sum, John would have a $10,000 ordinary gain from the land sale, a $5,000 ordinary loss from the SnowCat theft, and $15,000 ordinary loss from the building condemnation.

(d) Same as (a) except that one year before the current tax year, John had a $4,000 "net section 1231 loss."

In part (a), John's section 1231 gains for the year ($10,000) exceed his section 1231 losses for the year ($0). This excess (referred to as "net section 1231 gain") must be recaptured and treated as ordinary income to the extent of any "net section 1231 losses" from the preceding five years which have not previously been recaptured. IRC § 1231(c). Here, the net section 1231 gain of $10,000 would be treated as ordinary income to the extent of the $4,000 nonrecaptured section 1231 loss from the prior year (let's assume there were no other net ordinary losses in prior years). The remaining $6,000 of gain this year would be treated as long-term capital gain.

The effect of section 1231(c) recapture is to limit John's long-term capital gain this year to $6,000, which would have been the net long-term capital gain if he sold the land and had the $4,000 section 1231 loss in the same year.

18.2. Leo Tolstoy, who was employed as general counsel for a company, purchased a Kansas residence in Year 1. He occupied such residence until Year 8, when he moved to Pennsylvania due to his company relocating its offices. The property was continuously rented from Year 8 until it was sold in Year 12.

During the time the property was rented, Leo claimed depreciation deductions on the building and any improvements, and the property continued to be listed for sale. In Year 12, Leo realized a $7,000 loss on the sale. This was the only real estate sale he was ever involved in. Leo had no other gains or losses from property during the year. What are the tax consequences of the sale?

If the house is a capital asset within the meaning of section 1221 (i.e., property held for investment), the loss will be characterized as a capital loss subject to the limitations of sections 1211 and 1212. If the house is property described in section 1231(b) (i.e., property used in trade or business), the loss will be characterized as an ordinary loss.

In *Wasnok v. Commissioner*, cited in the Primary Authorities above, the Tax Court concluded that similar property was not a capital asset, but an asset described in section 1231. [Note that the Tax Court discussed the case of *Leland Hazard*, one of the key cases in this area.] *But see Grier v. United States* (concluding that the property in question was a capital asset; stating: "the activities with relation to the single dwelling, although of long duration, were minimal in nature. Activity to rent and re-rent was not required. No employees were regularly engaged for maintenance or repair."), also cited in the Primary Authorities above.

Leo lacked the broader activities stressed in many cases in this area that reach the "business" property result (e.g., regular and continuous activity involved in a large management operation—the constant need to get new rentals, the supplying of services, the keeping of the property in good repair, etc.). Leo's house is in the nature of property held for investment and not property used in a trade or business.

Chapter 19

Recapture of Depreciation

Overview

Section 1245 provides that gain recognized on the disposition of "section 1245 property" shall be recaptured and reported as ordinary income to the extent of any tax depreciation or amortization deductions previously taken with respect to the property. IRC § 1245(a).

Section 1245 property is defined generally as depreciable personal property. It includes both tangible and intangible personal property (not buildings). IRC § 1245(a)(3); Treas. Reg. § 1.1245-3(b). Section 1245 comes into play only when section 1245 property is "disposed of," a broad term that encompasses many transactions. However, certain transactions are excluded. For example, section 1245 does not apply to dispositions by gift. IRC § 1245(b) (providing several exceptions). Section 1245 also does not apply to conversions of depreciable property from business to personal use. Rev. Rul. 69-487, 1969-2 C.B. 165. However, in both cases (gifts and conversions), the recapture potential is still lurking in the property. For example, a donee of gifted depreciable property will be required to recapture as ordinary income any gain attributable to depreciation deductions claimed by the donor.

The amount treated as ordinary income under section 1245 is generally the lower of: (1) recomputed basis minus adjusted basis; or (2) amount realized minus adjusted basis. The second figure is easy to calculate, since it is merely gain realized on the transaction. The first figure seems more difficult since it requires figuring the "recomputed basis"; however, recomputed basis is simply the property's adjusted basis recomputed by adding back all the depreciation or amortization adjustments reflected in the adjusted basis. IRC § 1245(a)(2)(A). In most cases, recomputed basis is simply the property's original cost basis. So, the first figure is really the original cost minus current adjusted basis, or the depreciation/amortization deductions taken on the property. In sum, the amount treated as ordinary income is the lower of: (1) the depreciation deductions previously taken; or (2) the gain realized. A taxpayer will never have to recapture more than the depreciation deductions attributable to the property; and a taxpayer will never have to recapture and report as ordinary income more than the gain realized. Note that in determining recomputed basis, a taxpayer must add back not only depreciation deductions under section 167 and amortization deductions under section 197, but also amounts expensed under section 179. IRC § 1245(a)(2)(C).

While section 1245 applies to depreciable personal property, section 1250 applies to depreciable real property, such as residential rental property (apartment buildings) and non-residential real property (office buildings and warehouses). Interestingly, under that section, no depreciation is required to be recaptured as ordinary income for buildings acquired after 1986. Instead, gain from buildings attributable to depreciation deductions previously taken but not recaptured as ordinary income is taxed at a higher capital gains rate (maximum of 25%, which is higher than the 15% maximum rate applicable to most other long-term capital gains).

Primary Authority

Code: §§ 64; 179(d)(10); 1239(a), (b)(1), (c); 1245(a)(1)-(3), (b)(1)-(2), (c), (d); Skim § §1(h)(1), (3), (6); 267(b)-(c); 1250(a)(1)(A), (a)(1)(B)(v), (b)(1), (b)(3), (b)(5), (c); (d)(1)-(2), (g), (h).

Regulations: §§ 1.179-1(e); 1.1245-1(a)(1), (b), (c)(1), (d), -2(a)(1), (3), (6), (7).

Cases: None.

Rulings: Rev. Rul. 69-487, 1969-2 C.B. 165.

Problems

19.1. Otis, a calendar-year taxpayer, owns a Server that he uses solely in his business. Otis paid $20,000 for the Server on March 15, Year 1, and has taken the maximum allowable depreciation deductions under section 168. The Server is five-year property, and Otis did not elect to use section 179. You may assume that section 168(k) does not apply.

   (a)   What result to Otis if he sells the Server to Buyer on November 15, Year 3 for $26,000?

[This problem provides a good review of material covered in previous chapters-- i.e., Chapter 9 (depreciation), Chapter 17 (capital gains and losses), and Chapter 18 (quasi-capital assets). The second set of review problems in Chapter 21 will also help solidify these concepts.]

Amount of gain: The sale of the Server equipment is a realization event within the meaning of section 1001. Otis's amount realized on the sale is $26,000, the amount of money received. IRC § 1001(b). Otis's initial cost basis in the equipment of $20,000 (IRC § 1012) was decreased for depreciation allowances (IRC § 1016(a)(2)). The facts do not tell us what the depreciation deductions were, but we can figure them out. The equipment was depreciable property in Otis's hands, because it was subject to wear and tear and was used in Otis's trade or business. IRC § 167. To determine the allowable deductions under section 168, we must determine the applicable convention, the applicable recovery period, and the applicable depreciation method. IRC § 168(a). The *applicable convention* for the equipment is the default half-year convention (let's assume that Otis did not place a substantial amount of depreciable property in service during the last quarter of Year 1). IRC § 168(d)(1), (d)

(4)(A). The *applicable recovery period* is an arbitrary five years since the equipment is five-year property per the facts. IRC § 168(c). The *applicable depreciation method* is the 200% declining balance method, since the facts state that Otis has taken the maximum allowable depreciation deductions (that is, he did not elect to use the 150% declining balance method or straight line method). IRC § 168(b)(1). Using Revenue Procedure 87-57, referenced in Chapter 9, we can determine the following depreciation allowances for Years 1-3:

Depreciation Allowances

Year 1 .... $4,000
Year 2 6,400
Year 3 .... 1,920 (½ of $3,840 b/c half-year convention)
Total $12,320

Otis's adjusted basis in the equipment for purposes of determining gain or loss is $7,680 ($20,000 cost basis, minus $12,320 depreciation allowed). Otis's gain realized on the sale of the equipment is $18,320 ($26,000 amount realized, minus $7,680 adjusted basis). The gain realized is recognized per section 1001(c).

Character of gain: Capital gain or section 1231 gain: The next issue is the character of the $18,320 gain. Otis would like the gain to be characterized as long-term capital gain to receive preferential rate treatment. A long-term capital gain is defined as gain from the sale or exchange of a capital asset held for more than one year. IRC § 1222(3). The equipment is not a capital asset within the meaning of section 1221, because it is depreciable business property. It appears then that the $18,320 gain is characterized as ordinary income. But wait! Section 1231 may add to the characterization issue. Is the gain considered "section 1231 gain"? Section 1231 gain is defined as recognized gain on the sale or exchange of property used in the trade or business. IRC § 1231(a)(3)(A)(i). Is the equipment considered "property used in the trade or business" within the meaning of section 1231? The term "property used in the trade or business" means property used in the trade or business (YES!), of a character subject to the allowance for depreciation (YES!), held for more than one year (YES!). Therefore, this equipment is section 1231 property, and the gain is section 1231 gain to be placed in the section 1231 principal hotchpot to be netted with other section 1231 gains and losses to determine the ultimate character.

Section 1245 override: Depreciation recapture: Before we actually apply section 1231 and perform any netting, we must turn to section 1245 (the subject of this chapter) to see whether it applies. Section 1245 is an overriding provision. IRC § 1245(d). Section 1245 recapture comes into play whenever "section 1245 property" is "disposed of." IRC § 1245(a)(1). The equipment is section 1245 property because it is personal property (as opposed to realty) which is or has been property of a character subject to allowance for depreciation, and it is disposed of in a sale. IRC § 1245(a)(3). Accordingly, section 1245 will reach into our section 1231 principal hotchpot and pull out part or all of the section 1231 gain and characterize it as ordinary income. The amount treated as ordinary income under section 1245 is the lower of: (1) "recomputed basis" minus adjusted basis; or (2) amount realized minus adjusted basis. IRC § 1245(a)(1). Recomputed basis is simply the property's adjusted basis recomputed by adding back all adjustments reflected in the adjusted basis on account of deductions allowed or allowable to any taxpayer or to any other person for depreciation. IRC § 1245(a)(1)(A). Here, recomputed basis of $20,000 (that is, Otis's adjusted basis of $7,680 plus depreciation deductions allowed of $12,320) exceeds adjusted basis of $7,680, by $12,320 (the amount of depreciation deductions claimed by Otis). Amount realized of $26,000 exceeds adjusted basis of $7,680, by $18,320 (the amount of gain realized by Charlie). The lower of the two figures ($12,320) is the amount to be recaptured as ordinary income (the amount attributable to previous depreciation deductions taken with respect to the equipment).

Conclusion: In conclusion, section 1245 will reach into the section 1231 hotchpot and pull out $12,320 as ordinary income. The remaining $6,000 of gain recognized remains in the principal hotchpot to be netted with all other section 1231 gains and losses for during the year. There were no other section 1231 gains or losses. Accordingly, the $6,000 section 1231 gain comes out as long-term capital gain, because section 1231 gains for the year of $6,000 exceeded section 1231 losses for the year of $0. IRC § 1231(a)(1). Let's assume that section 1239 does not apply to characterize this gain as ordinary because Buyer is an unrelated third party.

(b) Same as (a) except that Otis elected to use section 179.

If Otis made the section 179 election in Year 1, he would have expensed the full $20,000 cost of the equipment in Year 1 and his basis would have been reduced to zero. IRC § 1016(a)(2). [The equipment is section 179 property, i.e., depreciable, tangible personal property acquired by purchase for use in the active conduct of a trade or business. IRC § 179(d)(1). The maximum allowable deduction for all qualifying property placed in service is $500,000. IRC § 179(b)(1). The $500,000 amount is reduced dollar-for-dollar by the amount by which the cost of qualifying property placed in service during the year exceeded $2,000,000. IRC § 179(b)(2). Assuming the equipment was the only section 179 property Otis placed in service during Year 1, and assuming the taxable income limitation of section 179(b)(3) was not an issue in Year 1, he would have been entitled to expense the full $20,000 cost of the equipment in that year.]

On later sale in Year 3, Otis would have gain realized and recognized of $26,000 ($26,000 amount realized minus $0 adjusted basis). Does section 1245 apply? Yes, because the equipment is considered "section 1245 property." IRC § 1245(a)(3). The amount treated as ordinary income under section 1245 is the lower of: (1) recomputed basis minus adjusted basis; or (2) amount realized minus adjusted basis. IRC § 1245(a)(1). In determining recomputed basis, a taxpayer must add back not only depreciation deductions under section 167, but also amounts expensed under section 179. IRC § 1245(a)(2)(C). In this problem, recomputed basis of $20,000 (that is, adjusted basis of $0 plus the section 179 expensed amount of $20,000) exceeds adjusted basis of $0, by $20,000. Amount realized of $26,000 exceeds adjusted basis of $0K, by $26,000 (the amount of gain realized). The lower of the two figures ($20,000) is the amount to be recaptured and treated as ordinary income. As with problem (a), the remaining gain of $6,000 is characterized as section 1231 gain. Assuming no other section 1231 gains or losses, it is characterized as long-term capital gain. IRC § 1231(a)(1).

(c) **Same as (a) except that Otis gives the Server to his daughter, and she immediately sells the Server for $26,000.**

Section 1245 comes into play only when section 1245 property is "disposed of," a broad term that encompasses many transactions. However, certain transactions are excluded. For example, section 1245 does not apply to dispositions by gift. IRC § 1245(b)(1). If Otis did not sell the equipment, but instead gave it to his daughter, section 1245 would not apply to Otis.

However, when his daughter later sells the equipment, she will be required to recapture as ordinary income any gain attributable to the depreciation deductions claimed by Otis. This is because "recomputed basis" is Daughter's adjusted basis (same adjusted basis Otis had at the time of gift per section 1015) plus "*all* adjustments reflected in such basis on account of deductions," including adjustments made by Otis. IRC § 1245(a)(2)(A). In short, Daughter will have $18,320 gain realized and recognized ($26,000 amount realized minus $7,680 adjusted basis). IRC § 1001. $12,320 of the gain will be recaptured and characterized as ordinary income under section 1245. $6,000 of the gain will be characterized as long-term capital gain (gain from the sale or exchange of a section 1221 capital asset).

(d) **Same as (a) except that Otis takes the Server home and converts it from business use to personal use.**

Are there any income tax consequences on the conversion? The conversion is not a realization event within the meaning of section 1001 (sale or other disposition). Does section 1245, an overriding provision, apply? As indicated by Revenue Ruling 69-487, section 1245 does not apply to conversions of depreciable property from business to personal use. Therefore, if Otis does not sell the equipment, but instead takes the equipment home and converts it to personal use, section 1245 would not apply. However, the recapture potential is still lurking in the equipment. If Otis later sells the equipment, gain from the sale will be characterized as ordinary income to the extent of the previous depreciation deductions taken.

(e) **Same as (b) except that Otis takes the Server home and converts it from business use to personal use.**

Although this conversion from business use to personal use would not trigger section 1245 recapture, as explained above, it would trigger section 179(d)(10) recapture since a section 179 deduction was taken with respect to the equipment. IRC § 179(d)(10); Treas. Reg. § 1.179-1(e). The amount included in ordinary income would be the benefit Otis derived from electing section 179 treatment. The benefit derived from making a section 179 election is not $20,000. Rather, the benefit is the deduction he took under section 179 ($20,000) minus the deductions he could have taken under sections 167/168 if a section 179 election had not been made ($12,320). Treas. Reg. § 1.179-1(e)(1). This amount would be added to the basis of the equipment at the time of conversion.

19.2. Oil tycoon John Rockefeller, a calendar-year taxpayer, purchased from his competitor a secret technique for refining crude oil for $180,000,000 on January 1, Year 1, and immediately began applying the technique in his refinery business. What result to John if, after taking the maximum allowable amortization deductions under section 197, he sells the secret process to Buyer on December 31, Year 5, for $160,000,000?

Section 197 intangibles include "know-how, formulas, processes, designs, patterns, formats, and similar items," regardless of whether acquired with a trade or business or acquired separately. IRC § 197(d)(1)(C)(iii); Treas. Reg. § 1.197-2(b)(5). The definition of know-how refers to secret processes, formulas and other secret information. *See* Rev. Rul. 64-56, 1964-1 (Part I) C.B. 133, *amplified by* Rev. Rul. 71-564, 1971-2 C.B. 179. Thus, the costs incurred by John to purchase the secret technique on how to refine crude oil must be amortized over fifteen years under section 197.

The amount of the section 197 amortization deduction each year is determined by amortizing the adjusted basis of the acquired trade secret ratably over a fifteen-year period. IRC § 197(a); Treas. Reg. § 1.197-2(a)(1). The fifteen-year period begins on the first day of the month in which the trade secret is acquired and held in connection with a trade or business (within the meaning of section 162). Treas. Reg. § 1.197-2(f)(1)(i)(A). Here, John must amortize ratably the $180,000,000 payment over 180 months (15 years × 12 months), or at $1,000,000 per month. Thus, John's amortization deduction each year is $12,000,000 (12 months @ $1,000,000 per month). By the end of Year 5, John will have claimed $60,000,000 of amortization deductions, reducing his adjusted basis to $120,000,000.

When John sells the trade secret at the end of Year 5, he will realize and recognize a gain of $40,000,000 (i.e., amount realized of $160,000,000 minus adjusted basis of $120,000,000). To what extent does section 1245 recapture apply? Section 1245 property is defined as depreciable personal property, which includes both tangible and intangible property. IRC § 1245(a)(3); Treas. Reg. § 1.1245-3(b). Section 1245 property encompasses intellectual property that is subject to the allowance for depreciation under section 167, as well as intellectual property that is subject to fifteen-year amortization under section 197 because section 197 intangibles are treated as property subject to the allowance for depreciation under section 167. IRC § 197(f)(7). Because all $40,000,000 of gain is attributable to amortization allowances (and none of it is attributable to economic appreciation in value), all $40,000,000 must be recaptured as ordinary income. None of the gain is considered section 1231 gain.

19.3. In Year 1, Sam purchased a parcel of commercial property at a cost of $150,000,000, of which $100,000,000 was properly allocated to the building

and $50,000,000 was properly allocated to the land. In Year 3, Sam sold the property for $200,000,000, of which $130,000,000 was properly allocated to the building and $70,000,000 was properly allocated to the land. During Years 1-3, Sam properly claimed $7,000,000 of straight-line depreciation with respect to the building. What are the tax consequences to Sam on the sale of the property? (No depreciation calculations are called for in this problem.)

Gain with respect to the land: Sam realized and recognized a $20,000,000 gain with respect to the land ($70,000,000 amount realized minus $50,000,000 adjusted basis). The gain is characterized as a section 1231 gain. No recapture rules apply.

Gain with respect to the building: While section 1245 generally applies to depreciable personal property, section 1250 generally applies to depreciable real property, such as residential rental property (apartment buildings) and non-residential real property (office buildings and warehouses). IRC § 1250(c). The amount treated as ordinary income under section 1250 is the "applicable percentage" (typically 100%) of the lower of: (1) "additional depreciation" or (2) gain realized. IRC § 1250(a). Additional depreciation, in the case of property held for more than a year, is defined as depreciation adjustments in excess of what would be allowed under the straight-line method. IRC § 1250(b)(1). Interestingly, for depreciable real property acquired after 1986, the straight line method must be used. Hence, for real property acquired after 1986, there will be no "additional depreciation" and, hence, no amount recaptured as ordinary income. However, "unrecaptured section 1250 gains" are taxed at a maximum rate of 25%, which is higher than the 15% or 20% maximum rate applicable to most other long-term capital gains. The term "unrecaptured section 1250 gain" means long-term capital gain from the sale of depreciable real property attributable to depreciation deductions taken that are not recaptured as ordinary income. IRC § 1(h)(6). Thus, gain attributable to depreciation deductions, while not taxed at ordinary income rates (up to 39.6%), are taxed at higher capital gains rates (up to 25%).

Sam's realized and recognized gain on the sale of the building is $37,000,000—that is, $130,000,000 amount realized, minus $93,000,000 adjusted basis ($100,000,000 cost basis less $7,000,000 depreciation allowances). IRC §§ 1001; 1016(a)(2). What is the character of the gain? The building is section 1250 property (depreciable real property). IRC § 1250(c). The amount recaptured as ordinary income is the applicable percentage (assume 100%) of the lower of additional depreciation or gain realized. IRC § 1250(a). Additional depreciation is zero since Sam did not take depreciation adjustments in excess of straight line. IRC § 1250(b)(1). Applying the lower of rule, the amount recaptured is 100% of $0, or $0. The entire $37,000,000 gain is section 1231 gain.

Assuming no other section 1231 gains or losses during the year, Sam has $20,000,000 section 1231 gain from the sale of the land and $37,000,000 section 1231 gain from the sale of the building. Because section 1231 gains for the year exceed section 1231 losses for the year, the entire $57,000,000 comes out of the section 1231 principal hotchpot as long-term capital gain. IRC § 1231(a)(1). However, $7,000,000 of the gain is "unrecaptured section 1250 gain" (i.e., gain attributable to depreciation not recaptured as ordinary income) and is taxed at a maximum rate of 25%. IRC § 1(h)(6). The remaining $50,000,000 of the gain is long-term capital gain taxed at a maximum rate of 20% (based on his bracket).

Chapter 20

The Charitable
Contribution Deduction

Overview

The application of the charitable tax deduction depends on a good understanding of characterization issues. That is why we are revisiting this topic, first introduced in Chapter 11.

Section 170(a) authorizes a deduction for a "charitable contribution." A charitable contribution is a gift to or for the use of an organization described in section 170(c). This includes governmental entities and various private non-profit entities that are deemed to do public good. While this requires some fleshing out, the essential point to observe at the outset is that not every gift from charitable impulses is entitled to a deduction. A gift to a homeless person or to a friend in need is not a charitable contribution for tax purposes. It must be a gift to a recognized charitable entity. For the most part those entities are "[c]orporations, and any community chest, fund, or foundation, organized and operated exclusively for religious, charitable, scientific, testing for public safety, literary, or educational purposes." IRC § 501(c)(3). The entities that are customarily thought of as charities typically qualify for tax exempt status under section 501. It should be noted that there can be no required consideration passing from the charity to the donor for the deductible part of a contribution. Treas. Reg. § 1.170A-1(c)(5). Thus, if a charity stages a play and charges standard market prices for tickets, the buyers are not entitled to a charitable deduction even if they choose not to attend the play. If the charity charges an amount above the market value of the admission price, it should designate what amount is considered a charitable contribution and only that amount can be deducted. Rev. Rul. 67-246, 1967-2 C.B. 104. It should also be noted that there is no charitable deduction for the contribution of services to a charity. Treas. Reg. § 1.170A-1(g). However, out-of-pocket expenses related to contributions of charitable services are deductible.

If a gift is made to a qualified charitable organization, the amount of the contribution must determined. In the case of donated property, the amount of the contribution is generally the fair market value of the property at the time of gift. In some cases, however, the amount of the contribution is reduced by the gain lurking in the property (which reduces the contribution amount from fair market value to adjusted basis). Whether gain must be wrung out depends on the character of the gain inherent in the property. If a hypothetical sale of the property at its fair market value would produce ordinary income or short term capital gain, the gain must be wrung out in all cases. If a hypothetical sale of the property would produce long term capital gain, the gain must be wrung out only in certain circumstances: (1) the property is tangible personal property and the use by the charity is unrelated to its charitable purpose; (2) the property is donated to a disfavored private foundation; (3) the property is intellectual property; or (4) the property is taxidermy property.

After determining the amount of the contribution, percentage limitations must be applied to determine the amount deductible in any given year. *See* IRC § 170(b)(1)(A) (general limitation for gifts to public charities); (b)(1)(B) (general limitation for gifts to disfavored private foundations); 170(b)(1)(C) (special rule for gifts of capital gain property to public charities); 170(b)(1)(D) (special rule for gifts of capital gain property to disfavored private foundations). Any excess contribution carries over for up to five years.

The gain wring out rules and percentage limitations are summarized in the chart below:

The Charitable Deduction Summarized

1. Start with the FMV of donated property. Treas. Reg. § 1.170A-1(c)(1).
2. Exclude non-long-term capital gains. (This includes both short-term capital gains and ordinary income.) IRC § 170(e)(1)(A).
3. If the gift is of tangible personal property to a public charity (PC) and the property donated is unrelated to its charitable function, exclude long-term capital gains. IRC § 170(e)(1)(B)(i).
4. If the gift is to a DPF (i.e., a private foundation other than a foundation described in § 170(b)(1)(E)), exclude long-term capital gains. IRC § 170(e)(1)(B)(ii) (but note section 170(e)(5) exception).
5. If the gift consists of intellectual property other than self-created copyrights, exclude long-term capital gains. IRC § 170(e)(1)(B)(iii). Section 170(m) may apply.
6. If the gift is to a public charity, limit the deduction to 50% of the donor's contribution base. *See* IRC § 170(b)(1)(G). Carry over the remainder. IRC § 170(b)(1)(A).
7. If the gift is to a DPF, limit the deduction to 30% of the contribution base (but this must be coordinated with step six when there are gifts to both PCs and DPFs). Carry over the remainder. IRC § 170(b)(1)(B).
8. If the gift is capital gain property given to a PC (to which step 3 or 5 did not apply), limit the deduction to 30% of the contribution base. Do not change step 7. If an election under section 170 (b)(1)(C)(iii) is made, exclude long term capital gains but do not apply the 30% limit to the remainder. Carry over any excess. (See below for further discussion.) IRC § 170(b)(1)(C).
9. If the gift is capital gain property given to a DPF, limit the deduction to the lesser of 20% of the contribution base or 30% of the contribution base

reduced by the section 170(b)(1)(C) amount. Carry over the remainder. IRC § 170(b)(1)(D).

With respect to step 8, if no section 170(b)(1)(C)(iii) election is made, follow these steps in this order. A step 8 limitation does not affect the step 7 computation. *See* IRC § 170(b)(1)(B)(ii) (parenthetical language). However, if a section 170(b)(1)(C) election is made, the step 6 and step 7 computations must be reworked. The regulations permit this result despite the apparent conflict with the parenthetical language of section 170(b)(1)(B)(ii). *See* Treas. Reg. § 1.170A-8(f), Ex. 15(a).

Primary Authority

Code:	§§ 170(a), (b)(1), (c), (d)(1)(A), (e)(1), (f)(8)(A)-(B); 1011(b). Skim §§ 170(f)(11), (m); 501(a)-(c); 511(a)(1).
Regulations:	§ 1.170A-1(c)(1), -1(c)(5), -1(g), -13.
Cases:	United States v. American Bar Endowment, 477 U.S. 105 (1986); Hernandez v. Commissioner, 490 U.S. 680 (1989); Sklar v. Commissioner, 282 F.3d 610 (9th Cir. 2002).
Rulings:	Rev. Rul. 67-246, 1967-2 C.B. 104; Rev. Rul. 81-163, 1981-1 C.B. 433.

Problems

20.1. Ilya, who is an industrialist, has a contribution base of $500,000. What is his current charitable deduction and carryover, if any, in the situations below?

(a) Ilya gave $1,000,000 cash to Metropolitan Museum, a public charity.

This is a gift to a qualified charitable organization. The amount of the contribution is $1,000,000, the amount of money contributed. Because of the percentage limitations, however, only $250,000 (50% of Ilya's contribution base) is allowed as a deduction in the current year. IRC § 170(b)(1)(A). The remaining $750,000 carries over to next year. IRC § 170(d)(1)(A). The $750,000 would be a section 170(b)(1)(A) deduction in the next year.

(b) Instead of cash, Ilya gave Metropolitan an industrial-size shredder used in his business worth $1,000,000 to be used by the museum to shred confidential files as it converts to digital recordkeeping. Ilya's basis in the shredder is $350,000. The shredder has $100,000 of section 1245 depreciation recapture inherent in it.

The *beginning* amount for purposes of determining the deduction is the fair market value of the property contributed. Treas. Reg. § 1.170A-1(c)(1).

The $100,000 section 1245 gain is wrung out under section 170(e)(1)(A). Since the shredder will be used in Metropolitan's business, the long-term capital gain under section 1231 is not wrung out under section 170(e)(1)(B)(i). *See* Treas. Reg. § 1.170A-4(b)

(3) (defining "unrelated use"). Note section 170(e)(1) flush language states that section 1231 property is treated as a capital asset. Hence, the gain in excess of the section 1245 gain is deemed long-term capital gain for section 170(e)(1)(B) purposes. [Note: Even if the shredder is used by Metropolitan, the section 1231 gain would be excluded if the shredder is sold by Metropolitan in the year in which the contribution is made. IRC § 170(e)(1)(B)(i)(II). If the shredder is sold by Metropolitan within three years, the donor must include in income (in the year of disposition) an amount equal to the excess of the donor's deduction over the donor's basis in the property at the time of contribution. IRC § 170(e)(7).]

Since this a gift of capital gain property to a public charity to which section 170(e) (1)(B) did not apply, the current deduction is limited to 30% of Ilya's contribution base ($150,000). IRC § 170(b)(1)(C)(i). Ilya can elect to wring out the long-term capital gain to avoid this rule. IRC § 170(b)(1)(C)(iii). Whether he should do so depends on various factors including his gifting plans for future years and his income expectations in the future. If he does not make the election, his deduction is $150,000 with a $750,000 carryover under section 170(b)(1)(C)(ii). If he makes the election, his current deduction is $250,000 and his carryover is $100,000.

(c) **Same as (b) except that the shredder is given to City Zoo which, in turn, sells it to Metropolitan Museum for $1,000,000.**

Again the $100,000 section 1245 gain is wrung out under section 170(e)(1)(A). The section 1231 gain is also wrung out under section 170(e)(1)(B)(i)(I) since it is a gift of tangible personal property that is not related to the charity's charitable function. *See also* IRC § 170(e)(1)(B)(i)(II). This is the same outcome as if the election is made in (b).

(d) **Same as (b) except that all of the gain is section 1245 gain and Metropolitan takes the shredder subject to a non-recourse mortgage of $400,000.**

This is a bargain sale since the debt relief constitutes an amount realized to Ilya. *See* Treas. Reg. § 1.1011-2(a)(3). *See also* Rev. Rul. 81-163. Under section 1011(b), the transaction is divided into a sale and a gift and each is treated separately. The property's basis is divided according to this formula:

$$\frac{\text{Amount Realized}}{\text{Fair Market Value}} \times \text{Adjusted Basis} = \text{Basis allocated to sale}$$

Here that means that $140,000 of basis is allocated to the sale.

$$\frac{\$400,000 \text{ AR}}{\$1,000,000 \text{ FMV}} \times \$350,000 \text{ AB} = \$140,000 \text{ Basis allocated to sale}$$

Thus, Ilya has $260,000 of section 1245 gain to recognize. ($400,000 AR – $140,000 AB = $260,000).

A difficult point that is finessed by eliminating the section 1231 gain from the problem is how to allocate the gain between sections 1245 and 1231 if both types of gain were present . The regulations indicate the recapture would be apportioned just like basis. *See* Treas. Reg. § 1.1011-2(c), Ex. 7.

The charitable contribution initially is $600,000 ($1,000,000 FMV – $400,000 AR = $600,000). The remaining portion of Ilya's basis ($210,000) is allocated to the gift. Since all the gain is section 1245 gain it is wrung out under section 170(e)(1)(A). Since it has no section 1231 gain, the shredder is not deemed capital gain property so the 30% limit under section 170(b)(1)(C)(i) does not apply. *See* IRC § 170(b)(1)(C) (iv). This would mean his current deduction is $210,000 and there is no carryover.

(e) Ilya makes a $200,000 cash gift to Metropolitan Museum and a $150,000 cash gift to the Schreck Family Foundation, a DPF.

The cash gift to the PC is fully deductible since it does not exceed 50% of Ilya's contribution base. IRC § 170(b)(1)(A). The current deduction for the cash gift to the DPF is limited to $50,000 (the lesser of 30% of Ilya's contribution base ($150,000) or 50% of his contribution base reduced by his gift to the public charity ($250,000 – $200,000 = $50,000)). The rest carries over as a gift to a DPF under section 170(b) (1)(B) flush language.

(f) Same as (e) except that Ilya gives $50,000 cash to Metropolitan and $300,000 cash to the Schreck Family Foundation.

The cash gift to the PC is fully deductible since it does not exceed 50% of Ilya's contribution base. IRC § 170(b)(1)(A). The current deduction for the cash gift to the DPF is limited to $150,000 (the lesser of 30% of Ilya's contribution base ($150,000) or 50% of his contribution base reduced by his gift to the public charity ($250,000 – $50,000 = $200,000)). The rest carries over as a gift to a DPF under section 170(b) (1)(B) flush language.

20.2. John Galsworthy owns the copyright of a novel entitled Badly Demented and has held it for more than a year. It is worth $100,000. John's contribution base is $200,000. What are the charitable deduction consequences to John under the following circumstances?

(a) John wrote the book and his basis in it is zero. John gives the copyright to his local Humane Society.

The copyright is not a capital asset in John's hands. IRC § 1221(a)(3). All of the gain would be ordinary and thus is wrung out by section 170(e)(1)(A). However, under section 170(m) if the Humane Society receives royalty payments within the next ten years, John should receive a deduction in each of those years that is a specified percent of the income received by the charity. The gift must be of "qualified intellectual property." This means that it cannot be made to a DPF. *See* IRC § 170(m)(9). [Note: "Qualified intellectual property" is defined as property described in section 170(e)(1)(B)(iii). IRC § 170(m)(9). That provision, interestingly, refers to any copyright "other than a copyright described in section 1221(a)(3)." IRC § 170(e) (1)(B)(iii). John's self-created copyright is described in section 1221(a)(3). Does that mean John cannot take future charitable deductions under section 170(m) even if the donee earns income from his donated copyright? That seems inconsistent with the legislative history of section 170(m). The exception for self-created copyrights in the gain wring out rule of section 170(e)(1)(B)(iii) is perhaps justified by the fact that self-created copyrights are subject to the gain wring out rule of section 170(e)(1)(A).]

(b) Same as (a) except that John bought the copyright from Ernest Hemingway Joyce for $50,000 as an investment.

The copyright is a capital asset so now section 170(e)(1)(A) does not apply. Neither does section 170(e)(1)(B)(i). But section 170(e)(1)(B)(iii) applies to wring out the gain. The deduction is $50,000. Section 170(m) will apply but only to the royalties in excess of the $50,000 already deducted. *See* IRC § 170(m)(2).

(c) Same as (b) except that John is a publisher and the copyright is part of his inventory.

The copyright is not a capital asset in John's hands. IRC § 1221(a)(1). All of the gain would be ordinary under section 1221 (and thus is wrung out by section 170(e)(1)(A)). The deduction is $50,000. Section 170(m) will apply but only to the royalties in excess of the $50,000 already deducted. *See* IRC § 170(m)(2).

20.3. Angelo and Madonna , a married couple, send their two children, Matthew and Penelope, to the Church of Numerology Day School. In the morning of each school day the children do conventional schoolwork. In the afternoon of each school day the children study principles of Numerology. These principles are a blend of philosophical and ethical principles derived from divine, mystical and other special relationships between numbers and some coinciding events. The church charges $10,000 a year to attend the morning sessions and $10,000 a year to attend the afternoon sessions. Students can attend either or both sessions. Matthew and Penelope attend both sessions. Angelo and Madonna want to deduct the costs of their children's attendance at the afternoon sessions as charitable deductions. What are the arguments for and against deduction? Would it change anything if the church gave Angelo and Madonna a statement that the value of childcare services it provides in the afternoons is $5,000 per year per child?

A threshold question might be whether the church of Numerology is a church at all? If it is not, perhaps no deduction is permitted for any part of the payment or gift.

Beyond that, however, this question tests our understanding of the *Sklar v. Commissioner* case and the authorities discussed in it. The holding of *Sklar*, relying on *Hernandez v. Commissioner,* suggests that no deduction is available since there is a quid pro quo being received. However the narrow holding of *Sklar* is that the documentation requirements of section 170(f)(8) were not satisfied. In the problem, unlike *Sklar,* the tuition for the religious education is billed separately. Moreover, the religious education is separated temporally from the secular education. Should this matter? As to the second part, arguably it strengthens the case for deduction to have the child care costs wrung out because of the dual benefit analysis in the *United States v. American Bar Endowment* case. Arguably, the situation is now more like the auditing and training fees the Scientologists charge. The IRS has allowed deduction of those fees.

The two arguments that trump any factual variation we might offer are: (1) if there is a quid pro quo, including intangible religious benefits, there is no deduction; and (2) it is irrelevant whether the IRS is improperly granting a deduction to Scientologists since equal protection does not require granting an improper benefit to a similarly situated taxpayer.

20.4. Jack has a very high contribution base and has three assets of equal value he is considering giving away to a DPF. The first is highly appreciated publicly traded stock. The second is highly appreciated closely held stock. The third is publicly traded stock in which his basis substantially exceeds its value. Which asset should he use for the gift?

The publicly traded stock, probably. This is because a gift of the closely held stock will have the gain wrung out under section 170(e)(1)(B)(ii). The wring out will not apply to the publicly traded stock. IRC § 170(e)(5). The stock with a loss should not be given since the loss will be lost. (The *beginning* amount for purposes of determining the deduction is the fair market value of property contributed. Treas. Reg. § 1.170A-1(c)(1).) Alternatively, Hugo might sell the loss stock, recognize the loss, and give the cash to the charity. This would avoid the 20% of contribution base limit in section 170(b)(1)(D). In this case the contribution base may be so high that the limits don't matter.

Chapter 21

Second Set of Review Problems

The following problems are designed to review what has been addressed in the preceding four chapters on characterization of gains and losses, and to help integrate what has been learned.

21.1 Bill, who is single and has no dependents, has a calendar taxable year and reports on the cash receipts and disbursements method. For many years, Bill has been in the business of catching and selling lobster on the Maine coast. He owns two assets that he has used in his business—a lobster boat and a vacant lot used to store lobster traps.

During the current year (Year 1), Bill had $30,000 of *ordinary* taxable income (before the property transactions below). In addition, two unfortunate events occurred that forced Bill out of business:

- On September 1, Year 1, Bill's lobster boat sank in a horrible storm. Bill paid $10,000 for the boat nine years ago and has claimed the maximum annual depreciation allowances. (Fishing boats used in one's fishing business are 7-year property under IRC § 168.) In December, Year 1, Bill received $25,000 in insurance proceeds as the boat was fully insured against sinking. Bill does not intend to use the cash received to purchase any other property.
- On September 10, Year 1, the government condemned the vacant lot that Bill used in his business. In December, Year 1, the government paid a condemnation award in the amount of $90,000. Bill does not intend to use the cash received to purchase any other property. Bill paid $100,000 for the lot six years ago.

(a) Determine Bill's income tax liability for Year 1, using the rate structure set out in Revenue Procedure 2015-53 (which can be found in the Appendix). In completing this part, please: (1) fully analyze the two property transactions and their impact on taxable income; (2) compute Bill's net capital gain for the year; and (3) explain the maximum rate(s) that will apply to the net capital gain. You may assume that no credits are available to Bill.

Analysis of the two property transactions: The *boat casualty* is a realization event. Bill realizes a gain of $25,000 ($25,000 amount realized, minus $0 adjusted basis). IRC §§ 1001, 1016 (requiring downward adjustment for the maximum ACRS depreciation allowances Bill claimed under section 168). The gain is recognized per section 1001(c) since section 1033 does not apply here. [Section 1033(a)(2), the subject of Chapter 25, does not apply since Bill does not intend to use the insurance proceeds to purchase qualified replacement property.]

What is the character of the $25,000 gain? Bill would like the gain to be characterized as long term capital gain to receive preferential treatment. A long term capital gain is defined as gain from the sale or exchange of a capital asset held for more than one year. IRC § 1222(3). The reimbursement for the sinking is not a "sale or exchange" and the boat is not a "capital asset" per section 1221(a)(2). It appears then that the entire gain is ordinary income. But wait! Section 1231 may add to the characterization issue. Is the gain considered "section 1231 gain"? Section 1231 gain includes recognized gain from the involuntary conversion (as a result of storm) into money of property used in trade or business. IRC § 1231(a)(3)(A)(ii)(I). The term "property used in the trade or business" means property used in the trade or business, of a character which is subject to the allowance for depreciation, held for more than one year. Therefore, the boat is "section 1231 property," and the gain appears to be section 1231 gain to be placed in the section 1231 preliminary (casualty) hotchpot for later netting.

However, before we actually apply section 1231 and perform any netting, we must turn to section 1245 to see if recapture applies. Section 1245 is an overriding provision. IRC § 1245(d). Section 1245 recapture comes into play whenever "section 1245 property" is "disposed of." IRC § 1245(a)(1). The boat is section 1245 property because it is "property which is or has been property of a character subject to allowance for depreciation," and it is disposed of in a casualty transaction. IRC § 1245(a)(3). Accordingly, section 1245 will reach into our section 1231 casualty pot and pull out some of the section 1231 gain and characterize it as ordinary income. The amount treated as ordinary income under section 1245 is the lower of: (1) recomputed basis minus adjusted basis; or (2) amount realized minus adjusted basis. IRC § 1245(a)(1). In determining recomputed basis, a taxpayer must add back not only depreciation deductions under section 167, but also amounts expensed under section 179. IRC § 1245(a)(2)(C). In this problem, recomputed basis of $10,000 (that is, adjusted basis of $0 plus the section 168 ACRS amounts of $10,000) exceeds adjusted basis of $0, by $10,000. Amount realized of $25,000 exceeds adjusted basis of $0K, by $25,000 (the amount of gain realized). The lower of the two figures ($10,000) is the amount to be recaptured and treated as ordinary income. Thus, of the $25,000 total gain, $10,000 is ordinary, and the remaining $15,000 is a section 1231 gain (in the preliminary hotchpot). The character of the section 1231 gain will be determined at the end of the year when we do our section 1231 netting.

The *condemnation of the vacant lot* is a realization event (sale or other disposition of property within the meaning of section 1001(a)). The loss realized is $10,000 ($100,000 adjusted basis minus $90,000 amount realized). The loss is recognized. And the loss is deductible, since it was a loss incurred in a trade or business. IRC § 165(a), (c)(1). What is the character of the loss? Bill would prefer the loss to be characterized as ordinary to avoid the capital loss limitation rule of section 1211(b).

The vacant lot is not a capital asset because of section 1221(a)(2), but it is a quasi-capital asset described in section 1231(b)—real property used in a trade or business held for more than one year. IRC § 1231(b). The $10,000 loss is a section 1231 loss (recognized loss from the compulsory conversion of property used in a trade or business described in section 1231(b)). IRC § 1231(a)(3)(B) (referring to IRC § 1231(a)(3)(A)(ii)(I)). Because the loss resulted from condemnation, it is placed in the principal hotchpot (and not the preliminary hotchpot) for netting at the end of the year with other section 1231 gains and losses.

Assuming no other property transactions, we can apply section 1231 to determine the character of the $15,000 section 1231 gain from the sinking of the boat and the $10,000 section 1231 loss from the condemnation of the vacant lot. We net the preliminary hotchpot first. Because the $15,000 casualty gain exceeds the casualty losses ($0), the casualty gain drops down to the principal hotchpot. IRC § 1231(a)(4)(C). Because the section 1231 gain ($15,000) exceeds the section 1231 loss ($10,000), the gain is characterized as long-term capital gain and the loss is characterized as long-term capital loss. IRC § 1231(a)(1). This assumes there were no unrecaptured section 1231 losses from prior years. IRC § 1231(c). In sum, Bill had the following:

$10,000 Ordinary income	Sinking of boat (§ 1245 recapture)
15,000 LTCG	Sinking of boat (§ 1231 gain)
10,000 LTCL	Condemnation of vacant lot

Application of § 1211(b) capital loss limitation: Because the loss from the condemnation of the vacant lot was characterized as a long term capital loss, we must address the capital loss limitation rule to determine whether it is deductible in full this year. For individuals, capital losses are allowed to the extent of capital gains, plus if such losses exceed such gains, then up to $3,000 are allowed to offset ordinary income. IRC § 1211(b). Here, Bill's $15,000 capital gain is sufficient to absorb the $10,000 capital loss. The full $10,000 LTCL is allowed this year; there is no "net capital loss" to carryover.

Determination of "net capital gain" for the year: Although Bill has recognized $15,000 of long-term capital gains, he has a "net capital gain" of only $5,000 (the amount by which the net long-term capital gain ($5,000) exceeds the net short-term capital loss ($0)). *See* IRC § 1222(11) (defining net capital gain), 1222(7) (defining net-long term capital gain), 1222(6) (defining net short-term capital loss). The following chart illustrates the determination of net capital gain:

NCG	=	NLTCG	−	NSTCL
$5,000	=	LTCG − LTCL	−	STCL − STCG
		$15,000 − $10,000	−	$0 − $0
		$5,000	−	$0

The $5,000 net capital gain will get the preferential rate treatment of section 1(h).

Applicable rate(s) on net capital gain: Now that we know Bill's net capital gain for the year ($5,000), it is necessary to determine the applicable capital gain rate(s). Here, the net capital gain is made up solely of adjusted net capital gain (i.e., gain that is not classified as 28-percent rate gain or unrecaptured section 1250 gain). Adjusted net capital gain is taxed at: (1) 20% if the taxpayer's ordinary marginal tax rate is 39.6%; (2) 15% if the taxpayer's ordinary marginal tax rate is 25%, 28%, 33%, or 35%; and (3) 0% if the taxpayer's ordinary marginal tax rate is 10% or 15%.

The appropriate capital gain rate will depend on Bill's marginal tax rate on ordinary income. Using the rate schedule for single filers in Table 3-Section 1(c) of Revenue Procedure 2015-53, included in the Appendix, we see that Bill's marginal tax rate on ordinary taxable income is 25%. The ceiling of the 25% bracket for single filers is $91,150. Bill has $40,000 of ordinary taxable income ($30,000 ordinary taxable income before the property transactions, and $10,000 ordinary § 1245 recapture income from the boat casualty). Assuming Bill has no other income and no deductions, the last dollar of ordinary income is taxed at 25%.

Bill's ordinary income has utilized only $2,350 of the 25% bracket (ceiling of $91,150). When we layer on the $5,000 adjusted net capital gain, we see that it will be taxed at 15% (none of it falls within the 10% or 15% brackets which would yield a 0% rate).

Assuming Bill has no credits, his income tax liability for the year is $6,521.25, determined as follows:

$5,771.25   The first $9,275 of ordinary income is taxed at 10%; income over $9,275 but not over $37,650 is taxed at 15%; and income over $37,650 is taxed at 25%. Using Table 3 of Rev. Proc. 2015-53 his tax on the *ordinary income* is $5,183.75 plus $587.50 (25% of $2,350) which equals $5,771.25.

  750.00   15% tax on *adjusted net capital gain* ($5,000 × 15%).
$6,521.25

(b) Same as (a) above except that Bill had $150,000 of ordinary taxable income in addition to the two property transactions described above.

Assuming Bill has no credits, his income tax liability for the year is $21,886.75, determined as follows:

$37,836.75   The first $9,275 of ordinary income is taxed at 10%; income over $9,275 but not over $37,650 is taxed at 15%; income over $37,650 but not over $91,150 is taxed at 25%; and income over $91,150 is taxed at 28%. Using Table 3 of Rev. Proc. 2015-53 his tax on the *ordinary income* is $18,558.75 plus $19,278 (28% of $68,850) which equals $37,836.75.

+ $750.00
$38,586.75

Bill is in the 28% tax bracket (i.e., the last dollar of ordinary income is taxed at the marginal rate of 28%). The ceiling of the 28% bracket is $190,150. When we layer on the $5,000 adjusted net capital gain, we see that it will be taxed at 15% (none of it falls within the 10% or 15% brackets which would yield a 0% rate). In sum, the $5,000 adjusted net capital gain is taxed at 15%. Assuming Bill has no credits, his total income tax liability for the year is $38,586.75.

IRC § 1(h)(1)(A): Tax on Ordinary Income. The income tax on Bill's $160,000 of ordinary income (ordinary income before the property transactions, plus the recapture income from the boat casualty) is $37,836.75.

IRC § 1(h)(1)(B): 0% Tax on Adjusted Net Capital Gain. Bill has already utilized his 10% and 15% brackets with ordinary income. Therefore, none of the $5,000 adjusted net capital gain is taxed at 0%.

IRC §1(h)(1)(C): 15% Tax on Adjusted Net Capital Gain. The entire $5,000 of adjusted net capital gain is taxed at 15%, resulting in a **$750.00** tax.

IRC § 1(h)(1)(D): 25% Tax on Unrecaptured Section 1250 Gain. Not applicable here because Bill had no unrecaptured section 1250 gain.

IRC § 1(h)(1)(E): Tax on 28-Percent Rate Gain. Not applicable here because Bill had no 28-percent rate gain (e.g., gain from the sale of a collectible).

(c) What will happen to Bill's current year capital gain in (a) above if he also has a $7,000 long-term capital loss carry over from the previous year under IRC § 1212 as a result of the sale of stock held for investment.

With the capital loss carry over from last year, Bill has the following gains and losses for the current year:

$10,000	Ordinary income	Sinking of boat (§ 1245 recapture)
15,000	LTCG	Sinking of boat (§ 1231 gain)
10,000	LTCL	Condemnation of vacant lot
7,000	LTCL	Carry over from prior year

For individuals, capital losses are allowed to the extent of capital gains, plus if such losses exceed such gains, then up to $3,000 are allowed to offset ordinary income. IRC § 1211(b). Here, Bill's $15,000 LTCG is sufficient to absorb only $15,000 of his capital losses. The remaining capital losses ($2,000) are deductible and will offset ordinary income of $2,000 (because that amount is less than $3,000). In sum, all $17,000 of Bill's LTCLs are deductible this year and there is no net capital loss to carry over to next year. Of that amount, $15,000 will offset capital gains and $2,000 will offset ordinary income.

Although Bill has recognized $15,000 of long-term capital gains, he has a "net capital gain" of $0:

NCG	=	NLTCG	–	NSTCL
$0	=	LTCG – LTCL	–	STCL – STCG
		$15,000 – $17,000	–	$0 – $0
		$0 (no excess)	–	$0

None of his LTCG will get the preferential rate treatment of section 1(h). He shouldn't complain . . . because he got the benefit of deducting $15,000 of his capital losses! And his remaining capital loss carryover will reduce his taxable ordinary income to $38,000.

> **(d) Same as (a) above. In addition to the two property transactions, Bill is considering selling some stock in ABC Company before the close of Year 1. He acquired the stock eighteen months ago for $4,000. Its current value of $1,000 is projected to remain steady. He can wait until January, Year 2 to sell, however, and he asks your tax advice whether he should. What advice do you give and why?**

If Bill were to sell the stock at the end of Year 1, he would have a $3,000 LTCL which would offset $3,000 of LTCG otherwise taxed at 15% (rather than offset ordinary income taxed at 25%). It might be advisable for Bill to sell the stock next year to take advantage of the lower capital gains rates this year. If Bill had no capital gains next year, he would be entitled to deduct the full $3,000 LTCL against ordinary income next year. This advice is even more attractive if Bill's ordinary income is consistently high from year to year (e.g., he might be in the 28% or higher bracket next year). Offsetting $3,000 of LTCG this year would save $450 in taxes ($3,000 × .15), whereas wiping out $3,000 of ordinary income next year would save $750 in taxes ($3,000 × .25) assuming he'll remain in the same bracket next year—a tax savings of $200 just by waiting to sell.

21.2. You are minding your own business at a cocktail party, when Debbie approaches you with a question. Debbie tells you that she soon plans to donate a painting to charity, and she asks you, "What is the proper tax treatment of the charitable gift of the painting?" You reply, "It depends." She responds, "It depends on what?" How do you respond to Debbie? In particular, (1) list the additional information you need, and (2) explain why this information is relevant in determining the proper tax treatment of the charitable gift of the painting.

The following questions will help determine the tax treatment of the gift:

1. *Who is the charity?* This information is necessary for several reasons. First, the charity must be an organization described in section 170(c). Second, gifts to private foundations (as opposed to public charities) are subject to special rules. Any long term capital gain lurking in the painting must be wrung out (reducing the contribution amount from fair market value to adjusted basis) if the charity is a disfavored private foundation (DPF). Further, a taxpayer's charitable gifts to DPFs are limited to the lesser of 30% of the taxpayer's contribution base or the excess of 50% of contribution base over the amount given to public charities. IRC § 170(b)(1)(B). Stricter limitations apply if the gift is capital gain property. *See* IRC § 170(b)(1)(D) (stating that deductions for gifts of capital gain property to DPFs are limited to the lesser of 20% of the taxpayer's contribution base or the excess of 30% of the contribution base over the section 170(b)(1)(C) amount).

2. *Will Debbie be receiving anything from the charity?* There can be no consideration passing from the charity to the donor for the deductible part of a contribution. Treas. Reg. § 1.170A-1(c)(5). If Debbie does receive some consideration (e.g., she sells the painting to the charity at less than its fair market value), she will engage in a bargain sale to a charity. *See* IRC § 1011(b) (providing rule for determining how much of the taxpayer's basis to allocate to the sale and how much to allocate to the gift).

3. *What is the fair market value of the painting?* The beginning amount for purposes of determining the deduction is the amount of the fair market value of the painting contributed. Treas. Reg. § 1.170A-1(c)(1). In some cases, unrealized gain lurking in the property must be wrung out, reducing the contribution amount to the property's adjusted basis. The next few questions focus on the gain wring out rules.

4. *Did Debbie create the painting herself? If so, what is her adjusted basis in the painting?* If Debbie painted the painting herself, then ordinary income is lurking in the painting. IRC § 1221(a)(3) (providing that a self-created work of art is not a capital asset); IRC § 1231(b) (providing a similar exclusion). Under section 170(e)(1)(A), that ordinary gain must be wrung out, reducing Debbie's contribution to her adjusted basis. Her adjusted basis is most likely zero (or very low), as "qualified creative expenses" are not subject to the uniform capitalization rule of section 263A (see IRC § 263A(h)), but can be expensed when paid under section 162 provided she is in the painting trade or business.

5. *Did Debbie purchase the painting? If so, when did she purchase the painting and how much did she pay for it?* If Debbie purchased the painting (instead of creating it), then capital gain is lurking in the painting (assuming it was held for investment). If she held the painting for one year or less, then STCG is lurking in the painting and it must be wrung out, reducing her contribution amount to her adjusted basis (cost). IRC § 170(e)(1)(A). If she held the painting for more than one year, then LTCG is lurking in the painting and it may or may not have to be wrung out depending on what the charity does with the painting. IRC § 170(e)(1)(B)(i)(I). See next question.

6. *What does the charity intend to do with the painting?* If the painting (an item of tangible personal property) is unrelated to the charity's purpose, any long term capital gain in the property must be wrung out, reducing the amount of the contribution from fair market value to adjusted basis. IRC § 170(e)(1)(B)(i)(I). Even if the painting is related to the public charity's purpose, the long term capital gain in the property is wrung out if the property is sold by the charity in the year in which the contribution is made. IRC § 170(e)(1)(B)(i)(II). Note that if the painting is sold by the charity within three years, then Debbie must include in income (in the year of disposition) an amount equal to the excess of her deduction over the her basis in the property at the time of contribution. IRC § 170(e)(7).

7. *What is Debbie's contribution base (AGI)?* As a general rule, in any single year a taxpayer's charitable deduction for gifts to *public charities* may not exceed 50% of the taxpayer's contribution base. IRC § 170(b)(1)(A). [An individual taxpayer's

contribution base generally is the same as adjusted gross income. IRC § 170(b)(1)(G).] Section 170(b)(1)(C)(i) limits the deduction to 30% of the taxpayer's contribution base if the gift is *capital gain property* given to a *public charity* to which subjection (e)(1)(B) did not apply (i.e., the long term capital gain was not wrung out). There are special rules for gifts to disfavored private foundations (DPFs). A taxpayer's charitable deduction for gifts to DPFs is limited to the lesser of 30% of the taxpayer's contribution base or the excess of 50% of contribution base over the amount given to public charities. IRC § 170(b)(1)(B). But deductions for gifts of capital gain property to DPFs are limited to the lesser of 20% of the taxpayer's contribution base or the excess of 30% of the contribution base over the section 170(b)(1)(C) amount. If any of the above limits apply, the excess deduction carries over for up to five years.

8. *Has Debbie made any other charitable contributions during the year?* Because of ordering rules in the contribution base limitations discussed above, we need to know all other contributions Debbie has made during the current year, as well as any carryovers from prior years. For example, if Debbie made gifts to both public charities and DPFs this year, the gifts to public charities are deducted first. IRC § 170(b)(1)(B). If Debbie has made gifts of cash as well as the painting to a public charity, she would deduct the cash gifts first. IRC § 170(b)(1)(C)(i) (final sentence). Gifts of capital gain property to DPFs are taken into account after all other charitable contributions. IRC § 170(b)(1)(D)(i) (flush language).

9. *Is Debbie prepared to properly substantiate the contribution?* If the claimed deduction is in excess of $250, Debbie must obtain a contemporaneous written acknowledgement of the gift from the charity. IRC § 170(f)(8). If the gift is in excess of $500, Debbie must provide a description of the property with her tax return. If the gift is in excess of $5,000, she must obtain a professional appraisal of the property. Treas. Reg. § 1.170A-13(f).

21.3. Auguste Rodin is a sculptor who has a contribution base of $100,000. What are the tax consequences of the following transactions:

   (a) Rodin makes a gift to The Museum of Modern Art (public charity) of one of his sculptures he created, which now has an appraised value of $8,000. The museum will include the sculpture as part of its permanent display. You may assume the sculpture has a zero basis in his hands.

No deduction is allowed since the sale would yield $8,000 of ordinary income. IRC § 1221(a)(1), (a)(3). All gain is wrung out by section 170(e)(1)(A). Taxable income remains at $100,000 (all ordinary income).

   (b) Same as (a) except the sculpture was by Rodin's friend, Constantin Brancusi. Rodin bought it for investment nine months ago for $3,000, which was its appraised value then.

The amount of the contribution is $3,000—i.e., the fair market value of $8,000 minus the short term capital gain of $5,000 lurking in the property. In other words, the $5,000 of STCG is wrung out by section 170(e)(1)(A), yielding a contribution amount equal to the sculpture's adjusted basis. The $3,000 contribution does not exceed 50% of Rodin's contribution base, so there is no carry over. Taxable income is reduced to $97,000.

(c) Same as (b) except Rodin bought the sculpture from Brancusi twelve years ago for $3,000, which was its appraised value then.

Since the sculpture is tangible personal property *related* to the charity's purpose, none of the $5,000 long term capital gain is wrung out under section 170(e)(1)(B)(i). The contribution amount is the property's value of $8,000 (and not the property's adjusted basis as in part (b) above). Because long term capital gain was not wrung out by section 170(e)(1)(B), section 170(b)(1)(C)(i) limits the deduction to 30% of Rodin's contribution base. That is not a problem here, so there is no carry over. Taxable income is reduced to $92,000.

(d) Same as (c) except the sculpture is given to a local food bank (public charity) to auction off.

Since the sculpture is tangible personal property *unrelated* to the charity's purpose, the $5,000 long term capital gain is wrung out under section 170(e)(1)(B)(i). The contribution amount is the property's adjusted basis of $3,000 (and not the property's fair market value as in part (c) above). The $3,000 contribution does not exceed 50% of Rodin's contribution base, so there is no carry over. Taxable income is reduced to $97,000.

(e) Same as (d) except the sculpture is given to a not-for-profit retirement home (public charity) to display for its residents.

The issue is whether the sculpture (tangible personal property) is related or unrelated to the retirement home's purpose. The IRS would most likely agree that the sculpture is related to the charity's purpose, yielding the result in part (c) above. *See* Priv. Ltr. Rul. 8247062 (ruling that paintings donated to a retirement center were related to the exempt function of the center by enriching and enhancing the lives of the residents and helping provide stimulation by keeping its residents motivated and alert and by stimulating artistic creativity); Priv. Ltr. Rul. 8143029 (ruling that donated porcelain art objects to a retirement center for display were related to the retirement home's purpose of creating a living environment for its residents).

(f) Rodin donates his studio to The Museum of Modern Art, which will house the museum's entire sculpture collection. Rodin bought the studio years ago for $80,000. The studio is worth $120,000. It has been depreciated under the straight-line method, and Rodin's adjusted basis is $60,000.

The amount of the contribution is $120,000, the fair market value of the donated studio. (None of the gain is wrung out because (1) none of the lurking gain is ordinary recapture income under section 1250; (2) the studio is not an item of tangible personal property; and (3) the museum is not a disfavored private foundation.)

However, the deduction this year may not exceed 30% of Rodin's contribution base. IRC § 170(b)(1)(C)(i). Here, the 30% limit is exceeded. Any excess contribution carries over for up to five years. IRC § 170(b)(1)(C)(ii). He could elect to have the gain wrung out and have the 50% limit apply. IRC § 170(b)(1)(C)(iii). Given the large amount of gain inherent in the gift, he would probably not make the election.

Note that if Rodin sold the studio to the museum for $120,000 rather than donate it, Rodin would realize and recognize $60,000 of section 1231 gain. $20,000 of the gain would be nonrecaptured section 1250 gain taxable at a maximum rate of 25%. *See* IRC § 1(h)(1)(D). $40,000 would be regular LTCG most likely taxed at 15%.

(g) Same as (f) except that Rodin sells the studio to The Museum of Modern Art for $60,000 even though it is worth $120,000.

This is a part sale part gift. Rodin's basis is allocated 50-50. IRC § 1011(b). The sale yields $30,000 of gain ($10,000 of the gain is nonrecaptured section 1250 gain taxable at a maximum rate of 25%. $10,000 is regular LTCG taxed at 15%.) The gift will yield a $60,000 charitable deduction. Again, the 30% limit is exceeded and there will be carryover. IRC § 170(b)(1)(C)(i)-(ii). Note that the recapture is allocated in a part sale part gift transaction in the same way as the transferor's basis. *See* Treas. Reg. § 1.1011-2(c), ex. 7. He could elect to have the gain wring out and have the 50% limit apply. IRC § 170(b)(1)(C)(iii). Given the large amount of gain inherent in the gift, he would probably not make that election.

Chapter 22

Residential Real Estate

Overview

Congress believes that widespread home ownership is an important policy goal, and it uses the tax law to achieve it. The goal is achieved in part by exempting from taxation the imputed rental value of owner-occupied housing. That goal is also achieved in part by providing taxpayers itemized deductions for real property taxes and mortgage interest on personal residences. These matters were addressed in Chapter 11. For many persons, one of the most important tax benefits of home ownership is the substantial exclusion of gain from the sale of a principal residence provided by section 121. That provision is considered in this chapter. This gain exclusion provision in conjunction with the deductions for mortgage interest and property taxes constitutes a massive tax subsidy for housing.

The tax benefits of home ownership provided some planning opportunities that were greater than Congress intended. These opportunities involved the careful mixing of personal and profit-oriented activities by taxpayers. The response was section 280A. This provision is confusingly drawn because it seeks to address two distinctly different matters without clearly delineating when it is addressing one and when it is addressing the other. The two matters in question are (1) the use of some portion of one's residence for business purposes and (2) the use of one's vacation home as a rental property for some portion of the year. The problems below will consider those two matters as well as the section 121 gain exclusion rules.

Primary Authority

Code: §§ 121; 280A(a)-(c)(1), (3), (5), (d)(1), (e), (f)(1), (g). Skim §§ 163(a), (h)(1)-(4); 164(a)-(d)(2)(A).

Regulations: § 1.121-1(a), -1(b)(1)-(4), -1(c)(1)-(2), (4), -2, -3, -4(a)–(b), (g); Prop. Treas. Reg. § 1.280A-2(i)(5), -3(d)(3).

Cases: Guinan v United States, 2003-1 U.S.T.C. (CCH) ¶50,475 (D. Ariz. 2003); Popov v. Commissioner, 246 F.3d 1190 (9th Cir. 2001); Commissioner v. Soliman, 506 U.S. 168 (1993).

Rulings: None.

Problems

22.1. Lady May is a self-employed, professional singer who performs several nights per week at various venues. Although one of the venues provides her with a small room where she could develop and practice her songs, she rarely uses it. Instead, she uses a 400 square foot room in her 4,000 square foot home that she has converted to an office. She spends four-to five hours per day practicing in the home office. She also uses the office to contact venues and musicians regarding scheduling, prepare for performances, and maintain billing records.

(a) Does Lady's home office qualify as her principal place of business for deducting expenses for its use? Why?

This problem affords an opportunity to consider *Popov v. Commissioner*, which applied the *Commissioner v. Soliman* tests, and section 280A(c)(1).

Lady's home office qualifies as her principal place of business for deducting expenses for its use. Lady conducts administrative or management activities for her business as a professional cabaret singer at her home office, and she has no other fixed location where she conducts substantial administrative or management activities for this business. Her choice to use her home office instead of the small room provided by one of the venues does not disqualify her home office from being her principal place of business. Her performance of substantial non-administrative or non-management activities at fixed locations outside her home also does not disqualify her home office from being her principal place of business.

(b) Assume Lady's home office qualifies as her principal place of business, and that the gross income from her singing activity was $70,000. To what extent may Lady deduct the following expenses: home mortgage interest–$20,000; real estate taxes–$10,000; business expenses not related to the use of her home, such as advertising, office telephone, supplies–$17,000; fire and casualty insurance–$1,000; utility charges (other than home telephone)–$3,000. If the home were fully depreciable, the depreciation allowance would have been $8,000.

Lady can deduct the $17,000 of business expenses not related to the use of her home. In addition, Lady can deduct the $30,000 of home mortgage interest and real estate taxes, allowable under section 280A(b) without regard to business use of the home.

Deductibility of the remaining $12,000 of expenses (for insurance, utilities, and depreciation) depends on the percentage of the home used for business. Since the square footage of the home office is 10% of the total square footage of the home, Lady could deduct $100 for insurance (10% × $1,000), $300 for utilities (10% × $3,000), and $800 for depreciation (10% × $8,000)—or a total of $1,200. The overall limitation under section 280A(c)(5) is not a problem since gross income from the singing activity was $70,000. [The overall limitation under section 280A(c)(5) is $50,000—income from the business ($70,000), minus business expenses not related to the office ($17,000) and the portion of interest and taxes attributable to the business ($3,000).]

(c) How would your answer to (b) change if the gross income from Lady's singing activity was only $21,000 (and she had $50,000 of interest income)?

Here we must consider the section 280A(c)(5) limitation. The ordering rules in Prop. Treas. Reg. § 1.280A-2(i)(5), and the example in Prop. Treas. Reg. § 1.280A-2(i)(7) should be used in answering this problem.

Lady's gross income from the singing activity is $21,000. The "total expenditures not allocable to the use of the unit" are $17,000. Accordingly, "gross income derived from the use of the unit" is $4,000. *See* Prop. Treas. Reg. § 1.280A-2(i)(2)(iii). Under Prop. Treas. Reg. § 1.280A-2(i)(5), business deductions with respect to the business use of a dwelling (here, the mortgage interest, real estate taxes, insurance, utilities, and depreciation) are allowable in the following order and only to the following extent:

Category 1: Allocable portions of amounts allowable as deductions with respect to the dwelling unit without regard to any use of the unit in trade or business (here, 10% of the $30,000 in mortgage interest and real estate taxes). Rule: Allowable to the extent of the gross income derived from use of the unit ($4,000). *Sum: $3,000 of Category 1 expenses allowed.*

Category 2: Amounts otherwise allowable as deductions by reason of the business use of the dwelling unit (*other than those which would result in adjustment to the basis of property*) (here, 10% of the $1,000 insurance and $3,000 utilities). Rule: Allowable to the extent the gross income derived from the use of the unit ($4,000) exceeds the deductions allowed under Category 1 ($3,000). *Sum: $100 of insurance and $300 of utilities allowed as Category 2 expenses.*

Category 3: Amounts otherwise allowable as deductions by reason of the business use of the dwelling unit *which would result in an adjustment to the basis of property* (here, $800 of depreciation). Rule: Allowable to the extent of the gross income derived from use of the unit ($4,000) exceeds the Category 1 and Category 2 deductions allowed ($3,400). *Sum: Only $600 of Category 3 depreciation expense allowed, with the remaining $200 carried over to the next year.*

To summarize, Lady had $21,000 of gross income from her singing activity. She may deduct from that amount: $17,000 in business expenses not related to the use of her home, $3,000 for taxes and mortgage interest, $100 for insurance, $300 for utilities, and $600 for depreciation–total deductions of $21,000.

Lady may claim the remaining $27,000 for taxes and mortgage interest as itemized deductions on Schedule A. However, the remaining expenses for insurance, utilities, and depreciation cannot be deducted against her interest income.

Chart Summarizing Results Obtained

Gross income from singing activity $21,000
    Business expenses not allocable to use of unit − 17,000
    Gross income derived from use of unit $4,000

Deductions allowable under Category 1
    Mortgage interest and real estate taxes (10% × $30,000)
    Amount allowable − 3,000
Limit on further deductions $1,000

Deductions allowable under Category 2
    Insurance (10% × $1,000)
    Utilities (10% × $3,000)
    Amount allowable − 400
Limit on further deductions $600

Deductions allowable under Category 3
    Depreciation (10% × $8,000) $800
    Amount Allowable 600
Carryover $200

22.2. Mehmet, a doctor, owns a home in the Rocky Mountains not far from several major ski resorts. In the current year he spends 30 days vacationing at the house and rents it to unrelated third persons for another 60 days. Gross rental income from renting the house is $18,000. Expenses relating to the house are as follows:

Property Taxes	**$ 6,000**
Mortgage Interest	**$ 9,000**
Insurance	**$ 1,200**
Utilities	**$ 4,500**
Maintenance	**$ 6,000**
Depreciation	**$18,000**
Total	**$44,700**

(a) **Applying the allocation method supported by the proposed regulation § 1.280A-3, what amount of the expenses are deductible for the rental activity? What is the amount of Mehmet's carry over deduction, if any?**

Under the proposed regulation, we would allocate $10,000 of the Category 1 expenses (taxes and interest) to the rental activity (60/90 × $15,000 = $10,000). This would leave only another $8,000 of deductions from Categories 2 (insurance, utilities and maintenance) and 3 (depreciation) before encountering the income cap. We would then deduct those expenses as follows:

Insurance	$ 1,200	×	2/3	=	$ 800
Utilities	$ 4,500	×	2/3	=	$3,000
Maintenance	$ 6,000	×	2/3	=	$4,000
Depreciation	$18,000	×	2/3	=	$ 200 (+$11,800 disallowed)
Total	$29,700				$8,000

Remember that any of the Category 1 expenses that are disallowed under section 280A(c)(5) remain deductible under the regular deduction rules for property taxes and mortgage interest. *See* IRC §§ 62; 163; 164; 280A(b). The $11,800 disallowed depreciation deductions carry over to the next year.

(b) Applying the allocation method supported by the case law, what amount of the expenses are deductible for the rental activity? What is the amount of Mehmet's carry over deduction, if any?

If we use the allocation method supported by the case law we would allocate about $2,466 of the Category 1 (taxes and interest) expenses to the rental activity (60/365 × $15,000 = $2,466). This would leave another $15,534 of deductions from Categories 2 (insurance, utilities and maintenance) and 3 (depreciation) before encountering the income cap. We would then deduct those expenses as follows:

Insurance	$ 1,200	×	2/3	=	$ 800
Utilities	$ 4,500	×	2/3	=	$3,000
Maintenance	$ 6,000	×	2/3	=	$4,000
Depreciation	$18,000	×	2/3	=	$7,734 (+$4,266 disallowed)
Total	$29,700				$15,534

Remember that any of the Category 1 expenses that are disallowed under section 280A(c)(5) remain deductible under the regular deduction rules for property taxes and mortgage interest. *See* IRC §§ 62; 163; 164; 280A(b). The $4,266 disallowed depreciation deductions carry over to the next year.

22.3. **On January 1, Year 1, Nicole, who is single and unemployed, purchased a principal residence in Fort Lauderdale, Florida, for $200,000. Determine the amount of gain that must be reported in the following situations:**

(a) **Three years after the purchase, Nicole sold the Fort Lauderdale residence for $500,000.**

Nicole realizes a gain of $300,000 from the sale of her principal residence ($500,000 amount realized minus $200,000 adjusted basis). She may exclude $250,000 from income since she has owned and occupied the residence as her principal residence for the last three years. IRC § 121(a), (b)(1). [We're assuming that Nicole has not used the section 121 exclusion within the last two years. IRC § 121(b)(3)(A) (providing that the exclusion applies to only one sale or exchange every two years).]

(b) **Eighteen months after the purchase, Nicole sold the Fort Lauderdale residence for $600,000 because she obtained a job in Gainesville, Florida, (277 miles from her Fort Lauderdale residence).**

Nicole fails to meet the two-year ownership and use requirements for the maximum exclusion of $250,000. Because the sale is a function of a change in place of employment, however, Nicole will be entitled to a reduced maximum exclusion under section 121(c). Section 121(c) provides that when a sale is because of a change in employment, health, or unforeseen circumstances, the ownership and use requirements and the one-sale-every-two-years rule are relaxed and a percentage of the general exclusion amount (e.g., $250,000) can be used. Here, Nicole is eligible to exclude up to $187,500 of the gain ($250,000 × 18 months/24 months).

(c) **What result in (b) if Nicole sold the Fort Lauderdale residence for $600,000 because she obtained a job in Miami, Florida, (25 miles from her Fort Lauderdale residence)?**

Is the sale here by reason of a change in place of employment, entitling Nicole to claim a reduced maximum exclusion under section 121(c)? Her new job is merely 25 miles away, and many taxpayers commute daily between Miami and Fort Lauderdale.

The regulations provide guidance, including several safe harbor provisions, for determining when a sale or exchange is by reason of a change in employment, health, or unforeseen circumstances. Treas. Reg. § 1.121-3. If the change of employment safe harbor does not apply, a sale is by reason of a change in place of employment only if the primary reason for the sale is a change in place of employment (a facts and circumstances test). Treas. Reg. § 1.121-3(b).

Under the change of employment "distance safe harbor," a sale is deemed to be by reason of a change in place of employment if "the distance between the qualified individual's new place of employment and the residence sold or exchanged is at least 50 miles." Treas. Reg. § 1.121-3(c). Because the distance between Nicole's new place of employment and the Fort Lauderdale house is only 25 miles, the sale is not within the distance safe harbor. As noted above, all may not be lost. The reduced exclusion may be available if Nicole's primary reason for the sale was the change in place of employment. The regulations list factors that may be relevant in determining Nicole's primary reason for the sale. Treas. Reg. § 1.121-3(b)(1)-(6).

Note that if Nicole had already been employed, the distance safe harbor requires that the new place of employment must be "at least 50 miles farther from the residence sold or exchanged than was the former place of employment." Treas. Reg. § 1.121-3(c)(2)(ii).

(d) **Six months after the purchase, Nicole married Keith who, at that time, moved into the Fort Lauderdale residence. Title remained in Nicole's name alone. Eighteen months after the marriage, Nicole sold the Fort Lauderdale residence for $600,000, and filed a joint return with Keith.**

We must consider the possible application of the $500,000 exclusion in section 121(b)(2).

Nicole and Keith make a joint return for the tax year of sale. IRC § 121(b)(2)(A). Nicole meets the two-year "ownership" requirement with respect to the property. IRC § 121(b)(2)(A)(i). [Note that only one spouse needs to meet the ownership requirement with respect to the property.] Neither Nicole nor Keith are ineligible for the benefits of the exclusion by reason of the one-sale-every-two-years rule. IRC § 121(b)(2)(A)(iii), (b)(3).

The problem here is that Keith does not meet the two-year "use" requirement with respect to the property. IRC § 121(b)(2)(A)(ii). [Note that both spouses must meet the use requirement with respect to the property in order to enjoy the larger exclusion amount.] Accordingly, the maximum exclusion of $500,000 is not available. You might raise the question of why section 121(d)(1) does not make the full $500,000 exclusion available. The answer seems to be that section 121(d)(1) makes reference only to subsections (a) and (c) and not (b).

All is not lost if the requirements for a maximum exclusion of $500,000 are not met, as the exclusion is determined on an individual basis. Nicole is still entitled to exclude up to $250,000 of the $300,000 gain on the joint return. In other words, nothing prevents Nicole from claiming the exclusion she would otherwise be entitled to. IRC § 121(b)(2)(B).

(e) **What result in (d) if Keith had been living in the Fort Lauderdale residence since January 1, Year 1?**

Now, Keith meets the two-year "use" requirement with respect to the property. IRC § 121(b)(2)(A)(ii). As a result, up to $500,000 of gain may be excluded. In sum, none of the $300,000 gain need be reported on the joint return.

(f) **Six months after the purchase, Nicole married Keith who, at that time, moved into the Fort Lauderdale residence. Twelve months later, Nicole died and bequeathed title to the residence to Keith who continued to use it as his principal residence. Six months after Keith inherited the house, Keith sold it for $600,000.**

The basis step up under section 1014 may make the section 121 issue irrelevant. If there is any post-inheritance appreciation in the home, is Keith entitled to exclude any of the gain from the sale of the house? He has *used* the property as his principal residence for only eighteen months, and has *owned* the property for only six months. It would seem he could not exclude any of the gain.

Section 121(d)(2), however, provides that a taxpayer who receives property from a deceased spouse is treated as owning and using the property for the period the deceased spouse owned and used the property before death. Assuming that Keith has not remarried and that he otherwise qualifies for the exclusion, he could exclude up to $250,000 of gain. [If Keith (surviving spouse) files a joint return with Nicole (deceased spouse) for the year of death, the maximum exclusion of up to $500,000 would not be available. Review IRC § 121(b)(2)(A)(ii), (b)(4).]

(g) What result in (f) if Keith did not inherit the residence twelve months after marriage, but instead received title under the terms of a divorce settlement twelve months after marriage and then six months later Keith sold the home for $600,000?

Nicole transferred the property to Keith in a transaction described in section 1041(a). As a result, under section 121(d)(3)(A), the period Keith *owns* the property includes the period that Nicole owned the property. This would give Keith the requisite two-year ownership.

Note, however, that under section 121(d)(3)(A), the period that Nicole *used* the property is not included in the period that Keith used the property. Keith would still have to satisfy the two-year use requirement in order to qualify for the exclusion. His actual use was only eighteen months. Accordingly, none of the gain is excludable. He should have waited another six months before he sold the house.

Chapter 23

Hobby Losses

Overview

Section 183(a) generally prohibits any deductions attributable to a hobby—*an activity not engaged in for profit*. Yet, section 183(b) goes on to permit deductions attributable to a hobby, but only to the extent of income attributable to the hobby. The approach taken by section 183 should not come as a surprise. Expenses and losses from personal hobby activities should not be allowed to shelter income from other sources. However, if a personal hobby activity produces reportable income, then expenses and losses incurred to produce that income should be allowed to offset that income.

Section 183(c) defines an *activity not engaged in for profit* by incorporating the standards applied by sections 162 and 212, which we looked at in Chapter 7. Fortunately, the regulations under section 183 provide an independent set of principles to help determine whether an activity is or is not engaged in for profit. The regulations provide nine factors that should be taken into account in determining whether or not an activity is or is not engaged in for profit. *See* Treas. Reg. § 1.183-2(b). The Code creates a rebuttable presumption that an activity is engaged in for profit if the activity was profitable (e.g., gross income exceeded deductions) for three or more years in the five-year period ending with the year in question. IRC § 183(d). In ascertaining whether two or more activities may be treated as one activity, all the facts and circumstances should be considered, including the degree of organizational and economic interrelationship, the business purpose served by the undertakings, and the similarity of the undertakings. Treas. Reg. § 1.183-1(d).

If an activity is not engaged in for profit, deductions attributable to the activity are deductible only to the extent permitted by section 183(b). Although section 183(b) establishes two tiers of permitted deductions, the regulations split the second tier into two parts—effectively marshalling deductions into one of three tiers. Tier 1 deductions (those that would be allowable in full regardless of whether the activity was engaged in for profit) are allowed in full. Tier 2 deductions (those that would be allowable if the activity had been conducted for profit but that do not result in basis adjustments) are allowed only to the extent that gross income from the activity exceeds the total Tier 1 deductions. Tier 3 deductions (those that would be allowable if the activity had been conducted for profit but that do result in basis adjustments) are allowed only to the extent gross income exceeds the sum of Tier 1 and Tier 2 deductions. Treas. Reg. § 1.183-1(b)(1)-(3).

Primary Authority

Code: § 183(a)-(d). Skim § 280A(f)(3), (e)(1).

Regulations: §§ 1.183-1(a), (b)(1)-(2), (c)(1), (d)(1)-(2), (e); 1.183-2.

Cases: Nickerson v. Commissioner, 700 F.2d 402 (7th Cir. 1983).

Rulings: None.

Problems

23.1. Bode, who was employed full-time as vice president of a bank and who maintained a home with his wife in New York, was a regular skier in the northern Vermont area. Because of the development of several skiing facilities in the area, and because of the apparent boom in downhill and cross-country skiing, Bode believed that there was a demand for overnight lodging during the winter ski season and that a lodge, which provided such accommodations, would be a viable investment opportunity. Bode was aware that he would not be able to rent the lodge during the insect and mud season (April 15 to July 4), and that it would be difficult to secure summer and fall rentals. In Year 1, Bode purchased land on which he constructed a lodge that could accommodate 12 overnight guests. In Years 2-3, the lodge was rented to family groups. In Years 4-6, the lodge was a licensed inn offering food and lodging to transients primarily on a weekend basis with Bode managing the inn and cooking and serving all meals. In Year 7, Bode concluded that the lodge could not be operated profitably on a weekend basis, so in Years 8-10, the lodge was available for full-season rental, under which a tenant leased the premises from Bode for the entire ski season for an agreed rent and assumed all the costs of operating the lodge (e.g., fuel oil, electricity, snow removal). Although this rental arrangement proved more successful than the weekend operation, Bode continued to lose some money because there was very little snow in the area during those years and because many other lodges were constructed in the area during those years. In response to the declining demand for full-season rentals, Bode offered short-term leases during Years 11-12. However, because of the weather, competitors, and the gasoline shortage in those years, Bode's rental revenue decreased dramatically. In all years (Years 1-12), Bode advertised the inn for rent in several papers and also listed the lodge with real estate brokers in the area. For the most part, repairs, maintenance, and cleaning were performed by Bode; on occasion, however, Bode would hire two neighbors to perform such services. Bode and his wife remained in the lodge overnight when they were there for cleaning, repairing, or preparing it for use by a tenant. When vacationing or skiing in the Vermont area, however, they rented a room from their neighbor. The inn has appreciated in value since its purchase. But Bode has sustained net losses from the operation of the lodge each year during Years

1-12, with the annual net losses about the same each year. Are Bode's losses subject to the limitations of section 183?

This problem requires us to consider whether Bode's losses from operation of the lodge are fully allowable each year under sections 162 or 212 (i.e., allowable to reduce taxes due from his bank employment income) or whether such losses are limited as provided in section 183(b) (allowed only to the extent of the income from the lodge activity). The presumption in section 183(d) does not apply. IRC § 183(d). No inference is to be drawn from a failure to establish the presumption. Treas. Reg. § 1.183-1(c)(1). You should rely on the factors in Treas. Reg. § 1.183-2(b) in evaluating Bode's profit objective.

Some may point to the following in asserting that Bode's lodging activity *was profit motivated*:

1. Before purchasing the land and constructing the lodge, Bode familiarized himself with the skiing industry in Vermont. The development of other skiing facilities in the area spelled the beginning of dramatic growth in downhill and cross-country skiing in the area. Treas. Reg. § 1.183-2(b)(1).

2. Even though Bode had no prior knowledge of operating a lodge, there appeared to be a market for a lodge providing overnight accommodations, and Bode spent a good deal of time investigating the lodge business and various construction alternatives for the lodge. Treas. Reg. § 1.183-2(b)(2).

3. Once the lodge was completed, Bode operated it in a business-like manner. He kept adequate books and records for the lodge, and placed advertisements in several newspapers and listed the property with local real estate agents and brokers in their efforts to generate summer and winter rentals. Treas. Reg. § 1.183-2(b)(1).

4. Although Bode had a record of losses over a number of years, the regulations provide that a series of losses during the startup phase of an activity may not necessarily be an indication that the activity is not engaged in for profit. The regulations further provide that if losses are sustained because of unforeseen circumstances beyond the control of the taxpayer, then such losses are not an indication that the activity is not engaged in for profit. Treas. Reg. § 1.183-2(b)(6). Here, Bode sustained losses beyond his control. Investors quickly entered the market for seasonal lodging in Vermont, with the result that the marketplace soon became saturated with similar lodges. In addition, several years of below average snowfall and the gasoline shortage caused the rental income from the lodge to decline dramatically. Due primarily to the continuing losses, Bode experimented with different modes of operating the lodge in hopes of producing a profit. Initially, he rented the lodge to family groups. When that arrangement proved unsuccessful, he operated the lodge as a licensed inn providing overnight accommodations and dining facilities for weekend skiers. Though this proved to be more successful than his earlier arrangement, it did not produce a profit. Therefore, he began accepting full season rentals. However,

because of the weather and gasoline shortage, he had difficulty renting the lodge for the entire ski season; he was forced to accept weekly or monthly rentals. As stated in Treas. Reg. § 1.183-2(b)(1), a "change of operating methods, adoption of new techniques or abandonment of unprofitable methods in a manner consistent with an intent to improve profitability may also indicate profit motive." It is fair to conclude that Years 1-12 encompassed a start-up period. His losses were sustained during the start-up phase of the lodge activity and were the result of unforeseen circumstances beyond his control.

5. Bode's bank employment income was his only other source of income. He likely engaged in the lodge activity to provide for his retirement. Treas. Reg. § 1.183-2(b)(8).

6. Although he sustained substantial current losses, he hoped in the long run to realize a profit because the lodge appreciated in value. The appreciation in value may, or may not, offset the aggregate operating losses, but the prospect of realizing a profit on the sale of the lodge was bona fide when he decided to invest in the lodge and is sufficient to explain his willingness to continue to sustain operating losses. Treas. Reg. § 1.183-2(b)(4).

7. Most importantly, Bode never used the lodge for his own personal enjoyment. Only in connection with the management of the lodge did he stay in it overnight. At all times, the lodge was either rented, available for rent, or being prepared to be rented. Thus, it offered him no recreational benefits. Treas. Reg. § 1.183-2(b)(3). Renting a lodge is not an activity which by itself would cause a taxpayer to derive the kind of personal pleasure or gratification which could supplant profit motivation. Treas. Reg. § 1.183-2(b)(9). Similarly, there are no elements of personal pleasure, including aesthetic or other benefits, inherent in such activity.

Others may point to the following in asserting that Bode's activity *was not engaged in for profit*:

1. Bode failed to operate his lodge activity in a businesslike manner. There is nothing in the facts to suggest that he created or followed a written business plan, or that he prepared written profit or loss statements or balance sheets for the lodge activity. Treas. Reg. § 1.183-2(b)(1).

2. Prior to Year 1, Bode knew how to ski, but he had no knowledge about how to successfully operate a lodge. And there is nothing in the facts to suggest that he sought the appropriate type and quality of advice from other inn owners. This is not indicative of an intent to engage in an activity for profit. Treas. Reg. § 1.183-2(b)(2).

3. Bode undoubtedly derived a significant amount of personal pleasure from skiing. For a large part of each year, he did not spend a substantial amount of time on the lodge activity considering his full-time job as Vice President of a bank. Treas. Reg. § 1.183-2(b)(3).

4. Bode's consistent history of losses (12 years) is persuasive evidence that he did not expect to make a profit. Indeed, a history of unexplained losses over an

extended period is persuasive evidence of the absence of a profit motivation. Twelve years should not be considered a "startup period" phase for any lodge activity. Treas. Reg. § 1.183-2(b)(6).

5. According to the regulations, substantial income from sources other than the activity in question, particularly if the activity's losses generate substantial tax benefits, may indicate that the activity is not engaged in for profit. Treas. Reg. § 1.183-2(b)(8). Bode had substantial independent sources of income which permitted him to sustain the losses. The net losses from operation of the lodge should not be able to shelter his bank employment income.

The facts of this problem are drawn from Allen v. Commissioner, 72 T.C. 28 (1979). The Tax Court held for the taxpayer, and concluded that the taxpayer intended to derive a profit from renting his lodge. Accordingly, the court held that the losses incurred in the lodge activity were fully deductible.

23.2. Assume Bode's lodge activity in part 1, above, is subject to section 183. In Year 12, Bode had $20,000 of gross income from operating the lodge. To what extent are the following expenses deductible in Year 12?

Property taxes on the inn	**$4,000**
Interest on the inn mortgage	**$3,000**
Guests' food and other supplies	**$5,000**
Advertising	**$1,000**
Repairs and maintenance	**$4,000**
Depreciation on building	**$5,000**

Assuming the lodge activity is not engaged in for profit, Bode's expenses attributable to the activity are deductible only to the extent permitted by section 183(b).

The Tier 1 deductions total $4,000 (property taxes). They are allowed in full regardless of whether the lodge activity is engaged in for profit. Treas. Reg. § 1.183-1(b)(1)(i).

The Tier 2 deductions total $13,000 ($3,000 interest, $5,000 food and supplies, $1,000 advertising, and $4,000 repairs). [These are deductions that would be allowable if the lodge activity had been conducted for profit but that do not result in adjustments to basis of property.] Since gross income of $20,000 exceeds the Tier 1 deductions by $16,000, the $13,000 Tier 2 deductions are allowed in full. Treas. Reg. § 1.183-1(b)(1)(ii).

The Tier 3 deductions total $5,000 (depreciation on building). [Tier 3 deductions are those that would be allowable if the activity had been conducted for profit but, unlike Tier 2 deductions, result in basis adjustments.] Gross income of $20,000 exceeds both Tier 1 and Tier 2 deductions by $3,000. Therefore, only $3,000 of depreciation is deductible this year. Treas. Reg. § 1.183-1(b)(1)(iii).

Chapter 24

Like Kind Exchanges

Overview

Ordinarily a sale or exchange of property will trigger the recognition of gain or loss on the transaction by operation of section 1001(c). However, there are a number of provisions that overrule section 1001. These are known collectively as *non-recognition provisions*. One of the most prominent of these is section 1031, which addresses what are known as like kind exchanges. The like kind exchange is a widely employed tax avoidance technique, especially in the area of commercial real estate transactions. It will grant complete non-recognition when a taxpayer swaps real property for other real property of equal value. It may grant partial non-recognition in other cases. There is a catch, however. Non-recognition usually means deferral of, not exemption from, gain recognition. This results because the basis of the like kind property received is not stepped-up. *See* IRC § 1031(d), discussed below.

The fundamental thrust of section 1031 is to grant non-recognition of gain or loss on the exchange of business or investment property for like kind business or investment property. IRC § 1031(a)(1). The general rule for determining like kindness is that the properties exchanged must be similar in "*nature or character*." Treas. Reg. § 1.1031(a)–1(b). In this context any sort of fee interest in real estate is similar in nature or character to any other form of fee interest in real estate. Thus, for example, an exchange of farmland for an apartment building can qualify as a like kind exchange. *See* Treas. Reg. §§ 1.1031(a)–1(b) & (c); 1.1031(b)–1(b), ex. 1. *See also* Commissioner v. Crichton, 122 F.2d 181 (5th Cir. 1941). Implicit in this example is the further point that a taxpayer is within section 1031 if she exchanges real property held for investment for real property to be used in a trade or business or vice versa. Treas. Reg. § 1.1031(a)–1(a).

Often the taxpayer who wants to do a like kind exchange will have difficulty finding a buyer who holds just the sort of like kind property that is being sought. This lack of fit does not pose an insuperable barrier, however, because of the possibility of a *three cornered exchange*. This typically involves a buyer first purchasing the desired exchange property from a third party and then engaging in the exchange with the seller who is seeking non-recognition. *See* Revenue Ruling 77-297, 1977-2 C.B. 304. The regulations permit the use of qualified intermediaries to facilitate exchanges. Treas. Reg. 1.1031(k)-1(g).

It is often difficult to find like kind properties that are precisely equal in value. Often one party may have to pay some cash or transfer some non-like kind property

to equalize the deal. This equalizing payment is called *boot*. Since boot is by definition not like kind, the Code provides that the recipient of the boot (which also
includes relief of liabilities) must recognize gain to the extent of the *lesser* of gain
realized or the value of the boot received. IRC § 1031(b). However, the recipient
of boot is not allowed to recognize a loss on the like kind property given up. IRC
§ 1031(c). We should note that this non-recognition of loss rule does not prevent
loss recognition on losses resulting from *giving* boot. That is, if a taxpayer gives up
non-like kind loss property, the loss on that property is recognized.

As noted above, section 1031 grants deferral of gain recognition rather than complete forgiveness. This deferral derives from the basis rules. The taxpayer's basis in
the newly acquired property is governed by section 1031(d) as embellished upon in
the regulations. Essentially, section 1031(d) provides that the taxpayer's basis in the
property received is her basis in the property given up minus any money received,
plus any gain recognized, and minus any loss recognized. The beginning basis number is the aggregate of the bases in all property given up and includes the amount of
any cash given as well. Treas. Reg. § 1.1031(d)-1(a). Liability assumptions are treated
the same as cash payments. *See* IRC § 1031(d) (last sentence).

It is possible to bring residential rental property within the operation of section 1031 even when there has been some personal use of the property by the
owner. The Service has set out guidelines for this in Revenue Procedure 2008-16,
2008-1 C.B. 547.

Primary Authority

Code: §§ 1001(c); 1031(a)-(d); 1245(b)(4); 1250(d)(4).

Regulations: §§ 1.1031(a)-1(a)(1) 1st par., -1(b), -1(c), -2(a); 1.1031(b)-1(c); 1.1031(d)-2 ex. 2.

Cases: Click v. Commissioner, 78 T.C. 225 (1982); Commissioner v. Crichton, 122 F.2d 181 (5th Cir. 1941).

Rulings: Rev. Proc. 77-297, 1977-2 C.B. 304; Rev. Proc. 2008-16, 2008-1 C.B. 547.

Problems

**24.1. You are an associate at a local law firm. You run into the Senior Partner
who tells you that he plans soon to swap his log cabin near Vail, Colorado,
for a friend's log cabin near Aspen, Colorado, and he states: "I've been told
that the exchange will be tax free! Is that true?" You reply, "It depends." He
responds, "It depends on what?" How do you respond to the Senior Partner? In particular, (1) list the additional information that you need, and
(2) explain why this information is relevant in determining the proper tax
treatment of the exchange of log cabins.**

The following information is needed to determine the tax treatment of the exchange for the Senior Partner:

1. *Did Senior Partner hold his Vail cabin for productive use in a trade or business or for investment?* Section 1031 requires that the property given up in the exchange be held for productive use in business or for investment. The operative word is "held." Most likely, Senior Partner's cabin is currently held for personal use and he would not qualify. Could he argue that despite the personal use, the Vail cabin is held for "investment?" After all, property near a ski resort is likely to increase in value. Courts have held that personal use is inconsistent with business or investment motives. Perhaps he could benefit from section 1031 nonrecognition if he were to actually rent the Vail cabin as a preliminary to a section 1031 exchange. But then the question arises as to how long the property must be held for rental. Section 1031 provides no specific rules on how long property must have been held for business or investment. In Rev. Proc. 2008-16, the IRS established a safe harbor for when a dwelling unit qualifies as property held for productive use in a trade or business or for investment for purposes of section 1031. Senior Partner would qualify for the safe harbor if the Vail cabin (the relinquished property): (1) was owned by Senior Partner for at least 24 months immediately before the exchange (the "qualifying use period"); and (2) within the qualifying use period, in each of the two 12-month periods immediately preceding the exchange, his personal use of the cabin has not exceeded 10 percent of the number of days during the 12-month period that the dwelling unit is rented at a fair rental. Under this safe harbor, additional requirements would have to be satisfied with respect to the Aspen cabin (the replacement property), discussed below.

2. *Does Senior Partner intend to hold the Aspen cabin for productive use in a trade or business or for investment?* Under section 1031, the acquiring property must be trade or business or investment property. (Note: property held for trade or business may be exchanged for property held for investment. And property held for investment may be exchanged for property held for trade or business. Treas. Reg. § 1.1031(a)-1(a).) Intent must be determined at the time of exchange. *Click v. Commissioner.* Here, Senior Partner must intend to hold the Aspen cabin for productive use in business or for investment. To meet the safe harbor in Rev. Proc. 2008-16, the Aspen cabin (the replacement property): (1) must be owned by Senior Partner for at least 24 months immediately after the exchange (the "qualifying use period"); and (2) within the qualifying use period, in each of the two 12-month periods immediately after the exchange, Senior Partner rents the Aspen cabin to another person or persons at a fair rental for 14 days or more, and has no personal use of the cabin exceeding the greater of 14 days or 10 percent of the number of days during the 12-month period that the dwelling unit is rented at fair rental value.

3. *Will Senior Partner receive anything other than the Aspen cabin (e.g., money) in the exchange?* Often properties exchanged are not of equal value, and additional cash or property is received in an exchange. If there is adjusting property—in addition to qualifying "like kind" property—section 1031(a) does not literally apply because the exchange is not "solely" for property of like kind. Does this mean that the taxpayer must recognize all the realized gain? No. Section 1031(b) modifies

the rules of section 1031(a). The taxpayer must only recognize the lesser of (1) the realized gain or (2) the cash/FMV of the non-qualifying property received (a/k/a "boot"). The basis of the like kind property received will be impacted if boot is received. *See* IRC § 1031(d) (requiring the basis of the like kind property received to be adjusted downward for the boot received and adjusted upward for the gain recognized).

4. *Are there liabilities encumbering the two cabins, and, if so, will Senior Partner experience a relief of debt when the liabilities are netted (e.g., Senior Partner will assume a mortgage encumbering the Aspen cabin and his friend will assume a mortgage encumbering the Vail cabin)?* The last sentence of subsection (d) of section 1031 applies for purposes of all of section 1031, including the boot gain rule of subsection (b). Thus, relief of debt is treated as money received and may cause immediate gain recognition. We say "may" because gain recognition may be avoided if the taxpayer who is transferring property subject to a liability is also paying money or taking on a liability. The regulations make it clear that in determining the boot paid or received, we should take into account both liabilities relieved and assumed and net them. Only net liability relief is treated as boot received. *See* Treas. Reg. § 1.1031(d)-2(c), ex. 2.

5. *Will Senior Partner receive title to the Aspen cabin within 180 days after he transfers the Vail cabin to his friend?* Senior Partner has already identified the replacement property (i.e., the Aspen cabin). But the Code requires that the Aspen cabin be received within 180 days after Senior Partner transfers the Vail cabin. IRC § 1031(a)(3)(B).

24.2. **Same as problem 1 above. Assume, based on the information provided by the Senior Partner, that the Vail cabin currently does not qualify under section 1031 as "property held for productive use in a trade or business or for investment." What should the Senior Partner do if he wants the exchange to qualify under section 1031?**

Most tax advisors would recommend that Senior Partner actually rent out the Vail cabin at fair value before engaging in the exchange. But many may disagree over the amount of time the Vail cabin should be rented. The safest approach would be to satisfy Rev. Proc. 2008-16, which establishes a safe harbor for when a dwelling unit qualifies as property held for productive use in a trade or business or for investment for purposes of section 1031.

Senior Partner qualifies for the safe harbor if:

(a) The Vail cabin (the relinquished property):

(1) Was owned by Senior Partner for at least 24 months immediately before the exchange (the "qualifying use period"); and

(2) Within the qualifying use period, in each of the two 12-month periods immediately preceding the exchange, his personal use of the cabin

does not exceed 10 percent of the number of days during the 12-month period that the dwelling unit is rented at a fair rental; and

(b) The Aspen cabin (the replacement property):

    (1) Is owned by Senior Partner for at least 24 months immediately after the exchange (the "qualifying use period"); and

    (2) Within the qualifying use period, in each of the two 12-month periods immediately after the exchange, Senior Partner rents the cabin to another person or persons at a fair rental for 14 days or more, and has no personal use of the cabin exceeding the greater of 14 days or 10 percent of the number of days during the 12-month period that the dwelling unit is rented at fair rental value.

24.3. Doc Holliday owns five acres of swampland located in Okeechobee, Florida ("Swampland"). Doc acquired Swampland, which has bad drainage and abuts a small highway, several years ago as an investment. In the current year, Doc exchanges Swampland for a small plot of land in Miami Beach, Florida owned by Wyatt Earp ("Cityland"). Although Wyatt currently holds Cityland for investment, Doc plans to use Cityland in his current trade or business. What are the tax consequences of this exchange for Doc, assuming the following:

(a) At the time of exchange, Doc's Swampland is unencumbered with a fair market value of $100,000 and an adjusted basis in Doc's hands of $50,000. Wyatt's Cityland is unencumbered with a fair market value of $100,000.

Doc has met all the requirements of section 1031(a). Note that this is a like kind exchange since this is real estate for real estate, and even though Doc held Swampland for investment but intends to use Cityland for business. Treas. Reg. § 1.1031(a)-1(a), -1(b).

Step 1. What is Doc's gain realized? Doc has a gain realized of $50,000.

	$100,000	Fair market value of Cityland received
+	0	Cash received
+	0	Liability transferred (treated like cash received) (*Crane*)
−	0	Liability assumed (treated as boot paid) (reverse-*Crane*)
	$100,000	Amount realized
−	50,000	Adjusted basis of Swampland
	$ 50,000	Gain realized

Step 2. What is Doc's gain recognized? His gain recognized is $0 since he received no boot (i.e., non-like kind property). The $50,000 of gain realized that is not recognized is preserved through his basis in the Cityland received.

Step 3. What is Doc's basis in Cityland? His basis is $50,000 pursuant to section 1031(d).

$50,000	Swampland's adjusted basis
− 0	Cash received (including net liability relief)
+ 0	Gain recognized
$50,000	Cityland's adjusted basis

Step 4. What is Doc's holding period in Cityland? Doc's holding period in Swampland will be tacked onto the holding period in Cityland because (1) the basis in Cityland was determined by reference to the basis in Swampland, and (2) Swampland was a capital asset under section 1221 (held for investment). IRC § 1223(1).

> **(b) At the time of exchange, Doc's Swampland is unencumbered with a fair market value of $100,000 and an adjusted basis in Doc's hands of $75,000. Wyatt's Cityland is unencumbered with a fair market value of $50,000. To equalize the exchange, Wyatt also gives Doc $50,000 in cash.**

Step 1. What is Doc's gain realized? Doc has a gain realized of $25,000.

$50,000	Fair market value of Cityland received
+ 50,000	Cash received
+ 0	Liability transferred (treated like cash received) (*Crane*)
− 0	Liability assumed (treated as boot paid) (reverse-*Crane*)
$100,000	Amount realized
− 75,000	Adjusted basis of Swampland
$25,000	Gain realized

Step 2. What is Doc's gain recognized? Because Doc is receiving some cash in addition to the like kind property, section 1031(b) applies. Section 1031(b) modifies the rules of section 1031(a), but does not completely do away with the benefits of nonrecognition. Many readers might jump to the erroneous conclusion that Doc must recognize $50,000—the cash received. But that is incorrect, since Doc's gain realized was only $25,000. Section 1031(b) actually requires Doc to recognize the lesser of the realized gain ($25,000) or the cash received ($50,000). Thus, Doc must recognize $25,000. Because all of the gain realized was recognized, there is no gain to defer through basis mechanism. Note the character of the gain is long term capital gain—gain from the sale or exchange of a capital asset held for more than a year. IRC §§ 1221, 1222(3).

Step 3. What is Doc's basis in Cityland? His basis is $50,000 pursuant to section 1031(d).

$75,000	Swampland's adjusted basis
− 50,000	Cash received (including net liability relief)
+ 25,000	Gain recognized
$50,000	Cityland's adjusted basis

Thus, if Doc were to sell Cityland soon after the exchange for its value of $50,000, he would realize $0 gain.

Step 4. What is Doc's holding period in Cityland? Doc's holding period in Swampland will be tacked onto the holding period in Cityland because (1) the basis in Cityland was determined by reference to the basis in Swampland, and (2) Swampland was a capital asset under section 1221 (held for investment). IRC § 1223(1).

 (c) **At the time of exchange, Doc's Swampland has a fair market value of $65,000 and an adjusted basis in Doc's hands of $20,000. Swampland is also subject to a mortgage of $5,000. Wyatt's Cityland is unencumbered with a fair market value of $50,000. To equalize the exchange, Wyatt also gives Doc $10,000 in cash and assumes the $5,000 mortgage encumbering Doc's Swampland.**

Step 1. What is Doc's gain realized? Doc has a gain realized of $45,000.

$50,000	Fair market value of Cityland received
+ 10,000	Cash received
+ 5,000	Liability transferred (treated like cash received) (*Crane*)
− 0	Liability assumed (treated as boot paid) (reverse-*Crane*)
$65,000	Amount realized
− 20,000	Adjusted basis of Swampland
$45,000	Gain realized

Step 2. What is Doc's gain recognized? At a minimum, it would seem that Doc should recognize $10,000 worth of cash received. But what about the $5,000 mortgage relief? The last sentence of section 1031(d) states that relief of the $5,000 is also treated as money received. Thus, Doc must currently recognize $15,000 of gain—the lesser of the gain realized ($45,000) or the money received ($15,000). IRC § 1031(b). (The remaining $30,000 of gain realized will be deferred until Doc disposes of Cityland in a taxable transaction.) Note that the character of the $15,000 of gain is long term capital gain—gain from the sale or exchange of a capital asset. IRC §§ 1221, 1222(3).

Step 3. What is Doc's basis in Cityland? His basis is $20,000 pursuant to section 1031(d).

$20,000	Swampland's adjusted basis
− 15,000	Cash received (including net liability relief)
+ 15,000	Gain recognized
$20,000	Cityland's adjusted basis

Thus, if Doc were to sell Cityland soon after the exchange for its value of $50,000, he would realize $30,000 of gain, the amount of gain that was deferred in the exchange.

Step 4. What is Doc's holding period in Cityland? Doc's holding period in Swampland will be tacked onto the holding period in Cityland because (1) the basis in Cityland was determined by reference to the basis in Swampland, and (2) Swampland was a capital asset under section 1221 (held for investment). IRC § 1223(1).

(d) **At the time of exchange, Doc's Swampland has a fair market value of $125,000 and an adjusted basis in Doc's hands of $10,000. Swampland is also subject to a mortgage of $75,000. Wyatt's Cityland has a fair market value of $100,000, and is subject to a mortgage of $50,000. To equalize the exchange, Doc will assume the $50,000 mortgage encumbering Cityland and Wyatt will assume the $75,000 mortgage encumbering Swampland.**

Step 1. What is Doc's gain realized? Doc has a gain realized of $115,000.

$100,000	Fair market value of Cityland received
+ 0	Cash received
+ 75,000	Liability transferred (treated like cash received) (*Crane*)
− 50,000	Liability assumed (treated as boot paid) (reverse-*Crane*)
$125,000	Amount realized
− 10,000	Adjusted basis of Swampland
$115,000	Gain realized

Step 2. What is Doc's gain recognized? Section 1031 is full of gaps. It talks about what happens if one transfers property subject to a liability, but it does not talk about what happens when one takes on a liability. Read carefully the last sentence of section 1031(d). As far as the Code is concerned, Doc would have to recognize $75,000. But intuition says otherwise. Indeed, while Doc is being relieved of a $75,000 liability, he is at the same time taking on a $50,000 liability. Intuitively, from an economic standpoint, Doc is relieved of a liability of $25,000. Fortunately, the regulations take care of the deficiency in the Code and require us to net the two liabilities to determine net liability relief (treated as money/boot received). Treas. Reg. § 1.1031(d)-2(c), Ex. 2. Doc must recognize $25,000 of gain—the lesser of the gain realized ($115,000) or the boot received ($25,000). The character of the gain is long term capital gain—gain from the sale or exchange of a capital asset. IRC §§ 1221, 1222(3). $90,000 of gain is deferred via basis, determined in Step 3 below.

Step 3. What is Doc's basis in Cityland? His basis is $10,000 pursuant to section 1031(d).

$10,000	Swampland's adjusted basis
− 25,000	Cash received (including net liability relief)
+ 25,000	Gain recognized
$10,000	Cityland's adjusted basis

Thus, if Doc were to sell Cityland soon after the exchange for its value of $100,000, he would realize $90,000 of gain, the amount of gain that was deferred in the exchange.

Step 4. What is Doc's holding period in Cityland? Doc's holding period in Swampland will be tacked onto the holding period in Cityland because (1) the basis in Cityland was determined by reference to the basis in Swampland, and (2) Swampland was a capital asset under section 1221 (held for investment). IRC § 1223(1).

(e) **At the time of exchange, Doc's Swampland has a fair market value of $75,000 and an adjusted basis in Doc's hands of $10,000. Swampland is also subject to a mortgage of $50,000. Wyatt's Cityland has a fair market value of $100,000, and is subject to a mortgage of $75,000. To equalize the exchange, Doc will assume the $75,000 mortgage encumbering Cityland and Wyatt will assume the $50,000 mortgage encumbering Swampland.**

Step 1. What is Doc's gain realized? Doc has a gain realized of $65,000.

$100,000	Fair market value of Cityland received
+ 0	Cash received
+ 50,000	Liability transferred (treated like cash received) (*Crane*)
− 75,000	Liability assumed (treated as boot paid) (reverse-*Crane*)
$ 75,000	Amount realized
− 10,000	Adjusted basis of Swampland
$ 65,000	Gain realized

Step 2. What is Doc's gain recognized? None of the gain is currently recognized because when we net the transferred liability ($50,000) against the liability Doc took on ($75,000), there is no net liability relief treated as money received. Here Doc ends up $25,000 in the hole, which is treated as a constructive payment.

Step 3. What is Doc's basis in Cityland? His basis is $35,000 pursuant to section 1031(d).

$10,000	Swampland's adjusted basis
− 0	Cash received (including net liability relief)
+ 25,000	Cash paid (the net liability assumed) Treas. Reg. § 1.1031(d)-1(a).
$35,000	Cityland's adjusted basis

Thus, if Doc were to sell Cityland soon after the exchange for its value of $100,000, he would realize $65,000 of gain, the amount of gain that was deferred in the exchange.

Step 4. What is Doc's holding period in Cityland? Doc's holding period in Swampland will be tacked onto the holding period in Cityland because (1) the basis in Cityland was determined by reference to the basis in Swampland, and (2) Swampland was a capital asset under section 1221 (held for investment). IRC § 1223(1).

24.4. **Del owns and operates an unencumbered ranch that has greatly appreciated in value since she purchased it 20 years ago. Del, who would like to get out of the "ranching" business and go into the "farming" business, recently noticed a "For Sale" sign on a farm owned by Phyllis. Del approached Phyllis about the possibility of doing a like-kind exchange, but Phyllis is not interested in Del's ranch; Phyllis wants cash from a sale so that she can retire and move to Florida. Is there anything Del can do to achieve her goals without recognizing gain?**

Del could find a buyer ("Buyer") who wants her ranch and who is willing to pay cash. Buyer would first purchase Phyllis' farm for cash, and then Del and Buyer would engage in a section 1031 like kind exchange. At the end of the day, everyone would be happy: (1) Phyllis would have cash, (2) Buyer would own Del's ranch, and (3) Del would own Phyllis' farm. Most likely, Buyer will not agree to engage in this mess—i.e., buy Phyllis' farm and then go through a section 1031 exchange of that farm for Del's ranch. In addition, there are substantial risks for both Del and Buyer. There is a risk for Del that Buyer will go out and purchase the wrong farm. There is a risk for Buyer that Del might change her mind after Buyer purchases Phyllis' farm.

Fortunately, the regulations authorize the use of a "qualified intermediary." Treas. Reg. § 1.1031(k)-1(g). So, Del can utilize the services of a person or entity (who is not a "disqualified person") to accommodate the exchange. Treas. Reg. § 1.1031(k)-1(k). More specifically, Del could transfer her ranch to the intermediary, who would (1) sell the ranch to Buyer for cash, (2) use the proceeds from the sale to acquire property designated by Del (i.e., the farm owned by Phyllis), and (3) transfer the farm to Del. The receipt of cash by the intermediary does not jeopardize section 1031 treatment for Del; in other words, Del will not be in actual or constructive receipt of money. It should be noted that the regulations permit direct deeding, so that the intermediary can remain outside the chain of title. Treas. Reg. § 1.1031(k)-1(g)(4).

Chapter 25

Involuntary Conversions

Overview

Section 1033 is a non-recognition provision that potentially applies when property is involuntarily converted into other property. Under section 1033(a)(1), if property is involuntarily converted directly into similar-use property, the gain realized, if any, will not be recognized. Under section 1033(a)(2), if property is involuntarily converted into money (e.g., condemnation award or fire insurance proceeds), the gain realized, if any, will be recognized unless the taxpayer elects non-recognition treatment by purchasing similar property within a prescribed time period. However, gain is recognized to the extent that the conversion proceeds exceed the cost of the replacement property. The policy behind section 1033 is similar to that of section 1031 (covered in the previous chapter): non-recognition is warranted if a taxpayer's investment is continued and the taxpayer has not really changed his or her economic position.

Section 1033 applies only to gains (not losses) and only if property is *compulsorily or involuntarily converted* as a result of certain events: (1) destruction in whole or in part; (2) theft; (3) seizure; or (4) requisition or condemnation (or sale made under threat or imminence thereof). Further, non-recognition of gain is available only if a taxpayer acquires qualified replacement property; that is, property *similar or related in service or use* to the converted property (or a controlling stock interest in a company owning such property), which is more stringent that the like kind standard of section 1031. With respect to *owners-users* of property, courts have applied a "functional use test," under which the physical characteristics and end uses of the converted and replacement properties must be closely similar. With respect to *owners-lessors* of property (investors), courts have applied a "relation of the properties to the taxpayer" test—one that considers the nature of the business risks connected with the converted and replacement properties, and what such properties demand of the taxpayer in the way of management, services and relations to her tenants. *See* Clifton Inv. Co. v. Commissioner, 312 F.2d 719 (6th Cir. 1963); Rev. Rul. 64-237, 1964-2 C.B. 319. *But see* IRC § 1033(g) (allowing condemned business or investment real property to be replaced by like kind property).

Non-recognition of gain upon the involuntary conversion of property hinges on whether the taxpayer acquires similar use property within the time period prescribed by section 1033. As a general rule, the replacement period ends two years after the close of the taxable year in which gain is first realized (i.e., when proceeds in excess of basis become available to the taxpayer). IRC § 1033(a)(2)(B). *But see* IRC § 1033(g) (applying a three-year replacement period to condemnations of business or investment real property).

If property is involuntarily converted into similar use property and gain is not recognized pursuant to section 1033(a)(1), then the basis of the replacement property is the same as the taxpayer's basis in the converted property. IRC § 1033(b)(1). If property is involuntarily converted into money and the taxpayer elects not to recognize gain pursuant to section 1033(a)(2), then the basis of the replacement property is the cost of the replacement property minus the amount of unrecognized gain on the conversion. IRC § 1033(b)(2).

Primary Authority

Code: §§ 1001(c); 1033(a)(1)-(2), (b)(1)-(2), (g)(1)-(2), (4), (h)(2). Skim §§ 1245(b)(4); 1250(d)(4).

Regulations: § 1.1033(b)-1(b).

Cases: Clifton Inv. Co. v. Commissioner, 312 F.2d 719 (6th Cir. 1963); Liant Records v. Commissioner, 303 F.2d 326 (2d Cir. 1962); Ponticos v. Commissioner, 338 F.2d 477 (6th Cir. 1964).

Rulings: Rev. Proc. 64-237, 1964-2 C.B. 319; Rev. Rul. 76-391, 1976-2 C.B. 243.

Problems

25.1. Buddy, who owned and operated an auto repair business, received $1 million in insurance proceeds when the building used in his business was totally destroyed by a tornado. Which of the following transactions qualify for nonrecognition of gain under section 1033?

Buddy will qualify for nonrecognition of gain under section 1033 only if the replacement property is similar or related in service or use to the converted property. In answering this problem, students should rely on *Clifton Investment Co. v. Commissioner* and Revenue Ruling 64-237, both of which are cited in the Primary Authorities above. As these materials illustrate, for *owners-users* of property (as opposed to *owners-lessors* of property) courts apply the so-called "functional test" or "end-use test," which takes into account the actual physical end use to which the properties involved are put.

(a) Buddy used all the proceeds to construct another building that he used in his auto repair business.

The new building is similar or related in service or use to the old building. This transaction qualifies for nonrecognition of gain.

(b) Buddy used all the proceeds to construct another building that he leased to a tenant engaged in auto repairs.

Here, the new building is not similar or related in service or use to the old building. This transaction does not qualify for nonrecogntion of gain.

(c) **Buddy used all the proceeds to purchase a gas station that Buddy operated as a business. The gas station business involved sales of gasoline, cigarettes, and lottery tickets in addition to auto repair services.**

Although the new building involves sale of merchandise, it is also used for auto repair services. Thus, it is most likely similar or related in service or use to the old building. This transaction probably qualifies for nonrecognition of gain. But an argument could be made that it does not.

(d) **Would your answers above change if the original building was condemned?**

Although section 1033(a)(2) requires converted property to be replaced by property that is "similar or related in service or use," section 1033(g) allows certain converted real property to be replaced by "like-kind" property. The special rule only applies to real property held for business use or investment (and not to property held for personal use such as a residence), and only applies if the property is converted by reason of seizure, requisition or condemnation, or threat or imminence thereof (and not by reason of fire, flood, or other catastrophe).

If Buddy's auto repair building were condemned, he would qualify for the special rule in section 1033(g), and would only have to satisfy the like-kind standard of section 1031 (which is less stringent than the "related in service or use standard" of section 1033). Recall from the last chapter that land for land, however improved, is considered like kind.

25.2. Michelle, owner-lessor of a residential apartment building, received $1 million in insurance proceeds when the building was totally destroyed by fire. Which of the following transactions qualify for nonrecognition of gain under section 1033?

Michelle will qualify for nonrecognition of gain under section 1033 only if the replacement property is similar or related in service or use to the converted property. As noted in *Clifton Investment Co.* and Revenue Ruling 64-237, for *investors* of property (i.e., *owners-lessors* of property) courts do not apply the functional/end-use test discussed above. Instead of focusing on physical end uses by tenants, courts apply a "relation of the properties to the taxpayer" test. In this problem, we should focus on what the properties demand of Michelle in the way of management, services, and relations to her tenants—we must compare the extent and type of Michelle's management activity, the amount and kind of services rendered by her to the tenants, and the nature of her business risks connected with the properties.

(a) **Michelle used all the proceeds to purchase an office and warehouse building that Michelle leased to tenants.**

The leased warehouse building is similar or related in service or use to the leased apartment building. *See Ponticos v. Commissioner; see also Liant Records v. Commissioner,* which is discussed in *Clifton Investment Co.* This transaction qualifies for nonrecognition of gain.

(b) Michelle used all the proceeds to purchase a single-family home that Michelle leased to tenants.

What is demanded of Michelle by the single family investment home in terms of services to tenants and management activity most likely materially differs from what was demanded of her by the residential apartment building. The nature of her business risks also are likely materially varied. Thus, the new single family home is not similar or related in service or use to the apartment building. The transaction does not qualify for nonrecognition of gain.

(c) Michelle used all the proceeds to purchase unimproved farmland that Michelle leased to tenants.

The leased farmland may not be considered similar or related in service or use to the leased apartment building. *See, e.g.,* Rev. Rul. 76-391. We should consider what the two properties require in the way of Michelle's services to the tenants, management activity, risks, etc. Review *Clifton Investment Co.*

(d) Would your answers above change if the original building was condemned?

As noted in Problem 1(d) above, section 1033(g) allows certain converted real property to be replaced by "like-kind" property. The special rule only applies to real property held for business use or investment (and not to property held for personal use such as a residence), and only applies if the property is converted by reason of seizure, requisition or condemnation, or threat or imminence thereof (and not by reason of fire, flood, or other catastrophe).

If Michelle's apartment building were condemned, she would qualify for the special rule in section 1033(g), and would only have to satisfy the like-kind standard of section 1031 (which is less stringent than the "related in service or use standard" of section 1033). Recall from the last chapter that land for land, however improved, is considered like kind.

25.3. ABC, Inc., a calendar-year taxpayer, manufactures widgets. Its manufacturing plant (a factory building of 8,000 square feet located on 1 acre of land) was completely destroyed by fire on August 10, Year 1, when the plant building's adjusted basis was $180,000. On November 30, Year 1, ABC received $200,000 of insurance proceeds on account of the fire, and estimated that the entire $200,000 would be used to replace the original manufacturing plant with a new plant.

(a) What is ABC's gain realized on the casualty?

The fire casualty is a realization event under section 1001. ABC's gain realized is $20,000 ($200,000 amount realized minus $180,000). IRC § 1001(a), (b). None of the gain is recognized in Year 1 if ABC elects to postpone recognition by purchasing qualified replacement property within the appropriate time period. IRC

§§ 1001(c), 1033(a)(2). The election is made by not reporting the gain on the Year 1 tax return. All the details in connection with the casualty (including those relating to replacement of the destroyed property) should be provided in an attached statement to the Year 1 tax return. Notice that the statute of limitations for assessment of a deficiency remains open. IRC § 1033(a)(2)(C)(i).

(b) What is the latest date ABC has to purchase qualified replacement property to not recognize the gain?

The general period within which qualified property must be replaced is "2 years after the close of the first taxable year in which any part of the gain upon the conversion is realized." IRC § 1033(a)(2)(B)(i). (However, this rule is applied by substituting "3 years" for "2 years" in the case of a condemnation of real property held for productive use in trade or business or for investment. IRC § 1033(g)(4).) Accordingly, ABC must purchase qualified replacement property by December 31, Year 3—that is, 2 years after the close of December 31, Year 1, which is the year gain was realized (when insurance proceeds in excess of basis became available to ABC).

Note: Section 1033(a)(2)(B)(ii) allows the Service to extend the replacement period upon taxpayer application. *See* Treas. Reg. § 1.1033(a)-2(c)(3). Such extensions are typically granted for one-year upon showing of reasonable cause for failing to timely secure replacement property.

(c) Are there any restrictions on the type of property ABC may purchase?

As discussed above in Problems 25.1 and 25.2, ABC will qualify for nonrecognition of gain under section 1033 only if the replacement property is similar or related in service or use to the converted property. *See Clifton Investment Co.* and Revenue Ruling 64-237. Section 1033(g) allows certain converted real property to be replaced by "like-kind" property. The special rule, however, only applies to real property held for business use or investment (and not to property held for personal use such as a residence), and only applies if the property is converted by reason of seizure, requisition or condemnation, or threat or imminence thereof (and not by reason of fire, flood, or other catastrophe). ABC does not qualify for the special "like-kind" standard in section 1031, and must meet the more stringent "similar or related in service or use" standard of section 1033.

(d) Assume ABC purchased qualified replacement property (a factory building of 10,000 square feet located on 3 acres of land) within the prescribed time limit. The total purchase price is $700,000, of which $200,000 is allocable to the building itself and $500,000 is allocable to the land. What is ABC's basis in the new property?

ABC's basis in the replacement building is $180,000—that is, the cost of the replacement building ($200,000) minus the amount of gain not recognized on the conversion ($20,000). IRC § 1033(b)(2). The basis in the land is $500,000. As can be seen, section 1033 does not permanently exclude gain, but instead defers gain until disposition of the replacement property.

(e) **Assume ABC paid only $190,000 for the new plant building within the prescribed time limit, what is the amount of gain recognized on the insurance proceeds (to be reflected on an amended return), and what is ABC's basis in the new property?**

Under section 1033(a)(2), gain realized ($20,000) is recognized to the extent that the casualty proceeds ($200,000) exceed the cost of the replacement property ($190,000). ABC must recognize $10,000 of gain. ABC must file an amended tax return for Year 1—the year in which gain was realized but not reported—and pay the additional tax liability on that gain. The Service usually sends a bill for interest.

ABC's basis in the replacement building is $180,000—that is, the cost of the replacement property ($190,000) minus the amount of gain not recognized on the conversion ($10,000). IRC § 1033(b)(2).

(f) **Would any of your answers above change if the original building was condemned instead of destroyed by fire?**

Section 1033(g) allows certain converted real property to be replaced by "like-kind" property (instead of property similar or related in service or use). The special rule, however, only applies to real property held for business use or investment (and not to property held for personal use such as a residence), and only applies if the property is converted by reason of seizure, requisition or condemnation, or threat or imminence thereof (and not by reason of fire, flood, or other catastrophe). If ABC's building were condemned, it would qualify for the special "like-kind" standard in section 1031, and it would not have to meet the more stringent "similar or related in service or use" standard of section 1033.

Furthermore, if ABC's building were condemned, it would have 3 years instead of 2 years to acquire qualified replacement property. Thus, ABC must purchase qualified replacement property by December 31, Year 4—that is, 3 years after the close of December 31, Year 1, which is the year gain was realized (when insurance proceeds in excess of basis became available to ABC).

Chapter 26

Installment Sales

Overview

It is not unusual for sellers and buyers of property to agree that payment will be made in installments over time rather than all at once. Section 453 fosters these installment sale contracts by permitting the seller to recognize the tax gain on such sales over time. Thus, the installment method of reporting is favorable to taxpayers because it defers tax liability until the cash payment (as distinguished from the installment note) is received. This is different from the outcome that would normally arise under either the cash method or the accrual method of accounting.

An installment sale is a sale where at least one payment comes after the end of the year in which the disposition occurs. IRC § 453(b)(1). Some sales are excluded from installment sale treatment, including dealer dispositions and sales of inventory. IRC § 453(b)(2). Nor does the installment method apply to gains arising from the recapture of depreciation. IRC § 453(i). The key to applying the installment method is found in section 453(c). It provides that the tax gain recognized on each payment is that proportion of the payment "which the gross profit . . . bears to the total contract price." This may be stated as a formula applying what is known as the gross profit ratio.

Gross Profit Ratio Formula

Payment × [Gross Profit ÷ Total Contract Price] = Gain Recognized on Payment

The terms "gross profit" (GP), "total contract price" (TKP), and "payment" all have precise definitions set out in the regulations. *Gross profit* means "selling price" (SP) minus the seller's adjusted basis. Treas. Reg. § 15A.453-1(b)(2)(v). *Total contract price* means selling price reduced by "qualifying indebtedness" (QI) not in excess of seller's basis. Treas. Reg. § 15A.453-1(b)(2)(iii). Qualifying indebtedness is the buyer's acquisition indebtedness assumed from the seller. Treas. Reg. § 15A.453-1(b)(2)(iv). *Payment* does not include the evidences of indebtedness that the seller receives from the buyer. Treas. Reg. §§ 1.453-4(c); 15A.453-1(b)(3)(i). Nor does payment include any debt assumption by the buyer to the extent that the debt does not exceed the seller's adjusted basis. *Id.* Nor does the gross profit ratio apply to payments of interest (which are ordinary income to the seller under section 61).

These definitions have great significance when an installment sale involves property transferred subject to a mortgage. In particular, the exclusion of the buyer's assumption of qualifying indebtedness not in excess of basis from treatment as a payment has the effect of allowing the seller to avoid current gain recognition on such assumptions and permits the seller to reduce basis instead.

Transfers of installment notes are subject to a number of special rules. Generally speaking, the transfer of an installment obligation, even as a gift, triggers gain or loss recognition. IRC § 453B(a). If the transfer is a sale, gain or loss recognition is determined by reference to the difference between amount realized and adjusted basis. If the transfer is by gift, the fair market value of the obligation is deemed the amount realized. The adjusted basis of the obligation is determined by deducting from its face value an amount equal to the gain that would have been realized had the installment obligation been paid in full. IRC § 453B(b). Two significant exceptions to the recognition rule of section 453B(a) are transfers at death and transfers between spouses or incident to divorce. IRC § 453B(c) & (g). In both cases, the transferee takes the transferor's basis. IRC §§ 691(a)(4), 1014(c), 453B(g)(2). Thus, the gain remains lurking in the note to be recognized by the transferee.

Primary Authority

Code: §§ 453(a)-(d), (e)(1), (4), (f)(3), (i); 453B(a)-(c), (g)(2); 691(a)(4); 1014(c); 1271(a). Skim §§ 1272(a); 1273(a); 1274(a)-(b).

Regulations: §§ 1.453-4(c); 15A.453-1(b)-(c).

Cases: Shapfa Realty, 8 B.T.A. 283.

Rulings: Rev. Rul. 79-371, 1979-2 C.B. 294.

Problems

26.1. **Jeff, a cash method taxpayer, owns an incorporated newspaper business that has been in his family for generations. His basis in the stock is $10,000,000. In the current year, Jeff sold his stock in the business to his daughter, Kalpana, for $40,000,000. Under the terms of the agreement Jeff receives $2,000,000 cash in the current year and nineteen notes of $2,000,000 each. The notes bear adequate interest at the rate of 3% compounded semi-annually and come due sequentially over the succeeding nineteen years. What are the tax consequences to Jeff in the current and succeeding years in the following circumstances? (Ignore the application, if any, of section 1202.)**

(a) **Jeff does not elect out under section 453(d).**

The installment method applies. IRC § 453(a). Thus, the gross profit formula is utilized to measure Jeff's gain in each year as payments are made.

GP/TKP × payment = income in current year. IRC § 453(c).

His gross profit is $30,000,000 ($40,000,000 SP − $10,000,000 AB = $30,000,000 GP). The gross profit ratio is 3/4 (30 divided by 40). The gross profit percentage is 75%. Thus, the payment received in the current year is $1,500,000 gain and $500,000 return of basis. The same will be true for each note as it is paid. Observe that when all the notes have been paid, Jeff will have will have reported $30,000,000 gain just as if he sold for cash. The difference is one of timing. But 19 years of deferral is a good deal. The character of the gain is not altered by section 453. The interest payments are ordinary income under section 61.

(b) What if in (a) Jeff had borrowed $6,000,000 using the stock as security and Kalpana assumed the debt as part of the sale and only 16 notes are given by Kalpana?

Notice that the selling price is still $40,000,000, the sum of the cash, the notes and the debt assumed.

The debt assumption is only treated as a payment to the extent it exceeds his adjusted basis. *See* Treas. Reg. § 1.453-4(c). Here it does not.

For purposes of computing the gross profit ratio the debt which does not exceed basis is deducted from selling price to arrive at total contract price (making it $34,000,000). *See* Treas. Reg. § 15A.453-1(b)(iii). This is taxpayer favorable since in effect it allows reduction of basis rather than current recognition of *Crane* gain.

Here the effect is to create a gross profit ratio of 15/17ths (approximately 88%). Thus, $3,529,412 of each payment is gain. *See* Treas. Reg. § 15A.453-1(b)(3)(i).

(c) What results in (b) if the mortgage is $12,000,000 and Kalpana gives 13 notes?

Notice that the selling price is still $40,000,000, the sum of the cash, the notes and the debt assumed.

The $2,000,000 of debt assumed in excess of Jeff's basis is a payment. For purposes of computing the gross profit ratio the debt assumed which does not exceed basis is deducted from selling price to arrive at total contract price (making it $30,000,000). *See* Treas. Reg. § 15A.453-1(b)(2)(iii). Thus the gross profit ratio is 1/1.

In Year 1, Jeff has $2,000,000 of *Crane* gain recognized currently and $2,000,000 of gain from the cash payment. In each succeeding year he will recognize $2,000,000 of gain as payment is made.

(d) What if in (a) Jeff sells the 19 notes for $36,000,000?

This triggers section 453B gain recognition on the difference between the amount realized on sale of the notes and his basis in the notes. IRC § 453B(a)(2).

Basis in the notes is determined by taking the face amount of the note and deducting the amount which would have been income had it been paid in full. IRC § 453B(b). $2,000,000 (face) − $1,500,000 (gain) = $500,000 basis × 19 (# of notes) = $9,500,000 AB. $36,000,000 (AR) − $9,500,000 (AB) = $26,500,000 gain realized and recognized.

The character of the gain is same as that on sale of the asset. *See* IRC § 453B(a) (last sentence).

(e) **What if in (a) Jeff gives the 19 notes (which have a fair market value of $36,000,000) to his grandson, Howard , prior to collecting them? What is Howard's basis in the notes?**

This also would constitute a section 453B disposition. We use the fair market value of the notes to calculate the gain recognized. *See* IRC § 453B(a)(2). So the result to Jeff is the same as in (d).

His gain recognition steps up his basis so Howard takes a $36,000,000 basis in the notes ($1,894,737 in each note). IRC § 1015(a). *See* Revenue Ruling 79-371. The character of the notes in Howard's hands is capital but prior to a law change in 1997 when he received payment he would not have been involved in a sale or exchange. *See Shapfa Realty.* Thus, the gain would have been ordinary. Now section 1271(a) provides for sale or exchange treatment on retirement of a note. Observe also that Howard can tack his holding period for the notes. IRC § 1223(2).

As an aside it might be mentioned that Jeff has potential gift tax and generation skipping transfer tax liabilities to pay. It could also be noted that section 1015(d) of the Code provides that if property is acquired by gift, the basis is increased (but not above the fair market value of the property at the time of the gift) by the amount of gift taxes paid with respect to such gift.

(f) **What if in (a) Jeff dies before collecting on the notes and bequeaths them to Howard?**

Section 453B does not apply so no gain is recognized at the time of the bequest. *See* IRC § 453B(c). However, neither does section 1014(a) apply, so there is no date of death basis step up. *See* IRC § 1014(c). Howard succeeds to Jeff's basis of $500,000 in each of the 19 notes and recognizes $1,500,000 of gain ($2,000,000 − $500,000 = $1,500,000) as each is paid just as Jeff would have. The character of the gain will also be determined by reference to its character had Jeff received the payments. *See* IRC § 691(a)(3) & (4). Thus, it will be long-term capital gain.

As an aside it might be noted that the notes would be included in Jeff's gross estate. His estate could owe federal estate tax. Chapter 41 takes a brief look at the gratuitous transfer taxes.

26.2. **Henry is a sculptor who runs his business as a sole proprietor. He agrees to sell a special oven designed to cast large bronze sculptures to Dale, an employee who wants to use the oven to start his own sculpting business. The terms of sale provide that Dale will pay Henry $240,000 in eight annual installments of $30,000 each. The first installment is due in cash upon delivery of the oven. The other seven installments are due over the next seven years and are evidenced by notes bearing interest at 4%. In addition to the payments of cash and the notes, Dale takes the oven subject to a mortgage of $90,000, which Dale assumes. Henry's basis in the oven is $180,000. He has taken $60,000 of depreciation on the oven. What are the income tax consequences of the sale to Henry?**

Note at the outset that selling price is not stated in the problem. One might forget to include the mortgage assumption in the selling price. In any event selling price does include the debt assumption and, thus, is $330,000 ($240,000 + $90,000). *See* Treas. Reg. § 15A.453-1(b)(2)(ii).

The $60,000 depreciation recapture is recognized immediately as ordinary income. IRC §§ 453(i), 1245(a).

This amount is then added to basis for computing the section 453 gross profit of $90,000. ($330,000 SP – $240,000 AB = $90,000 GP).

Since the mortgage does not exceed basis, its assumption is not treated as a payment. *See* Treas. Reg. § 1.453-4(c); *see also* Treas. Reg. § 15A.453-1(b)(2)(iii), (iv). For purposes of computing the gross profit ratio the debt which does not exceed basis is deducted from selling price to arrive at total contract price (making it $240,000). *See* Treas. Reg. § 15A.453-1(b)(2)(iii). Here the effect is to create a gross profit ratio of 90/240 or 3/8 (37.5%). Thus, $11,250 of each $30,000 payment is gain. *See* Treas. Reg. § 15A.453-1(b)(3)(i). This means that in the year of sale Henry has $60,000 of ordinary income and $11,250 of section 1231 gain. The gain is section 1231 gain because the oven is excluded from treatment as a capital asset by § 1221(a)(2) and included within § 1231 by the definition of trade or business property in § 1231(b)(1).

26.3. **Santiago bought a patent for a biological mechanism for healing damaged nerves for $3,000,000,000 as an investment. Three years later he sold the patent to a major drug company for 4% of the earnings from the patent for 10 years up to a maximum stated sales price of $15,000,000,000. He received $1,500,000,000 a year for ten years.**

(a) **What are the income tax consequences of the sale to Santiago?**

The maximum stated sales price is used as the selling price to determine the gross profit. Treas. Reg. § 15A.453-1(c)(2).

$15,000,000,000 – $3,000,000,000 = $12,000,000,000 Gross Profit

$15,000,000,000 = Total Contract Price

4/5 = Gross Profit Ratio

4/5 × 1,500,000,000 (each payment) = $1,200,000,000 gain

The gain is long-term capital gain since the property was held for investment. IRC § 1221(a).

The interest payments are ordinary income to Santiago. IRC § 61.

(b) **What are the tax consequences to Santiago if there is no maximum stated sales price?**

Santiago will recover his basis ratably over 10 years ($300,000,000 per year). IRC § 453(j)(2). Thus, $1,200,000,000 of each payment is gain. *See* Treas. Reg. § 15A.453-1(c)(3).

Chapter 27

Limitations on Deductions

Overview

Some ventures can produce tax benefits without producing any significant economic risk. (Recall Crane v. Commissioner, 331 U.S. 1 (1947), considered in Chapter 3, which created opportunities for taxpayers to lawfully gain large depreciation tax deductions with minimal economic outlays by including non-recourse borrowing in their basis.) This chapter looks at two congressional enactments designed to disallow or defer some deductions otherwise allowable in these situations. The first enactment is section 465, the at risk rules. The second is section 469, the passive loss rules.

Section 465 applies to most business activities for profit in which one participates as a sole proprietor, partner, or a shareholder of a small corporation. *See* IRC § 465(a) (1), (c)(3). Its central message is that an investor is *not* permitted to deduct a loss from such an activity in excess of that investor's amount *at risk* in that activity. IRC § 465(a), (d) (defining a "loss" as the excess of deductions allocable to the activity over income derived from the activity). Generally speaking, the investor's at risk amount is his investment. His investment is equal to his cash contributions, the basis of property contributed, and some borrowed or pledged contributions. IRC § 465(b)(1) & (2). Borrowed contributions that are not included in the investor's at risk amount include funds borrowed directly or indirectly from co-investors and certain non-recourse borrowings. IRC § 465(b)(3) & (4). Any loss that is disallowed in the current year under section 465 carries over to the next year. IRC § 465(a)(2). The carryover is indefinite.

It is implicit in what we have said so far that losses not in excess of a taxpayer's at risk amount in an activity may be used to offset income from another activity. However, each time such a loss is deducted it reduces the taxpayer's amount at risk in the activity that generated the loss. IRC § 465(b)(5). Similarly, a distribution from the business to the investor reduces the investor's at risk amount. Thus, the taxpayer's at risk amount in a particular activity can change from year to year as losses are deducted and distributions are made.

Section 469, the passive loss provision, was enacted in 1986 as part of the most extensive overhaul of our income tax system of the past half century. The provision's plain purpose was to attack tax shelters. But, the attack was somewhat indirect. It separates out a certain class of business activities—passive activities. Gain and loss from these activities are separately aggregated. A net loss from such activities is not permitted to offset income from non-passive activities. IRC § 469(a)(1). Similar rules apply to tax credits in excess of income from passive activities.

A passive activity is a trade or business in which the taxpayer does *not* "materially participate." IRC § 469(c)(1). Material participation is participation in the activity on a "regular," "continuous," and "substantial" basis. IRC § 469(h)(1). The regulations set out detailed criteria for meeting the material participation standard. These include some bright line tests. For example, a person who works in the activity for more than 500 hours in a year is deemed to materially participate and one who works in the activity for less than 100 hours is deemed not to materially participate. *See* Treas. Reg. § 1.469-5T(a)(1), (b)(2)(iii). Because limited partnerships are particularly common tax sheltering mechanisms, a limited partner is automatically deemed *not* a material participant unless the limited partner is also a general partner or meets other requirements. IRC § 469(h)(2); Treas. Reg. § 1.469-5T(e)(1), (2), & (3)(ii). *But see* Thompson v. United States, 87 Fed. Cl. 728 (2009), *acq.* AOD 2010- 02, 2010 I.R.B. 515 (holding that an LLC member materially participated even though he had limited liability). Because rental businesses are common tax shelter devices, a rental activity is automatically deemed passive. IRC § 469(c)(2) & (4). There are exceptions to this rule. One exception is for rental real estate professionals and for those who provide substantial services as part of their rental activity. *See* IRC § 469(c)(7); Treas. Reg. § 1.469-1T(e)(3). Another exception, albeit a limited one, is for rental real estate activities in which the taxpayer who is at least a 10 percent owner "actively participates." IRC § 469(i). If this exception applies, the losses are treated as non-passive up to $25,000. IRC § 469(i)(1) & (2). However, this amount is reduced by one dollar for every two dollars by which the taxpayer's adjusted gross income (determined without regard to passive losses) exceeds $100,000. IRC § 469(i)(3)(A).

A "passive activity loss" is the net loss from all of a taxpayer's passive activities for the year. IRC § 469(d)(1). Thus, for example, if a taxpayer is a limited partner in two activities and one yields a $10,000 loss and the other gives him $2,500 of income, the taxpayer has a $7,500 passive activity loss. The effect of having a passive activity loss, is that it is disallowed. IRC § 469(a). That is, it cannot be deducted against non-passive income. Instead it carries over as a deduction for the next year where it can be used to offset passive income. IRC § 469(b) & (d)(1). It is important to note that portfolio income such as a stock dividend, which seems passive, is not deemed passive for purposes of section 469. IRC § 469(e)(1). Thus, passive losses cannot offset portfolio income. It is also important to remember that dispositions of passive activities by sale can serve to release some or all of the previously disallowed losses for deduction against non-passive income. IRC § 469(g).

Primary Authority

Code: §§ 465(a)(1)-(2), (b)(2), (b)(4), (b)(6)(A)-(B), (e)(1); 469(a)-(b), (c)(1)-(2), (c)(7), (d)(1), (e)(1)(A), (g), (h)(1)-(2), (i)(1)-(3)(A), (i)(6), (j)(6).

Regulations: §§ 1.469-4(c), -5T(a)(1).

Cases: None.

Rulings: None.

Problems

27.1. Andy established a sole proprietorship, TopDog, that manufactures and sells high-end racing bikes for professional triatheletes. Andy contributed $50,000 and a piece of land worth $100,000 in which he had a basis of $75,000. He also borrowed $300,000 on a non-recourse basis. What are the consequences under section 465 in the following circumstances?

(a) In its first year of operation, TopDog lost $175,000.

Andy's beginning at risk amount is $125,000, the sum of the cash and the basis in the contributed property. IRC § 465(b)(1)(A). Thus, only $125,000 of the loss is currently deductible. The loan is clearly not qualified non-recourse financing since it is not for a real estate holding activity. IRC § 465(b)(6)(B). The remaining $50,000 of losses carry over as a deduction next year. IRC § 465(a)(2). Andy's at risk amount falls to zero. IRC § 465(b)(5).

(b) Same as (a) except that the lender has recourse against Andy personally on the $300,000 debt.

Andy's beginning at risk amount is $425,000, the sum of the cash, the basis in the contributed property, and the debt. IRC § 465(b)(1)(A) & (B). Thus, all $175,000 of the loss is currently deductible. Andy's at risk amount falls to $250,000. IRC § 465(b)(5).

(c) Same as (a) except the following year TopDog had net earnings of $100,000.

The $25,000 of suspended losses from Year 1 can be deducted from the second year's earnings. IRC § 465(a)(2).

(d) Same as (b) except that in the following year TopDog has net earnings of $12,000 and the bank agrees to convert the debt, still $300,000, to non-recourse.

The conversion of the debt from recourse to non-recourse causes his at risk amount to fall to – $50,000 ($250,000 – 300,000 = – $50,000). The $12,000 of current year earnings will offset that amount so that Andy is only obliged to report $38,000 of recapture income under section 465(e)(1)(A). Andy will then be entitled to carry over a deduction of that amount into the following year. IRC § 465(e)(1)(B).

27.2. In Year 1, Lionel earns $900,000 of taxable income as a lawyer specializing in mergers and acquisitions. He has another $100,000 of interest income from an investment in corporate bonds. Lionel invests $1,000,000 as a limited partner in SkinSaver LP. SkinSaver holds the patent on a device the size of a quarter that, when carried on a person, effectively blocks all UV rays

by emitting radio signals. This device, known as a UV blocker, is expected to be a big seller eventually. Unfortunately, at the moment it produces some adverse side effects for human beings, including headaches, nausea, and sudden uncontrollable rages. It has not gained government approval for sale to the public but research is continuing. Discuss the consequences under section 469 to Lionel under the following circumstances:

(a) In Year 1, SkinSaver loses money. Lionel's share of those ordinary losses is $100,000. For the year he spends approximately 20 hours, mostly in meetings, managing his interest in SkinSaver.

The income from his legal practice is not passive. IRC § 469(c)(1). Neither is the dividend income. IRC § 469(e)(1)(A)(i)(I). The limited partnership interest is a passive activity. IRC § 469(c)(1), (h)(2). The loss cannot be deducted against Lionel's non-passive income. IRC § 469(a) & (d). The $100,000 loss carries over to next year. IRC § 469(b). Lionel has $1,000,000 of taxable income.

(b) In Year 2, Lionel's earnings from his practice and his bond interest income are the same as in Year 1. Again he has $100,000 of losses from SkinSaver (aggregating to $200,000), but he also invests as a limited partner in Titan LP, which produces titanium and aluminum alloy hip joints that are the gold standard in hip replacements. Lionel has $50,000 of ordinary income from his investment in Titan in Year 2.

Again the SkinSaver loss cannot be deducted against Lionel's non-passive income. IRC § 469(a) & (d). However, the income from Titan is passive income, which can be aggregated with the losses from SkinSaver for a $150,000 net passive activity loss. IRC § 469(a)(1)(A) & (d)(1). The $150,000 aggregate loss carries over to next year. IRC § 469(b). Lionel's Year 2 taxable income is still $1,000,000.

(c) In Year 3, Lionel's earnings from his practice and his bond interest income are the same as in Year 1. This year, SkinSaver again produces $100,000 of losses for Lionel, and again he has $50,000 of income from Titan. However, SkinSaver makes a partial breakthrough in combating the side effects of the UV blocker (milder headaches and fewer sudden rages) and Lionel is able to sell his entire interest in SkinSaver to a major medical supplies manufacturer for a $50,000 long-term capital gain.

The sale of his entire interest in SkinSaver releases his $150,000 carried loss and his $100,000 current loss for recognition against non-passive income. IRC § 469(g)(1)(A) (flush language). But the loss is first allowed against income from the SkinSaver limited partnership interest ($50,000 LTCG in this case), IRC § 469(g)(1)(A)(i), next against gains and income from other passive activities ($50,000 from Titan), IRC § 469(g)(1)(A)(ii). The legislative history of section 469 says that gain from the sale of the activity is treated first as passive income and should be offset by suspended losses from the activity. Sen. Rep. 99-313, 99th Cong. 2d Sess. (1986), 1986 C.B. 3. It may seem unusual to offset capital gains with ordinary losses but it makes sense in this context. This is because the gain arose from the basis reductions in his partnership interest caused by the losses. *See* IRC § 705. This means that $150,000 of losses from Years 1, 2, and 3 can be used to offset non-passive ordinary income in Year 3. Thus, in Year 3, Lionel has $850,000 of taxable income.

Note: Using ordinary losses to offset capital gains is a variation on the assignment of income doctrine. It prevents taking ordinary deductions at the cost of lower taxed capital gains.

> **(d) Same as (c) except that, instead of selling his interest, on December 31ˢᵗ of Year 3, Lionel gifts his partnership interest to his daughter, Mia , at a time when it is worth $1,200,000 and his basis stands at $700,000.**

Since the gift occurred at the end of the year, Lionel will deduct $50,000 of the Year 3 losses against the $50,000 of passive income from Titan. However, Lionel loses his ability to carry over the losses. Instead, Mia is permitted to step up her section 1015 basis by the amount of the $200,000 of carried losses to $900,000. IRC § 469(j)(6).

> **(e) Same as (d) except that Lionel dies on December 31ˢᵗ of Year 3 and leaves his partnership interest to Mia. At the time of Lionel's death, the partnership interest is worth $775,000 and his basis is $700,000.**

Since the death occurred at the end of the year, Lionel's executor will deduct $50,000 of the Year 3 losses against the $50,000 of passive income from Titan on his final return. Death also releases the carried losses for deduction on the decedent's final tax return except to the extent of the basis step up the beneficiary receives under section 1014. IRC § 469(g)(2). Since Mia's basis is stepped up by $75,000 to $775,000 under section 1014(a), only $125,000 of losses are deductible on Lionel's final return ($150,000 carried losses + $50,000 passive losses in excess of passive income in current year – $75,000 basis step up = $125,000).

> **27.3. Ozzie and Harriet jointly own, in its entirety, a ten-unit apartment building which they actively manage and maintain. In the current year, the building generates a $30,000 tax loss because of a glut of rental properties on the market. What are the tax consequences to Ozzie and Harriet in the following circumstances?**

> **(a) The loss from the apartment building aside, Ozzie and Harriet have $90,000 of adjusted gross income and file a joint return.**

The general rule is that rental activities are deemed passive. IRC § 469(c)(2). But since they actively participate in this rental real estate activity, they can deduct $25,000 of the loss. IRC § 469(i)(1) & (2). This yields a new adjusted gross income of $65,000. The phase out rule of section 469(i)(3) does not apply. Note that the dollar limit in section 469(i)(2) would be split if they filed separately. IRC § 469(i)(5)(A)(i). The $5,000 excess loss carries over to next year. IRC § 469(b).

(b) Same as (a) except that their adjusted gross income is $130,000.

Now the phase out rule of section 469(i)(3) does apply since their adjusted gross income (determined without regard to their passive loss) exceeds $100,000. Their deductible loss is reduced one dollar for every two dollars of such excess. IRC § 469(i)(3)(A), (i)(3)(F)(iv). Here the reduction is $15,000. Thus, they can only deduct $10,000 of the loss currently. This yields an adjusted gross income of $120,000 and a loss carryover of $20,000. IRC § 469(b).

27.4. Michael is a general partner in two businesses in San Francisco. The first is a very profitable high-end shop selling women's clothing that Michael manages on a full time basis. The second is a mildly profitable upscale jewelry store in which Michael does not materially participate. Michael and his partners plan to open a fashion shop and a jewelry store in Portland. Michael will also be a general partner in each new business, but he does not plan to manage either of them on a daily basis. The Portland jewelry store is the riskier of the two new enterprises and also involves the larger capital outlay. If it does not reach breakeven status within two years, the partners plan to close it and liquidate its assets. Assuming all four businesses will have identical ownership arrangements, how should Michael seek to structure his business interests under section 469?

He could group his two jewelry store interests into one activity and the two fashion shops as one activity since they are probably appropriate economic units. *See* Treas. Reg. § 1.469-4(c)(2). If so, he can meet material participation requirements for both fashion shops but not for the jewelry stores. Treas. Reg. § 1.469-5T(a), -4(c). Any losses from the Portland jewelry store could be offset against his share of the income from the San Francisco jewelry store. However, if the Portland jewelry store losses exceed the San Francisco jewelry store income, they would be suspended. Moreover, if the Portland jewelry store fails, his losses could fail to qualify for release under section 469(g)(1)(A) since it would not be a disposition of his entire interest in the activity.

He could treat the San Francisco businesses as one activity and the Portland businesses as one activity and thus be passive as to the Portland operation. *See* Treas. Reg. § 1.469-4(c)(2)(iv), -4(c)(3), ex. 1. Since both Portland businesses may have losses initially, this does not seem particularly beneficial. Moreover, as above, if the Portland jewelry store fails, his losses could fail to qualify for release under section 469(g)(1)(A) since it would not be a disposition of his entire interest in the activity.

He could treat all four businesses as separate activities. This would make all but the San Francisco fashion shop passive. Since it has the most income that is probably not the best route to take. However, it does have the advantage of freeing up the losses under section 469(g)(1)(A) of any business if he sells his interest.

He could seek to treat all four businesses as one activity since they have common ownership. *See* Treas. Reg. § 1.469-4(c)(2)(iii). If so, he can meet material participation requirements for all four businesses. Treas. Reg. § 1.469-5T(a), -4(c). This is the most favorable route to follow since any losses from the Portland activities could be applied against the income of the San Francisco fashion shop, the most profitable of the businesses.

Once he chooses his treatment he cannot change it easily. Treas. Reg. § 1.469-4(e)(1).

Chapter 28

Intellectual Property Development and Acquisitions

Overview

Intellectual property has become enormously important in recent years as valuable business assets are frequently found in the form of intangibles, such as patents, trade secrets, copyrights, trademarks, trade names, and computer software. Although many of the general tax principles we have considered in this book are applicable to most types of intellectual property, there are some special tax rules that exclusively govern certain types of intellectual property. This chapter addresses the tax treatment of intellectual property creation and acquisitions. The next chapter addresses the tax treatment of intellectual property sales and licenses.

Intellectual Property Creation. Under the general capitalization rules of sections 263 and 263A, considered in Chapter 8, a taxpayer is required to capitalize amounts paid to create intangible assets. Treas. Reg. § 1.263(a)-4(b). But, for various tax policy reasons (e.g., to encourage intellectual property creation, to close tax loopholes and remove tax inequities, or to simplify rules and eliminate uncertainties), the government has created a number of exceptions to the general capitalization rules. *See, e.g.*, IRC § 174 (research and experimental expenditures), § 181 (qualified film production costs), § 263A(h) (qualified creative expenses); Treas. Reg. § 1.263(a)-4(b)(3)(iv) (computer software development costs), -4(b)(3)(v) (package design costs); Rev. Proc. 2000-50 (computer software development costs); Rev. Rul. 92-40 (advertising costs). The result is that some intellectual property creation costs are deductible in full at the time of expenditure; some development costs are permitted to be deducted only over a prescribed time period; and some development costs are not deductible at all, and can be recovered only upon abandonment or the eventual transfer of the developed intellectual property (in the form of an offset of the selling price). Some intellectual property creation costs are eligible for a tax credit instead of a deduction.

Intellectual Property Acquisitions. Royalties paid under a license for the use of intellectual property are typically deductible in the year paid. IRC § 162(a)(3). In contrast, amounts paid to purchase intellectual property are not currently deductible but rather must be capitalized. Treas. Reg. § 1.263(a)-4(b)(1)(i). The capitalized costs of purchasing intellectual property may be recovered over a certain time period through an appropriate depreciation or amortization allowance. Section 197 provides an arbitrary fifteen-year recovery period for many types of intellectual property. IRC § 197(a), (d). If section 197 does not apply, depreciation continues to be governed by pre-section 197 law—or section 167. Treas. Reg. § 1.167(a)-14. Under section 167, acquired intellectual property that is not subject to section 197 can be depreciated if the intellectual property has a useful life that can be determined with reasonable accuracy. Treas. Reg. § 1.167(a)-3. The most common depreciation methods are the straight line method and the income forecast method, which are addressed in the problems below.

Primary Authority

Code: §§ 167(a), (c), (f)(1), (g); 174; 197(a)-(d), (e)(3)-(4), (f)(4)(C); 263(a); 263A(a), (b)(1), (c)(2), (h); 1253(d). Skim §§ 41(a)(1), (c)(4), (d)(1); 179(d); 181(a), (d).

Regulations: §§ 1.167(a)-1(b), -3(a), -14(a), (c)(4); 1.167(b)-1(a); 1.174-2(a); 1.197-2(a), -2(b)(1), (5), (10), -2(c)(4)-(5), (7), -2(d)(2)(i), -2(e)(1)-(2), -2(f)(1)-(2), -2(g)(8). Skim § 1.263A-1(e)(2)-(3), -2(a)(2).

Cases: Avery v. Commissioner, 47 B.T.A. 538 (1942); Cleveland v. Commissioner, 297 F.2d 169, 173 (4th Cir. 1961); Diamond v. Commissioner, 92 T.C. 423 (1989), *aff'd*, 930 F.2d 372 (4th Cir. 1991); Houston Chronicle Publ'g Co. v. United States, 481 F.2d 1240 (5th Cir. 1973); Kantor v. Commissioner, 998 F.2d 1514 (9th Cir. 1993); Kilroy v. Commissioner, 41 T.C.M. (CCH) 292, 295 (1980); Lockheed Martin Corp. v. Network Solutions, Inc., 985 F. Supp. 949 (C.D. Cal. 1997); Louw v. Commissioner, 30 T.C.M. (CCH) 1421 (1971); Nabisco v. Commissioner, 76 T.C.M. (CCH) 71 (U.S. Tax Ct. 1998); Reinke v. Commissioner, 41 T.C.M. (CCH) 1100, 1102 (1981); Saykally v. Commissioner, T.C. Memo 2003-152; Schneider v. Commissioner, 65 T.C. 18 (1975); Snow v. Commissioner, 416 U.S. 500 (1974); Spellman v. Commissioner, 845 F.2d 148 (7th Cir. 1988); Wildman v. Commissioner, 78 T.C. 943 (1982); Zink v. United States, 929 F.2d 1015 (5th Cir. 1991).

Rulings: Rev. Rul. 60-358, 1960-2 C.B. 68, amplified by Rev. Rul. 79-285, 1979-2 C.B. 91; Rev. Rul. 69-484, 1969-2 C.B. 38; Rev. Rul. 73-20, 1973-1 C.B. 133; Rev. Rul. 92-80, 1992-2 C.B. 57; Rev. Proc. 2000-50, 2000-2 C.B. 601; IRS Field Service Advice 200125019s.

Problems

28.1. Jasmina, Inc., a successful perfume manufacturing company, decides to create a new perfume to sell to teenage girls. Discuss the deductibility of expenses incurred by Jasmina during the current year:

(a) Jasmina spent $150,000 to conduct consumer surveys to determine the preference of potential customers. Jasmina then spent the following amounts to create the new perfume: (1) $50,000 to acquire a new

machine to be used in connection with research and experimentation activities; (2) $100,000 to actually develop the basic scent; (3) $25,000 to determine whether the perfume causes an allergic reaction; and (4) $35,000 to develop alternative perfumes with different scents and colors. Later, Jasmina spent $35,000 in attorneys' fees in the prosecution of a patent application, and $50,000 on the development of graphic and package designs for the new perfume.

We should focus on whether these costs are deductible under section 174, since section 174 is not subject to the capitalization rules of section 263 or section 263A. *See* IRC §§ 263(a)(1)(B), 263A(c)(2). If section 174 does not apply, then costs must be capitalized unless an exception to capitalization exists that would open the door for current deduction under section 162. For example, expenditures for advertising are specifically excluded from section 174 under the theory that such expenses do not relate to the actual development of a new product (see Treas. Reg. § 1.174-2(a) (3)(v)). However, expenditures for ordinary product advertising have long been held currently deductible under section 162 despite the fact that advertising expenditures often produce long-term benefits. Rev. Rul. 92-80.

$150,000 to conduct consumer surveys: Jasmina will not be able to deduct the $150,000 under section 174. Certain expenditures incurred in the development of intellectual property are specifically excluded from the definition of "research and experimental expenditures" and will not qualify for section 174 treatment. The regulations specifically provide that business management expenses, such as efficiency surveys, management surveys, and consumer surveys do not qualify as research or experimental expenditures. Treas. Reg. § 1.174-2(a)(3)(ii)-(iv).

If we view the consumer surveys as "advertising," then Jasmina could deduct the $150,000 under section 162 (ordinary and necessary expense in carrying on a trade or business). *See* Rev. Rul. 92-80.

$50,000 to acquire a new machine to be used in connection with R&D: Section 174 does not apply to amounts spent to acquire depreciable property even if the taxpayer uses the property in connection with its R&D activities. IRC § 174(c); Treas. Reg. § 1.174-2(b). However, any depreciation allowances with respect to depreciable property that is used by a taxpayer in connection with research and experimentation are considered as research and experimental expenditures for purposes of section 174 (to the extent that the property is used in connection with research). *Id.*

$100,000 to actually develop the basic scent: This expenditure is currently deductible. Section 174 research or experimental expenditures are broadly defined as "expenditures incurred in connection with the taxpayer's trade or business which represent research and development costs in the *experimental or laboratory sense*," and generally include "all costs incident to the development or improvement of a product." Treas. Reg. § 1.174-2(a)(1) (emphasis added). A product, for these purposes, "includes any pilot model, process, formula, invention, technique, patent, or similar

property" that is either "used by the taxpayer in its trade or business [or] held for sale, lease, or license" by the taxpayer. Treas. Reg. § 1.174-2(a)(2). "[T]he nature of the product or improvement being developed or the level of technological advancement the product or improvement represents" is not relevant in determining whether the related expenditure qualifies as a section 174 research or experimental expenditure. Treas. Reg. § 1.174-2(a)(1). Instead, the focus is on the "nature of the activity to which the expenditures relate." *Id.*

The regulations expand on the definition of research and experimental expenditures by clarifying that expenditures are incurred in the "experimental or laboratory" sense if they are incurred in "activities intended to discover information that would eliminate *uncertainty* concerning the development or improvement of a product." *Id.* (emphasis added). If (1) the capability or method for developing or improving the product, or (2) the appropriate design of the product, are not established by the information available to the taxpayer, then "uncertainty" exists. *Id.* Under this uncertainty test, the information available to a taxpayer does not have to be information reasonably available. Rather, the focus should be on information that is actually available and on procedures actually involved as opposed to procedures generally in the nature of research activities. Also, the process of determining the appropriate design of a product qualifies as research, even though a taxpayer knows at the outset that the product development project will be successful.

In this problem, Jasmina has decided to create a new perfume to sell to teenage girls. The costs of developing the basic scent should qualify under section 174. If you are in doubt, review IRS Field Service Advice 200125019. This field service advice concluded that expenditures incurred to design, develop, modify, and improve athletic footwear constituted "research and experimental expenditures" under section 174.

$25,000 to determine whether the perfume causes an allergic reaction: The costs relating to the functional aspects of the perfume, such as whether it causes an allergic reaction, qualify as section 174 expenditures. Some may suggest that the $25,000 is for "quality control testing," and that the section 174 regulations exclude from the definition of research or experimental expenditures those expenditures for inspection of materials or products for quality control. Treas. Reg. § 1.174-2(a)(3). But Treas. Reg. § 1.174-2(a)(4) provides that the exclusion for quality control testing does not apply to testing to determine whether the design of the product is appropriate. As noted by IRS Field Service Advice 200125019, "[i]f a taxpayer finds that the design of its product is inappropriate, then the research is not completed and the taxpayer must resume its research activities."

$35,000 to develop alternative perfumes with different scents and colors: In Field Service Advice 200125019, the Service clarified that any distinction between the functional and nonfunctional aspects of the product is irrelevant. Here, the fact that Jasmina's activities are with respect to the development or improvement of any nonfunctional aspects of the perfume product is, by itself, not a supportable basis for disallowance under section 174. The $35,000 costs of developing alternative perfumes

(with different scents and colors) should qualify under section 174, even though the alternatives do not alter the basic design specifications of the perfume.

$35,000 in attorney's fees in the prosecution of a patent application: The regulations under section 174 specifically provide that the costs of obtaining a patent are research and experimental expenditures. Treas. Reg. § 1.174-2(a)(1). Such costs include not only expenses incurred in creating patentable technology, but also attorney's fees in the prosecution of patent applications. *Id.*

$50,000 on the development of graphic and package designs for the new perfume: The $50,000 advertising/promotion costs associated with the development of graphic and package designs for the new perfume do not constitute research and experimental expenditures under section 174. Treas. Reg. § 1.174-2(a)(3)(v). Section 174 does not apply under the theory that such expenses do not relate to the actual development of a new product. Advertising typically occurs after research is completed for the purpose of evaluating and disseminating the results of the research. *See* IRS Field Service Advice 200125019.

Although advertising costs are not deductible under section 174, they are typically deductible under section 162—notwithstanding the fact that the advertising will likely produce benefits that continue well beyond the year. Review Revenue Ruling 92-80, wherein the Service ruled that ordinary business advertising expenditures are not subject to the general capitalization rules and are currently deductible under section 162 even though they produce long-term future benefits. Under that ruling, advertising costs must be capitalized only in the unusual circumstance where advertising is directed towards obtaining future benefits significantly beyond those traditionally associated with ordinary product advertising or with institutional or goodwill advertising. *See also Nabisco, Inc. v. Commissioner* (applying Revenue Ruling 92-80 and holding that both "advertising campaign expenditures" and "advertising execution expenditures" were deductible as an ordinary and necessary business expenses under section 162 even though some of the costs provided long-term, intangible benefits).

Does it matter here that the advertising costs relate to the development of graphic and package designs for the perfume? Prior to 2004, the Service's position was that package design costs were distinguishable from advertising costs and were, therefore, nondeductible capital expenditures. *See* Rev. Proc. 2002-9, 2002-3 I.R.B. 327 (app. § 3.01); Rev. Proc. 97-35, 1997-2 C.B. 48 (§ 5); Rev. Rul. 89-23, 1989-1 C.B. 85. In January 2004, the Service issued final regulations under section 263 that require capitalization of amounts paid to create separate and distinct intangible assets. Treas. Reg. § 1.263(a)-4(b)(1)(iii). These regulations provide, however, that an amount paid to create a package design is *not* treated as an amount that creates a separate and distinct intangible asset. Treas. Reg. § 1.263(a)-4(b)(3)(v) (describing the term "package design" as "the specific graphic arrangement or design of shapes, colors, words, pictures, lettering, and other elements on a given product package, or the design of a container with respect to its shape or function"). Accordingly, any portion of the costs allocable to package designs for the perfume are deductible under section 162.

    (b) Same as (a), above, except that instead of incurring in-house expenses to create the new perfume (e.g., salaries for researchers and materials and supplies used in the course of research), Jasmina paid a third party to create the perfume, which Jasmina manufactured, marketed, and sold.

Section 174 applies not only to costs paid or incurred for research undertaken directly by the taxpayer, but also to costs paid or incurred for research carried on in the taxpayer's behalf by another person or organization (e.g., payments to a research institute, foundation, engineering company, or similarly contractor). Treas. Reg. § 1.174-2(a)(2); Rev. Rul. 69-484 (ruling that payments made by an airline to an aircraft manufacturer were section 174 expenditures); Rev. Rul. 73-20 (ruling that payments by a utility company to a nonprofit research group were section 174 expenditures). Whether payments to others are for research or some other purpose is a question of fact. *See Reinke v. Commissioner.* In sum, the results should be the same as in (a), above.

    (c) Would your answers to (a) or (b), above, change if Jasmina was a new start-up company developing its first perfume, which it planned to manufacture, market, and sell? What if Jasmina was a new start-up company that merely expected to license the patent to another perfume manufacturing company?

Expenditures incurred in the development of the perfume are deductible under section 174 if incurred "in connection with a trade or business." IRC § 174(a). Because Jasmina, Inc. is currently engaged in manufacturing perfume, it satisfies the "in connection with" requirement. What if Jasmina were a start-up business enterprise? Would the "in connection with" requirement of section 174 be met? The Supreme Court in *Snow v. Commissioner* analyzed whether the section 174 deduction applies to start-up businesses. As interpreted by the Supreme Court, the "in connection with" standard does not require that a taxpayer actually be carrying on an existing, ongoing business in order to deduct intellectual property creation costs. In fact, the taxpayer need not be currently producing or selling any product in order to utilize section 174. (As a result of *Snow*, the "in connection with" requirement of section 174 is more lenient than the "in carrying on" requirement under section 162.) Although a taxpayer need not be currently conducting a business in order for research or experimental expenditures to meet the "in connection with a trade or business" requirement under section 174, it must, however, demonstrate a realistic prospect of entering into a trade or business that will exploit the technology under development. *See Kantor v. Commissioner; Zink v. United States; Spellman v. Commissioner; Diamond v. Commissioner.* In sum, the answers above would not change if Jasmina was a new start-up company developing its first perfume, which it planned to manufacture, market, and sell.

If Jasmina merely intended to exploit the patent through license, however, the results above may be different. As a general rule, the receipt of royalties alone does not constitute a trade or business. H.R. Rep. No. 97-201, at 113 (1981), 1981-2 C.B.

352. *See Saykally v. Commissioner* (holding that a computer software developer could not claim section 174 deductions where his research and development activities amounted to nothing more than the development of property rights that he intended to license to his wholly-owned company for use in the company's business). Courts have held, however, that in-house research activities and exploitation of the resulting inventions by sale or license may constitute a trade or business. *See Avery v. Commissioner; Kilroy v. Commissioner; Louw v. Commissioner.* Although such cases permitting deductions typically involve an inventor who has had a series of inventions, multiple inventions are not necessary to establish a trade or business of inventing and exploiting inventions by sale or license. *See Cleveland v. Commissioner.*

28.2. ABC, Inc., a company that publishes general reference books, decides to publish textbooks for use in high schools. ABC incurs expenses to develop the theme and topic of each textbook, obtain manuscripts from authors, edit the textbooks, and obtain illustrations.

(a) What is the general tax treatment of ABC's expenditures?

Costs incurred by a commercial publisher in creating works that are subject to copyright protection are generally not currently deductible under section 174 or section 162.

Section 174 does not apply because expenses in producing copyrightable works do not constitute "research and experimental expenditures" within the meaning of section 174. Section 174 expenditures are limited to "research and development costs in the experimental or laboratory sense" (i.e., costs incident to the development or improvement of a product, including any pilot, model, process, formula, invention, technique, or similar property). Treas. Reg. § 1.174-2(a)(1), -2(a)(2). Section 174 does not apply to costs "for research in connection with literary, historical, or similar projects" including costs incurred in the production of films, sound recordings, video tapes and books. These costs must be capitalized unless an exception exists. Treas. Reg. § 1.174-2(a)(3).

Section 162 generally does not apply to the costs paid or incurred by publishers in producing copyrightable books. Section 263A requires a taxpayer to capitalize all direct and indirect expenditures incurred to produce tangible personal property as part of a trade or business or activity conducted for profit. IRC § 263A. The phrase "tangible personal property" is defined under the Code to include a film, sound recording, video tape, book, or similar property that embodies the words, ideas, concepts, images, or sounds by the creator thereof. IRC § 263A(b); Treas. Reg. § 1.263A-2(a)(2)(ii). "Similar property" is defined under the regulations as "intellectual or creative property for which, as costs are incurred in producing the property, it is intended (or is reasonably likely) that any tangible medium in which the property is embodied will be mass distributed by the creator or any one or more third parties in a form that is not substantially altered." Treas. Reg. § 1.263A-2(a)(2)(ii). As can be seen, section 263A clearly applies to the costs of producing a book.

Section 263A(h) provides an important exemption from the capitalization requirements of section 263A. But the exemption provision of section 263A(h) is narrow in that it is limited to only certain individuals—writers, photographers, and artists as those terms are defined in the statute. A "writer" is defined as an individual whose personal efforts create, or may be expected to create, a literary manuscript, musical composition, or dance score. IRC § 263A(h)(3)(A). A publisher, such as ABC, would obviously not qualify for the exemption.

Because the exemption provision of section 263A(h) does not apply to a commercial publisher, ABC's expenditures must be capitalized under the uniform capitalization rules of § 263A. *See* Treas. Reg. § 1.263A-2(a)(2)(ii)(A)(1) (clarifying that the capitalization rules apply to prepublication costs by commercial publishers, including the costs of writing, editing, compiling, illustrating, and designing books or similar property). The costs that must be capitalized include all direct material and direct labor costs, as well as indirect material and labor costs. IRC § 263A(a)(2)(A); Treas. Reg. § 1.263A-1(e)(2)(I), -1(e)(3)(ii). Certain costs, however, do not need to be capitalized. For example, selling and distribution costs, such as marketing, selling, and advertising costs, do not fall within the ambit of section 263A. Treas. Reg. § 1.263A-1(e)(3)(iii)(A). Moreover, costs incurred in the rendition of services are not within the uniform capitalization rules of section 263A, even if the rendition of services results in the production of intellectual property. Treas. Reg. § 1.263A-2(a)(2)(ii)(B)(2).

The costs will be capitalized into ABC's book inventory, and recovered as the books are sold.

(b) Will the individual authors generally be entitled to deduct fully their expenses in preparing and writing the manuscripts?

The first issue is whether the uniform capitalization rules of section 263A(a) apply to individual authors writing a book, as with commercial publishers. As noted above, section 263A requires a taxpayer to capitalize all direct and indirect expenditures incurred to produce tangible personal property as part of a trade or business or activity conducted for profit. IRC § 263A(a). Although § 263A mentions "tangible personal property," the phrase actually applies to several types of intellectual property that are considered intangible property. The phrase "tangible personal property" is defined under the Code to include a film, sound recording, video tape, book, or similar property that embodies the words, ideas, concepts, images, or sounds by the creator thereof. IRC § 263A(b); Treas. § 1.263A-2(a)(2)(ii). "Similar property" is defined under the regulations as "intellectual or creative property for which, as costs are incurred in producing the property, it is intended (or is reasonably likely) that any tangible medium in which the property is embodied will be mass distributed by the creator or any one or more third parties in a form that is not substantially altered." Treas. Reg. § 1.174-2(a)(2)(ii). Accordingly, section 263A(a) applies to costs incurred by the individual authors in preparing and writing the manuscripts. [In sum, with respect to the production of books, the uniform capitalization rules apply, regardless of whether the taxpayer is a commercial publisher or an individual author writing a book. *See* H.R. Conf. Rep. No. 99-841, at II-308 (1986), *reprinted in* 1986 U.S.C.C.A.N. 4079, 4396 fn. 1 (1986) (clarifying that the uniform capitalization rules were expanded to apply to the costs of "researching and writing a book").]

The second, and perhaps most important issue, is whether the individual authors will qualify for the exemption provided in section 263A(h). As noted above, section 263A(h) provides an important, but narrow, exemption from the capitalization requirements of section 263A in the case of certain writers, photographers, and artists. Section 263A(h), which was added to the Code in 1988, provides that "qualified creative expenses" are not required to be capitalized. IRC § 263A(h); H.R. Rep. No. 100-795, at 531 (1988); H.R. Conf. Rep. No. 100-1104, at 145 (1988), *reprinted in* 1988 U.S.C.C.A.N. 5048, 5205 (noting the purpose of the exemption was to relieve writers, photographers, and artists from the burden of the uniform capitalized rules, especially when their activities may not generate income for years). A qualified creative expense is defined as any expense paid or incurred by an individual in the trade or business of being a "writer," "photographer," or "artist," which, except for the uniform capitalization rules of section 263A, would be otherwise deductible for the taxable year. IRC § 263A(h)(3).

The exemption provision of section 263A(h) is narrow in several respects. First, the exemption is not so broad as to include all individuals engaged in any creative activity. Rather it is limited to only certain individuals—writers, photographers, and artists as those terms are defined in the statute. A "writer" is defined as an individual whose personal efforts create, or may be expected to create, a literary manuscript, musical composition, or dance score. IRC § 263A(h)(3)(A). [Although not relevant in this problem, "photographers" and "artists" are defined at IRC § 263A(h)(3)(B) & (C).] Second, the exemption provision of section 263A(h) is limited only to individuals who are writers, photographers, or artists whose activities rise to the level of a trade or business within the meaning of the Code. If an individual's activities do not rise to the level of a trade or business, then the uniform capitalization rules apply. Finally, even if an individual is engaged in the trade or business of being a writer, photographer, or artist, not all expenses are deemed to be "qualified creative expenses." The Code specifically provides that a qualified creative expense does not include "any expense related to printing, photographic plates, motion picture films, video tapes, or similar items." IRC § 263A(h)(2).

The exemption provision of section 263A(h) should apply to the individual authors in this problem. Accordingly, qualified creative expenses paid or incurred by the authors in writing the books are not subject to the uniform capitalization rules of section 263A, and may be deductible if the elements of section 162 are satisfied. Under section 162, the qualified creative expenses must be "ordinary and necessary." Moreover, the qualified creative expenses must be paid or incurred by an individual in "carrying on" an existing "trade or business" as opposed to one that is associated with the development of a new business.

28.3. LenderTree, Inc., a new company that is in the business of lending money, spent $10,000 to register the federal trademark "LenderTree" (official fees paid to the U.S. Patent and Trademark Office and fees paid to a trademark attorney who took care of the process). LenderTree also paid $5,000 to purchase the domain name "lendertree.com" from a third party who already owned that domain name, and paid $3,000,000 to purchase the domain name "loans.com" from a third party who already owned that domain name.

(a) Is the federal trademark "LenderTree" a section 197 intangible amortizable over fifteen years?

Yes. In 1993, Congress enacted section 197, which provides for a fifteen-year recovery period for certain intangible assets. Although not applicable to self-created patents, trade secrets, know-how, and copyrights (*see* IRC § 197(c)(2)); Treas. Reg. § 1.197-2(d)(2)), section 197 does apply to self-created trademarks and trade names (*see* IRC § 197(d)(1)(F); Treas. Reg. § 1.197-2(b)(10)). As a result, the capitalized costs incurred in connection with the registration of the trademark "LenderTree" are to be amortized over fifteen years.

(b) Is the domain name "lendertree.com" a section 197 intangible amortizable over fifteen years?

Yes. Purchased domain names are not mentioned in section 197. Purchased trademarks, however, are listed as section 197 intangibles. IRC § 197(d)(1)(F) (listing trademarks as section 197 intangibles). For purposes of section 197, the term "trademark" includes any word, name, symbol, or device, or any combination thereof, adopted and used to identify good or services and distinguish them from those provided by others. Treas. Reg. § 1.197-2(b)(10). Domain names have dual functions. In addition to the technical function of locating a site on the Web, a domain name can function as a trademark if it is used to identify the source of goods or services. *See* Lockheed Martin Corp. v. Network Solutions, Inc., 985 F. Supp. 949 (C.D. Cal. 1997). Accordingly purchase costs allocable to domain names that function as trademarks (like "lendertree.com") are to be amortized ratably over a 15-year period.

(c) Is the domain name "loans.com" a section 197 intangible amortizable over fifteen years?

The answer is not clear. Take a look at the list of section 197 intangibles in section 197(d) and consider whether or not generic domain names fit within any of the categories.

The IRS recently issued Chief Counsel Advice 201543014, which concluded that a generic domain name is a customer-based intangible as defined in Treas. Reg. § 1.197-2(b)(6) if (a) the generic domain name is associated with a website that is already constructed and will be maintained by the purchaser, and (b) such taxpayer acquired the generic domain name for use in its trade or business. This assumes that the taxpayer is aquiring an already existing site. It does not suggest what would happen if the domain name was purchased from someone who simply owned the name but was not using it.

28.4. On January 1, Year 1, American Seating Company purchased from a young inventor a patented leveling device for tables and chairs for $100,000, and immediately began using the patented device. American Seating Co. estimated that the patented invention would produce $160,000 of income during its 8-year useful life, after which it would have no salvage value. The patent, which was not acquired as part of the acquisition of a trade or business and which had a remaining legal life of 18 years, actually produced $80,000 of income within the first taxable year, $40,000 of income in the second year, and only $1,600 of income in the third year.

(a) Is the patent amortizable under section 197?

If a patent is not acquired with a trade or business or substantial portion thereof, it is excluded from the application of section 197. As a result, the purchase costs of the separately acquired patent are not subject to amortization on a fifteen-year schedule. IRC § 197(e)(4)(C); Treas. Reg. § 1.197-2(c)(7).

(b) If the answer to (a) is no, is the patent depreciable under section 167?

As was the case under pre-section 197 law, a separately-acquired patent is an intangible asset that is eligible for depreciation under section 167. [Treas. Reg. § 1.167(a)-14 provides rules for the depreciation of certain assets not covered by section 197. For separately-acquired patents, the rules of Treas. Reg. § 1.167(a)-14(c)(4) are similar to the pre-section 197 rules (e.g., the basis is depreciated either ratably over its remaining useful life OR under section 167(g) (income-forecast method).] In fact, the regulations under section 167 list patents as examples of intangible assets that may be depreciated, provided the useful life of the patent can be reasonably estimated, and the taxpayer is engaged in either a trade or business or an activity conducted for profit. IRC § 167(a); Treas. Reg. § 1.167(a)-3.

(c) Assuming section 167 applies, what are the proper deductions for Years 1-3 under the straight-line method and income-forecast method?

There are different methods of depreciating the capitalized costs of purchased patents under section 167. The regulations provide that depreciation must be determined in accordance with a "reasonably consistent plan." Common methods are the straight-line method and the income-forecast method, both of which are considered in this problem. Some methods are generally not available. For example, the sliding-scale method, under which amortization is typically computed based on a declining rate of exhaustion over time, is typically unavailable. *See* Rev. Rul. 60-358, which was amplified by Rev. Rul. 79-285. Likewise, the cost-recovery method, under which a taxpayer can recover all costs before reporting any income, is generally unavailable. *See Schneider v. Commissioner.*

Straight-line method: The simplest depreciation method is the straight-line method, under which the capitalized costs of acquiring property (less salvage value) are deducted ratably over the period the taxpayer expects the property to be useful in its trade or business. [Note: The regulations contemplate use of the straight-line method unless a "different acceptable method" has been adopted. Treas. Reg. § 1.167(b)-1(a).] It should be noted that patent costs do not have to be amortized over the remaining legal term (in this case eighteen years). The regulations provide that the useful life of property is not necessarily the useful life inherent in an asset, but rather the "period over which the asset may reasonably be expected to be useful to the taxpayer in his trade or business or in the production of income." Treas. Reg. § 1.167(a)-1(b). Further, a taxpayer needs only to establish useful life with "reasonable accuracy." Treas. Reg. § 1.167(a)-3. According to one court, "[e]xtreme exactitude in ascertaining the duration of an asset is a paradigm that the law does not demand. All that the law and the regulations require is a reasonable accuracy in forecasting the asset's useful life." *Houston Chronicle Publ'g Co. v. United States*. In this case, the regulatory definition of useful life permits a faster recovery of the costs of acquiring the patented leveling device. In short, assuming that salvage value was zero, American Seating Company would be entitled to depreciation deductions of $12,500 in each of Years 1–3 ($100,000/8 years) using the straight-line method.

Income-forecast method. A permitted, alternative depreciation method is the "income-forecast" method. The IRS originally permitted use of the income-forecast method to amortize films, taped shows, and "other property of a similar character." *See* Rev. Rul. 60-358. It later extended its definition of "other property of a similar character" to include patents. *See* Rev. Rul. 79-285. The Code now limits the use of the income-forecast method to (1) motion picture films, video tapes, and sound recordings; (2) copyrights; (3) books; (4) patents; and (5) other property to be specified in the regulations. IRC § 167(g)(6). The income-forecast method is appropriate for these types of property (including the patent on the leveling device in this problem) because they possess unique income earning characteristics. For instance, the income potential of the leveling device will vary as a direct result of its popularity; the patent's economic usefulness cannot be measured adequately by the passage of time.

Under the income-forecast method, patent acquisition costs are recoverable as income is earned from the exploitation of the patent (*e.g.*, amortization flows from income). Under the income-forecast method, the taxpayer takes a depreciation deduction each year equal to a certain percentage of the basis in the patent. The percentage is determined through a fraction. The numerator of the fraction is the income from the asset for the taxable year. The denominator is the forecasted or estimated total income to be earned in connection with the asset during its useful life. American Seating Company's depreciation deduction each year using the income-forecast method would be:

Year 1's depreciation would be $50,000 [($80,000/$160,000) × $100,000].
Year 2's depreciation would be $25,000 [($40,000/$160,000) × $100,000].
Year 3's depreciation deduction would be $1,000 [($1,600/$160,000) × $100,000].

Comparison of Methods. After comparing the results of using both the straight-line and income-forecast methods, consider the relevant benefits and drawbacks of each method. The benefit of using the income-forecast method is that it may permit a taxpayer to recover patent acquisition costs more quickly than the straight-line method would allow. The problem with the income-forecast method is that it is often difficult to determine how much income is earned in a particular year in connection with a patent (the numerator), and estimate all future income to be generated by the patent (the denominator), in which case the income-forecast method is not available. Another potential problem with choosing the income-forecast method is that no amortization deduction is allowed for any year in which no income is earned. In this problem, the income-forecast method provides large depreciation deductions in Years 1 and 2, compared to the straight-line method. In Year 3, however, the income-forecast method only produces a $1,000 depreciation deduction, because the patent produced very little income (the numerator) for that year. In Year 3, where the patent fails to generate much income, American Seating Company may wish to switch to the straight-line method to get a larger depreciation deduction. However, the company would first have to obtain the consent of the Service before changing methods. IRC § 446(e); *Wildman v. Commissioner* (holding that the taxpayer was not allowed to switch from the income-forecast method to an accelerated method without the consent of the IRS).

28.5. You are an associate at a local law firm. You run into the Senior Partner who tells you that the firm plans soon to purchase computer software, and he asks you, "What is the proper tax treatment of the software purchase?" You reply, "It depends." He responds, "It depends on what?" How do you respond to the Senior Partner? In particular, (1) list the additional information that you need, and (2) explain why this information is relevant in determining the proper tax treatment of the software acquisition costs.

1. *Will the computer software be "bundled software?"* Acquired computer software that is bundled with hardware without a separately stated cost is subject to depreciation rules governing the hardware. As addressed in Chapter 9, section 168 (ACRS) provides depreciation rules for tangible personal property, such as computers. Under section 168, computers are depreciated using an accelerated depreciation method (as opposed to the straight line method) over an arbitrary five-year recovery period (as opposed to the computer's useful life). IRC § 168(b)(1), (c), (e)(3)(B)(iv), (i)(2). Instead of depreciating the software and hardware costs over the depreciation period for the hardware, the taxpayer may be eligible to currently deduct such costs in full in the year paid under section 179.

2. *Will the computer software be off-the-shelf software or custom software?* If the software is off-the-shelf software (i.e., readily available for purchase by the general public, subject to a nonexclusive license, and not substantially modified), section 197 does not apply. IRC § 197(e)(3)(A)(i); Treas. Reg. § 1.197-2(c)(4). Rather, an election may be made under section 179 to expense currently the cost of the off-the-shelf

software. IRC § 179(d)(1)(A)(ii). If the software is custom software, the tax treatment depends on whether the custom software was acquired separately or in a transaction involving the acquisition of a trade or business.

3. *Will the software be acquired separately or in a transaction involving the acquisition of a trade or business?* If the software is custom software that will be acquired in a transaction (or series of related transactions) involving the acquisition of assets constituting a trade or business or substantial portion thereof, then the custom software is a section 197 intangible amortizable over fifteen years using the straight-line method. IRC § 197. However, if the software is custom software that will be acquired separately, the custom software is not a section 197 intangible. IRC § 197(e)(3)(A)(ii); Treas. Reg. § 1.197-2(c). Instead, the custom software costs are to be depreciated over three years using the straight-line method. IRC § 167(f)(1).

Chapter 29

Intellectual Property Sales and Licenses

Overview

Two common ways to exploit intellectual property are through licenses and sales—with significant tax differences depending on how the transfer is characterized. If an intellectual property transfer is considered a *sale* for tax purposes, then the transferor is permitted to recover tax free any remaining basis in the property transferred, and the resulting gain may be taxed at preferential capital gains rates rather than the much higher ordinary income rates. If, however, the transfer is characterized as a *license* for tax purposes, the transferor is not permitted to recover any basis in the property, and the full amounts received must be reported and taxed as ordinary income rather than capital gain.

Characterizing the transfer of intellectual rights under general tax principles is not always easy. Courts have established the basic criteria of a sale under general tax rules. A patent owner, for example, must transfer the exclusive right to make, use, and sell the patented article for the remaining life of the patent; anything short of that is not a sale but a license. Waterman v. Mackenzie, 138 U.S. 252 (1891). But questions still arise, including what restrictions or limitations in particular patent agreements preclude a finding of a sale for tax purposes.

As discussed in Chapter 17, long-term capital gain consequences require a sale or exchange of a capital asset held for longer than one year. If a transaction does not constitute a sale or exchange or if a transaction does not involve a capital asset, the transaction will give rise to ordinary income unless a special characterization provision applies. There are special characterization provisions that apply to intellectual property transfers. Section 1235 (which provides long-term capital gain treatment for certain dispositions of patent rights) and section 1253 (which imposes ordinary income treatment on certain transfers of trademarks and trade names) are considered in the problems below.

Primary Authority

Code: §§ 61(a)(7); 197(f)(1), (f)(7); 1221(a)(1)-(3); 1235; 1239; 1245(a)(1)-(3)(A); 1253(a)-(c). Skim §§ 453(a)-(d); 483(a)-(c)(1), (d)(4); 1274(a)-(c)(1), (c)(3)(C), (c)(3)(E), (d).

Regulations: §§ 15A.4531(c)(2)(i), -1(c)(3)(i), -1(c)(4), -1(d)(2)(i), -1(d)(2)(iii); 1.1221-1(c)
               (1), -1(c)(3); 1.1235-1(b), -1(c)(2), -2(a)-(d); 1.1239-1(b), -1(c)(5); 1.1245-3(b).
               Skim § 1.483-1(a)(2)(ii).

Cases: Busse v. Commissioner, 479 F.2d 1147 (7th Cir. 1973), aff'g 58 T.C.
               389 (1972); Cascade Designs, Inc. v. Commissioner, 79 T.C.M. (CCH)
               1542 (2000); Gable v. Commissioner, 33 T.C.M. (CCH) 427 (1974);
               Gershwin v. United States, 153 F. Supp. 477 (Ct. Cl. 1957); Gold-
               man v. Commissioner, 34 A.F.T.R.2d 6019 (E.D. La. 1974); Herwig v.
               United States, 105 F. Supp. 384 (Ct. Cl. 1952); Kronner v. United States,
               100 F. Supp. 730 (Ct. Cl. 1953); McClain v. Commissioner, 40 T.C. 841
               (1963); Newton Insert Co. v. Commissioner, 61 T.C. 570 (1974); Stern v.
               United States, 164 F. Supp. 847 (E.D. La. 1958); Poole v. Commissioner,
               46 T.C. 392 (1966); Stokely USA, Inc. v. Commissioner, 100 T.C. 439
               (1993);Watson v. Commissioner, 222 F.2d 689 (10th Cir. 1955).

Rulings: Rev. Rul. 60-226, 1960-1 C.B. 26; Rev. Rul. 67-136, 1967-1 C.B. 58;
               Rev. Rul. 69-482, 1969-2 C.B. 164; Rev. Rul. 85-186, 1985-2 C.B. 84,
               revoking Rev. Rul. 72-528, 1972-2 C.B. 481.

Problems

**29.1. Jack is the author of a well-known book, "My Sister Eileen," which por-
trays the adventures of two main characters, the "neat-and-uptight" and
"easygoing-and-disorganized" sisters. Jack assigned the radio and television
rights in the characters and stories to Arthur, an independent writer and
producer of radio and television programs, who was interested in creating
and producing a serial television program utilizing the two main characters.
The assignment was for a period to begin upon commencing of production
and was to remain in force so long as production was continued. Jack was
to receive a percentage of what Arthur obtained. Does the assignment constitute a "license" or a "sale" for tax purposes? Why does it matter?**

The IRS and some courts once took the position that a copyright was indivis-
ible, and that a transfer of less than all of the copyright was not a sale, but rather a
license, for tax purposes. Later, the IRS conceded and courts adopted the view that
a copyright was divisible, making tax law consistent with substantive copyright
law. In Revenue Ruling 60-226, the Service ruled that a sale arises whenever the
copyright holder transfers "the exclusive right to exploit the copyrighted work in
a medium of publication throughout the life of the copyright." See Gershwin v.
United States (holding that a transfer of motion picture rights in musical compositions was a sale despite the reservation of certain rights in the grantor); Herwig
v. United States, (holding the transfer of entire motion picture rights in one book
was a sale, stating: "We believe that it is not only logical but also practical and just
to consider the exclusive and perpetual grant of any one of the 'bundle of rights'
which go to make up a copyright as a 'sale' of personal property rather than a
mere 'license.'").

Because the assignment by Jack was not limited, but rather was "so long as production was continued," we believe there is an argument that the assignment was a sale for tax purposes. (Some advisors, however, may argue that serial television programs seldom last as long as the legal lives of copyrights, suggesting Jack has merely licensed radio and tv rights in the characters and stories). The fact that payments are contingent will not prevent the transfer from being considered a sale. *See* Rev. Rul. 60-226.

Why does it matter? If the transfer is characterized as a sale, Jack is permitted to recover any unadjusted basis in calculating gain (using installment sale reporting rules under section 453). If the transfer is characterized as a license, the full amounts received must be reported as income. Note that the character of the income would be ordinary in either case, because self-created works are not capital assets under section 1221(a)(3) or quasi-capital assets under section 1231(b).

29.2. Charles Lindbergh, who conceived, invented, and perfected a new and different windshield construction to be used on aircraft, applied for a patent and then granted to Lockheed Aircraft Corp., a publicly traded company, the "sole and exclusive right, privilege and license to use, manufacture, produce and sell the invention covered by the patent application for a period of 20 years."

(a) What is the proper tax treatment of the assignment assuming Charles receives a lump sum payment of $200,000?

Section 1235 is a special characterization rule that provides all three requirements for long-term capital gains treatment (sale or exchange, capital asset, and requisite holding period) in connection with the transfer of all the substantial rights to a patent. Specifically, section 1235 provides that a transfer (other than by gift, inheritance, or devise) of all substantial rights to a patent, or of an undivided interest in all such rights to a patent, by a statutorily defined holder to a person other than a related person constitutes the *sale or exchange of a capital asset held for more than one year.*

To benefit from section 1235, a transaction must involve the *transfer* by a *holder* of *all substantial rights* to a *patent*. We consider each element below.

Transfer. There is a section 1235 "transfer" here (assuming Charles is not an employee of Lockheed Aircraft Corporation and the transfer is not in exchange for compensation pursuant to an employment contract). *See* Treas. Reg. § 1.1235-1(c)(2).

Holder. Section 1235 (capital gains treatment) applies only if the transferor is a statutorily defined "holder" of the patent. The holder of a patent is defined as (1) any individual whose personal efforts created the patent property, or (2) any other individual who acquired his interest in the patent property from the original inventor in exchange for money or money's worth prior to the actual reduction to practice of the invention covered by the patent (e.g., a "financial backer"). IRC § 1235(b)(1)(2); Treas.

Reg. § 1.1235-2(d)(1)(i)(ii). An individual may qualify as a holder whether or not he is in the business of making inventions or in the business of buying and selling patents. Treas. Reg. § 1.1235-2(d)(3). Accordingly, Charles is a qualified holder even if he is a professional inventor or holds inventions primarily for sale to customers in the ordinary course of a trade or business.

All Substantial Rights. Section 1235 only applies to a transfer "of all the substantial rights" to a patent or an "undivided interest" therein. IRC § 1235(a). The term "all substantial rights" refers to all rights (whether or not then held by the grantor) that are of value at the time the rights to the patent (or an undivided interest in it) are transferred. Treas. Reg. § 1.1235-2(b)(1). Therefore, to qualify for the benefits under section 1235, a transferor must typically transfer the entire bundle of rights under a patent (i.e., convey the exclusive right to make, use, and sell the patent in all geographical regions and in all fields of use). Because Charles is transferring the "sole and exclusive right, privilege and license to use, manufacture, produce and sell the invention covered by the patent application" for the life of the patent (twenty years), he is transferring "all substantial rights."

Patent. Section 1235 applies only to patents and not to other forms of intellectual property, such as copyrights and trademarks. Although the Code does not define a "patent" for purposes of section 1235, the regulations provide that the term "patent" means a patent granted under the provisions of Title 35 of the United States Code, as well as any foreign patent granting rights generally similar to those under a United States patent. Treas. Reg. § 1.1235-2(a). The regulations under section 1235 also provide that it is not necessary that the patent or patent application for the invention be in existence if the requirements of section 1235 are otherwise met. *Id.* Thus, section 1235 can apply to inventions for which a formal patent application has not yet been made. Although Charles has just filed a patent application and has not obtained a patent, the payments received may qualify for capital gains treatment under section 1235.

Section 1235 applies only to the transfer of a patent and not the provision of services. In other words, if Charles receives payment for the patent and for significant or unrelated services, he must allocate the payment and separately state that portion accorded long-term capital gains treatment and that portion taxable as ordinary income. Such allocation is not necessary, however, if the services rendered are ancillary to the patent transfer. In *Gable v. Commissioner,* the Tax Court held that the ancillary services provided by the inventor in connection with the transfer of the patent rights do not affect the capital nature of the payments received by the inventor. This decision reflects the recognition that a patent transfer is primarily a transfer of knowledge.

Based on the foregoing, the $200,000 lump sum payment received by Charles should be entitled to capital gains treatment under section 1235. We can assume that Charles' basis in the invention was low (perhaps zero) in light of the fact that his development costs most likely qualified as section 174 research and experimental expenditures, deductible in the year paid or incurred.

Another issue is whether section 1245 requires any of the gain to be recaptured as ordinary income. Section 1245, considered in Chapter 19, provides that gain recognized on the disposition of "section 1245 property" shall be reported as ordinary income to the extent of any depreciation or amortization deductions taken with respect to the property. IRC § 1245(a)(1). Section 1245 property is defined as depreciable personal property, which includes both tangible and intangible personal property. IRC § 1245(a)(3); Treas. Reg. § 1.1245-3(b). As a general rule, section 1245 property encompasses patents that are subject to the allowance for depreciation under section 167. However, patent applications, which are not depreciable, are not subject to the depreciation recapture rules of section 1245. Also, patents, the creation costs of which were currently deducted under section 174, are not subject to section 1245 recapture. *See* Rev. Rul. 85-186, *revoking* Rev. Rul. 72-528. Accordingly, Charles does not need to worry about the recapture rules.

(b) Same as (a) except that instead of receiving a lump sum payment, Charles receives a percentage of the gross receipts realized by Lockheed Aircraft from the sale of the product.

Section 1235 provides favorable long-term capital gains treatment regardless of whether the payments received are payable periodically over a period generally coterminous with the transferee's use of the patent or are contingent on the productivity, use, or disposition of the property transferred. IRC § 1235(a). Accordingly, Charles' sale of the invention may receive preferential capital gains treatment even though the sale is for contingent payments.

The more interesting issue has to do with timing–especially if Charles has some unrecovered basis in the invention. When an invention is sold on a contingent-use basis, as is the case here, it is difficult to determine the total selling price (amount realized) in the year of sale and, hence, the proper amount and timing of gain from the sale. Should Charles' total gain be reported in year of sale or, instead, spread out as payments are received? Should Charles' gain be reported only after he has recovered tax-free the property's basis (assuming there is still some unrecovered basis)? You may recall from Chapter 26 that contingent payment sales are governed by the installment reporting rules of section 453.

Section 453 provides that "income" from an "installment sale" is to be reported under the "installment method." IRC § 453(a). An "installment sale" occurs when at least one payment of the total purchase price is to be received after the close of the taxpayer year in which the sale or other disposition occurs. IRC § 453(b)(1). As can be seen, this definition includes Charles' sale on a contingent basis. Because section 453 applies, Charles' gain is included in income only as payments are received from Lockheed Aircraft, regardless of whether he reports his income using the cash method or accrual method. In other words, Charles' gain is spread over the life of the payments (the total gain on the sale is prorated over the total payments received). If there is still some unrecovered basis, the percentage of each payment that must be reported as income (*i.e.*, the income portion of any payment) is determined by multiplying the amount of each payment by a fraction. The numerator is the gross profit realized on the sale or to be realized when payment is completed, and the denominator is the total contract or aggregate selling price. IRC § 453(c). This ratio of gross profit to total contract price is known as the gross profit ratio.

Determining the gross profit ratio would seem impossible in the case of Charles' contingent payment sale, because gross profit (numerator) or total contract price (denominator) cannot be readily determined in the year of sale when payments are contingent on use, productivity, or disposition of the intellectual property. Nevertheless, the regulations deal with contingent payment sales (Treas. Reg. § 15A.453-1(c)) and provide the following guidance: First, if the sale is subject to a "stated maximum selling price," then this maximum selling price is to be treated as the "selling price" for purposes of computing the gross profit ratio and determining the income portion of each payment. Treas. Reg. § 15A.453-1(c)(2). Second, if a maximum selling price is not known, but a maximum period of time over which payments may be received is known, then the taxpayer's basis in the intellectual property transferred is allocated over that "fixed period" in equal annual amounts. Treas. Reg. § 15A.453-1(c)(3). Finally, if there is no maximum selling price or fixed period over which payments may be received, then the transaction "will be closely scrutinized" to see whether a sale has occurred and if so, the basis in the intellectual property transferred is allocated ratably over a fifteen-year period. Treas. Reg. § 15A.453-1(c)(4).

Charles' adjusted basis in the invention is probably low (perhaps zero) since expenditures incurred in the development of the invention were most likely deducted under section 174, which was addressed in the last chapter. If Charles' adjusted basis in the transferred invention is zero, then each payment he received would be reported in income. In other words, since he would have fully recovered his invention costs via a current deduction under section 174(a), there would be no remaining costs (basis) to recover ratably as payments are received over time.

It should be noted that if intellectual property is sold on a contingent-payment basis, the parties must provide for adequate interest on the unpaid balance (adequate interest must be stated and paid annually). If adequate interest is not provided, minimum interest will be imputed by the Code, and a portion of the selling price (each deferred payment) will be recharacterized as interest. With the selling price adjusted accordingly, the seller will have less capital gain and some ordinary interest income; the purchaser will receive less depreciation and have interest expense. Minimum interest is required under either section 1274 (called "OID") or section 483 (called "unstated interest"), depending on the size of the contract. Interestingly, contingent payments received in a section 1235 transfer are excluded from the interest imputation rules of section 1274 and section 483. IRC §§ 483(d)(4), 1274(c)(3)(E).

(c) **Would your answers in (a) or (b), above, change if Charles was an employee of Lockheed Aircraft Corp. who was hired as a layout draftsman to design window installations for aircraft being developed?**

It depends. Section 1235 does not apply to a transfer by an employee to an employer of the rights to an invention if the transfer was in exchange for compensation pursuant to an employment contract. Treas. Reg. § 1.1235-1(c)(2) (providing that "[p]ayments received by an employee as compensation for services rendered as an employee under an employment contract requiring the employee to transfer to the employer the rights to any invention by such employee are not attributable to a transfer to which section 1235 applies"). The reason for this exception is that an employee who is hired by an employer to invent cannot make a "transfer" of intellectual property inventions in which he or she has no rights. An employee paid by an employer to invent receives compensation for services rendered (taxable as ordinary income), and not consideration for the assignment of inventions constituting capital assets (taxable as long term capital gains under section 1235).

Whether payments received by Charles from his employer are treated as compensation for services rendered by Charles or treated as proceeds derived from the transfer of patent rights is a question of fact. *Id.* Consideration is given not only to all the facts and circumstances of the employment relationship, but also to whether the amount of such payments depends upon the production, sale, or use by, or the value to, the employer of the patent rights transferred by Charles. *Id.* We need additional facts to determine whether Charles was, indeed, hired to invent (e.g., what was Charles expressly hired to do; did the employment contract provide for the royalty payments here in dispute or was the contract silent as to any payments over and above wages?). This problem is actually based on *McClain v. Commissioner*, wherein the Tax Court, deciding in favor of the taxpayer, stated: "It is clear that petitioner was not hired to invent, and Lockheed, without quibble, paid him the amounts in dispute in full compliance with its successive patent plans. These amounts were not gifts, and it is equally clear from the facts that they were not mere wages, but were attributable to the transfer of the patent rights."

(d) Would your answers in (a) or (b), above, change if Charles transfers the patent application to a corporation in which Charles owns one-third of the outstanding stock?

The capital gains benefits of section 1235 are not available when an individual transfers a patent to a "related person." IRC § 1235(d). This limitation was added to "prevent possible abuses arising from the sale of patents within essentially the same economic group." S. Rep. No. 83-1622, at 441 (1954), *reprinted in* 1954 U.S.C.C.A.N. 4621, 5084. A transferor and a corporation in which the transferor holds a 25% or greater ownership interest are treated as related. IRC § 267(b). [Note: The 50% stock ownership test in section 267(b) is replaced with a 25% stock ownership test for purposes of section 1235. IRC § 1235(d).] Accordingly, the transfer to Charles' corporation would not qualify for section 1235 treatment.

Even though Charles' transfer does not qualify for long-term capital gains treatment under section 1235, the transfer may still qualify for capital gains treatment under other Code provisions. *See* Treas. Reg. § 1.1235-1(b). In *Poole v. Commissioner*, the Tax Court held that section 1235 was the exclusive means by which a holder could qualify for capital gains treatment. Later, in Revenue Ruling 69-482, the Service stated that it would not follow *Poole* and ruled that the fact that a transfer does not qualify for long-term capital gains treatment under section 1235 (because a holder transferred all substantial rights to a related person) will not prevent it from qualifying for such treatment under general characterization provisions. The Tax Court later changed its position and followed Revenue Ruling 69-482 in *Cascade Designs, Inc. v. Commissioner.* Accordingly, Charles' transfer will qualify for long-term capital gains treatment under general characterization provisions if the transfer constitutes a *(1) sale or exchange (2) of a capital asset (3) held for more than one year.* Each of these elements is considered next

Sale. Charles' assignment constitutes a sale under general principles because he is transferring the exclusive right to make, use, and sell for the life of the patent. *See Watson v. Commissioner.*

Capital Asset. For a transfer of a patent outside the scope of section 1235 to qualify for capital gains treatment, the patent must qualify as a capital asset under section 1221 or a quasi-capital asset under section 1231. A patent in the hands of a professional inventor does not qualify as a capital asset under section 1221 or a quasi-capital asset under section 1231 because both definitions specifically exclude "stock-in-trade," "inventory" and "property held primarily for sale to customers in the ordinary course of trade or business." IRC §§ 1221(a)(1), 1231(b)(1)(A) & (B). Property used in the transferor's trade or business and that is depreciable under section 167 is excluded from the definition of capital asset under section 1221. IRC § 1221(a)(2). Charles' invention is most likely a capital asset. There is nothing in the facts to indicate that he is a professional inventor, and, hence, subject to the capital asset exclusion of section 1221(a)(1). Moreover, patent applications are not depreciable property subject to the exclusion of section 1221(a)(2).

Holding Period. A patent that qualifies as a capital asset under section 1221 must be held for more than one year to qualify for long-term capital gains treatment. IRC § 1222(3). For self-created patents, the holding period begins when the invention is actually reduced to practice. 35 U.S.C. §102(g); *Kronner v. United States* (finding that the inventor held his invention beyond the requisite holding period prior to assignment so that the payment received may be taxed as capital gains; the holding period of the invention began on the date on which the original invention was reduced to practical applications).

Assuming all of the elements above are met (sale, capital asset, requisite holding period), Charles would receive preferential capital gains treatment. As noted in (a), above, none of his gain would have to be recaptured as ordinary income under section 1245.

[As noted above, contingent payments received in a section 1235 transfer are excluded from the interest imputation rules of sections 1274 and 483. IRC §§ 483(d)(4), 1274(c)(3)(E). Interestingly, transfers by holders to related parties (which are not eligible for section 1235 treatment) are nevertheless transfers described in section 1235 and, as such, are not subject to the interest imputation rules. *See Busse v. Commissioner* (holding that payments received pursuant to a transfer of a patent to a related party were exempted from treatment as unstated interest) *Goldman v. Commissioner*.]

    (e) **Assume that Lockheed Aircraft in (b), above, purchased the invention for a percentage of the gross receipts realized by Lockheed Aircraft from the sale of the product. Pursuant to the agreement, Lockheed paid Charles $20,000 in Year 1 and $40,000 in Year 2. At the beginning of Year 3, Lockheed Aircraft sold all substantial rights in the patent to an unrelated third party for $300,000. What is the amount of Lockheed Aircraft's gain on the sale? Will any gain be recaptured as ordinary income under section 1245? Does it matter?**

Lockheed's gain realized on the sale is the amount by which amount realized ($300,000) exceeds adjusted basis. IRC § 1001(a). What is Lockheed's adjusted basis in the patent? A taxpayer who purchases a separately-acquired patent (that is not subject to section 197) for contingent payments adds such payments to the basis of the patent in the taxable year paid but then amortizes the full amount paid in that year. *See Associated Patentees, Inc. v. Commissioner; see also* Rev. Rul. 67-136; Treas. Reg. 1.167(a)-14(c)(4) (following *Associated Patentees*). Because Lockheed was permitted an immediate deduction for the $20,000 payment in Year 1 and the $40,000 payment in Year 2, its adjusted basis in the patent is zero. Hence, the gain equals $300,000. The character of the gain on the sale of the patent (depreciable trade or business property) would most likely be long-term capital gain under section 1231. But wait! What impact, if any, will section 1245 have?

Section 1245 property is defined as depreciable personal property, which includes both tangible and intangible personal property. IRC § 1245(a)(3); Treas. Reg. § 1.1245-3(b). Section 1245 property encompasses intellectual property that is subject to the allowance for depreciation under section 167, as well as intellectual property that is subject to fifteen-year amortization under section 197 (because section 197 intangibles are treated as property subject to the allowance for depreciation under section 167). IRC § 197(f)(7). The important question here is whether section 1245 encompasses intellectual property that has been depreciated in accordance with the method approved in *Associated Patentees, Inc.* Courts have said yes. *See Newton Insert Co. v. Commissioner.* Gain in the amount of those previous payments to Charles (which served as deductions for Lockheed), will be treated as ordinary income. Gain in excess of those amounts most likely will treated as capital gain under section 1231.

29.3. Juanita sells her restaurant, which is named for her and is famous for its fruit pies, to Bob for $500,000 in cash. As part of the transaction, Juanita transfers to Bob several "section 197 intangible" assets. Juanita grants to Bob the right to continue using Juanita's name as the name of the restaurant in perpetuity subject to the following two restrictions: (1) the right of

Juanita to prescribe ingredients that may be used in making the pies for five years; (2) the right of Juanita to train all new chefs at the restaurant for five years; and (3) a limitation against using Juanita's name on clothing for twenty years. What is the tax treatment of the sale? What if Bob agreed to pay $100,000 in cash and 5% of the gross income of the business for the next five years?

Section 1253 imposes ordinary income treatment on noncontingent payments received for the transfer of a trademark or trade name if the transferor retains any significant power, right, or continuing interest with respect to the subject matter of the mark or name. IRC § 1253(a). The Code sets out six potentially significant powers, any one of which, if retained, would require ordinary income treatment. *See* IRC § 1253(b)(2)(A)-(F). This list of retained powers that may qualify as significant is not exhaustive. IRC § 1253(b)(2). Rather, consideration is given to all the facts and circumstances existing at the time of a transfer when determining whether an unenumerated power constitutes a significant power.

The duration of the relevant restriction is important in determining whether the restriction is significant. Any one of the enumerated retained rights could be objectively insignificant if the retained right is not coextensive in duration with the interest transferred. For example, the Tax Court in *Stokely USA, Inc. v. Commissioner* held that a transferor's five-year right to disapprove a transfer was not significant because the restriction was not co-extensive with the duration of the interest transferred.

Here, as was the case in *Stokely*, the transfer of the trademark rights as a whole is in perpetuity. However, there are restrictions having a limited duration. We should analyze whether these restrictions fall within section 1253(b). If it is determined that some or all of the restrictions do not fall within subjection (b), we should analyze the restrictions under section 1253(a). We should keep in mind that the duration of the relevant restriction is important in determining whether the restriction is significant.

What if Bob agreed to pay $100,000 in cash and 5% of the gross income of the business for the next five years? Section 1253 imposes ordinary income treatment on all payments that are *contingent*. IRC § 1253(c). Note also that the fixed amount here ($100,000) could also become tainted under section 1253(b)(2)(F).

Chapter 30

Assignment of Income

Overview

Because of the progressive rate structure in section 1 of the Code, related taxpayers have some incentive to shift income among themselves in order to take advantage of the lower tax brackets more than once and, sometimes, to avoid the higher brackets altogether. As we will see, however, a taxpayer's ability to engage in this sort of "assignment of income" has been substantially curtailed. There are many strands of the court-made "assignment of income doctrine." We will focus on two of these strands: (1) assignments of earned income, and (2) assignments of income from property. We will also take note of assignments designed to convert ordinary income into capital gains.

Assignments of Income from Services. The foundational case on the assignment of income doctrine is *Lucas v. Earl*, 281 U.S. 111 (1930). There the Supreme Court held that income is taxed to the person who earned it. This remains the general rule with respect to earned income. However, Poe v. Seaborn, 282 U.S. 101 (1930), decided the same year as *Earl,* introduced an immediate complexity. *Seaborn* involved the interaction between federal tax law and the community property law of the State of Washington. There, the Court held that half of a husband's earnings were taxed to his wife since by operation of law the earnings belonged to her from the instant they were earned. Though the husband had the authority to spend those earnings, his authority to act arose from an agency relationship rather than from his ownership of the earnings. Thus, income earned by an agent acting for a principal is taxed to the principal, at least when state law creates the agency relationship automatically. The holding in *Seaborn* was one of the reasons Congress adopted the joint filing system that is in place today. Any married couple who jointly files is automatically treated for tax rate purposes as if each of the spouses earned half of their aggregate income. See Chapter 14.

It should be noted that the IRS accepts that a person who earns a fee while acting on behalf of his employer and who, by prior agreement, endorses that fee over to his employer, is not taxable on those earnings. Rev. Rul. 74-581, 1974-2 C.B. 25. In the Service's view, it is essential that the obligation to transfer the funds to the employer arose before the act of earning occurred.

It is possible to disclaim income from services so as not to be subject to tax. A disclaimer, in the immediate context, is an unconditional refusal to accept earnings to which one is entitled. If the person making the disclaimer does so before the right to receive the income has been fixed, she will not be taxed on the earnings. Rev. Rul. 66-167, 1966-1 C.B. 20. In order to qualify as unconditional, the disclaimant cannot direct the earnings to another. Commissioner v. Giannini, 129 F.2d 638 (9th Cir. 1942). Thus, for example, a disclaimant who refuses her Christmas bonus and asks that it be given to her mother remains taxable on the bonus if her request is granted.

Assignments of Income from Property. Normally the owner of the property is taxed on the income from the property. But what if the owner of the property transfers the right to receive the income from the property to another person while retaining the property itself? Who is taxable on that income now? Generally speaking, if the assignment of the income from property is gratuitous, the owner of the property remains taxable on the income. Helvering v. Horst, 311 U.S. 112 (1940). [A more nuanced question arose in Blair v. Commissioner, 300 U.S. 5 (1937). In *Blair,* the taxpayer inherited an income interest in trust for life and then transferred an undivided portion of the income interest to his children. The Supreme Court held that the assignment was successful in transferring the tax liability to the children because of the lack of a differentiated retained interest. All Blair owned was an income stream and he gave part of that away. He did not retain the source of the income (indeed he never owned it).]

Income from property can be assigned to another person for tax purposes if one is willing to transfer the property to the assignee. This leaves some planning opportunities for more affluent members of society. Congress thought these planning opportunities were too generous and attacked them in three ways. First, Congress established the grantor trust rules in sections 671–79. These rules provide that if a grantor sets up a trust but retains any of a number of different rights, including the right to revoke and certain rights of reversion, then the trust income remains taxable to the grantor. If the grantor trust rules do not apply, there is another attack known as the Kiddie Tax. *See* IRC § 1(g). With some exceptions it provides that the unearned (i.e. investment) income of children under the age of 18 is taxed at the child's parents' top marginal rate. Thus, in a limited way, the combination of joint filing by married couples and the Kiddie Tax treats the nuclear family as the taxable unit. The third attack is that the rate structure applicable to entities such as trusts and corporations is less graduated than the rate structure for individuals. For example, the top tax rate for income taxed to trusts quickly reaches 35%. *See* IRC § 1(e) & (i).

Generally an assignment of the property that produces the income will cause the assignee to become liable for the taxes on the income from the property. But a significant caveat to this principle is that income that is already realized at the time of the assignment remains with the assignor for tax purposes. *See* Salvatore v. Commissioner, 29 T.C.M. 89 (1960). Just as realized income is taxed to the owner at the time of realization, so too is accrued income taxed to the person who owned the property at the time of accrual.

Thus far we have focused on assignments of income in the form of gifts. But what if a taxpayer *sells* the right to future income while retaining the property that produces the income? If your inclination is to treat this as a transaction governed by section 1001, you are on the right track. By definition one has a zero basis in pre-tax income. Thus, if one sells the right to future income, one's amount realized is itself pure income. From this one can see that a sale of future income does not on its face raise the same tax avoidance concerns as a gratuitous assignment of income. Indeed it results in an acceleration of tax liability. Thus, the general rule is that a sale of future income will be respected for tax purposes. *See* Estate of Stranahan v. Commissioner, 472 F.2d 867 (6ᵗʰ Cir. 1973).

Assignments Designed to Convert Ordinary Income into Capital Gains. Ordinary income is generally taxed at higher rates than long-term capital gains. It is not surprising then that taxpayers have long sought to transmute one into the other. A leading case in this area is Commissioner v. P.G. Lake Inc., 356 U.S. 260 (1958) (though its precise holding has since been reversed by statute). In *P.G. Lake,* an oil company sold a portion of its future income from wells in which it owned a working interest. It took the position that the sale of a portion of a capital asset produced a capital gain. The Supreme Court held that one who converts future ordinary income to present income will find that present income also to be ordinary. The retention of a continuing interest in the oil property was central to the Court's analysis.

Primary Authority

Code: §§ 1(g)(1)-(3); 7872(a), (c)(1)-(2).

Regulations: None.

Cases: Blair v. Commissioner, 300 U.S. 5 (1937); Estate of Stranahan v. Commissioner, 472 F.2d 867 (6ᵗʰ Cir. 1973); Commissioner v. Ferrer, 304 F.2d 125 (2ⁿᵈ Cir. 1962); Commissioner v. Giannini, 129 F.2d 638 (9th Cir. 1942); Heim v. Fitzpatrick, 262 F.2d 887 (2d Cir. 1959); Helvering v. Horst, 311 U.S. 112 (1940); Hundley v. Commissioner, 48 T.C. 339 (1967); Lucas v. Earl, 281 U.S. 111 (1930); Lattera v. Commissioner, 437 F.3d 399 (3ʳᵈ Cir. 2006); Metropolitan Building Co. v. Commissioner, 282 F.2d 592 (9ᵗʰ Cir. 1960); Commissioner v. P.G. Lake Inc., 356 U.S. 260 (1958); Poe v. Seaborn, 282 U.S. 101 (1930); Salvatore v. Commissioner, 29 T.C.M. 89 (1960); Watkins v. Commissioner, 447 F.3d 1269 (10ᵗʰ Cir. 2006).

Rulings: Rev. Rul. 58- 275, 1958-1 C.B. 22; Rev. Rul. 66-167, 1966-1 C.B. 20; Rev. Rul. 74-581, 1974-2 C.B. 25; Rev. Rul. 79-121, 1979-1 C.B. 61.

Problems

30.1. Serena earns a $1,200,000 annual fee for endorsing a clothing line for Nike Apparel Inc. She is normally paid $100,000 at the beginning of each month. What are the tax consequences to Serena of the following events?

  (a) At the beginning of the year Serena directs Nike to pay $100,000 to Augusta Country Club for her membership.

She's taxed on all $100,000. She earned the income and simply made a directed disposition to another. *Lucas v. Earl; Old Colony Trust.*

> **(b) After winning the Dancing With the Stars competition, Serena receives a diamond tiara worth $300,000. Prior to the contest Serena had promised her niece that she could have whatever she won, and Serena later directed that the tiara be delivered directly to her niece.**

Same as above. The promise is probably not legally enforceable. Even if it were, it is still a garden variety assignment of income. The niece would have no income from the gift and would take Serena's $300,000 tax cost basis. IRC §§ 102(a) & 1015(a).

> **(c) Same as (b) except that under her contract with her dance instructor, Fred Astaire, Fred was entitled to 10% of any prizes earned by Serena. Serena wrote Fred a check for $30,000.**

Serena is still the earner here. Her assignment to Fred is legally binding but still nothing differentiates this case from *Lucas v. Earl*. But now Serena has a section 162 deduction. *See Hundley v. Commissioner.*

> **(d) Halfway through the year Serena declared that she had earned enough and asked Nike to pay the $600,000 remainder of her fee to the International Rescue Agency, a public charity.**

While again Serena may be entitled to a deduction, this time under section 170, she is still taxed on the income because she directed it to another. *See* Rev. Rul. 79-121.

> **(e) Same as (d) except that Serena told Nike to give it to any "charity" the Board of Directors chose.**

Arguably there is no income to Serena under the *Commissioner v. Giannini* case. This is because the payment was disclaimed prior to being earned without being directed to a named recipient. The Service construes *Giannini* narrowly. *See* Rev. Rul. 79-121.

> **(f) Serena makes appearances at sports conventions, which include paid autograph signing sessions. Nike sponsors these events and her appearances are part of her agreement with Nike. The autograph fees are collected by Nike and retained by it.**

Nike is taxed rather than Serena. *See* Rev. Rul. 74-581. Serena is an agent of Nike for fund receipt purposes because she is bound to turn over the fees to it. Revenue Ruling 74-581 involved a law school clinician who was obliged to turn any fees earned over to the school.

30.2. Aristotle owns a tanker ship that is leased to an oil company. The rent, $1,000,000 a month, is payable on the 1st day of each month. The rent is paid in advance. How are Aristotle and his daughter, Christina, treated for tax purposes in the following circumstances?

(a) **On March 1ˢᵗ Aristotle assigns Christina all rent from the tanker for the rest of the year.**

Aristotle is taxed on the rent as it is paid to Christina since Aristotle kept the tanker. *Helvering v. Horst. See* Rev. Rul. 58-275. Aristotle's accounting method should control the timing of the income.

(b) **On March 1ˢᵗ Aristotle assigns Christina all rent from the tanker for the next five years.**

Aristotle is taxed on the rent as it is paid to Christina since he kept the tanker. *Horst. See* Rev. Rul. 58-275. Again Aristotle's accounting method should control the timing.

(c) **On March 1ˢᵗ Aristotle transfers the tanker and all future rent to Christina.**

Christina is taxed on the rent. Aristotle gave the tree with the fruit. *Blair v. Commissioner.*

(d) **On March 31ˢᵗ Aristotle transfers the tanker and all of the year's rent, including the January through March rent, to Christina.**

Same as above except that the January through March rent is taxed to Aristotle since it was earned before the assignment. *Salvatore v. Commissioner.*

(e) **On March 1ˢᵗ Aristotle sells the right to the next three years of rent to Christina for $30,000,000 which represents the present value of the future payments.**

Aristotle has $30,000,000 current income under *Estate of Stranahan v. Commissioner.* Christina will ultimately have $4,000,000 of income. ($34,000,000 amount realized − $30,000,000 adjusted basis = $4,000,000). Basis is recovered ratably over the life of the payments.

30.3. Doc invented and patented a mechanism for time travel. He sold his patent to a major corporation in exchange for a royalty interest in the sales of the mechanism. Doc then assigned his royalty interest to his protégé, Michael. Who is taxed on the royalty income?

Michael. *See Heim v. Fitzpatrick. Heim* follows the *Blair* analysis even though Heim was the inventor of the patent and thus once held the entire income producing property.

30.4. Longfellow won the Megaburst lottery. This entitled him to twenty annual payments of $10,000,000 each. A year later he sold his interest in the remaining payout for one $125,000,000 payment. What is the character of his gain from that payment?

Ordinary. Even though one might contend that the rights to future payments are capital assets, the payment is still a substitute for ordinary income. *Watkins v. Commissioner; Lattera v. Commissioner.*

But note this is not a carve out case like *Commissioner v. PG Lake, Inc.* since he retained nothing. The rationale for this outcome is that treating this as capital gain would unduly advantage the seller as compared with someone who took a lump sum payment in the first place.

30.5. David wrote a play about the life of Marilyn Monroe. Reese entered into a contract with David with respect to the play. David retained legal and equitable title to the play; however, in the contract David gave Reese the exclusive right to stage the play for five years in exchange for a share of the profits if she did so. The contract also gave Reese the right to prohibit the production of the play into a film for the longer of five years or as long as the play was running on Broadway. Finally, the contract gave Reese the right to receive 30% of the net profits to star in the play for five years and 25% of the net profits to star in any film version of the play that was produced within five years. A little more than a year later, Spike approached David and Reese about the possibility of turning the play into a film without it ever being brought to the stage. Ultimately David and Reese agreed to this proposal. Under the agreement between David, Reese and Spike, the contract between David and Reese was cancelled. In consideration for agreeing to the cancellation of the contract with David, Reese received $9,000,000 from Spike. Of this amount, $3,000,000 was for giving up the exclusive right to stage the play, $3,000,000 was for giving up the right to prohibit the production of a film version of the play, and $3,000,000 was for agreeing to give up the right to receive 25% of the net profits for starring in the film version of the play. (Spike thought Reese was not right for the role.) Assuming that Reese had a zero basis in the contract with David, what is the character of the income she received for cancelling the contract?

This problem raises the question of what constitutes a capital asset. It is adapted from the case of *Commissioner v. Ferrer*, referenced in the Primary Authorities. In that case, the actor Jose Ferrer contracted to produce a play about the life of Toulouse Lautrec. Under *Ferrer* the surrender of the right to stage the play is, like the sale of the lease by the lessee in *Metropolitan Building Co. v. Commissioner*, the sale of a capital asset. Thus, Reese would have $3,000,000 in capital gain. Similarly the transfer of the right to prohibit production of a film for five years is considered the sale of a capital asset. It was in the nature of an encumbrance on the motion picture rights. Again Reese would have $3,000,000 of capital gain. But the payment for surrender of the right to star in the film is deemed a payment for services. It is comparable to the payment one might receive for entering into a non-competition agreement or other agreement where one agrees to forego a compensable service activity. Thus, the $3,000,000 payment for foregoing the right to star in the film is ordinary income.

Chapter 31

Alimony & Support

Overview

In this chapter and the next, we are going to take a look at the tax consequences of divorce. For tax purposes, there are three possible ways to treat payments from one spouse to another as part of a divorce. A payment is either alimony, child support, or a property settlement. Alimony is ordinary income to the payee and is deductible by the payor. Child support is neither income to the payee nor deductible by the payor. A property settlement is a non-recognition event for both parties and results in a transferred basis. A lawyer representing a party to a divorce must be alert to these differing tax treatments of payments and transfers because of the advantages and disadvantages that come with each designation. In this chapter we will look at alimony and child support.

Section 71(a) provides for the inclusion of alimony or separate maintenance in the gross income of the payee spouse or former spouse. Section 215(a) provides for a deduction from gross income for the payor spouse or former spouse. The payor's deduction is measured by reference to the payee's inclusion. *See* IRC § 215(b). Whether a payment is alimony is to a significant degree a matter for negotiation between the parties. Within some limits then, the parties can decide who gets taxed on the income. It's a bargaining chip. Obviously the payor has an incentive to have any payment denominated as alimony rather than as child support or a property settlement since the first is deductible and the other two are not. As a practical matter the payor may have some leverage to force the payee to accept this designation since the payor often is wealthier or has more income than the payee. As we will see, section 71(f) seeks to restrain the parties from characterizing as alimony payments that are really property settlements. The definition of alimony in section 71(b) also acts as a restraint on this tendency. Section 71(b)(1) sets out specific criteria for a payment to constitute alimony for tax purposes. A *cash* payment is alimony if:

a. it is received under a "divorce or separation instrument";
b. it is not designated as a *non*-alimony payment;
c. it is made at a time when the payor and payee are not members of same household (if the divorce is final or there is a legal separation); and
d. there is no liability to make further payments after the death of the payee.

The most complex provision concerning alimony is section 71(f). This provision recaptures what otherwise qualifies for treatment as alimony so that the payor has gross income and the payee has a deduction in a later year. IRC § 71(f)(1). It is intended to prevent property settlements from being characterized as alimony by discouraging "front-loading." Front-loading occurs when there are early large cash payments that dwindle in size over a short time, usually three years. The recapture occurs in the third year of post-separation payments, but it arises by reference to an analysis of first and second year post-separation payments. The clock does not begin to run on this analysis until the first year when alimony is paid. IRC § 71(f)(6).

Payments of cash to someone other than the former spouse can be alimony if the other requirements of section 71(b) are met. *See* IRC §71(b)(1)(A) (parenthetical language "on behalf of"). Thus, for example, payments on the mortgage of a house owned by the payee spouse can be alimony. The key is that the payment must satisfy an exclusive obligation of the payee spouse. Thus, payments on the mortgage of a house owned by the payor cannot be alimony even if the payee spouse resides in the house. *See* Treas. Reg. § 1.71-1T(b) Q&A 6.

Payments denominated as child support are not deductible by the payor and are not included in the gross income of the payee. IRC § 71(c)(1). This is consistent with the tax treatment of payments in support of the children of non-divorced spouses. While it is possible to disguise child support payments as alimony there are a number of hurdles to prevent this characterization. One of these is the requirement that alimony must terminate upon the death of the payee. Normally one would not want child support to do this. Other hurdles to disguising child support as alimony are the rules of section 71(c) providing that payments which are reduced by the happening of *contingencies relating to the child* such as death, marriage or reaching a certain age are treated as child support. *See* Treas. Reg. § 1.71-1T(b) Q&A 17–18.

When a payor is obliged to pay both alimony and child support, any shortfall in meeting those obligations first reduces the alimony deemed paid. IRC § 71(c)(3). In other words the payor gets no alimony deduction until first fully satisfying the payor's child support obligation.

Primary Authority

Code: §§ 71; 215(a)-(b). Skim §§ 166(a)-(b), (d); 212.

Regulations: § 1.71-1T(b) & (c).

Cases: Berry v. Commissioner, T.C. Memo 2005-91.

Rulings: None.

Problems

31.1. Juliana and Chris were married for several years and have two young daughters, Elizabeth and Mary. Chris and Juliana begin living apart and a decree of divorce is entered that directs Chris to pay Juliana $50,000 a year for five years or until her death, whichever is sooner. How are the payments treated for tax purposes in the following circumstances?

(a) Chris makes the first year payment to Juliana in cash.

This qualifies as alimony under section 71(b) since it is:

1. cash,
2. pursuant to a divorce decree as defined in section 71(b)(2),
3. not designated as non-alimony,
4. they do not live together, and
5. there is no post-death liability.

(b) Chris makes the first year payment by transferring a diamond ring worth $50,000 to Juliana.

This is not alimony since it is not a cash payment and it is not child support since it is not designated as such. *See* IRC § 71(b) (opening sentence), (c)(1). Thus, this is a section 1041 transfer, the subject of Chapter 32.

(c) Same as (a) except that at the direction of the decree Chris pays off a $50,000 note secured by a diamond ring owned by Juliana.

An indirect payment mandated by the decree is sanctioned as alimony by the regulations. Treas. Reg. § 1.71-1T(b) Q&A 6.

This qualifies as alimony under section 71(b) since it is:

1. cash,
2. pursuant to a divorce decree as defined in section 71(b)(2),
3. not designated as non-alimony,
4. they do not live together, and
5. there is no post-death liability.

(d) Same as (c) except that Chris pays the note at Juliana's written request.

An indirect payment made at the written request of the payee spouse is sanctioned as alimony by the regulations. Treas. Reg. § 1.71-1T(b) Q&A 7.

Again this qualifies as alimony under section 71(b) since it is:

1. cash,
2. pursuant to a divorce decree as defined in section 71(b)(2),
3. not designated as non-alimony,
4. they do not live together, and
5. there is no post-death liability.

(e) Same as (a) except that the Chris and Juliana have a written separation agreement that says the payments are not alimony.

The payment is not alimony. IRC § 71(b)(1)(B). *See also* Treas. Reg. § 1.71-1T(b) Q&A 8. This illustrates the negotiability of alimony tax treatment.

(f) Same as (a) except the decree directs that the payments shall be reduced by $12,000 per year for each child that achieves an earned income level of $10,000 or more per year.

Only $26,000 per year is alimony. The other $24,000 per year is deemed child support since it is reduced as a result of a contingency relating to the children. IRC § 71(c)(2)(A). *See also* Treas. Reg. § 1.71-1T(c) Q&A 17. It is irrelevant whether the contingency actually occurs.

(g) Same as (f) except that in the first year, Chris has a liquidity problem and only pays $40,000.

The first $24,000 is deemed child support and so Chris only has a $16,000 alimony deduction and Juliana has only a $16,000 inclusion. This is because section 71(c)(3) sets up the presumption that child support is paid first.

31.2. Lucia and Bruce divorced in Year 1. In Year 1, there was a property settlement but no alimony was paid. In Years 2-4, Lucia made cash payments to Bruce that met the definition for alimony in section 71(b) in the following amounts: $140,000 (Year 2); $100,000 (Year 3); and $60,000 (Year 4).

(a) What are the tax consequences in Year 4 for Lucia and Bruce resulting from these payments?

In each of the three years the payments are deductible by Lucia and includable in gross income by Bruce. But in Year 4 (which is the third post-separation year under IRC § 71(f)(6)) there will be recapture of income by Lucia and a deduction by Bruce of $82,500 computed as follows:

1. Year 2 Excess Payment: IRC § 71(f)(4)

$\underline{\$25,000} = \$100,000$ 2nd yr pmt $- (\$60,000$ 3rd yr pmt $+ \$15,000)$

2. Year 1 Excess Payment: IRC § 71(f)(3)

$$\underline{\$57,500} = \$140,000 \text{ 1st yr pmt} - \left(\frac{(100,000 \text{ 2nd yr pmt} -25,000 \text{ 2nd yr EP} + 60,000 \text{ 3d yr pmt})}{2} + 15,000\right)$$

3. Total Excess Payments for Years 1 & 2

$25,000
+$57,500
$82,500

For Year 4, Lucia will report $82,500 of income (while also deducting the Year 4 payment of $60,000) and Bruce will deduct $82,500 (while also reporting the Year 4 payment as income).

(b) Same as (a) except that Bruce remarries at the end of Year 3 and no payments are made in Year 4.

There is no recapture since the payments cease by reason of remarriage before the close of the third post separation year. IRC § 71(f)(5)(A).

(c) Same as (a) except that the payments are a fixed portion of the rent from an office building owned by Lucia.

For purposes of section 71(f), these payments are not treated as alimony, thus there is no recapture. IRC § 71(f)(5)(C). This is because the fluctuations in amount are outside the control of the payor.

31.3. Alicia and Jay, who have three minor sons, divorce in Year 1. Jay is granted custody of the boys. The decree specifies that Alicia will pay Jay $60,000 a year in "family support" for ten years. These payments meet the requirements of sections 71(b)(1)(A)-(C). The decree does not specify whether the payments will end upon Jay's death. Under state law "family support" combines child support and spousal support without designating the amount to be paid for child support and the amount to be paid for spousal support. State law provides that the obligation to pay family support terminates upon the death of the payee spouse. However, state law also provides that any successor custodian to the minor children may bring an action for renewed child support upon the death of the payee spouse. Are the family support payments from Alicia to Jay alimony for federal tax purposes? Why or why not?

Under the *Berry v. Commissioner* case, the payments qualify as alimony since they terminate at death under local law. This is true despite the fact that some portion of the payments are plainly child support and may continue after the death of the payee spouse. The court reaches this result by noting that under earlier law undifferentiated payments combining alimony and child support were deemed alimony. It further asserts that this construction is necessary in order to give section 71(c)(1) any meaning. This analysis seems rather strained. Perhaps the best reason to accept this outcome is that it is likely that upon the death of the payee spouse, the payor spouse will assume custody. If this happens then the obligation to make support payments *under the decree* will cease in its entirety. Of course the payor will continue to be legally obligated to support the minor children as their legal custodian.

Chapter 32

Transfers of Property Between Spouses or Incident to Divorce

Overview

Generally, property transfers, other than gifts, trigger gain or loss recognition under section 1001. Under section 1041, however, property passing from one spouse to another or from one former spouse to another in settlement of their respective property rights has no immediate income recognition consequence unless it fits the definition of alimony. More specifically, section 1041 prevents recognition of gain or loss by the transferor. IRC § 1041(a). It also indirectly provides that the transferee has no income by specifying that the transfer is treated as a gift. IRC § 1041(b)(1). *See* IRC §102(a). It further provides for a transferred basis *in all cases* for the transferee. IRC § 1041(b)(2). In this last respect it differs from section 1015(a), which sometimes denies a transferred basis for loss recognition purposes. Note that the transferred basis also means that the transferee will get the transferor's holding period. IRC § 1223(2). Though section 1041 is a relatively straightforward provision, it has many nuances, some of which are explored in this problem set.

Any transfer of property between spouses is governed by section 1041. However, with respect to former spouses it only applies to transfers "incident to the divorce." IRC § 1041(a)(2). A transfer between former spouses is deemed incident to the divorce if it occurs within one year from the date on which the marriage ends or is "related to the cessation of the marriage." IRC § 1041(c). A transfer is related to the cessation of the marriage if it is pursuant to a divorce or separation instrument (as defined in section 71(b)(2)) and the transfer occurs within six years of the marriage's end. Treas. Reg. § 1.1041-1T Q&A 7.

Under limited circumstances a transfer of property to a third party can qualify for treatment under section 1041. Essentially, section 1041 will apply when either the divorce decree or a written agreement between the spouses authorizes a spouse or former spouse to make the payment on behalf of the other spouse or former spouse. Treas. Reg. § 1.1041-1T(c) Q&A 9. The effect is to grant non-recognition to the transferor spouse in the same way as if the transferor had made the transfer to the other spouse. Thereafter the non-transferor spouse is treated as if he or she had made a taxable transfer to the third party. Thus, normally transfers to third parties cause the deemed transferee spouse or former spouse to recognize gain or loss.

It is not uncommon for married couples to own businesses together. Often, when such couples divorce one party (the remaining spouse) will buy out the other party's (the departing spouse's) interest in the business. Generally, section 1041 applies to such transactions in a straightforward fashion. But special problems can arise for buyouts in which the business is conducted as a corporation. There are basically three ways to structure the purchase of the departing spouse's stock: (1) a straight purchase; (2) a distribution combined with a purchase, or (3) a redemption. Each of these forms requires a different analysis for tax purposes:

(1) Straight Purchase. A straight purchase is a sale of the stock to the remaining spouse in which the remaining spouse uses his or her own funds for the purchase. This is a classic section 1041 transaction in which the departing spouse receives non-recognition and the remaining spouse takes a carry over basis.

(2) Distribution Followed by Purchase. In this scenario, the funds for the purchase are distributed from the corporation to the remaining spouse who then transfers them to the departing spouse in exchange for the departing spouse's stock. Tax treatment of distributions are governed by section 301. Typically, the remaining spouse is treated as having dividend income. The purchase is treated as a section 1041 transaction. Thus, the remaining spouse gets taxed and the departing spouse gets non-recognition. Notice that despite recognizing income the remaining spouse gets no basis adjustment in the stock received from the departing spouse. IRC § 1041(b)(2). This tax payment without basis step up makes this an unappealing option to the remaining spouse.

(3) Redemption. A redemption is a purchase of the shareholder's stock by the issuing corporation. With some exceptions, the regulations under section 1041 provide that if the buyout is structured as a redemption of the departing spouse's stock, section 1041 will *not* apply. Treas. Reg. § 1.1041-2(a)(1). In other words, the form of the transaction will be respected for tax purposes. Thus, the redemption will usually be a gain or loss recognition event for the departing spouse. However, the regulation creates an exception to this general rule for a redemption that as a matter of law would be treated as a constructive distribution to the remaining spouse. Treas. Reg. § 1.1041-2(a)(2). The typical situation in which the law will imply a constructive distribution to the remaining spouse is when the redemption is carried out to satisfy the remaining spouse's "primary and unconditional obligation" to buy the shares from the departing spouse. *See* Treas. Reg. § 1.1041-2(d), ex. 1. If the constructive distribution exception applies, the transaction is treated as though the distribution was made to the remaining spouse who then buys the departing spouse's stock and surrenders it back to the corporation. In other words, it is the *remaining* spouse who is treated as having engaged in a redemption with the corporation. *See* Treas. Reg. § 1.1041-2(a)(2). Under this scenario the departing spouse will get nonrecognition under section 1041. The remaining spouse's redemption will likely fail to qualify for sale or exchange treatment and instead will be treated as a dividend. *See* IRC § 302(a), (b)(3), (d). To complicate things further (but in a taxpayer friendly way), the regulation permits the parties to override both the main redemption rule and its

constructive distribution exception by agreement. In other words, they can agree to flip flop the outcomes just described. *See* Treas. Reg. § 1.1041-2(c)(1), (2).

Often the spouses' pensions and retirement account rights are the most valuable assets of the marriage. Thus, proper division of these accounts upon divorce is vitally important. Typically under state law each spouse will own some portion of the other spouse's pension. In most cases, pensions and retirement accounts are forms of deferred compensation that have not yet been taxed to the earner. Thus, a division of such an account could be viewed as an assignment of income from the earner spouse to the non-earner spouse. There was a time when the Service took the view that section 1041 did not apply to transfers of rights to ordinary income and, instead, the assignment of income doctrine applied unless a more specific statute controlled. However, the Service has begun to retreat from that position. *See* Revenue Ruling 2002-22, 2002-1 C.B. 849. Note that for qualified pensions there is a specific provision that obviates any question of the assignment of income doctrine applying. Instead it makes clear that the payee is the one who is taxed. *See* IRC § 402(e)(1)(A). A point of practical importance is that, under the Employee Retirement Income Security Act (ERISA), divisions of pensions and retirement accounts must be carried out through "qualified domestic relations orders" (QDROs). Otherwise they will not be respected by pension managers. QDROs have various technical requirements. *See* 29 U.S.C. § 1056(d). Failure to properly draft a pension division as a QDRO can have serious adverse consequences. *See, e.g.,* Hamilton v. Wash. State Plumbing & Pipefitting Indus. Pension Plan, 433 F.3d 1091 (9th Cir. 2005).

Primary Authority

Code: §§ 402(a), (e)(1)(A); 1041; 1223(2). Skim §§ 83(a)-(b); 301(a), (c)(1); 302(a), (b)(3), (d); 414(p)(1).

Regulations: §§ 1.1041-1T (b)–(d); 1.1041-2.

Cases: Craven v. United States, 215 F.3d 1201 (11th Cir. 2000); Hamilton v. Wash. State Plumbing & Pipefitting Indus. Pension Plan, 433 F.3d 1091 (9th Cir. 2005).

Rulings: Rev. Rul. 2002-22, 2002-1 C.B. 849.

Problems

32.1. Jennifer and Mark are cash method taxpayers who were divorced in Year 1. What are the tax consequences of the following transactions?

> **(a) In Year 1, pursuant to their divorce decree, Jennifer transferred to Mark her half interest in a piece of investment land they had owned for years as community property. Her share of their basis was $350,000 and her interest was worth $750,000.**

No gain or loss to Jennifer on the transfer. IRC § 1041(a).

Mark has no income. IRC §§ 1041(b)(1), 102(a).

Mark takes a $350,000 basis in her half. IRC §§ 1041(b)(2), 1015(e). Assuming that his basis in his own half was also $350,000, his aggregate basis is now $700,000.

(b) Same as (a) except that Mark pays Jennifer $750,000 cash for her interest.

There is no change in the previous answer. Jennifer takes the cash without recognizing any gain, and Mark gets no basis step up. We should note that the lack of a basis step up for a cash purchase such as this might serve as a point for negotiating a lower purchase price.

(c) Same as (b) except that Mark pays only $300,000 but assumes Jennifer's half of a $900,000 mortgage on the property.

There is no change. The liability assumption is irrelevant under section 1041 even when the liability exceeds the transferor's basis. *See* Treas. Reg. § 1.1041-1T(d) Q&A 12.

(d) Same as (b) except that the property transferred are accounts receivable from their closely held business.

This raises the question of whether the assignment of income doctrine should override section 1041 where ordinary income rights are being transferred. The IRS now appears to accept that it does not. Rev. Rul. 2002-22. This is the better rule since applying the doctrine selectively introduces an undesirable degree of uncertainty. Thus,

No gain or loss to Jennifer on the transfer. IRC § 1041(a).

Mark has no income. IRC §§ 1041(b)(1), 102(a).

Mark takes a zero basis in her half. IRC §§ 1041(b)(2), 1015(e). Thus his aggregate basis is still zero. If they had been accrual method taxpayers, of course, the basis would be $1,500,000 rather than zero.

Since Mark is now facing being taxed on $1,500,000 of ordinary income when the receivables are collected, he might seek to negotiate a lower price for this buyout. Or, more likely, he might propose that they split the accounts receivables equally with each being taxed on his or her share.

(e) What if in (a) Mark immediately sold the land for $1,500,000 in cash to a third party?

Since his basis is $700,000, he recognizes $800,000 of gain. IRC § 1001. All of the gain would be long-term capital gain since he is entitled to tack her holding period to his. IRC § 1223(2).

(f) Same as (a) except that Jennifer transferred the interest to Ben in satisfaction of a $750,000 debt that Mark owed Ben.

Now Mark will recognize $400,000 of long-term capital gain under the indirect transfer rules of Treas. Reg. § 1.1041-1T(c) Q&A 9. This is because Jennifer is treated as having made a non-taxable section 1041 transfer to Mark followed by Mark's taxable transfer to Ben. Again tacking of holding period applies so all of the gain is long term. IRC § 1223(2).

32.2. Charlie and Ping started a successful music streaming business, Street-Song, Inc., shortly after their marriage. They each owned 50% of the StreetSong stock with each having a $1,000,000 basis in their respective blocks of stock. Fifteen years later they divorced. Assuming there are no agreements other than those described, what are the tax consequences to Charlie and Ping of the following transactions? (Ignore the application, if any, of section 1202.)

    (a) Pursuant to the divorce instrument Charlie sells his StreetSong stock to Ping for $50,000,000.

This problem is designed to illustrate the basic rules associated with ending co-ownership of a corporation as part of a divorce. The tax outcome is dramatically different depending on how the transaction is structured even though in all cases Ping ends up owning all of the outstanding StreetSong stock. This is the most important point to understand.

This first transaction is straightforwardly governed by section 1041. Charlie will not recognize gain (pursuant to section 1041(a)) and Ping will take a $1,000,000 transferred basis in the stock (section 1041(b)(2)). Obviously this is highly advantageous to Charlie. For the remaining parts the key authority is Treasury Regulation § 1.1041-2.

    (b) Pursuant to the divorce instrument, Charlie sells his StreetSong stock back to StreetSong for $50,000,000. Ping had no obligation to buy the stock.

The form of the transaction will govern the outcome. This will be treated as a redemption of Charlie's stock by the corporation. Treas. Reg. § 1.1041-2(a)(1). Thus, section 1041 will not apply. Treas. Reg. § 1.1041-2(b)(1). In all likelihood, Charlie will receive sale or exchange treatment under sections 302(a) and (b)(3) since he is completely terminating his interest in the corporation. In short, he will recognize $49,000,000 of long-term capital gain. Ping is unaffected. Obviously, this is advantageous to Ping.

    (c) The divorce instrument places a primary and unconditional obligation on Ping to buy Charlie's StreetSong stock for $50,000,000. However, the parties agreed that the funds for the buyout would come from Street-Song. StreetSong issued a check for $50,000,000 to Charlie and Charlie transferred his stock to Ping

This is a constructive distribution from the corporation to Ping under the laws of most states since she had an unconditional obligation to buy the stock from Charlie. Treas. Reg. § 1.1041-2(a)(2). She will be treated as though she received a cash distribution from StreetSong and used the money to purchase Charlie's stock in a section 1041 transaction. The constructive distribution is governed by section 301 and is most likely a dividend. Charlie receives non-recognition treatment under section 1041(a). Treas. Reg. § 1.1041-2(b)(2), -2(d), ex. 1.

(d) Same as (c) except that Charlie transferred his stock to StreetSong.

This is still a constructive distribution from the corporation to Ping since she had an unconditional obligation to buy the stock from Charlie. Treas. Reg. § 1.1041-2(a)(2). She will be treated as though she purchased Charlie's stock in a section 1041 transaction and then sold that stock to the corporation for the cash. This latter transfer will not qualify as a redemption for sale or exchange purposes under section 302(b). It will, thus, be a distribution under section 301 and is most likely a dividend. Charlie receives non-recognition treatment under section 1041(a). Treas. Reg. § 1.1041-2(b)(2), -2(d), ex. 1.

32.3. Diego and Kim, who are both age 60, were married for 35 years before divorcing. A major property interest acquired during the marriage is Kim's deferred compensation retirement account. On the date of the divorce the account was worth $1,000,000. All of the funds in this account were contributed on a pre-tax basis and will be ordinary income to someone when distributed. Who will be taxed on the distributions described below?

(a) As part of the divorce it is agreed that when Diego reaches age 65, Kim will begin making payments to Diego of $4,000 per month in settlement of Diego's claims against Kim's retirement account. When Kim and Diego reach age 65, Kim begins receiving distributions of $8,000 per month from Kim's retirement account. Kim then pays $4,000 of that amount to Diego each month.

The entire $8,000 distributed each month will be taxed to Kim since Kim is the "distributee." IRC § 402(a). The payment from Kim to Diego is governed by section 1041. Relying on Revenue Ruling 2002-22, Kim might seek to argue that in substance $4,000 of the $8,000 belongs to and should be taxed to Diego. However, the ruling involved direct payment from the employer to the alternate payee in one case and a transfer of stock options that were not immediately taxable in the other. Moreover, the availability of a method that explicitly transfers tax liability to the alternate payee (i.e., a QDRO) also argues in favor of treating Kim as taxable on the full $8,000. Certainly, that is the way the retirement account payor will report the matter to the IRS.

(b) As part of the divorce the judge enters a qualified domestic relations order (QDRO) equally dividing the retirement account into two retirement accounts, one for Kim and one for Diego. When Kim and Diego reach age 65 each begins receiving distributions of $4,000 per month from their respective retirement accounts.

Each distributee will be taxed on $4,000. IRC § 402(a). The QDRO causes the division of the account into two accounts. As the alternate payee on one of those accounts, Diego is the "distributee" on that account and will be taxed as the distributions are made to him. *See* IRC § 402(e)(1)(A). Many of the detailed requirements for a properly drawn QDRO are found at IRC § 414(p). In our experience fund managers often have their own preferred QDRO form.

Chapter 33

Education Benefits and Costs

Overview

This chapter addresses the income tax treatment of education. As explored in the problem set that follows, some education expenses are deductible as business expenses under section 162. Treas. Reg. § 1.162-5(a)(1)-(2), (b)(2)-(3). More often, however, education is treated as a personal matter within the meaning of section 262 even though much of education may be devoted to preparing to enter a job or profession. In addition, the cost of education is often considered a capital expenditure within the scope of section 263 rather than as a current expense. To counter these principles of tax policy, Congress has enacted several provisions that allow either a deduction or a credit for educational expenses that are not otherwise deductible under section 162. IRC §§ 25A, 222. Congress also has enacted varying exclusion provisions relating to scholarships and grants (§ 117), employer-provided educational assistance (§§ 127, 132(d)), and educational savings (§§ 135, 529, 530). Many of these deductions, credits, and exclusions apply not only to the taxpayer, but also to the taxpayer's spouse and dependents.

Primary Authority

Code: §§ 25A; 108(f); 117; 127; 132(d); 221; 222. Skim §§ 135; 529; 530.

Regulations: § 1.25A-5(e)(3); Prop. Treas. Reg. § 1.117-6(c)(2), (d), Ex. 5.

Cases: Bingler v. Johnson, 394 U.S. 741 (1969); MacDonald v. Commissioner, 52 T.C. 386 (1969).

Rulings: Rev. Rul. 2008-34, 2008-28 I.R.B. 76.

Problems

33.1. Frank has been a full-time law enforcement officer at the local police department for the past five years. May Frank deduct the costs of the following education as an ordinary and necessary business expense under section 162?

(a) Frank spends $100 to attend a two-hour training program on cultural diversity.

This training program likely maintains or improves skills in Frank's trade or business. Treas. Reg. § 1.162-5(a)(1). The training program might even be required by Frank's employer as a condition to retention of employment. Treas. Reg. § 1.162-5(a)(2). In either case, the $100 is deductible under section 162.

(b) Frank spends $2,000 to audit an evening course on criminal procedure at State University Law School.

Because Frank is not enrolled in the law school's J.D. program that would lead to a degree that would qualify Frank to enter a new business (i.e., lawyer), he may deduct the $2,000 as a business expense for the reasons stated in (a) above.

(c) Frank spends $6,000 to take three evening courses at State University Law School. Frank is enrolled in the law school's J.D. program, but he does not plan to practice law when he receives his J.D. degree in four years. He plans to remain a full-time police officer (hopefully with a higher rank).

The $6,000 tuition is not deductible under section 162. Although Frank does not plan to practice law with his J.D., the degree nevertheless qualifies him for a new trade or business—the practice of law. Treas. Reg. § 1.162-5(b)(3). Although not eligible for deduction under section 162, Frank may be entitled a Lifetime Learning Credit.

(d) After receiving his J.D. degree, and practicing criminal law at a local law firm for two years, Frank spends $40,000 to earn his LL.M. degree in criminal law.

The LL.M. degree does not qualify Frank for a new trade or business. Because he has been engaged in the practice of law for two years, this would be viewed as a deductible expense in carrying on an existing trade or business—the practice of law. Treas. Reg. § 1.162-5(a)(1). *See* Blair, T.C.M. 1980-488.

(e) Same as (d) above except that the LL.M. degree is in tax law.

The result is the same as in (d) above. A graduate degree in tax will make Frank a better criminal lawyer (think tax crimes!), and not qualify him for a new trade or business. His existing business is that of practicing law.

33.2. The following eight students are taking classes at State University Law School, which has a full-time J.D. program the tuition of which is $20,000 per year. Unless noted otherwise, assume that each student is enrolled full-time in Law School's J.D. program. Describe generally the tax consequences for each of the following:

(a) Alice, who has impressive academic credentials, receives a full tuition scholarship from Law School. Alice is not required to perform services to Law School as a condition of receiving the scholarship.

This amount is excluded under section 117(a). Alice is a degree candidate (includes a degree at graduate level), Prop. Treas. Reg. § 1.117-6(c)(4), at an educational organization, IRC §§ 117(a), 170(b)(1)(A)(ii). The amount received is a qualified scholarship since it is used for "qualified tuition and related expenses" (i.e., tuition,

enrollment fees, books, and supplies). IRC § 117(b); Prop. Treas. Reg. § 1.117-6(c)(3)
(i). The scholarship would not be excluded to the extent it covered personal expenses,
such as meals and lodging. Prop. Treas. Reg. § 1.117-6(c)(2). Tuition funded with the
excludable scholarship under section 117(a) would not qualify as an expense under
sections 25A or 222. IRC §§ 25A(g)(2), 222(d)(1).

**(b) Bob receives a full tuition scholarship from a reputable tax law firm. As
a condition to receiving the scholarship, Bob agrees to work for the law
firm after graduation. Bob has no previous relationship with the law firm.**

The scholarship does not qualify for exclusion under section 117(a) since Bob is
under a contractual obligation to render future services (i.e., the payment represents
payment for future services). IRC § 117(c); Prop. Treas. Reg. § 1.117-6(d). *See Bingler
v. Johnson* (holding employer-employee scholarship to be taxable compensation).
Even absent a contractual obligation, the educational scholarship would be taxable
if there was a clear expectation that Bob would work for the firm. *See MacDonald
v. Commissioner. See also* Prop. Treas. Reg. § 1.117-6(b)(1) (holding non-qualifying
scholarships are not excludable gifts under section 102).

Although not excludable under section 117(a), up to $5,250 may be excluded under
section 127 if Bob were considered an "employee" of the firm. IRC § 127(c)(2). Section 127 permits an employee to exclude up to $5,250 for amounts paid by the em-
ployer for educational assistance at either the undergraduate *or graduate levels* of
education if the employer's educational assistance program does not discriminate
in favor of highly compensated employees and meets other requirements (a formal
written plan open to everyone is required, which can be costly and burdensome for
employers). Tuition funded with assistance excluded under section 127 would not be
treated as qualified tuition under sections 25A or 222. IRC §§ 25A(g)(2), 222(d)
(1). [Note: Prior to 2001, section 127 did not apply to benefits with respect to any
graduate level course of a kind normally taken by an individual pursuing a program
leading to a law, business, medical, or other advanced academic or professional degree. That provision was stricken by the Economic Grown and Tax Reconciliation
Act of 2001. Thus, the section 127 exclusion applies at the graduate level now.]

Amounts not excludable under section 127 would not qualify for exclusion under
section 132(d) as working condition fringe benefits, as payment of the J.D. tuition by
Bob would not have been deductible by him under section 162. Treas. Reg. § 1.162-5.

**(c) Chris is a long-time employee at Law School who is now pursuing
a J.D. degree (in the school's part-time program). Because Chris has at
least five years of continuous full-time employment with Law School,
Chris receives a waiver benefit of 100% of the cost of tuition under Law
School's Post Graduate Tuition Benefits Program. Chris is not engaged
in teaching or research for Law School.**

Qualified tuition reduction programs offered to employees of educational organizations are non-taxable fringe benefits under section 117(d) even though they are

compensatory in nature. The problem for Chris is that the exclusion is limited to tuition reduction below the graduate level, or at the graduate level if the student is engaged in teaching or research activities. IRC § 117(d)(5). Because Chris is not engaged in teaching or research for Law School, the tuition reduction is not eligible for the section 117(d) exclusion.

Although not excludable under section 117(d), Chris may be able to exclude up to $5,250 of the benefit under section 127, if Law School has a formal written plan providing employer-provided educational assistance that is open to everyone. Amounts not excluded under section 127 would not qualify for exclusion under section 132(d) as working condition fringe benefits, as payment of the J.D. tuition by Chris would not have been deductible by him under section 162. Treas. Reg. § 1.162-5.

(d) **Don, who had a career before entering law school, has substantial savings that generate interest and dividend income. Don pays his own tuition with some of his savings. Don is not a dependent of any other taxpayer.**

As a law student, Don could claim the non-refundable Lifetime Learning Credit (but not the American Opportunity Tax Credit). The maximum amount of the credit is $2,000 per year (20% of qualified tuition and related expenses of up to $10,000 for each year). IRC § 25A(c). The credit is reduced if Don has too much income. IRC § 25A(d). Remember the AGI phase-out amounts are indexed for inflation. IRC § 25A(h)(2). If Don were a dependent of another taxpayer, the tuition Don paid would be deemed paid by the taxpayer. IRC § 25A(g)(3).

[Note: Prior to 2017, up to $4,000 of the tuition would qualify for an above-the-line deduction under section 222. But no deduction would be allowed if the Lifetime Learning Credit under section 25A was elected with respect to the expenses. IRC §§ 25A(g)(5), 222(c)(2)(A). Thus, prior to 2017, Don could choose between the deduction or the credit. Although the section 222 deduction is slated to expire at the end of 2016, Congress has extended the life of this provision on more than one occasion and it may do so again.]

(e) **Earl, who owns a home that has substantially increased in value since its purchase, takes out a home equity loan and pays tuition with the borrowed funds. Earl is not a dependent of any other taxpayer.**

The result is the same as in (d) above. In other words, Earl is entitled to a credit even though his tuition payment came from borrowed funds as opposed to his savings. Treas. Reg. § 1.25A-5(e)(3).

(f) **Fran's parents pay Fran's tuition with a combination of previous income and current income savings. Fran is 22 years old and her parents properly claim her as a dependent.**

Fran's parents can claim the non-refundable Lifetime Learning Credit (but not the American Opportunity Tax Credit). The Lifetime Learning Credit is a *per-taxpayer* credit for the taxpayer's payment of qualified tuition and related fees at an eligible institution of higher education for a student who is either the taxpayer or the tax-payer's spouse or the *taxpayer's dependent (as defined in section 152)*. IRC § 25A(f)(1)(A). As a per-taxpayer credit, Fran's parents could not claim a Lifetime Learning Credit for any other dependent who is a student, but if applicable, could claim an American Opportunity Tax Credit for the other dependent.

[Note: Prior to 2017, up to $4,000 of the tuition would qualify for an above-the-line deduction under section 222. But no deduction would be allowed if the Lifetime Learning Credit under section 25A was elected with respect to the expenses. IRC §§ 25A(g)(5), 222(c)(2)(A). Thus, prior to 2017, Fran's parents could choose between the deduction or the credit. Although the section 222 deduction is slated to expire at the end of 2016, Congress has extended the life of this provision on more than one occasion and it may do so again.]

(g) Gertrude pays her tuition with a $15,000 cash gift she received from Grandmother.

Gertrude can claim the non-refundable Lifetime Learning Credit (but not the American Opportunity Tax Credit), even though the tuition is funded by a gift that is excluded from gross income. IRC § 25A(g)(2)(C).

[Note: Prior to 2017, up to $4,000 of the tuition would qualify for an above-the-line deduction under section 222. But no deduction would be allowed if the Lifetime Learning Credit under section 25A was elected with respect to the expenses. IRC §§ 25A(g)(5), 222(c)(2)(A). Thus, prior to 2017, Gertrude could choose between the deduction or the credit. Although the section 222 deduction is slated to expire at the end of 2016, Congress has extended the life of this provision on more than one occasion and it may do so again.]

(h) Harry has no savings and receives no financial assistance to pay tuition. Harry thus borrows $8,500 in subsidized federal loans and the rest in private loans to attend law school. The interest on the federal loans is deferred, but Harry pays interest on the private loans each year.

Regarding interest, interest paid on the private law loans is potentially deductible above the line. IRC § 221.

Regarding tuition, a Lifetime Learning Credit, but not the American Opportunity Tax Credit, may be claimed by Harry for the tuition paid even though the tuition is paid with loan proceeds. Treas. Reg. § 1.25A-5(e)(3). The credit is claimed in the taxable year in which the tuition is paid, and may not be claimed in the taxable year in which the loan is repaid. *Id*. Loan proceeds disbursed directly to the law school will be treated as paid on the date the law school credits the proceeds to Greg's account. *Id*. [Note: Prior to 2017, up to $4,000 of the tuition would qualify for an above-the-line deduction under section 222. But no deduction would be allowed if the Lifetime Learning Credit under section 25A was elected with respect to the expenses. IRC §§ 25A(g)(5), 222(c)(2)(A). Thus, prior to 2017, Harry could choose between the deduction or the credit. Although the section 222 deduction is slated to expire at the end of 2016, Congress has extended the life of this provision on more than one occasion and it may do so again.]

(i) **Ira has been awarded a $15,000 loan to pay tuition as part of Law School's Foundation's Loan Repayment Assistance Program. The loan, which is evidenced by a promissory note bearing adequate interest, will be forgiven provided he remains employed on a full-time basis in a public interest job.**

As with Harry in part (h) above, Ira could claim the Lifetime Learning Credit, but not the American Opportunity Tax Credit, for the tuition even though the tuition is paid with loan proceeds. Treas. Reg. § 1.25A-5(e)(3). When the loan is subsequently discharged, Ira can exclude the loan forgiveness. IRC § 108(f). Revenue Ruling 2008-34 clarifies that law school loan forgiveness programs qualify for the section 108(f)(1) exception. Note that if the foundation loan was used to repay Ira's original student loans, the result would be the same. Rev. Rul. 2008-34.

33.3. Mr. and Mrs. Peyton are trying to figure out how best to save for their daughter's education, and can't decide between a Coverdell IRA and a 529 plan. What are the differences between the two savings plans?

There are many differences between the two plans. Here are a few:

1. 529 plans do not impose annual contribution limits, age limits, or income limits. Coverdells do; in fact, Coverdells have a low annual contribution cap ($2,000 per beneficiary).
2. Only the Coverdell allows you to self-direct your investments, as with investments in an IRA. (But many contributors are satisfied by the investment choices offered by 529 plans).
3. Coverdells can be withdrawn tax free for K-12 and college expenses, whereas 529 plans are limited to college expenses.
4. States may provide a state tax deduction for using a 529 plan.

Chapter 34

Personal Injury Recoveries and Punitive Damages

Overview

Section 104 excludes from gross income compensation received for certain personal injuries and sicknesses: (1) compensation under so-called "workmen's compensation acts," (2) damages on account of personal physical injury or physical sickness, (3) benefits under self-financed health and accident insurance policies, (4) disability pension arising out of certain government service, and (5) disability income received by officials who are violently attacked outside the country. IRC § 104(a)(1)-(5). These exclusions are restricted by an "except" clause, the effect of which is to include in gross income reimbursement of medical expenses that were deducted in a prior year. The problem set below focuses mainly on the tax treatment of (1) compensatory and punitive damages received on account of personal injuries and sickness, and (2) amounts received under insurance policies.

Damages Received on Account of Personal Injuries or Sickness. Section 104(a)(2) excludes damages received "on account of personal physical injuries or physical sickness." Damages received on account of non-physical injury or sickness (e.g., defamation, age discrimination, housing discrimination, injury to personal or business reputation) are not excludable from gross income. However, damages for non-physical injury or sickness that are "on account of" physical injury or sickness are excludable. The Code is explicit that "emotional distress" is not to be treated as a physical injury or sickness, except for related medical care expenses. IRC § 104(a), flush language. Neither the Code nor the regulations define what "physical" means. The IRS has taken the position that "direct unwanted or uninvited physical contacts resulting in observable bodily harms such as bruises, cuts, selling, and bleeding are personal physical injuries under section 104(a)(2)." Priv. Ltr. Rul. 200041022 (Oct. 13, 2000). Courts seem to accept the IRS's position of requiring physical contact causing observable bodily harm. *See, e.g.,* Stadnyk v. Commissioner, 367 Fed. Appx. 586 (6th Cir. 2010).

In contrast to compensatory damages, which may be excludable under section 104(a)(2), punitive damages are not excludable from gross income. Punitive damages are taxable whether or not related to a claim for damages arising out of physical injury or sickness.

Accident or Health Insurance Proceeds. Section 104(a)(3) excludes from gross income amounts received under self-financed accident and health insurance policies for personal injuries or sickness. Amounts received under employer-provided plans are not excludable under section 104(a)(3), but may be excludable under section 105. *See* Treas. Reg. § 1.104-1(d). It should be noted that the section 104(a)(3) exclusion pertaining to self-financed policies is not limited to actual expenses for medical care; the section 105(b) exclusion pertaining to employer-financed policies is so limited (in other words, the excess indemnification attributable to the employer's policy is includable in gross income).

Primary Authority

Code: §§ 104(a); 105(a)-(c), (e); 106(a).

Regulations: § 1.104-1(a)-(d).

Cases: Amos v. Commissioner, T.C. Memo 2003-329; Commissioner v. Schleier, 515 U.S. 323 (1995); Stadnyk v. Commissioner, 367 Fed. Appx. 586 (6th Cir. 2010).

Rulings: Rev. Rul. 69-154, 1969-1 C.B. 46; Priv. Ltr. Rul. 200041022 (Oct. 13, 2000); Internal Legal Memorandum 200809001; Chief Counsel Advice Memorandum 201045023.

Problems

34.1. Mary Jo sued Ted for injuries sustained when Ted, who was driving an automobile while intoxicated, ran over Mary Jo. Mary Jo won and received an award of $1 million allocated by the jury as follows: medical expenses ($200,000) (none of which had been previously deducted); lost wages ($150,000), pain and suffering ($350,000); and punitive damages ($300,000).

(a) What are the tax consequences to Mary Jo as a result of the jury award?

Section 104(a)(2) excludes from gross income "the amount of any *damages* (other than punitive damages) received (whether by suit or agreement and whether as lump sums or as periodic payments) *on account of personal physical injuries* or physical sickness." IRC § 104(a)(2) (emphasis added).

Mary Jo suffered a "personal physical injury." And, the damages were received "on account of" the personal physical injury. Therefore, all damages other than the punitive damages are excludable from Mary Jo's gross income. *See Commissioner v. Schleier* discussed in Priv. Ltr. Rul. 200041022. Note that Treas. Reg. § 1.104-1(c), which was amended in 2011, removes the first condition of *Schleier* (i.e., damages must be received in a tort-like cause of action).

We can analyze separately each component of the award:

Medical Expenses: The medical expenses of $200,000 were received on account of Mary Jo's personal physical injuries and were not previously deducted, and, thus, are excludable from her gross income. Mary Jo gets the exclusion now, but gets no medical expense deduction in the future. Review IRC § 213 (permitting a medical expense deduction to the extent not compensated by insurance or otherwise). [Note:

Mary Jo would get no exclusion now to the extent the amount represents reimbursement for medical expenses previously deducted by Mary Jo. *See* IRC § 104(a) ("except" clause). In that case, Mary Jo would have to include in gross income reimbursement of medical expenses that were deducted in a prior year.]

Lost Wages: We might mistakenly conclude that amounts representing lost income are not excludable under section 104(a)(2). In the automobile accident hypothetical in *Schleier*, the Supreme Court made clear that such amounts are excludable if on account of personal injuries. If an action has its origin in a physical injury or physical sickness, then all damages (other than punitive damages) that flow therefrom are treated as payments received on account of physical injury or physical sickness and are excludable. *See* H.R. Conf. Rep. No. 104-737 at 300 (1996). Mary Jo can exclude the $150,000 for lost wages.

Pain and Suffering: The $350,000 allocated to pain and suffering is excludable because they are attributable to a physical injury.

Punitive Damages: Punitive damages are not excludable under section 104(a)(2). Mary Jo must include $300,000 in gross income.

> **(b) Same as (a) except that Mary Jo witnessed Ted driving toward her but was able to jump out of the way before getting hit. As a result of the incident, Mary Jo experienced severe headaches, weight loss, sleeplessness, depression, anxiety, crying spells, nightmares, and alcohol abuse. She sued Ted for reckless infliction of emotional distress.**

The question here is whether Mary Jo has suffered a personal physical injury or physical sickness within the meaning of section 104(a)(2). There is little guidance on what constitutes a physical injury or physical sickness. The Code is explicit that "emotional distress" is not to be treated as a physical injury or sickness. IRC § 104(a) (flush language). And according to the legislative history, physical symptoms resulting from emotional distress (e.g., insomnia, headaches, and stomach disorders) are to be treated as emotional distress. Here, damages received based on a claim of emotional distress are not excludable from gross income except to the extent that damages are received for amounts paid for related medical care expenses.

> **(c) Same as (a) except that Mary Jo and Ted agreed to settle the suit out of court. Ted agrees to pay Mary Jo $500,000, which Mary Jo insisted be allocated entirely to pain and suffering. In return Mary Jo agreed not to defame Ted, publicize facts relating to the accident, or assist in any criminal prosecution against Ted with respect to the accident.**

The problem is designed to spark consideration of *Amos v. Commissioner*, and the proper nexus between damages and physical injury to satisfy the "on account of" standard in section 104(a)(2).

The dominant reason of Ted in making the settlement payment was to compensate Mary Jo for claimed physical injuries. It would seem, therefore, that all compensatory damages would be excludable as on account of Mary Jo's physical injuries. Under *Amos*, however, a portion of the settlement would be deemed expressly paid for reasons other than to compensate Mary Jo for personal physical injuries. In *Amos*, the Tax Court found that $120,000 of a $200,000 settlement was paid on account of physical injuries a photographer sustained when kicked by Dennis Rodman during the course of a NBA game, and that $80,000 was paid for the agreement not to defame Rodman, not to publicize the incident, or to assist in criminal prosecution against Rodman. Under *Amos*, Mary Jo could exclude only a portion of the settlement under section 104(a)(2). How much is unclear.

Do you think the Tax Court in *Amos* did the right thing? At least two arguments can be made that *Amos* was wrongly decided. First, section 104(a)(2) should be broadly interpreted to exclude all damages (other than punitive damages) whenever the exclusion applies (i.e., the statute excludes "any damages" on account of personal physical injury and does not require allocation of various types of damages that are taxable and non-taxable). Second, the agreement not to defame, publicize facts, or assist in criminal prosecution is boilerplate in many settlements and, as a result, *Amos* would require allocation of some portion of most all settlements; in addition, we all have a legal duty not to defame regardless of the boilerplate agreement.

34.2. What are the tax consequences to Plaintiff in each of the following situations:

    (a) **Plaintiff suffered a massive heart attack (but survived) when he witnessed his child get deliberately hit by a car driven by Defendant, who had a big grudge against Plaintiff and was looking to seek revenge on Plaintiff. Although Plaintiff was not physically hit by the car, he sued Defendant for intentional infliction of emotional distress and was awarded $100,000.**

In Private Letter Ruling 200041022, the Service gave its interpretation of the scope of the physical injury requirement. The ruling requires a physical touching that sets off a physical injury or physical illness. Here there was no physical contact by Defendant that caused any observable bodily harm to *Plaintiff*. Under this strict interpretation, Plaintiff could not exclude any of the damages (except for amounts paid for medical care).

Should, however, it make a difference that there was a physical injury to *Plaintiff's child*? Perhaps. According to the legislative history:

> If an action has its *origin* in a physical injury or physical sickness, then all damages (other than punitive damages) *that flow therefrom* are treated as payments received on account of physical injury or physical sickness *whether or not the recipient of the damages is the injured party*." For example, damages (other than punitive damages) received by an individual on account of a claim for loss of consortium due to the physical sickness of such individual's spouse are excludable from gross income.

H.R. Conf. Rep. No. 104-737 at 300 (1996) (emphasis added).

(b) Plaintiff sued the Catholic Church for alleged sex abuse that occurred twenty years ago. Plaintiff agreed to settle the suit out of court and received $5 million from the Catholic Church.

In Priv. Ltr. Rul. 200041022, the IRS concluded that damages the plaintiff received for unwanted physical contacts without any *observable bodily harm* were not received on account of personal physical injuries or physical sickness. In contrast, the damages the plaintiff received for pain, suffering, emotional distress, and reimbursement of medical expenses *after* the first assault were excludable under section 104 because they were attributable to physical injuries. This framework could prove difficult to apply to victims, like Plaintiff here, in the widely publicized Catholic Church sex scandal.

In Internal Legal Memorandum 200809001, the Service concluded that payments to settle a tort claim brought by an adult for injuries sustained as a child are excludable under section 104(a)(2), stating "it is reasonable for the Service to presume that the settlement compensated [the plaintiff] for personal physical injuries, and that all damages for emotional distress were attributable to the physical injuries." Under this ILM, Plaintiff can exclude the damages received for physical injuries without having to prove physical harm. Query: Does this ILM water down the observable bodily harm rationale? For commentary, see Robert W. Wood, *IRS Allows Damages Exclusion Without Proof of Physical Harm*, 2008 TNT 63-31 (Apr. 1, 2008).

(c) Plaintiff was detained by a pharmacy that was suspicious of Plaintiff's prescription. When the police arrived, they handcuffed and arrested Plaintiff. While Plaintiff was in jail, the police verified with her doctor that the prescription was authentic and that it was meant for her. Plaintiff sued the pharmacy and later received $20,000 in damages. Would it make any difference if while she was in jail Plaintiff was physically assaulted by a fellow inmate?

Stadnyk v. Commissioner suggests that in a claim for false imprisonment physical restraint is not necessarily a physical injury (i.e., although false imprisonment involves a physical act, it "does not mean that the victim is necessarily physically injured as a result of that physical act"). Thus, in the first part of the problem, Plaintiff could not exclude the damages received.

Would it make any difference if while she was in jail Plaintiff was physically assaulted by a fellow inmate? Yes. Chief Counsel Advice Memorandum 201045023 opens the door for exclusion of wrongful imprisonment recoveries. That memorandum involved an individual who suffered physical injuries while wrongfully incarcerated.

34.3. Luciaty MacColl was in a boating accident that caused permanent bodily injury. During the year, Luciaty paid total medical expenses of $10,000 and, as a result of her injury, was indemnified under two insurance policies (Policy A paid $9,000; Policy B paid $3,000). Luciaty took no deduction under section

213 for her medical expenses. To what extent are the insurance proceeds includible in Luciaty's gross income under each of the following:

(a)   Policy A and Policy B are both Luciaty's personal health insurance policies. Luciaty paid the annual premiums for both.

Section 104(a)(3) excludes from gross income amounts received under self-financed accident and health insurance policies for personal injuries or sickness *even if such amounts exceed expenses actually incurred.* In other words, the portion of excess indemnification received under medical insurance policies attributable to a taxpayer's contributions is not included in gross income.

Here Luciaty paid the annual premiums for two personal health insurance policies. Since she paid the entire premium for both policies, the $2,000 excess indemnification ($12,000 – $10,000) is not includible in Luciaty's gross income. *See* Situation 1 in Rev. Rul. 69-154.

(b)   Policy A is Luciaty's employer's general health insurance policy and Policy B is her employer's comprehensive supplemental health insurance policy. Luciaty's employer paid the entire annual premiums for both policies.

Amounts received under employer-provided plans are not excludable under section 104(a)(3), but may be excludable under section 105. *See* IRC § 105(b), (c). However, in contrast to the section 104(a)(3) exclusion pertaining to self-financed policies, the section 105 exclusion pertaining to employer-financed policies is limited to actual expenses for medical care. Treas. Reg. § 105-2. In other words, the excess indemnification attributable to the employer's policy is includible in gross income.

Here since Luciaty's employer paid the entire premium for both policies, the $2,000 excess indemnification ($12,000 – $10,000) is includible in Luciaty's gross income. *See* Situation 2 in Rev. Rul. 69-154.

(c)   Policy A is Luciaty's employer's health insurance policy for which the employer paid the annual premium. Policy B is Luciaty's personal health policy for which she paid the annual premium.

Here Luciaty is indemnified under both her employer's insurance policy (Policy A) and her personal insurance policy (Policy B), and the total amount received under both policies ($12,000) exceeds total medical expenses ($10,000).

The excess indemnification attributable to the employer's policy (Policy A) is includible in Luciaty's gross income. But what is the portion of the excess indemnification attributable to the employer's policy? Revenue Ruling 69-154 provides guidance. Under that ruling, the portion of the excess indemnification received by Luciaty attributable to her employer's contribution is determined as follows:

Indemnification from employer's policy	$ 9,000
Indemnification from employee's policy	3,000
Total indemnification received	$12,000

Amount of medical expenses attributable to employer's policy 9/12 × $10,000	$ 7,500
Amount of medical expenses attributable to employee's policy 3/12 × $10,000	$ 2,500
Total medical expenses incurred	$10,000
Excess indemnification attributable to the employer's policy $9,000 − $7,500	$ 1,500

Since Luciaty's employer paid the entire premium on Policy A, the $1,500 excess indemnification is the amount includible in Luciaty's gross income. *See* Situation 3 in Rev. Rul. 69-154.

Chapter 35

Attorney's Fees

Overview

In determining whether attorney's fees and other litigation costs are deductible under section 162 (business expenses) or section 212 (profit-seeking expenses), or are nondeductible under section 262 (personal expenses) or section 263 (capital expenditures), courts look to the origin and character of the claim with respect to which litigation costs are incurred. The origin of the claim test is not a purely mechanical test; it requires more than looking merely to the taxpayer's intent in filing the suit. One must also consider the issues involved, the nature and objectives of the litigation, the defenses asserted, the purposes for which the amounts claimed to be deductible were expended, the background of the litigation, and all facts pertaining to the controversy.

It should be noted that for legal fees to be deductible under section 212(1), they must relate to the production or collection of *taxable* income—amounts includible in gross income (e.g., fees to recover damages on account of non-physical injury, or fees paid to secure the right to alimony or to collect it). Legal fees paid in connection with the production or collection of *tax-exempt* income are generally not deductible in order to prevent what would, in effect, be a double benefit—and exclusion and a deduction. Treas. Reg. § 1.212-1(e) (citing IRC § 265). For example, attorney's fees paid in connection with the receipt of damages on account of personal physical injury are nondeductible since such damages are excludable from gross income under section 104(a)(2); likewise, attorney's fees paid in connection with the receipt of child support are nondeductible on the theory that child support is not taxable. IRC § 71(c). Legal or other professional fees paid or incurred in connection with the determination, collection, or refund of any tax are deductible under section 212(3). Treas. Reg. § 1.212-1(l). Fees for tax planning advice are also deductible. *See* Carpenter v. United States, 338 F.2d 366 (Ct. Cl. 1964); Rev. Rul. 89-68, 1989-1 C.B. 82 (permitting deduction for fees paid in connection with obtaining a private letter ruling). If a legal fee is partially deductible and partially nondeductible, the taxpayer must allocate the fee between the deductible and nondeductible portions. Treas. Reg. § 1.212-1(k).

Generally, attorney's fees related to a non-employee trade or business that are deductible under section 162 are considered above-the-line deductions (i.e., are taken into account in computing adjusted gross income), and other attorney's fees are miscellaneous itemized deductions (i.e., are subject to the section 67 limitation and the section 68 limitation). IRC § 62(a)(1). In an important exception, however, the Code provides an above-the-line deduction for attorney's fees and costs in connection with claims of "unlawful discrimination" and certain claims against the federal government. IRC § 62(a)(20), (e) (defining "unlawful discrimination" via a laundry list and a catchall category that largely covers employment discrimination claims).

In some lawsuits, plaintiffs will engage an attorney to represent them on a contingent fee basis. In such contingency fee arrangements, a taxpayer cannot exclude that portion of the recovery paid directly to an attorney, but must include the entire amount of damages in gross income and then claim a deduction for that portion of the award paid to the attorney. Commissioner v. Banks, 543 U.S. 426 (2005).

Primary Authority

Code: §§ 162(a); 212; 262; 263(a); 265(a)(1).

Regulations: §§ 1.212-1(e), (k)-(m); 1.262-1(b)(7); 1.263(a)-2(e).

Cases: Commissioner v. Banks, 543 U.S. 426 (2005); Carpenter v. United States, 338 F.2d 366 (Ct. Cl. 1964); Danskin, Inc. v. Commissioner, 331 F.2d 360 (2d Cir. 1964); Fleischman v. Commissioner, 45 T.C. 439 (1966); United States v. Gilmmore, 372 U.S. 39 (1963); Hylton v. Commissioner, 32 T.C.M. 1238 (1973); Merians v. Commissioner, 60 T.C. 187 (1973), acq., 1973-2 C.B. 2; Nadiak v. Commissioner, 356 F.2d 911 (2d Cir. 1966); Urquhart v. Commissioner, 215 F.2d 17 (3d Cir. 1954); Wild v. Commissioner, 42 T.C. 706 (1964).

Rulings: Rev. Rul. 89-68, 1989-1 C.B. 82.

Problems

35.1. Discuss the deductibility of the following attorney's fees paid. (Assume none of the fees were paid under a contingency fee agreement.)

(a) $10,000 incurred by Employee in connection with a suit against Employer for age discrimination.

This is deductible under section 212(1), because paid in connection with the production or collection of damages that are not excludable from gross income under section 104(a)(2). This is an above the line deduction because the action involves a claim of unlawful discrimination. IRC § 62(a)(20), (e).

(b) $1,500 incurred by Landlord to collect past due rent from Tenant.

This is deductible under section 212(1), because the legal fees relate to the collection of taxable rent. This is an above the line deduction because it is related to property held for production of rent. IRC § 62(a)(4). Note that if Landlord was deemed to be engaged in a rental trade or business, the legal fees would be deductible above the line as well. IRC § 62(a)(1).

(c) **$8,000 incurred by Plaintiff in connection with a suit against Defendant for assault and battery; and $15,000 incurred by Defendant to defend the assault and battery charge.**

The $8,000 incurred by Plaintiff is non-deductible because it is paid in connection with the production or collection of damages excludable from gross income under section 104(a)(2). *See* Treas. Reg. § 1.212-1(e) (citing IRC § 265).

The $15,000 incurred by Defendant is non-deductible as well. *See Nadiak v. Commissioner* and *Hylton v. Commissioner.*

(d) **$6,000 incurred by Divorcee to collect back child support.**

This is non-deductible because paid in connection with the production or collection of child support, which is not included in gross income under section 71(c). *See* Treas. Reg. § 1.212-1(e) (citing IRC § 265).

(e) **$6,000 incurred by Divorcee to collect unpaid alimony.**

This is deductible under section 212(1), because the legal fees relate to the collection of taxable alimony under section 71. *Wild v. Commissioner.* This is a miscellaneous itemized deduction. IRC § 67.

(f) **$50,000 incurred by Wife in attacking a prenuptial agreement and negotiating a property settlement; and $50,000 incurred by Husband in defending the prenuptial agreement and negotiating a property settlement.**

None of the legal fees are deductible. *Fleischman v. Commissioner,* following the origin of the claim doctrine established in *United States v. Gilmore,* holds that section 212(2) does not apply to expenses incurred in defending property settlement claims since they arise in the context of divorce, a personal matter. Whether *Fleischman* can be reconciled with *Wild v. Commissioner* is an interesting question that can be partially avoided by noting that they each interpret different parts of section 212.

(g) **$25,000 incurred by ABC, Inc. to contest condemnation of property used in the company's business.**

This is a non-deductible capital expenditure because the legal fees relate to defending title to property. Treas. Reg. §§ 1.263(a)-2(e); 1. 212-1(k).

(h) **$20,000 incurred in a copyright infringement action; and $30,000 incurred in a trademark infringement action.**

The $20,000 in legal fees incurred in the copyright infringement action are deductible, as costs incurred to recover lost profits that are themselves taxable are generally deductible expenses. [Note: *Urquhart v. Commissioner* held that legal fees incurred in a patent infringement action were deductible as ordinary and necessary expenses. In IRS Field Service Advisory 199925012, the IRS applied this rule to legal fees incurred in the pursuit and settlement of a copyright infringement action.]

In contrast to legal fees incurred in patent/copyright infringement actions, the $30,000 in fees incurred in the trademark infringement action, however, are non-deductible capital expenditures. The reason is that successful trademark infringement litigation increases the value of the trademark, secures the property right in the trademark, and removes threats of future infringement to the same trademark. Such benefits have a life of over one year; therefore, the litigation expenses are capital in nature and not entitled to immediate deduction in the year paid or incurred. *See Danskin, Inc. v. Commissioner.*

(h) $2,000 paid for tax advice on the deductibility of the legal fees in (h) above.

This is deductible under section 212(3) as a fee paid in connection with the determination of any tax. This is a miscellaneous itemized deduction. IRC § 67.

(i) $5,000 paid for estate tax planning advice.

This is deductible as a miscellaneous itemized deduction. *See Merians v. Commissioner.*

35.2. Lesley was forced to leave her job as an employee of Friendly Bank. Later, she hired an attorney under a contingent fee arrangement and filed a discrimination lawsuit against her former employer. This year, the parties settled the case for $5 million. Friendly Bank paid $3 million to Lesley and $2 million to Lesley's attorney pursuant to the attorney's fee agreement.

(a) What is the proper tax treatment of the $2 million attorney's fee?

Damages received on account of *non*-physical injury are includible in gross income; as a result, attorney's fees to recover such damages are deductible under section 212(1) as expenses for the production of income.

Should Lesley include the entire amount of damages ($5,000,000) in gross income and then take a deduction for the portion paid to the attorney ($2,000,000)? Or, should Lesley include only $3,000,000 in gross income and claim no deduction for the portion of the recovery paid to the attorney? Under *Commissioner v. Banks,* Lesley would have to include $5,000,000 in gross income and then take a $2,000,000 deduction. Fortunately, for Lesley, section 62(a) provides an above-the-line deduction for the deductible attorney's fees. IRC § 62(a)(20), (e). Had section 62(a) not applied, the attorney's fees would have been considered miscellaneous itemized deductions subject to the section 67 limitation and the section 68 limitation, and would not have been allowable as deductions in computing Lesley's alternative minimum tax.

(b) Would it make a difference if Leslie was not an employee of Friendly Bank and her suit was against Friendly Bank for false imprisonment?

The *Banks* decision becomes very significant here. The $2,000,000 attorney's fees are still deductible under section 212(1). But they do not qualify for "above the line" treatment under section 62(a). Instead, the fees are considered miscellaneous itemized deductions. As such, they are subject to the section 67 limitation and the section 68 limitation. Furthermore, as miscellaneous itemized deductions, they are not allowable as deductions in computing Lesley's alternative minimum tax. Lesley might end up paying more in attorney's fees and federal taxes than the $3,000,000 damage award she actually receives!

Chapter 36

Retirement Resources and Deferred Compensation

Overview

In this chapter, we take a broad look at taxation and retirement planning. Traditionally retirees rely on three sources for support during retirement: (1) personal savings; (2) deferred compensation; and (3) Social Security benefits.

(1) Savings. One of the most common forms of savings is home ownership. Although a basic tax and financial planning strategy is to structure one's home mortgage to be paid off by retirement, one who is planning for retirement should seek to build a nest egg independent of housing in order to maintain a level of financial solvency and liquidity. If one succeeds in doing so, the question then becomes how to preserve that solvency and liquidity for the remainder of one's life. Sometimes the answer is an annuity.

An annuity is a contract between a contract owner and an obligor. The obligor is usually an insurance company. The contract calls for a stream of future payments to an annuitant, usually for life, received for an up-front payment or payments to the obligor. An annuity can be for a single life or for multiple lives. A joint and survivor annuity is a common planning tool for married couples. An annuity can be for a term of years instead of for life. The amount of each payment to the annuitant is derived by an actuarial calculation that considers the life expectancy of the annuitant and the expected rate of return on the up-front payment. The taxation of annuities is governed by section 72. It provides for treating a portion of each payment received by the annuitant as a non-taxable return of basis and part as taxable income. In this context basis is called "investment in the contract." *See* IRC § 72(c)(1). The amount of basis recovery in each payment received is determined by reference to an "exclusion ratio" the numerator of which is investment in the contract and the denominator of which is the "expected return on the contract." IRC § 72(b)(1). The expected return on the contract is determined actuarially. If the annuitant out lives her life expectancy and, thus, fully recovers her investment in the contract, the full amount of all payments thereafter are taxable income. IRC § 72(b)(2). If the annuitant dies before recovering her full investment, the unrecovered investment amount is deductible on the decedent's final return. IRC § 72(b)(3) & (4). An annuity contract can be inherited in some circumstances. For example, an annuity may be purchased by a person who dies prior to the beginning of the pay out period. Anything the successor in interest receives in excess of the investment in the contract is treated as income in respect of a decedent under section 691. Thus, the beneficiaries will not receive a basis step up under section 1014. *See* IRC § 1014(c). Instead they will step into the annuitant's shoes for tax purposes. *See* Rev. Rul. 2005-30, 2005-1 C.B. 1015.

The reverse mortgage is a potential retirement planning tool for those whose main savings vehicle is their home. Under this arrangement a lender, usually a bank, agrees to make monthly payments to a homeowner in return for an ever growing share of the homeowner's equity. While a reverse mortgage resembles an installment sale, it is typically structured as a loan with deferred interest payments. The home is simply security for the loan. Thus, the payments do not trigger any gain recognition for the homeowner even if the limits of section 121 are exceeded. Revenue Ruling 80-248 addresses the treatment of the deferred interest payments by the cash basis borrower and lender.

(2) Retirement Plans. There are many types of retirement plans. They are characterized by reference to three overlapping dichotomies: employer funded versus individual funded; defined benefit versus defined contribution; and pre-tax contributions versus post-tax contributions. Many retirement plans ultimately become annuities.

Employer funded retirement plans fall into two broad categories, qualified plans and non-qualified plans. We will focus on qualified plans. These plans arise under the Employee Retirement Income Security Act of 1974 (ERISA). A plan is "qualified" when it is in compliance with government rules, primarily with respect to non-discrimination and financial set asides. In other words, such plans cannot discriminate in favor of highly compensated employees and they are obliged to partially fund their anticipated future obligations under the plan. In exchange for meeting these and other qualifications, the tax system confers an immediate tax deduction on the employer for those set asides and deferral of income to the employee until actual receipt of the compensation. This latter trait allows the funds that are set aside to grow tax-free.

An employer funded retirement plan may be either a "defined benefit" or a "defined contribution" plan. In either event the plan involves the creation of a trust to hold funds for the future well being of the employees. The chief distinction between the two types of plans is with respect to who bears the direct investment risk for the plan. A *defined benefit* is a promise to pay from employer to employee. Under these plans the employer has accepted the risk that the funds set aside in trust to fund the plan may not grow rapidly enough to pay the full amount to which the employee is entitled upon retirement. The employee's entitlement is based on some sort of formula that gives weight to years of service and level of compensation. A *defined contribution* plan, on the other hand, is an investment trust account into which the employer and, sometimes, the employee place funds for which risk of loss is on the employee. Usually the employer will contribute a percentage of the employee's salary to the account in each pay period. (There are dollar caps applicable to all qualified plans.) A typical defined contribution trust account is invested in broad based mutual funds. Upon retirement or certain other events the employee is only entitled to as much money as is represented by the value of those investments.

Under both defined benefit and defined contribution plans the payout to the employee is usually in the form of an annuity for life. Thus, the rules of section 72 are often implicated. If the employee is married, often he or she will select a joint life annuity in order to protect his or her spouse. In the case of the defined contribution plan, the annuity is purchased upon retirement with the funds in the account. If the account was funded with pre-tax dollars, the annuitant has no tax basis in the account. In other words, from a tax perspective the investment in the contract is zero. This means that the entire amount of the payments are taxable income to the annuitant as received. *See* IRC §§ 72(a), 402(a), & 403(a). If some post-tax dollars were used to fund the annuity, tax-free basis recovery is permitted on a statutory schedule. *See* IRC § 72(d). Some plans allow the employee to directly withdraw funds from the accounts. An employee who chooses not to annuitize the account upon retirement assumes the risk of running out of funds prior to death. As with the annuity, the pre-tax contributions and their earnings are taxable income to the employee as they are received. Normally, distributions from defined benefit accounts do not begin until retirement. Distributions from defined contribution accounts cannot usually begin without penalty until the employee reaches age 59½. The penalty for early withdrawal is 10 percent of the distribution. *See* IRC § 72(t)(1) & (2)(A)(i).

The modern trend in employer based retirement plans is toward defined contribution and away from defined benefit plans. The defined contribution plan carries direct investment risk for the employee but has certain advantages. These include portability, limited investment control, insulation from employer insolvency, and the ability to pass by inheritance in some cases.

Individuals have a number of options with respect to tax favored retirement planning through Individual Retirement Accounts (IRAs) and Cash or Deferred Arrangements (CODAs). *See, e.g.*, IRC §§ 408, 401(k). Functionally, IRAs and CODAs are similar, but CODAs are employer based and IRAs are not. Indeed, IRAs are primarily intended to benefit persons who lack adequate employer based retirement saving options. There are various annual limitations on how much money can be contributed to IRAs and CODAs. *See, e.g.*, IRC § 219(b)(1) & (5).

Like defined contribution plans, traditional IRAs and CODAs allow directing pre-tax dollars into investment accounts on a tax deferred basis. Again the taxpayer has a range of investment options. Both the IRA and the CODA are funded by the individual. In the case of the CODA an employee authorizes the employer to transfer a portion of the employee's compensation into the account. This sort of salary reduction agreement is sometimes called a "401(k) plan." This is a reference to the most prominent of the Code provisions that authorize these arrangements, but there are other Code provisions that authorize these accounts as well. *See, e.g.*, IRC § 403(b) (1)(E). Like the defined contribution accounts, IRAs and CODAs are subject to a withdrawal penalty of 10 percent on most distributions made before the distributee has reached age 59½. However, there are a number of exceptions to this rule most notably for qualified education expenses and for first time home purchases. *See* IRC § 72(t)(2)(E) & (F). The case of Gee v. Commissioner, 127 T.C. No. 1 (2006), illustrates how carefully one must apply these rules to avoid the penalty.

It is permitted under some circumstances to fund IRAs and CODAs with post-tax dollars. *See, e.g.,* IRC § 408A. These are known as "Roth" accounts. The advantage of this less favored front end treatment is that neither the principal nor the earnings on these accounts are taxed upon distribution as long as the distributions occur more than five years after establishing the IRA and after the beneficiary has reached age 59½. Economically, the traditional IRA or CODA and the Roth IRA or CODA are equivalent if we assume identical yields on investment, constant tax rates, and that the distributee has no other income. But these assumptions are hardly safe ones. The marginal tax rate that applies to an individual is affected both by acts of Congress and by changes in his or her overall income level. In this context it is worth noting that, unlike the traditional account, the Roth account is not income in respect of a decedent. The designated beneficiary who inherits a Roth account will take it free of any income tax.

(3) Social Security. Social Security is a federal government program designed to provide a modest amount of income to the elderly, the disabled, and their dependents. The statutory framework for Social Security is set out at 42 U.S.C. §§ 401-33. This scheme is fleshed out in a complex set of regulations beginning at 20 C.F.R. § 404. The source of Social Security support is a mandatory 12.4% payroll tax on earned income up to an inflation-adjusted maximum that in 2016 was $118,500. Half of the tax is withheld from the worker's pay and half is the responsibility of the employer. There is no actuarial component to benefits calculation. In other words, benefits are not tied to life expectancy. In addition, the statutory scheme includes provisions for periodic cost of living adjustments (COLAs). In 2016 the average monthly benefit was $1,341 and the maximum monthly benefit was $2,639. The latest figures on benefits may be found at www.ssa.gov.

Anyone born in 1929 or later needs 40 Social Security credits to be eligible for retirement benefits. A person can earn up to four credits per year, so one needs to work in at least 10 years to become eligible for retirement benefits. A person receives credits based on earnings. Each year the amount of earnings needed for a credit is adjusted for inflation. In 2016 a person received one credit for each $1,260 of earnings, up to a maximum of four credits per year. (A person can also gain eligibility for Social Security benefits by being married for ten years to a person who is eligible.) One can elect to begin receiving permanently reduced benefits at age 62 but full benefits do not begin until age 65 or older. Higher starting ages for full benefits are being phased in for persons born in 1939 and later. Under current law persons born after 1959 will receive full benefits at age 67. Spouses and former spouses of qualified workers are entitled to their own benefits based on their own employment histories or 50% of their spouse's benefit whichever ever is greater. A surviving spouse is entitled to the greater of his own benefits or 100% of his spouse's benefits.

In general Social Security benefits are not subject to income tax. There is a major exception to this rule with respect to the benefits of individuals whose adjusted gross income exceeds certain levels. *See* IRC § 86.

Primary Authority

Code: §§ 72(a)-(c)(1), (t)(1); 401(a)(1); 402(a); 403(a)(1); 691(a)(1); 1014(c). Skim: §§ 72(t)(2); 86, 404(a); 408(a), (d)(1).

Regulations: None.

Cases: Gee v. Commissioner, 127 T.C. No. 1 (2006).

Rulings: Rev. Rul. 80-248, 1980-2 C.B. 164; Rev. Rul. 2005-30, 2005-1 C.B. 1015.

Problems

36.1. Paul and Joanne are a retired couple living in a valuable home on a sunny ocean shore. They plan to live there as long as they are able. Paul is 75 and Joanne is 74. They have four adult children all of whom are fairly prosperous and who have children of their own. Paul and Joanne have relatively little income in retirement. Their home is their most valuable asset. They would like to see the home remain in the family as recreational property for their descendants. Their children have indicated a willingness to help make this a reality by contributing financially to their parents' retirement. An estate planner has presented three alternatives for the family's consideration. The first is for the kids to simply make cash gifts to their parents with the expectation that the home will be left to them by will. The second is an installment sale of the home from the parents to the kids coupled with a lease of the home to the parents by the kids. The third is a reverse mortgage financed by the kids.

(a) What income tax and non-tax advantages and disadvantages do you see with respect to these alternatives?

All three approaches involve having the kids, in effect, purchase some or all of their inheritance. The gift approach does not create any income for the parents. IRC § 102(a). The gift route gives the kids no protection against their parents' creditors should there be any. For example if the parents should end up in a nursing home supported by Medicaid, the state might have a claim against the home. Nor does it protect them if the parents have a change of heart and sell the home. It does give them a section 1014 basis step up if the plan is followed.

The installment sale gives the kids a cost basis under section 1012. If the home appreciates after the date of sale and before the parents' deaths, there is a loss of basis step up. This may not matter greatly if there are no plans to sell. The sale generates a reliable flow of cash for the parents that is largely tax free under section 121. The sale will generate current interest income for the parents and may generate interest deductions for the kids. A potential problem with the installment sale is that the parents want to continue to live in the home. Thus, they are either obliged to pay rent or the kids must make gifts of rent to them. The sale could be structured so that the installment payments are considerably greater than the rent payments, yielding a net positive cash flow to the parents. This also creates rental income for the kids.

The reverse mortgage gives some protection from creditors and preserves the section 1014 basis step up if the parents hold the property until death. The kids will have interest income when the mortgage is paid. The parents have a deduction at that time as well. *See* Rev. Rul. 80-248. If the parents die before the mortgage must be paid, the kids inherit the property subject to the debt owed to themselves. The debt is extinguished. Technically the parents retain the right to sell the property or to leave it to someone other than the kids.

(b) Do you see any ethical issues for the family's advisor?

Since tax and asset protection consequences are different for various family members under the various scenarios, there are potential conflicts of interest among the family members. Especially if the advisor is a lawyer or an accountant, the ethical rules of those professions come into play. At a minimum, a lawyer should outline these potential conflicts to the parties, identify who he or she is representing and advise the others to seek their own counsel.

36.2. Matt bought a single life annuity for $800,000. Under the annuity contract, Matt will receive $64,000 a year for life. His life expectancy is 25 years.

(a) In the first year of the annuity payments, how much income will Matt have?

$32,000.

The exclusion ratio under section 72(b) is 1:2, i.e., his investment in the contract of $800,000 divided by his expected return of $1,600,000 ($64,000 × 25 = $1,600,000). Thus, one half of the $64,000 received in Year 1 is return of basis and one half is income. Over 25 years, Matt will receive return of his entire investment ($32,000 × 25 = $800,000).

(b) How will Matt be taxed in Year 26?

All $64,000 is taxable income since his investment has been recovered. IRC § 72(b)(2).

(c) If Matt dies after twenty years, what is the effect of the annuity on his final tax return?

His executor will take a $160,000 deduction. IRC § 72(b)(3) & (4) ($800,000 investment minus the $640,000 recovered before death).

36.3. Warren is offered two alternative forms of deferred compensation in Year 1. The first alternative provides for a pre-tax payment of $10,000 invested tax-free in a trust account at 10% compounded annually for 7.2 years. After

7.2 years the funds in the trust account will be distributed to Warren and taxed to him. Under the second alternative, a post-tax payment of $6,000 ($10,000 pre-tax) will be invested tax-free in a trust account for 7.2 years, again at 10% compounded annually. After 7.2 years the funds in the trust account will be distributed to Warren without any further taxation.

(a) **If under both alternatives the applicable tax rate is a flat 40%, what is Warren's after-tax yield upon distribution of the accounts to him?**

In either case, Warren will have $12,000 after taxes when the trust account is distributed to him.

Applying the rule of 72, in 7.2 years a lump sum invested at 10% will double in value (72 divided by 10 equals 7.2). Thus, under either scenario the amount placed in trust will double. In the first scenario this will yield $20,000 before taxes and $12,000 after taxes ($20,000 × .4 = $8,000 tax). In the second scenario the tax has been applied at the outset and then the $6,000 fund grows tax free.

This illustrates the after tax equivalence of traditional and Roth IRAs and CODAs if we assume the same tax rates will apply in both cases. The choice between them turns primarily on whether one expects tax rates to rise or fall prior to distribution. This is illustrated below. Of course in a graduated income tax system the applicable rates may rise or fall due to changes in the taxpayer's overall income level. Most taxpayers may expect to be in a lower marginal tax bracket after retirement. This argues for going with the traditional deferred compensation arrangement. On the other hand current income tax rates are relatively low compared to those of the past two or three decades. Can we expect tax rates to rise over the next several years?

(b) **Same as (a) except in Year 7 the applicable tax rate is 20%.**

Now the first alternative yields $16,000 after taxes and therefore is preferable to the second.

(c) **Same as (a) except in Year 7 the applicable tax rate is 50%.**

Now the first alternative yields only $10,000 in after tax income and the second alternative, yielding $12,000, is preferable.

36.4. John and June are a long time married couple who are now eligible for full Social Security benefits. John worked full time for forty years. Based on his earnings history John is entitled to $800 in monthly benefits. June worked full time for forty years. Based on her earnings history June is entitled to $1,500 in monthly benefits. Richard and Patricia are also a long time married couple. Richard worked full time for thirty years. Based on his earnings history Richard is entitled to $2,500 in monthly benefits. Patricia has no earnings history.

(a) **What is the aggregate monthly Social Security benefit that John and June are entitled to?**

$2,300. Spouses are each entitled to the greater of the benefit their earnings history would produce or 50% of their spouse's benefit. Here John is entitled to $800 based on his earnings history. Thus, their aggregate benefit is $2,300 per month ($1,500 + $800 = $2,300).

(b) What is the aggregate monthly Social Security benefit that Richard and Patricia are entitled to?

$3,750. Though Patricia has no earnings history she is entitled to $1,250 (50% of Richard's $2,500 monthly benefit). ($2,500 + $1,250 =$3,750)

(c) Do you think the two outcomes above represent good policy?

The subsidy for stay at home spouses can be justified on the basis of the need to support those people who raise children. But note there is no legal requirement that Patricia be a parent or that she stay at home with her children.

The subsidy also encourages marriage rather than mere cohabitation (assuming that people are aware of the incentive).

With more information about their aggregate contributions to the system we could also show that John and June may be getting a smaller aggregate monthly benefit despite having contributed a larger aggregate amount to the Social Security system. To the extent that we see Social Security as a form of purchased insurance, this outcome may seem unfair.

36.5. Do you think that Social Security should have an actuarial component, that is, should people with longer life expectancies receive smaller monthly benefits?

This raises the issue of equal treatment as between genders and races. For example, African Americans have lower life expectancies than White Americans. Since there is no actuarial component to Social Security, equal contributing White and African Americans can expect to receive different total amounts of benefits.

Assuming a zero sum game with respect to the total amount of money available for benefits, women would be the big losers if Social Security had an actuarial component since women tend to live considerably longer than men. Given that women on average already have lower lifetime earnings than men, the overall impact would likely be to leave more women in poverty during old age.

Chapter 37

Overview of Entity Taxation

Overview

Most individuals prefer not to operate their businesses as sole proprietorships, but instead choose to operate through a business form of statutory creation. There are various non-tax reasons for this preference including: the ability to pool capital, centralized management, and limited liability. (Entities often serve important estate planning functions as well. For example, parents may wish to prepare their children to take over a family business while keeping control for the near term. Transfers of minority stock or limited partnership interests can serve this purpose.) A variety of state-law entities are available, including the corporation, the partnership, the limited liability company (LLC), and the trust. (As will be discussed, trusts are more often used for estate planning than for business planning.) Tax considerations often play an important role in determining which entity to use.

A. Corporations

A corporation is a legal entity distinct from its owners. State law formalities must be met to create the legal entity. The corporation's owners (shareholders) own stock, which represents legal ownership and a stake in assets and future profits of the corporation. The corporation is solely responsible for its debts and obligations. Shareholders are not personally liable for debts of the corporation, unless they have entered into an agreement to the contrary (e.g., a personal guarantee). They are typically at risk to lose only their investment in the shares. For federal tax purposes, a corporation formed under state corporate law is either a C corporation, taxed under the rules of subchapter C of the Code, or an S corporation, taxed under the rules of subchapter S of the Code. To be taxed under subchapter S, the corporation must meet certain eligibility requirements and make a valid election.

C Corporations. A corporation formed under state law that does not elect to be treated as an S Corporation is a C corporation, taxed under the provisions of subchapter C of the Code. *See* IRC §§ 301–85. Almost all publicly traded stocks are in C corporations. A C corporation is a separate taxable entity distinct from its shareholders, and pays tax on the enterprise's taxable income. Though there are important differences, generally speaking a corporation determines its taxable income much the same way as an individual. The corporate income tax is imposed by section 11(a). When a C corporation's income is distributed to shareholders as a dividend, the shareholders are also taxed. IRC § 61(a)(7). When a C corporation liquidates, the liquidation is treated as a gain recognition event at both the corporate and at the shareholder level. *See* IRC §§ 331 & 336. As can be seen, the earnings of a C corporation are subject to two levels of tax—the first at the corporate level (when earned) and the second at the shareholder level (either when the corporation makes a dividend distribution or a liquidating distribution).

S Corporations. Certain qualified domestic corporations, newly formed under state law or preexisting, may elect to be treated as S corporations for federal tax purposes and, hence, taxed under the Code provisions of subchapter S, rather than the provisions of subchapter C. *See* IRC §§ 1361–77. An S corporation generally is not a separate taxpaying entity; rather income and deduction items are allocated to the individual shareholders and reported on their individual tax returns. Hence, S corporation income is taxed only once at individual shareholder rates rather than twice. Each owner's share of the corporation's income and deduction items is determined by reference to the owner's share of the corporation's stock. *See* IRC § 1366. Thus, for example, a person who owns 10 percent of an S corporation's stock will report and pay taxes on 10 percent of the corporation's taxable income. This is true without regard to whether that income is distributed. But the income allocated to the shareholder increases the shareholder's basis in his S corporation stock. IRC § 1367(a)(1). Any subsequent distribution from the S corporation is tax free to the shareholder as long as it does not exceed the shareholder's basis. IRC § 1368(b)(1). In many respects the S corporation tax rules resemble a simplified version of those for partnerships described below. The relative simplicity of S corporation tax rules is one of its main attractions both to their owners and to their tax advisors. The rules of subchapter S do not address all aspects of the formation, operation, and liquidation of an S corporation. These large gaps are filled in by subchapter C. *See* IRC § 1371(a).

B. Unincorporated Entities (Partnerships and Limited Liability Companies)

General Partnerships. A general partnership exists when two or more persons carry on as co-owners a business with the expectation of generating profits. A general partnership is a contractually-based, flexible business form that usually arises when two or more persons go into a business without much thought as to what their relationship is. Each partner is personally responsible for partnership debt and obligations. This unlimited personal liability is a significant drawback of the general partnership form.

Limited Partnerships. Unlike a general partnership, which often arises in informal circumstances, a limited partnership is a creature of state law that must satisfy filing requirements to come into existence. A limited partnership has one or more general partners and one or more limited partners. General partners have unlimited personal liability for partnership debts and obligations. Limited partners are not liable for debts and obligations of the partnership as long as they do not participate in control of the business. A limited partner's liability is generally limited to the capital that he or she contributes to the business.

Limited Liability Companies. A limited liability company (LLC) is a hybrid entity combining both corporate and partnership features. Despite being called a "company," an LLC is an unincorporated business entity formed under state law. Like a corporation and a limited partnership, an LLC can only be created by following state law requirements (i.e., filing articles of organization). LLC owners are known as members. There are no restrictions on the number or types of owners (as is the case with S corporations). All members of an LLC have limited liability protection regardless of their management activity. This is a significant advantage over the limited partnership form, wherein general partners have unlimited liability and limited partners may be personally liable if they participate in management.

Tax Classification and Treatment of Unincorporated Businesses. Treasury regulations permit most unincorporated business entities to elect, by "checking a box" on an election form, to be treated as either partnerships or corporations for federal income tax purposes. *See* Treas. Reg. § 301.7701-1 to -3. Specifically, under the check-the-box regulations, an unincorporated business entity with two or more members can freely elect to be taxed as a corporation (taxed under subchapter C or, if eligible, under subchapter S) or a partnership (taxed under subchapter K—IRC § 701-77). Treas. Reg. § 301.7701-2(a), -3(a). An unincorporated entity with a single member, such as the single-member LLC, can freely elect to be a corporation (taxed under subchapter C or, if eligible, under subchapter S) or to be "disregarded" for tax purposes (i.e., activities are treated in the same manner as a sole proprietorship and reported on Schedule C of the Form 1040). *Id.*

If an unincorporated entity chooses to be taxed under the rules of subchapter K, the entity is not a separate taxable entity for federal income taxes, but rather is a pass-through entity. Under subchapter K, items of income, gain, loss, deduction, and credit are determined at the entity level, but then flow through to individual partners and are reported on their individual returns. *See* IRC §§ 701, 702 & 704. The partners report these items without regard to whether the partnership makes any distributions. The payback for this treatment is that distributions are generally tax free to the partners but will reduce the partners' bases in their partnership interests. IRC §§ 731(a) & 705(a). Each partner's equity interest in the partnership is represented by a *capital account.* The regulations specify an elaborate scheme for keeping track of each partner's capital account. *See* Treas. Reg. § 1.704-1(b)(2)(iv).

One important tax difference between a partnership and an S corporation is that partnership tax rules permit tax items to pass through to the partners on a non pro rata basis if certain rules are followed. The rules for taxation of partnership income are highly nuanced and complex. The partnership tax rules are also very flexible and afford many opportunities for tax planning.

C. Trusts

Trusts are mechanisms by which legal and equitable title to property are divided. Legal title is placed with a *trustee.* Equitable title is lodged in one or more *beneficiaries.* The trustee stands in a fiduciary relationship to the beneficiaries of the trust and must manage the property for their benefit. The trust instrument (i.e., a written document executed according to the requirements of state law) establishes the relationship between the property and the interested parties. It guides the trustee's actions. Trusts often serve as a mechanism for dividing ownership of property on a temporal basis. Thus, for example, one beneficiary may be the life tenant receiving the income from the trust and another beneficiary may be the remainderman who is entitled to receive the trust assets upon the death of the life tenant. The ability to divide property on a temporal basis is one reason trusts are commonly used for estate planning purposes.

There are two main categories of trusts for tax purposes, grantor trusts and regular trusts. The grantor is the person who created the trust by transferring property to it. When the grantor maintains some degree of direct control over the trust after its formation the trust may be characterized as a grantor trust. The income from a grantor trust is usually taxed to the grantor as though the grantor owned the trust property directly. Whether the retained control is sufficient to cause this result is dictated by sections 671 through 679 of the Code. Some examples of retained rights that will trigger grantor trust treatment include: the right to revoke the trust, the right to change the beneficiaries, the right to a substantial reversion, and the right to borrow from the trust without adequate security.

There are two kinds of regular trusts, simple trusts and complex trusts. Simple trusts are obliged to distribute all of their income currently. Complex trusts may accumulate their income. The tax treatment of both kinds of regular trusts (and estates) is controlled by subchapter J of the Code. *See* IRC §§ 641–91. Regular trusts are at least nominally taxpaying entities. But, in fact, income from the trust assets may be taxed to the trust or to the beneficiaries depending on whether the trust income is currently distributed to the beneficiaries. The mechanism for achieving this result is a deduction granted to the trust for distributions. *See* IRC §§ 651 & 661. Thus, if a trust distributes all of its income currently, its distribution deduction will reduce its taxable income to zero. So much of its current income as is distributed is then taxed to the recipient beneficiaries. *See* IRC §§ 652 & 662. Conversely, if a trust retains any of its income, the trust will report and pay taxes on the retained income. Many complexities can arise in trust taxation. For example, how does one distinguish between distributions of income and distributions of trust principal? Or, if a trust has both capital gains and ordinary income, how does a beneficiary know the character of the distributions he or she is receiving? We have space here only to hint at the answers. The primary mechanism for answering these questions is the concept of *distributable net income* (DNI). *See* IRC § 643(a). DNI is essentially a trust's current taxable income prior to applying the distribution deduction rules. All distributions are deemed to be from DNI to the extent of DNI. The distributions are striped with their respective shares of DNI. This means, among other things, that the income has the same character in the beneficiary's hands as it did in the trust's hands.

Primary Authority

Code: §§ 11(a)-(b); 61(a)(7); 531; 541; 643(a); 651-652; 661-662; 671-679, 701-704; 705(a); 731(a); 752; 1361; 1366; 1367(a); 1368(b)(1); 1371.

Regulations: §§ 1.704-1(b)(2)(iv); 301.7701-2(a), -3(a), -3(b)(1).

Cases: None.

Rulings: None.

Problems

37.1. **Six of your clients—Monica, Ross, Phoebe, Joey, Rachel and Chandler— have just asked you for your advice. They are in the planning stages of a television studio, and would like your recommendation on the appropriate form of entity to be used. The estimated cost of purchasing the land and constructing the studio is $10,000,000. Your clients' equity contribution will be $4,000,000, and the remainder of the estimated costs will be borrowed from a local bank. They estimate that the project will produce large tax losses in the first few years of operation, but some positive cash flow by the second year. Ross will take an active role in management, while the others will take a passive role.**

   (a) **Would you recommend that a C corporation be used to own and operate the studio? Why or why not?**

   Probably not. If a C corporation is used, the large tax losses projected in early years will not flow through to the participants but will become net operating losses carried over to the next twenty years. IRC § 172. When the corporation becomes profitable, any taxable income will be subject to double taxation—once at the entity level (at section 11(b) rates) and then again at the owner level when distributed (at section 1 rates). A pass-through entity will most likely produce more beneficial results to the six friends.

   [Note: The regular C corporation may be the tax entity of choice for some small businesses and their owners. For example, a small or even moderate income private C corporation may end up paying less tax at the entity and owner levels combined than would occur under conduit taxation, especially when most of the owners' individual tax brackets are higher than the corporation's bracket, and if dividends are not going to be paid by the corporation.]

   (b) **Assume that your clients have considered using either a limited partnership with Ross as the general partner, a limited liability company, or an S corporation. Which would you recommend and why?**

   Non-tax Considerations:

   If the clients choose a *limited partnership* with Ross as the general partner, there will be some non-tax drawbacks. For example, Ross (as general partner) will be personally liable for the limited partnership's debts and obligations. In addition, Ross (as the sole general partner), might have greater decision making powers than the others deem acceptable. These problems could be solved with the use of a limited liability company or an S corporation. With an *LLC*, all participants enjoy limited liability regardless of management activity. Accordingly, Ross could be designated as the managing member with certain limits placed on his decision-making authority, and the others could be designated non-managing members with some participation rights. With an *S Corporation*, all shareholders enjoy limited liability protection. Accordingly, all six could serve on the company's board of directors (with decision making authority boards typically enjoy) and Ross could be designated as an officer with clearly defined managerial responsibilities. Whether to use an LLC or S corporation would be governed chiefly by the following tax considerations.

Tax Considerations–Subchapter K or Subchapter S:

With reference to the proposed venture, we should compare and contrast the treatment of a limited partnership or LLC (treated as a partnership) with the treatment of an S corporation. The following are a few considerations in determining whether subchapter K or subchapter S is best:

1. *Owner Eligibility*. In subchapter K, there are no limits on the number of owners or the type of owners. In subchapter S, however, there are. In order to be eligible for treatment as an S corporation, a corporation must be a "small business corporation" as defined in section 1361(b)(1) (e.g., the corporation can have no more than 100 shareholders, and only individuals (U.S. residents and citizens), estates, certain trusts, and certain tax exempt charitable organizations can be shareholders). [Here, if the venture will remain closely-held, owner eligibility would not be a problem.]

2. *Capital Structure*. In subchapter K, there are no limits on equity or debt. Accordingly, with a limited partnership or LLC (taxed as a partnership), Ross and the others could have multiple classes of partnership interests (i.e., could separate their profits interest from their capital interests and their profits and capital interests from their management interests). In subchapter S, this is more difficult. An S corporation may issue both stock and debt, but it may not have more than one class of stock (differences in voting rights are ignored). IRC § 1361(b)(1)(D), (c)(4). Every share of stock must confer identical rights to distribution and liquidation proceeds. Treas. Reg. § 1.1361-1(l). Debt treated as equity under general tax principles would create a second class of stock in violation of this requirement. *But see* IRC § 1361(c)(5) (straight debt safe harbor). [Here, we would need to know whether they plan to separate profits, management, and capital.]

3. *Allocation of Income/Deductions*: Both subchapter K and subchapter S entities are flow-through entities. Items of income and deduction are determined at the entity level, but then pass through to the owners to be reported on their individual returns. IRC §§ 701, 1363. Subchapter K and subchapter S differ chiefly in two respects: (1) how tax items flow through to the owners, and (2) how losses are limited.

4. *Special Allocations*: Subchapter K is much more flexible than subchapter S with respect to the allocation of tax items to participants. In subchapter K, the participants can agree in the partnership agreement how to allocated income, gain, loss, deductions, and credits. Indeed, subchapter K permits special allocations as long as those allocations have substantial economic effect. IRC § 704. In subchapter S, in contrast, special allocations are not permitted. Tax items are allocated on pro-rata, per-share, daily basis. IRC § 1377. [Here, if they wish to have flexibility in allocating tax items, they should use the limited partnership or the LLC.]

5. *Deductibility of Losses*: In subchapter K, participants can deduct their allocable share of partnership losses only to the extent of their tax basis in their partnership interest, *which includes their allocable share of partnership debt*. IRC §§ 704(d), 752. In subchapter S, shareholders can deduct their pro rata share of the corporation's losses only to the extent of their tax basis in their stock, *which does not include any portion of the corporation's debt*, and tax basis in shareholder loans made to the corporation. IRC § 1366(d). [Here, they anticipate large tax losses in early years. They also plan on having the entity borrow $6,000,000. If a limited partnership or LLC were used, each partner would get to include his share of the entity debt ($1,000,000 each if the borrowing were nonrecourse) in the basis in his partnership interest, which would ultimately allow more tax deductions and losses to be enjoyed at the owner level. If an S corporation were used, each shareholder would not increase basis for share of corporate debt, which might limit the amount of deductions enjoyed at the owner level. In the end, this might not make such a big difference, since partners and S corporation shareholders are subject to the at-risk limitations of section 465 and the passive activity loss limitations of section 469, both considered in Chapter 27. We would have to determine whether the $6,000,000 debt will be recourse, qualified nonrecourse, or nonrecourse financing. We also would have to determine each participant's material participation in the venture. With respect to S corporation shareholders, all seven material participation tests apply. *See* Treas. Reg. § 1.469-5T(a)(1)-(7). With respect to limited partners, however, only three of the seven tests apply. *See* Treas. Reg. § 1.469-5T(e)(3).]

6. *Cash Distributions*: In subchapter K, cash distributions are nontaxable to the extent of the partner's tax basis in his partnership interest. IRC § 731(a). Similarly, in subchapter S, cash distributions are nontaxable to the extent of the shareholder's tax basis in his stock. IRC § 1368(a), (b)(1). [Here, their venture will have positive cash flow by the second year. Cash distributions to them will be tax free provided they have enough tax basis in their interest. As noted above, tax basis will be higher if a partnership form is used, since partnership debt increases basis in partnership interests. Accordingly, distributions will more likely be tax free.]

7. *Payroll Tax Considerations*: A partner's allocable share of income from a trade or business carried on by the partnership is treated as net earnings from self employment. IRC § 1402(a); Treas. Reg § 1.1402(c)-1. An exclusion exists, however, for a limited partner. A limited partner's allocable share of partnership income is not subject to the self-employment tax. IRC § 1403(a)(13). Whether an LLC member's share of earnings will be subject to the self-employment tax depends on whether the

member will be treated as a limited partner for purposes of the section 1402(a)(13) exclusion. The Service has issued proposed regulations providing guidance in making that determination. Prop. Treas. Reg. § 1.1402(a)-2(h)(2). *See also* Chief Counsel Advice 201436049 (concluding income allocated to members of an LLC was subject to self-employment tax). In contrast to the treatment of partnerships and LLCs, income allocated to an S corporation shareholder is not subject to self-employment tax. *See* IRS Publication 533, "Self Employment Tax" (stating that S corporation income is not self-employment income). This is a significant advantage of the S corporation over the partnership forms. Note, however, the advantage is less significant if the S corporation shareholder is also an employee, since the Service will allocate a reasonable salary to an active S corporation shareholder, which will be subject to the self-employment tax. [Here, payroll tax considerations will be irrelevant for those who will be either limited partners in a limited partnership, non-managing members of an LLC, or non-active shareholders of an S corporation. Payroll tax considerations may, however, have implications for Ross, who will be an active manager.]

Recommendation: Although the S corporation has many advantages, the limited liability company taxed as a partnership might be the preferable choice. All six participants would enjoy limited liability protection regardless of their level of management activity. Subchapter K would give them great flexibility in expanding their business and in allocating tax items among themselves. In addition, subchapter K might allow them to enjoy greater deductions in the early years of the business and to receive a larger amount of distributions tax free (due to the fact that the tax basis of their LLC membership interests will be increased for their share of LLC debt).

(c) For the entity recommended in (b), what steps would you take to ensure desired classification for tax purposes?

If they desire partnership taxation and utilize either a limited partnership or an LLC, they would have to do nothing. Under the default rules in the check-the-box classification regulations, an unincorporated entity with more than one owner will be taxed as a partnership (subchapter K). Treas. Reg. § 301.7701-3(b)(1). If they insisted on filing a form, they would need to file IRS Form 8832, Entity Classification Election, with the Service center designated on the form. Treas. Reg. § 301.7701-3(c)(1)(i). [Note: There is no minimum duration for the initial election. However, if they choose to change the entity's classification, the entity could not change its classification again for 60 months. Treas. Reg. § 301.7701-3(c)(1)(iv).]

If they choose an S corporation, they would have to file IRS Form 2553. For rules and procedures for shareholders' consent to an S election, see Treas. Reg. § 1.1362-6. For the effective date of an S election, see IRC § 1362(b).

37.2. Mother creates a "simple trust" for the benefit of her two children, Son and Daughter, (the income beneficiaries) and her three grandchildren (the remainder beneficiaries). Under the terms of the trust, Trustee is required to distribute all of its income currently, including all realized capital gains, and may also distribute trust principal. In the current year, the trust has

$50,000 of rental income and $10,000 of long-term capital gains. In the current year, Trustee directs distributions from the trust of $60,000 to Son and $40,000 to Daughter. What is the proper tax treatment of the trust distributions?

The simple trust has $50,000 of rental income and $10,000 of long-term capital gains. Thus, the trust has distributable net income (DNI) of $60,000. IRC § 643(a). (This assumes that realized capital gains are required to be distributed currently.) Trustee directs distributions from the trust of $60,000 to Son and $40,000 to Daughter. Thus, the Trustee distributed $40,000 in excess of its income.

Since the trust distributed all of its current income, its distribution deduction will reduce its taxable income to zero. IRC § 651. The trust will owe no taxes in the current year.

Since Son received three fifths of the funds distributed, Son is deemed to have received three fifths of the rental income ($30,000), three fifths of the long-term capital gains ($6,000), and three fifths of the principal distributed ($24,000). IRC § 652(a). Since Daughter received two fifths of the funds distributed, Daughter is deemed to have received two fifths of the rental income ($20,000), two fifths of the long-term capital gains ($4,000), and two fifths of the principal distributed ($16,000). Son and Daughter will each report their respective shares of trust income on their current year tax return. The income will have the same character in their hands as it did in the trust's. IRC § 652(b).

Chapter 38

Corporate Formations

Overview

From a tax perspective, the formation of a corporation is essentially a sale or exchange between a corporation and its founding shareholders. The shareholders transfer cash or other property to the corporation and take back stock in the corporation. The corporation issues its stock for the cash or property received from the shareholders. Normally each party is deemed to give and receive property of equal value. Thus, in the absence of overriding rules, section 1001 would cause each party to recognize gain or loss. However, with good reason, Congress has chosen to treat corporate formations as non-recognition events under certain circumstances. *See* IRC § 351(a). As detailed below, the tax rules with respect to corporate formations bear a strong similarity to the like kind exchange rules studied in Chapter 24. The basic pattern is the grant of non-recognition of gain or loss but at the price of a carry over basis in the property acquired in the formation. *See* IRC § 358(a).

The key operative provision in most corporate formations is section 351. It prevents recognition of gains and losses by the transferors when property is contributed *solely* for stock of a corporation if afterwards the transferors are in "control" of the corporation. IRC § 351(a). Money is property for this purpose. Rev. Rul. 69-357, 1969-1 C.B. 101. Not even the depreciation recapture rules will override section 351(a) in most cases. *See* IRC § 1245(b)(3). The transferor takes a basis in the stock received equal to her basis in the property and cash given up. IRC § 358(a)(1). If the transferor receives more than one class of stock the basis is allocated between classes based on their relative values. Treas. Reg. § 1.358-2(b)(2). If the property given up by the transferor was capital gain property or section 1231 property, the transferor can tack the property's holding period to the stock's holding period. IRC § 1223(1). The provision that grants the corporation non-recognition is section 1032(a). This is important because normally the corporation will have a zero basis in its own stock. But rather than being obliged to take a zero basis in the property received for the stock, the corporation takes the transferor's basis in the property. IRC § 362(a).

Section 351 only grants non-recognition for transfers of "property" for stock. Thus, a person who receives stock for services is outside of the operation of section 351. *See* IRC § 351(d)(1); Treas. Reg. § 1.351-1(a)(1)(i). The shareholder who receives stock for services has compensation income measured by the value of the stock. IRC § 61.

For various reasons a contributing shareholder may receive cash or other property in addition to stock in the corporation as part of the formation. Just as with like kind exchanges, we refer to this other property as "boot." If boot is received by the transferor, realized gain (but not loss) is recognized by the transferor to the extent of the boot's value. IRC § 351(b). In other words, the transferor will recognize the *lesser* of gain realized or boot received. If the boot is cash, the transferor's basis in her stock is decreased to the extent of the cash received and increased to the extent of the gain recognized. IRC § 358(a)(1). If the boot is property other than cash, the transferor's basis in the stock is reduced by the value of the boot received and increased by the gain recognized. The non-cash boot will take a fair market value basis. IRC § 358(a)(2). The corporation's basis in the property it receives from the transferor is increased by the amount of gain recognized by the transferor. IRC § 362(a) (flush language).

Primary Authority

Code: §§ 351(a)-(b); 357(a), (c); 358(a), (d)(1); 362(a); 368(c); 1032(a). Skim §§ 83(a)-(b); 1223(1)-(2); 1245(b)(3).

Regulations: §§ 1.351-1(a)(1); 1.358-2(b)(2).

Cases: None.

Rulings: Rev. Rul. 64-56, 1964-1 C.B. 133; Rev. Rul. 66-7; 1966-1 C.B. 188; Rev. Rul. 69-357, 1969-1 C.B. 101; Rev. Rul. 74-477, 1974-2 C.B. 116.

Problems

38.1. Sheldon, Leonard, and Penny decide to form HighTech Corporation to operate a software development business near Silicon Valley. What are the tax consequences of this formation under the following circumstances?

(a) **Sheldon contributes investment land worth $1,000,000 in which he has a basis of $500,000. Leonard contributes $1,000,000 in cash. Penny, who is a programmer and entrepreneur, contributes a patent held as inventory and a license granting unlimited use of another patent. She purchased the license from an inventor third party. The patent is worth $200,000 and has a basis of $300,000. The license is worth $800,000 and has a basis of $400,000. Each of them receives 300 shares of HighTech common stock in exchange for their transfers.**

Section 351 non-recognition applies because each has transferred "property" to the corporation for stock. Money is property for this purpose. *See* Rev. Rul. 69-357. They are in control within the meaning of section 368(c).

Sheldon has a $500,000 realized gain but recognizes no gain and takes a $500,000 basis in his stock. IRC § 358(a)(1). He gets tacking of his holding period for the land to his stock holding period since the land was a capital asset. IRC § 1223(1).

Leonard has no gain and takes a $1,000,000 basis in his stock. If he were outside 351 the result would be the same for him but by classifying his money as property he allows the others to obtain section 351 treatment because the 80% control test is met.

Penny has a $100,000 realized loss on the patent but it is not recognized under section 351. She has a realized gain of $400,000 on the license transfer but this gain also goes unrecognized. Her basis in her stock is $700,000. IRC § 358(a)(1). No tacking occurs with respect to the patent because the inventory is not a capital asset or section 1231 property. *See* IRC § 1223(1). However, the license is probably section 1231 property.

HighTech recognizes no gain and takes carryover bases in the assets. IRC §§ 1032(a), 362(a). It gets tacking of holding periods of all assets. IRC § 1223(2).

(b) Same as (a) except that each receives 200 shares of common stock valued at $500,000 and 100 shares of preferred stock also valued at $500,000.

Assuming the preferred stock is not "nonqualified preferred stock" defined in section 351(g), there is no change in the analysis in (a) except their bases must be spread between the two classes of stock. This is done by allocating their bases in proportion to the fair market values of the two classes of stock. Treas. Reg. § 1.358-2(b)(2). Thus, Sheldon will take $250,000 basis in each class of stock. Leonard will take a $500,000 basis in each class. Penny will take a $350,000 basis in each class of stock.

(c) Same as (a) except that Sheldon's land is worth $1,100,000. To equalize the deal he receives $100,000 of cash in addition to the stock.

The result is the same as (a) for Leonard and Penny. Sheldon has received $100,000 of boot and must recognize that amount of gain under section 351(b) since his realized gain is $500,000. His gain is capital, presumably long term. IRC §§ 1221, 1222. His basis in the stock is still $500,000 ($500,000 beginning basis minus $100,000 boot received plus $100,000 gain recognized). IRC § 358(a)(1). The company's basis in the land is $600,000 per section 362(a).

(d) Same as (c) except that Sheldon's basis in the land is $1,050,000.

Now Sheldon's realized gain is only $50,000 so that is how much gain he will recognize. IRC § 351(b). His basis in the stock is $1,000,000 ($1,050,000 beginning basis minus $100,000 boot received plus $50,000 gain recognized). IRC § 358(a)(1). The company's basis in the land is $1,100,000 per section 362(a).

(e) Same as (a) except that Sheldon, Leonard, and Penny each receives 270 shares of stock worth $1,000,000 and Rajeesh, an expert programmer, receives 90 shares worth $300,000 of fully vested stock in exchange for agreeing to manage HighTech for ten years.

Now we have a shareholder receiving stock for services and thus that stock cannot be counted for purposes of the section 368(c) control test. Since the stock received is less than 20%, the control test is still met. Sheldon, Leonard and Penny all still receive non-recognition treatment. Rajeesh has $300,000 of ordinary income. IRC

§§ 61, 83(a). He will take a $300,000 cost basis in his stock. IRC § 1012. Tacking will not apply and his holding period will begin the day after he receives the stock. Rev. Rul. 66-7.

(f) **Same as (e) except that each of the four owners receive 225 shares worth $1,000,000.**

Section 351 non-recognition no longer applies because Rajeesh's interest is not received for property and exceeds the 20% threshold. Sheldon, Leonard, and Penny (the transferors of property) are not in control within the meaning of section 368(c).

Sheldon has a $500,000 realized and recognized gain and takes a $1,000,000 basis in his stock. IRC §§ 1001, 1012. (This presumes that the stock he receives is still worth $1,000,000.) He gets no tacking of his holding period for the land to his stock holding period.

Leonard has no gain and takes a $1,000,000 cost basis in his stock. IRC §§ 1001, 1012.

Penny has a $100,000 realized and recognized ordinary loss on the patent. She has a realized and recognized section 1231 gain of $400,000 on the license. IRC § 1001. Her basis in her stock is $1,000,000. IRC § 1012.

Rajeesh has $1,000,000 of ordinary income and takes a $1,000,000 basis in his stock. IRC §§ 61, 83, 1012.

HighTech recognizes no gain and takes carryover bases in the assets increased by the amount of gain recognized. IRC §§ 1032(a), 362(a). Thus its basis in each asset is:

cash—$1,000,000
employment contract—$1,000,000
land—$1,000,000 ($500,000 plus $500,000)
patent—$300,000
license—$800,000 ($400,000 plus $400,000).

(g) **Same as (a) except that Sheldon's land is worth $1,100,000 and is transferred subject to a $100,000 mortgage which HighTech assumes.**

Since the mortgage does not exceed Sheldon's basis, no gain is recognized. IRC § 357(a), (c). However, the mortgage assumption is treated as cash received for basis purposes. IRC § 358(d)(1). Thus, Sheldon's basis in his stock is $400,000 ($500,000 beginning basis minus the $100,000 debt relief). This illustrates how section 357 merely defers gain recognition.

HighTech's basis in the land is $500,000. IRC § 362(a).

(h) **Same as (g) except that the land is worth $1,600,000 and is subject to a $600,000 mortgage which HighTech assumes.**

Now the mortgage exceeds Sheldon's basis by $100,000 so he must recognize that amount of gain under section 357(c)(1). His basis in his HighTech stock is zero

($500,000 beginning basis plus $100,000 gain recognized minus $600,000 boot received). IRC § 358(a), (d)(1).

HighTech's basis in the land is $600,000. IRC § 362(a).

(i)   Same as (a) except that Leonard only contributes $900,000 of cash but also contributes secret physics knowledge that is worth $100,000. This knowledge allows computer programs to become self-aware and self-correcting.

The question is whether contributing secret physics knowledge is a contribution of "property" for section 351 purposes. On the authority of Revenue Ruling 64-56, it probably is. The most relevant portion of the ruling reads as follows:

> The term "property" for purposes of section 351 of the Code will be held to include anything qualifying as "secret processes and formulas" within the meaning of sections 861(a)(4) and 862(a)(4) of the Code and any other secret information as to a device, process, etc., in the general nature of a patentable invention without regard to whether a patent has been applied for (see G.C.M. 21507, C.B. 1939-2, 189; Wall Products Inc. v. Commissioner, 11 T.C. 51, at 57 (1948), acquiescence, C.B. 1949-1, 4; Ralph L. Evans v. Commissioner, 8 B.T.A. 543 (1927)), and without regard to whether it is patentable in the patent law sense. Other information which is secret will be given consideration as "property" on a case-by-case basis.

This is a secret process. It is possible that it could be patented but note that it need not be "patentable in the patent law sense." A different conclusion could be reached if Leonard is actually transferring his physics services. If so, then Leonard has $100,000 of ordinary income under section 83. The formation is still within section 351 since only 10 percent of his interest is received for services and the control test is met even without that 10 percent of his stock.

Chapter 39

Partnership Formations

Overview

Under the tax rules governing the operations of partnerships, found in subchapter K of the Internal Revenue (§§ 701–777), a partnership (or limited liability company treated as a partnership under check-the-box entity classification) is not a separate taxable entity for federal income tax purposes, but rather is a pass-through entity. This means that items of income, gain, loss, deduction, and credit are determined at the entity level, but then flow through to individual partners and are reported on their individual returns. As with corporate formations, Congress has generally chosen to treat partnership formations as non-recognition events.

The key operative provision in most partnership formations is section 721. It provides that no gain or loss shall be recognized by a *partner* upon a contribution of property to the partnership in exchange for a partnership interest. Section 721 parallels section 351, its corporate tax counterpart, in that a contribution must qualify as "property" and that property must be "exchanged" for an ownership interest in the new entity. Section 721 differs from section 351 in several respects. For example, section 721 does not have a "control" requirement. Thus, any contribution of property in exchange for a partnership interest, no matter how small, will generally be nontaxable. If section 721 applies to a contribution of property to a partnership, the reporting of gain or loss realized is postponed to a later year—for example, when the partnership interest received on formation is later sold or disposed of in a taxable transaction. Gain or loss is preserved by generally giving the partner the same basis in the partnership interest acquired (known as "outside basis") as he or she had in the property given up in the exchange. IRC § 722. A partner's outside basis represents the partner's *post-tax* investment in the partnership, and is later adjusted upward for the partner's share of profits and downward for the partner's share of deductions. IRC § 705. Since a partner's basis in the partnership interest is determined by reference to the partner's basis in property given up, the partner's holding period for the partnership interest received generally includes the holding period of the property given up. IRC § 1223(1).

Consistent with the tax treatment of corporations that issue stock for property, *partnerships* do not recognize gain or loss when they issue partnership interests in exchange for money or property. IRC § 721. A partnership that receives property in exchange for its partnership interests in a nontaxable formation steps into the shoes of the transferor. Thus, a partnership's basis in any property received in a section 721 exchange (known as "inside basis") is the same as the transferor partner's basis. IRC § 723. The partnership's holding period in such property includes the holding period of the transferor. IRC § 1223(1).

As a general rule, a partner who receives a partnership interest in exchange for services must report as ordinary income the value of the partnership interest received. IRC § 61. It is sometimes difficult to value certain partnership interests. The receipt of a *capital interest* (an interest in the current value of the partnership) for services provided to or for the benefit of a partnership should be currently taxable as compensation since a capital interest is easy to value. Treas. Reg. § 1.721-1(b)(1). McDougal v. Commissioner, 62 T.C. 720 (1974), addresses the tax consequences to a partner who receives a capital interest in exchange for past services rendered. Sometimes it is difficult to determine the extent to which a mixed contribution of property and services qualifies as "property" for purposes of section 721. United States v. Frazell, 335 F.2d 487 (5th Cir. 1964), concerns that issue.

Although section 721 does not have a "solely in exchange" for requirement, a partner who receives money in addition to receiving a partnership interest at formation may have to report some gain. Under section 731, a partner generally recognizes no gain on a distribution of cash. However, if the cash distribution exceeds a partner's adjusted basis in his or her partnership interest (which is determined by reference to the adjusted basis of the property contributed), then the excess is treated as gain from the sale or exchange of a partnership interest. IRC § 731. Taxation is deemed appropriate when a cash distribution exceeds a partner's outside basis, since the partner is apparently receiving something more than previously taxed income or a return of capital. In contrast to this rule for boot distributions of cash, no gain or loss is recognized on boot distributions of property. Gain recognized by a partner as a result of a boot distribution of cash is typically characterized as capital gain unless the partnership has a lot of inventory or accounts receivable. IRC §§ 741, 751. The partner's adjusted basis in the partnership interest must be reduced, but not below zero, by the amount of the distribution. IRC § 733.

Many partnership formations involve the contribution of encumbered property by a partner. To determine the impact of liabilities at formation, we must look to section 752, which governs the treatment of partnership liabilities in several transactions including formations. Consistent with *Crane v. Commissioner*, discussed in Chapter 3, section 752(b) treats a partnership's assumption of a partner's liabilities as if it were a cash distribution by the partnership to the partner, and section 752(a) treats an increase in a partner's share of partnership liabilities as if it were a cash contribution by the partner to the partnership. The regulations under section 752 provide for netting of the two figures to determine the ultimate net deemed cash distribution or contribution. Treas. Reg. § 1.752-1(f). A net deemed cash distribution is treated as boot and taxable under section 731 to the extent the deemed distribution exceeds the partner's basis in the partnership interest (which is determined by reference to the adjusted basis of the property contributed).

The rules of subchapter K are quite complex. For example, the so-called "disguised sales" rules under section 707 may trump the above treatments when there is a cash distribution (or deemed cash distribution) at formation. These rules are beyond the scope of this chapter.

Primary Authority

Code: §§ 705(a); 721; 722; 723; 731(a)(1); 733; 752(a)-(b); 1223(1)-(2); 1245(b)(3). Skim §§ 83(a)-(c); 704(c)(1)(A); 707(a)(2)(B); 709; 724.

Regulations: §§ 1.704-1(b)(2)(iv)(b); 1.721-1(b). Skim § 1.752-1, -2, -3.

Cases: McDougal v. Commissioner, 62 T.C. 720 (1974); Stafford v. United States, 727 F.2d 1043 (11ᵗʰ Cir. 1984); United States v. Frazell, 335 F.2d 487 (5ᵗʰ Cir. 1964).

Rulings: Rev. Rul. 66-7, 1966-1 C.B. 188.

Problems

39.1. Al (A) and Bob (B) are planning to organize a general partnership, Kup-Kake (K), to engage in the operation of a bakery in Brooklyn, New York. A will contribute to K a vacant lot, and B will contribute $200,000 of cash to be used in the construction of a building. The land has a fair market value of $200,000, and A's adjusted basis is $100,000. K will issue to both A and B a general partnership interest representing a 50% interest in the capital, profits, and losses of K in exchange for the contributions.

(a) What are the tax consequences to A, B, and K upon formation of the partnership? Your analysis should address gain realization, gain recognition, inside basis, outside basis, holding period, and capital account balances.

Tax Consequences to Al (A):

A's transfer of land in exchange for a 50% partnership interest in KupKake (K) is a realization event. A's gain realized is $100,000–that is, $200,000 amount realized (fair market value of the partnership interest received) minus $100,000 adjusted basis in the lot transferred. IRC § 1001(a), (b).

The $100,000 gain realized is *not* recognized. IRC §§ 1001(c), 721(a).

A's basis in the partnership interest ("outside basis") is $100,000. IRC §§ 722, 7701(a)(44) ("exchange" basis). Note that A's potential gain of $100,000 has been preserved; as soon as A sells the partnership interest, A will have taxable gain.

A's holding period for the partnership interest received includes the holding period for the land contributed, provided the land is a capital asset or section 1231 property. IRC § 1223(1).

A's initial capital account balance is $200,000, the fair market value of the property contributed. Treas. Reg. § 1.701-1(b)(2)(iv)(b)(2).

Tax Consequences to Bob (B):

B has no gain or loss because he is contributing cash, and his basis in the partnership interest ("outside basis") is $200,000. IRC §§ 721(a), 722. B's holding period starts the day after B receives his partnership interest (i.e., tacking does not apply). Rev. Rul. 66-7. B's initial capital account balance is $200,000 the amount of money contributed. Treas. Reg. § 1.704-1(b)(2)(iv)(b)(1).

Tax Consequences to KupKake (K):

K has no gain or loss recognition with respect to the land and cash it receives in exchange for the partnership interests issued. IRC § 721(a). K's basis for the land contributed by A ("inside basis") is the same basis A had in the land ($100,000). IRC §§ 723, 7701(a)(43) ("transferred" basis). K's holding period for the land includes A's holding period for the land (i.e., tacking applies). IRC § 1223(2).

[Note: What would happen if K sold the lot for its fair market value of $200,000? K would realize and recognize $100,000 of tax gain. Under section 704(a), gain is allocated to the partners in accordance with the partnership agreement. A and B have agreed to split profits equally, so it would appear that the $100,000 gain would be allocated equally–$50,000 to A and $50,000 to B. But this doesn't seem right. $50,000 of the gain would be allocated to B even though the entire $100,000 of gain is attributable to the period when A held the land. Section 704(c)(1)(A) fixes this problem by requiring all $100,000 of the tax gain to be allocated to the contributing partner–A.]

(b) **Same as (a) except that A's land is worth $210,000. In order to equalize the contributions of the two partners, K, as part of the transaction, distributes to A $10,000 of the $200,000 of cash contributed by B.**

Tax Consequences to A:

A's *amount realized* is $210,000–that is, the fair market value of the partnership interest received ($200,000) plus the amount of money received ($10,000). IRC § 1001(b). A's *adjusted basis* in the lot is $100,000, per the facts. Accordingly, A's *gain realized* is $110,000 ($210,000 AR – $100,000 AB). IRC § 1001(a). Is any of the gain *recognized*? IRC § 1001(c). A is receiving a partnership interest, and A is receiving cash. It is best to analyze this as two separate transactions.

Does A recognize any gain as a result of *receiving the partnership interest*? The answer is no. IRC § 721. A's initial outside basis is $100,000. IRC § 722. [Note, this initial outside basis will be helpful in determining the tax consequences of the receipt of $10,000 in cash, and will be adjusted downward for such receipt.] A's holding period of the partnership interest includes the holding period of the land contributed, provided such land was a capital asset or section 1231 property in A's hands. IRC § 1223(1). A's initial capital account balance is $210,000, the fair market value of the land contributed. Treas. Reg. § 1.704-1(b)(2)(iv)(b)(2).

Does A recognize any gain as a result of *receiving the cash*? Under section 731, no gain is recognized to A because the cash received ($10,000) does not exceed A's initial outside basis ($100,000). A's basis in cash is $10,000. A's basis in the partnership interest is reduced by the cash distributed, and is now $90,000. IRC § 733. [Note that pre-distribution outside basis of $100,000 has been allocated between the two assets–$10,000 for the cash and $90,000 for the partnership interest. We can test the outside basis figure. Assuming A sold his partnership interest for what it is worth ($200,000), A would have a $110,000 gain. This is the total realized gain that went unrecognized at formation.] A's capital account is reduced by $10,000 to $200,000. Treas. Reg. § 1.704-1(b)(2)(iv)(b)(4).

[Note: This answer (no gain recognition to A upon the distribution of boot) assumes that the transaction does not give rise to a transaction described in section 707(a)(2)(B). Under the disguised sales rules of section 707(a)(2)(B), if a partner transfers property to a partnership and the partnership makes a related transfer of money back to that partner, the two transfers, when appropriate, shall be considered the sale or exchange of property between the partnership and the partner acting in a non-partner capacity. The government has issued detailed regulations for determining when a contribution of property and a related distribution of money should be recast as a sale. *See* Treas. Reg. § 1.707-3.

Here, if A's contribution of land and K's distribution of $10,000 of boot is recast as a sale, the following will occur:

Sale in part: A will be treated as selling a portion (10/210ths) of the land with a value of $10,000 to the partnership in exchange for $10,000 cash. This would cause A to recognize $5,240 of gain–that is, $10,000 AR minus $4,760 AB (10/210 × $100,000).

Contribution in part: A will be treated as contributing to the partnership (in A's capacity as a partner) a portion (200/210ths) of the land with a value of $200,000 and an adjusted basis of $95,240. This contribution will be tax free. IRC §§ 721, 722.]

Tax Consequences to B:

The results to B are the same as in part (a) above. B has no gain or loss. B's basis in his partnership interest is $200,000. Tacking does not apply. B's initial capital account balance is $200,000.

Tax Consequences to K:

K does not recognize any gain on the distribution of a partnership interest in exchange for A's land. IRC § 721. Further, K does not recognize any gain or loss on the distribution of $10,000 cash to A. IRC § 731(b). K's basis in the land contributed by A is $100,000. IRC § 723 (with potential gain of $110,000 lurking in the property). [Note that total "inside basis" of $290,000 ($100,000 basis in the land and $190,000 basis in the cash) equals total "outside basis" of $290,000 ($90,000 outside basis for A's interest and $200,000 outside basis for B's interest).] Tacking applies. IRC § 1223(2).

(c) Same as (b) except that A's adjusted basis for the land is $5,000.

Tax Consequences to A:

A's gain realized is $205,000 ($210,000 AR minus $5,000 AB).

No gain is recognized by virtue of receiving a partnership interest. IRC § 721. A's initial outside basis is $5,000, the adjusted basis of the land contributed. IRC § 722. A's holding period of the land tacks onto the holding period of the partnership interest, provided the land is a capital asset or a quasi-capital asset. IRC § 1223(1). A's initial capital account balance is $210,000, the fair market value of the land contributed. Treas. Reg. § 1.704-1(b)(2)(iv)(b)(2).

Is any gain recognized by virtue of receiving $10,000 of cash? Under section 731(a), A must recognize $5,000 of gain (the amount by which the $10,000 distribution exceeds his initial outside basis of $5,000). The gain is treated as gain from the sale of a partnership interest, and will be treated as capital gain. IRC §§ 731(a), 741, 751. A's basis in the cash received is $10,000. A's basis in the partnership interest will be reduced by the distribution, but not below zero. IRC § 733. Accordingly, A's outside basis is reduced to $0. [A zero outside basis makes sense. If A were to sell his partnership interest for its value of $200,000, he would recognize $200,000 of gain. This was the exact amount of gain that was realized but not recognized at formation.] A's capital account will by decreased by the $10,000 money distributed to $200,000–the same as B's capital account balance. Treas. Reg. § 1.704-1(b)(2)(iv)(b)(4).

Tax Consequences to B:

The federal income tax consequences to B are the same as above. B has no gain or loss. B's outside basis is $200,000. Tacking does not apply. B's initial capital account balance is $200,000.

Tax Consequences to K:

K does not recognize any gain on the distribution of the partnership interests and the distribution of cash. IRC §§ 721, 731(b). K's basis in the land contributed by A is $5,000. IRC § 723. Tacking applies. IRC § 1223(2). [Note: In contrast to answer (b) above, total inside basis ($195,000) does not equal total outside basis ($200,000). If the partnership made a section 754 election, it could increase its basis in the land by $5,000. *See* IRC §§ 734, 754.]

(d) Same as (a) except that A's lot is subject to a nonrecourse liability of $120,000, and B contributes cash of $80,000. Assume that the partnership interest each receives has a fair market value of $80,000 because K has a net worth of $160,000 (i.e., $280,000 of assets and a $120,000 liability). Neither partner guarantees repayment of the debt.

Tax Consequences to A:

A's *amount realized* is $200,000 ($80,000 FMV of the partnership interest received plus $120,000 of liability relief). IRC § 1001(b); *Crane*. A's *adjusted basis* is $100,000 per the facts. Therefore, A's *gain realized* is $100,000 ($200,000 AR minus $100,000 adjusted basis). Is any of the gain *recognized*? IRC § 1001(c). Two things are going on here: A is receiving a partnership interest, and A is also being relieved of a liability. Let's analyze both issues separately.

Does A recognize any gain as a result of *receiving the partnership interest*? The answer is no. IRC § 721. A's initial outside basis is $100,000. IRC § 722. A's holding period of the partnership interest includes the holding period of the land contributed, provided such land was a capital asset or section 1231 property in A's hands. IRC § 1223(1). A's initial capital account balance is $80,000, the fair market value of the land contributed net of liabilities. Treas. Reg. § 1.704-1(b)(2)(iv)(b)(2).

Does A recognize any gain as a result of *receiving some liability relief*? A is being relieved of a $120,000 liability. Section 752(b) treats a partnership's assumption of a partner's liability as if it were a cash distribution to the partner. As we learned in parts (b) and (c) above, a cash distribution may cause gain recognition to the partner if the cash distributed exceeds the partner's outside basis. A's initial outside basis is $100,000, so it would seem as if A would have to recognize $20,000 of gain (the amount by which the section 752(b) deemed cash distribution exceeds outside basis). But wait! Although A is being relieved of an individual liability of $120,000, A–as a general partner—is taking on a share of the new partnership debt. Section 752(a) treats any increase in a partner's share of partnership liabilities as if it were a cash contribution by the partner to the partnership. A partner's share of partnership liabilities for purposes of section 752 depends on a number of factors, including the status of the partner (general versus limited) and the nature of the liability (recourse versus nonrecourse). *See* Treas. Reg. § 1.752-2 (providing that a partner's share of a recourse liability is that portion of the liability for which the partner bears economic risk of loss); Treas. Reg. § 1.752-3 (providing that nonrecourse liabilities are allocated to the contributing partner to the extent the liability exceeds the partner's basis in the contributed property and then is *generally* allocated among the partners in accordance with each partner's share of partnership profits). A's share of the nonrecourse liability is treated as a deemed cash contribution to the partnership.

In sum, A is being relieved of an individual liability of $120,000 (a deemed cash distribution by the partnership to A per section 752(b)). In addition, A is taking on a $70,000 share of partnership debt (a deemed cash contribution by A to the partnership per section 752(a)). (A is deemed to have contributed $20,000 of cash for that part of the non-recourse debt that exceeds his basis in the property. *See* Treas. Reg. § 1.752-3(a)(2). A is also deemed to have contributed another $50,000 of cash because he shares equally in profits with B. *See* Treas. Reg. § 1.752-3(a)(3)). The regulations say we can net the deemed distribution and the deemed contribution. Treas. Reg. § 1.752-1(f). Accordingly, there is a constructive distribution to A of only $50,000. This does not exceed A's initial basis in his partnership interest. Therefore, A has no gain as a result of the liabilities. IRC § 731. A's initial basis in his partnership interest of $100,000 is decreased by the deemed cash distribution of $50,000, and now stands at $50,000. IRC § 733. A's capital account remains at $80,000. Treas. Reg. § 1.704-1(b)(2)(iv)(c).

Tax Consequences to B:

B has no gain or loss recognition upon receiving the partnership interest. His initial outside basis is $80,000, the amount of money contributed. Under section 752(a), however, B's $50,000 share of the liability assumed by the partnership is treated as a constructive contribution of money by B to the partnership. Under section 722, B's outside basis is increased by $50,000 to $130,000. B's capital account balance is $80,000. Treas. Reg. § 1.704-1(b)(2)(iv)(b)(1), (c).

Tax Consequences to K:

No gain or loss is recognized by K. IRC §§ 721, 731(b). K's basis in the land contributed by A is $100,000. IRC § 723. Tacking applies. IRC § 1223(2).

(e) **Same as (a) except that A did not own a lot to contribute to K. A contributed instead a "letter of intent" in exchange for his partnership interest. The letter of intent recited that A and a landowner had begun negotiations to finance and construct a bakery, with the landowner providing a favorable land lease and loan. A assigned to K the agreement to lease and loan commitment and agreed to continue negotiations.**

A requirement for non-recognition of gain under section 721 is that "property" must be transferred. This problem is drawn from *Stafford v. United States.* The Eleventh Circuit in *Stafford* held that the letter of intent was "property" within the meaning of section 721 even though it gave no enforceable rights to the partnership. [The Eleventh Circuit reversed the lower court which held that both *value* and *enforceability* were necessary to conclude that the document was property for purposes of section 721. The lower court agreed that the letter of intent had value, but failed to perceive how the letter of intent was legally enforceable.]

Although the Eleventh Circuit found that the letter of intent constituted property, it remanded the case for a determination of the extent to which the receipt of the partnership interest was "partly in compensation for services and partly in exchange for property." According to the court, "the factfinder should determine the value of the property element (i.e., the letter of intent) and the value of the services element (i.e., the services to be rendered to the partnership by Stafford after formation of the partnership), . . . and allocate the value of the partnership share accordingly."

Here, A's letter of intent should constitute "property" for purposes of section 721. We should ask, however, whether A received the partnership interest wholly in exchange for the letter of intent he contributed. To the extent receipt of the partnership interest was compensation for services, section 721 would not apply. This was the theme in *United States v. Frazell.*

(f) **Same as (a) except that B did not contribute cash. Instead B receives his 50% capital interest in the partnership in exchange for his agreement to manage the business for five years.**

This is a very simple version of the *McDougal v. Commissioner* case.

The receipt of a "capital" interest is a gain recognition event for A and service income for B. *See* Treas. Reg. § 1.721-1(b)(1) (providing that the fair market value of the partnership interest received in exchange for services is includable in gross income under sections 61 and 83); *see also* Treas. Reg. § 1.722-1 (providing that income so recognized increases the partner's basis in the partnership interest). Section 83 provides rules for determining the proper year in which the value of the partnership interest must be included in income. Under section 83(a), income is included in the first year that the compensatory capital interest received by B is transferable and vested (not subject to a substantial risk of forfeiture). A special section 83(b) election can be made which will cause income recognition in the year it is received rather than year it becomes vested. [Note: Under recent regulations, the rules of section 83 will apply to all compensatory partnership interests (both capital interests and profits interests).]

In sum, B will have ordinary income at the time his compensatory capital interest vests. The value of the interest at the date of vesting may be greater than the value of the interest at the original grant date, which would cause B to have more ordinary income. To avoid this, B could elect to have the value of the partnership interest taxed currently as compensation by making a section 83(b) election.

Under *McDougal* A is treated as having sold one half of the land to B for its fair market value of $100,000. Thus, A recognizes $50,000 of long-term capital gain. A contributes the other half to the partnership and gets non-recognition and carryover basis treatment with respect to that transfer. IRC §§ 721, 722.

K will recognize no gain or loss and will take a $150,000 basis in the land. IRC §§ 721, 723.

Chapter 40

Overview of International Income Taxation

Overview

United States persons (citizens, resident aliens, domestic corporations) may derive income from sources outside the United States (i.e., foreign source income). Such persons engaged in activities abroad are generally taxed on their worldwide income (income earned in the United States as well as income earned in a foreign country) under the rates specified under either section 1 (individual citizens and resident aliens) or section 11 (domestic corporations). *But see* IRC § 911 (providing a limited exclusion from gross income for income earned abroad). Foreign source income may be taxed in a foreign country as well. To provide relief from double taxation, the United States allows a tax credit for foreign income taxes paid to any foreign country against U.S. income tax owed on the same income. IRC §§ 901-908. It also allows a deduction for foreign income taxes (§ 164(a)), but a taxpayer is not allowed to take both a deduction and a credit for the same foreign income tax and must choose between the two. IRC § 275(a)(4).

Non-U.S. persons (non-resident alien individuals and foreign corporations) may derive income from within the United States (i.e., U.S. source income). Under the Code, non-treaty, non-U.S. persons are taxed on most U.S. *business income* in the same manner that U.S. persons are. More specifically, a non-U.S. person engaged in a trade or business in the United States is taxed under the graduated rates of either section 1 (in the case of non-resident alien individuals) or section 11 (in the case of foreign corporations) on taxable income that is effectively connected with the conduct of the trade or business within the United States. IRC §§ 871(b), 882. (Note that the statutory concepts of *engaged in a trade or business* and *effectively connected income* that appear in the Code are replaced with thresholds much higher when there is an applicable income tax treaty.) Under the Code, non-treaty, non-U.S. persons are generally subject to a flat tax of 30% (as opposed to the rates of sections 1 or 11) each year on the amount of *non-business income* received from sources within the United States. IRC §§ 871(a), 881(a). The 30% flat tax is imposed on fixed or determinable annual or periodical income received, including passive income such as interest, dividends, rents, and royalties. (Note that most treaties impose a lower rate on non-business income than the 30% statutory rate; some treaties completely exempt certain income, such as royalties, from tax altogether.)

The Code contains rules that determine the source of income. *See* IRC §§ 861-865. These source rules are broken into categories of income (e.g., compensation, interest, dividends, rents, royalties, sales of real property interests, and sales of personal property). The following are examples: The source of *interest* income depends on the residence or place of incorporation of the obligor. IRC §§ 861(a)(1), 884(f)(1)(A). As with the interest source rule, the source rule for *dividends* is generally the residence of the payor. IRC §§ 861(a)(2), 884(a). The source rule for *personal services compensation* is based on where the services are performed. IRC § 861(a)(3). *Rents and royalties* are generally sourced according to the situs of the use of the property giving rise to the income. IRC § 861(a)(4). With respect to *real estate dispositions*, the situs of the real property is the critical factor. IRC § 861(a)(5). The source of gain from the sale of non-inventory personalty depends on the residence of the seller rather than where title passes. IRC § 865. The source of gain from the disposition of an intangible asset depends on the nature of the sale. If the sale proceeds are contingent on the productivity, use, or disposition of the property by the purchaser, the proceeds are treated as royalties and, hence, sourced according to where the property is used. IRC §§ 861(a)(4), 865(d). If the sale proceeds are not contingent, then any gain is sourced according the seller's residence. IRC § 865(a).

Many U.S. global companies attempt to reduce taxes on worldwide income by transferring their intellectual property and certain operations to controlled foreign subsidiaries located in low (or zero) tax countries. In a sale or license of intellectual property from the U.S. parent to the foreign subsidiary, there is an incentive for the foreign subsidiary to pay an artificially low price for the intellectual property. Setting license royalties as low as possible, for example, will maximize the amount of the foreign subsidiary's profits taxed at the low foreign tax rate and maximize the amount of U.S. tax deferral assuming those profits will not be distributed to the US parent. Congress has enacted a number of barriers aimed at U.S. companies that perform R&D in the United States, shift ownership (and related functions) of developed intellectual property to low-tax foreign countries where profitable operations occur, and then engage in advantageous transfer pricing practices. Two of these barriers include the so-called controlled foreign corporation rules of subpart F of the Code, and the transfer pricing rules under section 482. The U.S. government's approach to transfer pricing concerns has been to treat transactions between related parties, such as a U.S. parent company and its controlled foreign subsidiary, the same as if the transactions were between unrelated parties. Thus, related parties must be dealing with each other at arm's length, and the transactions and transfers of property between them must reflect arm's-length consideration. If this is not the case, the related parties risk that the government may make arm's-length transfer pricing adjustments to ensure that such transactions clearly reflect income. *See* IRC § 482.

Primary Authority

Code: §§ 482; 861-862; 864-865; 871; 881-882; 901-908; 911; 1441; 1442.

Regulations: None.

Cases: Boulez v. Commissioner, 83 T.C. 584 (1984).

Rulings: None.

Problems

40.1. Explain whether the following amounts received by USCo, a domestic corporation that sells widgets, are U.S. source income or foreign source income:

> **(a) $50,000 royalty payment from IrelandCo, a wholly-owned foreign subsidiary of USCo. USCo developed a new "high tech widget" and licenses for five years the non-U.S. rights to the patented technology to IrelandCo, which manufactures and sells the widget in Europe.**

Foreign source, because royalties from the licensing of intellectual property are sourced according to where the intellectual property is used (here Ireland). IRC § 861(a)(4).

> **(b) $1,000,000 gain from the sale of the patent in (a) above to IrelandCo, its wholly-owned foreign subsidiary.**

U.S. source, because gain from the sale of an intangible asset (if sale proceeds are not contingent) is sourced according to the seller's residence (here United States). IRC § 865(a), (g).

> **(c) $300,000 dividend payment received from IrelandCo, the wholly-owned foreign subsidiary of USCo.**

Foreign source, provided IrelandCo has only a de minimis U.S. business nexus (25%). *See* IRC § 861(a)(2)(B) (providing that any dividend received from a foreign corporation will be deemed foreign source if less than 25% of the gross income from all sources of such foreign corporation for a three-year period was effectively connected with the conduct of a trade or business within the United States).

> **(d) $15,000 dividend payment received from Apple, Inc., a publicly traded U.S. corporation that engages in business all over the world.**

U.S. source. IRC § 861(a)(2).

> **(e) $500,000 from widget inventory purchased in the United States and sold directly to distributors in Europe, with title passing in Europe.**

Foreign source. The source rule for sales of non-inventory personal property focus on the residence of the seller. The source rule for sales of inventory property, in contrast, focus on the jurisdiction in which title passes and not the residence of the seller. IRC § 861(a)(6).

40.2. Why are the source rules with respect to USCo, in problem 40.1 above, relevant since domestic corporations are taxed on their worldwide income anyway?

The source rules become relevant for U.S. persons in the calculation of the foreign tax credit. Section 904 limits the amount of the foreign tax credit to the amount of foreign income tax paid, but not in excess of an amount that is calculated by multiplying U.S. tax liability by a fraction, the numerator of which is foreign taxable income and the denominator of which is worldwide taxable income. Basically, the foreign tax credit is only available for foreign taxes paid with respect to foreign source income.

40.3. What might happen if the royalty payment in problem 40.1(a) above is unreasonably low?

In problem 40.1(a), USCo licenses intellectual property to its foreign subsidiary. There is an incentive for the foreign subsidiary to pay an artificially low price for the intellectual property. Setting the royalty payment as low as possible will maximize the amount of the foreign subsidiary's profits taxed at Ireland's low foreign tax rate (12.5%) and maximize the amount of U.S. tax deferral, assuming those profits will not be distributed to USCo. USCo will be subject to U.S. tax on the low royalties it receives.

If the royalties do not reflect arm's-length consideration, USCo and its subsidiary run the risk that the government may make arm's-length transfer pricing adjustments to ensure that the license transactions clearly reflect income. Section 482 authorizes the Service to "distribute, apportion or allocate gross income, deductions, credits, or allowances" among controlled businesses where "such distribution, apportionment or allocation is necessary in order to prevent evasion of taxes or clearly to reflect the income" of such controlled businesses.

40.4. USCo, a U.S. corporation, has developed and currently markets to customers around the world version 2.0 of a popular software application ("App"). USCo is considering developing a new version of App (version 3.0) to sell to U.S. and non-U.S. customers. Describe generally the benefits of establishing a wholly-owned foreign subsidiary corporation in a low-tax country, such as Ireland, the Netherlands, or Switzerland, to sell version 3.0 to customers outside the United States?

A U.S. company that conducts foreign business operations can lower its effective tax on worldwide income by moving its intellectual property assets and operations to a subsidiary company located in a low-tax foreign country like those mentioned in the problem. Any foreign income earned by the foreign subsidiary will be subject to foreign tax at a low rate, but will not be subject to current U.S. taxation. Consequently, U.S. tax on the foreign subsidiary's income can be purposefully avoided (or deferred) by keeping that income overseas instead of having it distributed to the U.S. parent company in the form of a dividend. There is nothing illegal about this international tax planning strategy. Indeed, it is used by many U.S. multinational entities principally to achieve two goals: (1) avoid current U.S. taxation on offshore profits; and (2) subject those offshore profits to as low a foreign tax as possible.

For example, assume USCo anticipates earning $10 million of profits from sales of version 3.0 to U.S. customers and $10 million of profits from sales of version 3.0 to non-U.S. customers. To lower its U.S. tax burden on non-U.S. sales, USCo can transfer non-U.S. rights in version 3.0 to its wholly owned subsidiary in Ireland, for example, to produce and sell version 3.0 to non-U.S. customers. The non-U.S. profits will be taxed to the foreign subsidiary at Ireland's 12.5% tax rate instead of being taxed to USCo at U.S.'s 35% tax rate, for a tax savings of $2,250,000. As long as those foreign profits stay in Ireland, they will escape U.S. taxation. [Note that USCo and its Irish subsidiary can enter into a cost-sharing arrangement for the co-development of version 3.0. More specifically, USCo can contribute version 2.0 (platform contribution) for further research to co-develop version 3.0. The Irish subsidiary must make an initial buy-in payment for the rights to co-develop and exploit the new property outside the United States. But because the new intellectual property will be jointly owned by both USCo and its Irish subsidiary, no royalties need to be paid to USCo.]

40.5. Hector Berlioz is a famous French conductor. He is a citizen of France and resides in Paris when he is not on tour. Recently, OMD (Online Music Digital), a New York corporation, offered to pay Hector $3 million over two years to conduct a group of musicians and record 10 new CDs. All the recording activities would occur at OMD's studio located in New York City. Hector typically owns the copyrights in his recordings, but he is open to the idea of assigning the copyrights in the 10 CDs to OMD. Hector asks you to provide tax advice on his future income.

This problem presents a *Boulez v. Commissioner*–type of problem: trying to determine the source of income earned by a foreign person. *Boulez* concerned the proper tax treatment of amounts paid to Pierre Boulez, a resident of Germany and a world-renowned conductor, for recordings made under a contract in the United States. The court held that under the income tax treaty between Germany and the United States, the payments to Mr. Boulez were not royalties exempt from tax by the United States, but were compensation for personal services, and thus were taxable by the United States.

Mr. Boulez signed a recording contract with CBS Records in 1969 and the contract was in effect during the calendar year 1975. Mr. Boulez timely filed a federal non-resident alien income tax return for the taxable year 1975. The Commissioner determined a deficiency in Mr. Boulez's individual income tax in the amount of $20,685.61 for 1975. Mr. Boulez argued that the payments received by him in the year of 1975 were royalties within the meaning of the applicable income tax treaty between Germany and the United States. Under the tax treaty, such royalty payments were exempt from U.S. taxation.

The Tax Court examined the contract between Mr. Boulez and CBS Records and concluded that the parties intended a contract for personal services, rather than one involving the sale or licensing of any intellectual property rights that Mr. Boulez might have in the recordings that were to be made in the future. Further, the Tax

Court reasoned, a person could not derive royalty income if the person had no ownership interest in the property whose licensing or sales give rise to the income. At the time Mr. Boulez and CBS Records executed the contract, Mr. Boulez had no copyrightable property interest in the recordings that he made for CBS Records under the Copyright Act of 1909. The Copyright Act of 1909 did not recognize copyrightable interest in recordings. Though the copyright law was later amended in 1971 to recognize copyrightable interest in recordings, Mr. Boulez did not modify his contract with CBS Records to reflect that he had copyright ownership in the recordings as recognized by the law and that he had licensable or transferable property rights in the recordings that he made for CBS Records. The copyrightable recordings made by Mr. Boulez were essentially works made for hire under the contract. Accordingly, the Commissioner was correct in taxing the payments received by Mr. Boulez from CBS Records as compensation for personal services. Under the tax treaty between Germany and the United States, such compensation for personal services was subject to U.S. taxation.

This problem requires us to ascertain whether the amounts received by Hector constitute payments for services, royalties for the license of intellectual property, or gain from the sale of intellectual property. If Hector *owns* the copyrights in the new recordings and licenses such copyrights to OMD, the amounts may be characterized as royalties. Under the treaty between France and the United States, Hector does not have to pay U.S. tax on the royalties. However, if the contract between Hector and OMD reveals that Hector is hired to perform the conducting services for OMD (and OMD owns and registers all the copyrights in the CDs), the amounts received by Hector are not "royalties," but are payments for service rendered in the United States and are subject to U.S. taxation. The facts state the Hector typically owns the copyrights in his works. If the compositions are not works for hire and he does own the copyrights therein, this suggests that the assignment is a sale for a lump sum payment. Under section 865(a)(2), the income is sourced according to Hector's residence (tax home under section 865(g)). Treaties impose a higher threshold to U.S. taxation (i.e., they favor residence based taxation), so the treaty would not likely change the result. We need more facts (e.g., duration of his stay in the United States, whether he has a permanent establishment in the U.S., etc.).

Chapter 41

Overview of Estate and Gift Taxation

Overview

A. The Estate Tax

The estate tax is borne by a decedent transferor's estate. It is computed by determining the "gross estate" (like gross income in the income tax) and taking certain deductions to derive the "taxable estate." The tax rate schedule is applied to the taxable estate. The resulting tentative tax liability is then reduced by the "unified credit" to arrive at a final tax owed.

The "gross estate" is a non-intuitive concept since it includes many things in addition to property the decedent owned at death. Moreover, significant valuation issues can also arise. The gross estate usually must be valued at its fair market value as of the date of death of the person whose estate is being taxed. IRC § 2031(a). It is useful to understand that the gross estate can consist of many things beyond the decedent's probate estate.

The taxable estate consists of the gross estate reduced by certain deductions. The more important deductions are the debt deduction (IRC § 2053), the charitable deduction (IRC § 2055), and the marital deduction. (IRC § 2056). The charitable deduction correlates in many respects with the same deduction for income tax purposes and has many technical limitations, especially for split interest transfers. The deduction for gifts between spouses also requires a further comment. This deduction rests on the idea that a married couple is a single economic unit and, thus, gifts between spouses should be ignored for transfer tax purposes. But not every gift between spouses qualifies for the deduction. Gifts of lifetime or term interests must be carefully structured in order to qualify. *See* IRC § 2056(b)(7). The marital deduction is a commonly used estate planning tool.

The rate structure for both the estate tax and the gift tax is set out in section 2001(c). *See also* IRC § 2502(a). The maximum rate under that provision is 40%.

The unified credit is the device that allows estates of less than $5,000,000 to go untaxed. It is set out in section 2010. The term "unified" refers to the way in which the credit's operation is integrated into a similar gift tax credit found in section 2505. The two credits are of equal amounts and both are annually adjusted for inflation since 2011. The two credits are unified in one important respect. The use of the gift tax credit has the effect of reducing the available estate tax credit. Thus, for example, a $500,000 taxable inter vivos gift means that a decedent's estate can only shelter $4,500,000 of property from taxation by use of the estate tax unified credit. The mechanics of the unified credit are a bit tricky. The statutes establish what is called an applicable exclusion amount" of $5,000,000 for the estate tax and for the gift tax. *See* IRC §§ 2010(c), 2505(a). The applicable exclusion amount is adjusted for inflation after year 2011. In 2016 it is $5,400,000. See Rev. Proc. 2015-53. The "applicable credit" is the amount of tax that would otherwise be owed on a transfer of the applicable exclusion amount under the section 2001(c) rate structure. A complicating factor is that under certain circumstances, a decedent's unused applicable exclusion amount can be used by the decedent's surviving spouse. *See* IRC § 2010(c).

B. The Gift Tax

The gift tax serves to backup the estate tax. Without a gift tax one could avoid tax on transfers from one generation to the next by the use of inter vivos gifts. Its structure is similar to that of the estate tax. Its provisions relating to such things as charitable gifts and inter-spousal transfers tend to mirror those of the estate tax. However, it does have a few unique rules some of which we will note below.

In Chapter 4, we considered the *Duberstein* case, which held that for income tax purposes a gift must arise out of "detached and disinterested generosity." This is not the rule in the gift tax context. Instead a gift occurs when there is a transfer of property for less than full and adequate consideration. *See* Treas. Reg. § 25.2511-1(g)(1). In order for a gift to be complete for gift tax purposes the donor must give up "dominion and control" over the property. Treas. Reg. § 25.2511-2(b). Thus, a transfer of property to a revocable trust, for example, is not a completed gift and is not currently taxable. If the trust makes distributions or later becomes irrevocable, the gift tax is triggered at that time. The gift tax is levied on the transferor (donor). The rates are established by section 2001(c). *See* IRC § 2502(a). Although an annual return is used, all gifts since 1932 are used to compute the tax rate. Thus, earlier years' gifts push current gifts into higher tax brackets.

The first $10,000 of a present interest gift to anyone is excluded from the gift tax. IRC § 2503(b). (This number is adjusted for inflation and was $14,000 in 2016.) This is known as the "annual exclusion" and, as its name describes, it arises anew each year. Thus, one can make gifts year after year with no gift tax consequences as long as the amount given to any particular person does not exceed the annual exclusion limit. This is an obvious planning opportunity. For example, a person can make gifts to her children and grandchildren over a span of years in order to spend down her estate to a level where little or no estate tax will apply when she dies. There are several nuances to the annual exclusion. Spouses may double their available exclusion by treating one another's gifts to third parties as being made half by each even though only one spouse actually made the gift. IRC § 2513. Gifts in trust to minor children can qualify if they meet certain terms. *See* IRC § 2503(c). Certain payments for education and for medical care for another are also excluded if made directly to the provider. IRC § 2503(e).

C. The Generation Skipping Transfer Tax

An ideal gratuitous transfer tax should apply once each generation. The generation skipping transfer tax (GSTT) is designed to foster that requirement. It is an excise tax on the transfer of property to a person who is more than one generation below the generation of the transferor. The tax is, in the main, a device for closing the loophole that exists in the estate and gift taxes for transfers of property from one generation to another without any tax.

The GSTT is triggered by any one of three events: (1) a direct skip; (2) a taxable distribution; or (3) a taxable termination. A *direct skip* is a transfer subject to estate or gift tax to a "skip person." IRC § 2612(c). A skip person is a natural person who is two or more generations below the transferor. IRC § 2613(a)(1). In addition, a trust is a skip person if all interests in the trust are held by skip persons or if no one other than a skip person can receive a distribution from the trust after the transfer creating the trust. IRC § 2613(a)(2). A *taxable distribution* is a distribution from a trust to a skip person (other than a taxable termination or a direct skip). IRC § 2612(b). A *taxable termination* is the termination of any interest held in trust unless after the termination the interest is held by a non-skip person or unless after the termination there can be no distributions from the trust to a skip person. IRC § 2612(a).

Generation assignment is a mechanical process. For lineal descendants of the transferor, you simply count generations (e.g., a grandchild is two generations below a grandparent.) IRC § 2651(b)(1). The spouses of lineal descendants are assigned to the descendant's generation. IRC § 2652(c)(2). Unrelated transferees are assigned generations according to a set of mechanical rules. *See* IRC § 2651(d). A spouse is assigned to the transferor's generation so there is no GSTT on a transfer between spouses no matter what their ages. IRC § 2651(c)(1).

The amount against which the tax is levied varies somewhat depending upon several factors including whether it arises out of a direct skip, taxable distribution, or taxable termination. But basically the amount is the fair market value of the property interest passing to the skip person (*see* IRC §§ 2621–2623) valued as of the time of the transfer. *See* IRC § 2624(a). The transferee is liable for the tax on a taxable distribution. The trustee is liable for the tax on a taxable termination. The transferor is liable for the tax on a direct skip. IRC § 2603. Where there is a direct skip, the GSTT paid by the transferor is treated as part of the gift for gift tax purposes. IRC § 2515.

There is an exemption from the GSTT equal to the inflation-adjusted applicable exclusion amount under section 2010(c). The transferor may allocate the exemption to any particular transfers she chooses. IRC § 2631. There are special rules for designating how the exemption is used in the absence of a specific election by the transferor. IRC § 2632. Inter vivos transfers that would otherwise be subject to the GSTT receive the benefit of the section 2503 annual exclusions. *See* IRC §§ 2642(c), 2611(b), 2612(c)(1). This is an important planning device since one can make annual gifts to grandchildren or to grandchildrens' trusts without attracting the GSTT.

Primary Authority

Code: §§ 2001(a)-(c); 2010; 2056(a); 2501; 2503(b); 2505(a). Skim §§ 2601-2613; 2631-2641; 2642(c); 2651(e)(1).

Regulations: None.

Cases: None.

Rulings: None.

Problems

In the problems that follow please ignore the inflation adjustments called for by section 2010(c) and, instead, assume that the applicable exclusion amount in sections 2010 and 2505 is a flat $5,000,000. You may also assume that the annual exclusion under section 2503(b) is $14,000.

41.1. In the current year, Commander Spock passed away with a gross estate of $9,100,000. His debts and the costs of administering his estate totaled $100,000. What is his estate's estate tax liability under the following circumstances?

(a) Spock had made no taxable gifts during life. Under his will everything passed to his children, Scottie and Uhuru.

The estate tax liability is $1,600,000 computed as follows

1.	Gross Estate (2031-44)	$9,100,000
2.	Total Deductions	
3.	Marital (2056)	
4.	Charitable (2055)	
5.	Casualties (2054)	
6.	Debts (2053) 100,000	
7.	Others	
8.	TOTAL	− 100,000
9.	Taxable Estate (2051, 2001(b)(1)(A))	9,000,000
10.	Adjusted Taxable Gifts (2001(b)(1)(B))	+ 0
11.	Tentative Taxable Estate	9,000,000
12.	Apply the 2001(c) rate	× rate
13.	Tentative Estate Tax (2001(b)(1), (c))	3,545,800
14.	Total Taxable Gifts _____ (2001(b))	
15.	Apply 2001(c) rate × rate	
16.	Gross Gift Tax _____ (2001(b)(2))	
17.	Unified Credit _−_ (2505)	
18.	Gift Tax Payable (2001(b)(2))	− 0
19.	Pre-Credit Estate Tax	3,545,800
20.	Unified Credit (2010)	− 1,945,800
21.	**Net Estate Tax Liability**	$1,600,000

(b) Same as (a) except that the Spock had made adjusted taxable gifts of $1,000,000.

The estate tax liability is $2,000,000 computed as follows:

1.	Gross Estate (2031-44)		$9,100,000
2.	Total Deductions		
3.	Marital (2056)		
4.	Charitable (2055)		
5.	Casualties (2054)		
6.	Debts (2053)	100,000	
7.	Others		
8.	TOTAL		− 100,000
9.	Taxable Estate (2051, 2001(b)(1)(A))		9,000,000
10.	Adjusted Taxable Gifts (2001(b)(1)(B))		+ 1,000,000
11.	Tentative Taxable Estate		10,000,000
12.	Apply the 2001(c) rate		× rate
13.	Tentative Estate Tax (2001(b)(1), (c))		3,945,800
14.	Total Taxable Gifts	1,000,000 (2001(b))	
15.	Apply 2001(c) rate	× rate	
16.	Gross Gift Tax	345,800 (2001(b)(2))	
17.	Unified Credit	−345,800 (2505)	
18.	Gift Tax Payable (2001(b)(2))		− 0
19.	Pre-Credit Estate Tax		3,945,800
20.	Unified Credit (2010)		− 1,945,800
21.	**Net Estate Tax Liability**		$2,000,000

This problem illustrates how the use of the section 2505 credit reduces the available section 2010 credit. Notice that the line 17 deduction reduces the line 18 reduction in tax liability. Thus, we are not using the credit twice even though it appears twice in the computation.

(c) Same as (a) except that Spock leaves $4,000,000 to his wife, Pring, and $5,000,000 to his children.

The estate tax liability is zero because of the marital deduction and the unified credit computed as follows:

1.	Gross Estate (2031-44)		9,100,000
2.	Total Deductions		
3.	Marital (2056)	4,000,000	
4.	Charitable (2055)		
5.	Casualties (2054)		
6.	Debts (2053)	100,000	
7.	Others		
8.	TOTAL	− 4,100,000	

9.	Taxable Estate (2051, 2001(b)(1)(A))		5,000,000
10.	Adjusted Taxable Gifts (2001(b)(1)(B))		+ 0
11.	Tentative Taxable Estate		5,000,000
12.	Apply the 2001(c) rate		× rate
13.	Tentative Estate Tax (2001(b)(1), (c))		1,945,800
14.	Total Taxable Gifts ____	(2001(b))	
15.	Apply 2001(c) rate × rate		
16.	Gross Gift Tax ____	(2001(b)(2))	
17.	Unified Credit ____	(2505)	
18.	Gift Tax Payable(2001(b)(2))		− 0
19.	Pre-Credit Estate Tax		1,945,800
20.	Unified Credit (2010)		− 1,945,800
21.	**Net Estate Tax Liability**		$0

This illustrates one of the most basic estate tax planning techniques, that is, the use of the marital deduction to avoid any estate tax in the estate of the first spouse to die. Note that the marital deduction only postpones the tax if the surviving spouse is also wealthy. The next problem illustrates a complete tax avoidance technique.

Charitable gifts are another tax avoidance technique. A $4,000,000 charitable gift instead of a marital gift would achieve the same result as above.

41.2. Barbara has three children and twelve grandchildren. This year she made outright gifts of $14,000 in cash to each of these fifteen people. These were her only gifts. What is her "total amount of gifts" within the meaning of section 2503(a)? *See* **IRC § 2503(b)(1).**

Zero. Section 2503(b) excludes the first $10,000 (adjusted for inflation) of a present interest gift from the "total amount of gifts." This illustrates one of the most basic gift and estate tax avoidance techniques. Annual gifts that are below the inflation adjusted annual exclusion amount pass outside of the transfer tax system. These gifts reduce her potential taxable estate. They also avoid the GSTT. *See* IRC §§ 2642(c), 2611(b), 2612(c)(1). In this example $210,000 escapes transfer tax. Over a number of years large sums can be passed tax free in this manner.

41.3. In the current year, Blythe gave $6,014,000 to her grandson, Moses. What are Blythe's transfer tax consequences under the following circumstances?

(a) **Her daughter, Juliana, Moses's mother, is still living at the time of the gift. Blythe has her full section 2505 tax credit remaining and she allocates $2,000,000 of her GSTT exemption to the gift. She requires Moses to pay any GSTT on the transfer.**

Her current gift tax liability is $435,000 computed as follows:

1.	Current gross gifts	6,014,000
2.	− Exclusions (§§ 2503(b), (c), (e); 2513)	− 14,000
3.	Total amount of gifts (§ 2503(a))	6,000,000

4.	– Deductions (e.g., § 2523 (marital deduction))	–	0
5.	Current taxable gifts § 2503(a)		6,000,000
6.	+ Prior years' taxable gifts	+	0
7.	Total tentative taxable gifts		6,000,000
8.	× Rate (§§ 2502(a)(1); 2001(c))	×	rate
9.	Tentative tax (§ 2502(a)(1))		2,345,800
10.	– Tax on prior years' gifts (§ 2502(a)(2) (pre-credit))	–	0
11.	Gift tax liability before credit		2,345,800
12.	– Unused unified credit (§ 2505(a))		– 1,945,800
13.	**Current Gift Tax Liability**		400,000

The GSTT liability is $1,662,000 since this is a direct skip computed as follows: Reduce the gift by the annual exclusion amount to $6,000,000.

$$\frac{2,000,000 \text{ (exclusion allocated)}}{6,000,000 \text{ (value of gift)}} = 1/3 \text{ (applicable fraction)}$$

1–1/3 (applicable fraction) = 2/3 inclusion ratio

40% (maximum federal rate) × 2/3 (inclusion ratio) = 27.7% applicable rate

6,000,000 × .277 = $1,662,000

Since she is requiring Moses to pay the GSTT there is no further gift tax liability.

(b) Same as (a) except that Juliana is no longer living.

The gift tax consequences are the same. But now there is no GSTT liability since Moses is reassigned to his mother's generation and is now only one generation below Blythe. IRC § 2651(e); Treas. Reg. § 26.2612-1(a)(2).

(c) Same as (a) except that Blythe had made a taxable gift of $500,000 in a prior year.

Now Blythe has partially used her unified credit in a prior year so her current gift tax liability will be greater.

Her current gift tax liability is $600,000 computed as follows:

1.	Current gross gifts		6,014,000
2.	– Exclusions (§§ 2503(b), (c), (e); 2513)	–	14,000
3.	Total amount of gifts (§ 2503(a))		6,000,000
4.	– Deductions (e.g., § 2523 (marital deduction))	–	0
5.	Current taxable gifts (§ 2503(a))		6,000,000
6.	+ Prior years' taxable gifts	+	500,000
7.	Total tentative taxable gifts		6,500,000
8.	× Rate (§§ 2502(a)(1); 2001(c))	×	rate
9.	Tentative tax (§ 2502(a)(1))		2,545,800
10.	– Tax on prior years' gifts (§ 2502(a)(2) (pre-credit))	–	155,800

11.	Gift tax liability before credit	2,390,000
12.	− Unused unified credit (§ 2505(a))	− 1,790,000
13.	**Current Gift Tax Liability**	$ 600,000

The GSTT liability is $1,662,000 just as in (a) computed in the same way.

Chapter 42

Tax Practice and Procedure

Overview

Typically, individuals must file their federal income tax returns by April 15th following the close of the calendar tax year. IRC § 6072(a). An individual may obtain an automatic six-month extension by filing Form 4868 before the return due date. IRC § 6081(a). Typically, payment of tax is also due by April 15th regardless of filing extensions. IRC § 6151. If unable to pay tax when due, an individual does have some options. *See* IRC § 6161; *see also* IRS Form 1127 (extension of time for payment); IRS Form 9465 (installment agreements). Penalties may be imposed for late filing and for late payment of tax. IRC § 6651(a)(1)-(2).

The IRS has various methods for determining which tax returns are audited, and there are different ways in which the IRS conducts audits. At the conclusion of an audit, the examiner may propose adjustments to the taxpayer's liability, in which case the taxpayer must decide whether to agree with or contest the proposed adjustments. If the taxpayer agrees with, or reaches a mutually acceptable agreement with the examiner, the taxpayer generally signs Form 870 and pays the deficiency. If, however, the taxpayer does not agree with the examiner, the IRS will issue a preliminary notice of deficiency (30-day letter), which permits the taxpayer to file a written protest and request IRS appeals consideration. If a taxpayer and the appeals division reach a mutually acceptable settlement, they generally memorialize that settlement in Form 870-AD. If they cannot reach an agreement, the IRS issues a notice of deficiency (90-day letter) under section 6212. Once the IRS issues the notice of deficiency, the taxpayer's recourse is to pay the tax or litigate the matter.

A taxpayer has choices regarding the forum in which to litigate. The taxpayer may first pay the asserted deficiency and commence a refund action in either the U.S. District Court or the U.S. Claims Court. Alternatively, the taxpayer may file a petition with the Tax Court for a redetermination of the proposed deficiency. IRC § 6213. There are several factors that should be considered in selecting the proper forum, including: (1) the prior precedential decisions of the three trial courts and their relevant appellate courts; (2) whether the taxpayer wants a jury trial, which is available only in the district court; (3) the expertise of the Tax Court judges in deciding tax matters; and (4) the level of discovery required in each trial court, with discovery in Tax Court being much less extensive than in district court.

The IRS cannot collect a tax without first "assessing" it, a term used to describe the IRS's formal recording of a tax liability. IRC § 6203. As a general rule, the IRS must assess tax within three years of when the return was filed. IRC § 6501(a). The statute of limitations is six years in some cases (i.e., substantial omission of items from gross income), and is unlimited if the taxpayer files no return, a false return, or a fraudulent return. IRC § 6501(c)(1)-(3), (e)(1)(A). Within sixty days of tax assessment, the IRS issues a notice and demand for payment, which opens the door to collection remedies provided in the Code. IRC § 6303. If a taxpayer fails to pay the assessed amount after a notice and demand for payment, the federal tax lien attaches to the taxpayer's property. IRC § 6321. With some exceptions, the federal tax lien is automatically perfected and is valid against the taxpayer and certain other parties.

A federal tax lien does not automatically result in the collection of a tax liability. The IRS must enforce the lien through an appropriate collection device (e.g., an administrative collection remedy or a judicial avenue). One device is the federal tax levy, which requires a third party to pay to the IRS amounts that he or she owes to the taxpayer. IRC §§ 6331(a), (e); 6343. Certain property is exempt from levy. IRC § 6334(a), (d), (e). Under its levy authority, the IRS can also seize property held by the taxpayer or a third party. IRC § 6331(b).

Tax lawyers are subject to special ethical standards when advising a client with respect to a tax return position or when giving written tax advice and opinions. *See* Treasury Circular 230.

Primary Authority

Code: §§ 6001; 6011; 6072(a)-(b); 6081(a)-(b); 6151; 6161; 6201; 6203; 6212; 6213; 6303; 6321; 6322; 6323; 6330; 6331; 6501(a), (c)(1)-(3), (e)(1)(A); 6502; 6503; 6851; 6861; 7429; 7430; 7502; 7602(a)(1). Skim §§ 6662(b)(6) & 7701(o).

Regulations: None.

Cases: The Colony, Inc. v. Commissioner, 357 U.S. 28 (1958).

Rulings: Circular 230, 10.34, 10.35, 10.37.

Problems

42.1. Leona, a single individual who uses the cash method and calendar year, is a full-time tax associate at a law firm. Leona also writes a daily Internet blog on tax law. To her surprise, she collected in Year 1 about $50,000 through an on-line tip jar administered by Paypal, for which she sends donors a "thank you" email.

(a) Assume Leona cannot file her Year 1 tax return by April 15, Year 2. What should she do?

Section 6081(a) authorizes the Service to "grant a reasonable extension of time for filing any return." For an automatic six-month extension, Leona should file Form 4868 on or before the due date of the return. Form 4868 requires Leona to properly estimate her tax liability for the year. The extension of time to file is not an extension of time to pay. Treas. Reg. § 1.6081-1(a).

> **(b) Assume Leona filed her Year 1 tax return on April 15, Year 2, but she did not report the $50,000 based on her belief that the amounts were "gifts" excludable from gross income under section 102. When is the last day the IRS may assess additional tax with respect to the Year 1 return?**

The IRS must assess additional tax within three years from the later of (1) the return's due date or (2) the return's filing date. Assuming Leona filed her Year 1 return on or before April 15, Year 2, the Service would have until April 15, Year 5.

Note: The statute of limitations on assessment is generally three years. Under section 6501(e), if the return reflects a substantial omission of items (i.e., an omission of an amount in excess of 25% of the amount stated in the return), a six-year statute of limitations applies. The Service might attempt to assert that the six-year statute of limitation applies to Leona's return. *See The Colony, Inc. v. Commissioner* (holding that the six-year statute of limitation does not apply unless *an entire item* was omitted). Leona omitted the tip from her return. She should be worried.

> **(c) Assume Leona filed her Year 1 tax return on April 15, Year 2, but she did not report the $50,000 in gross income. In Year 3, the IRS audited Leona's Year 1 return. At the conclusion of the examination, the IRS issued a 30-day letter, which contained the proposed adjustment (inclusion of the $50,000 as "tip" income) and recomputation of her tax liability showing a proposed deficiency in tax. What are Leona's options?**

Leona will have 30 days from the date of the 30-day letter to tell the IRS whether she will accept or appeal the proposed adjustment. Essentially, Leona can appeal to a local Appeals Office for an informal appeals conference. Most differences are settled at this level. *See* IRS Publication 556, Examination of Returns, Appeal Rights, and Claims for Refund (Rev. Sept. 2013).

> **(d) Same as (c). Assume that Leona failed to respond to the 30-day letter, and the IRS issued a statutory notice of deficiency (90-day letter). What are Leona's options?**

Leona could respond to the notice of deficiency by signing a Form 870 (waiving restrictions on assessment). If Leona wishes to litigate, she will have 90 days from the date of the notice to file a petition with the Tax Court. Alternatively, she could pay the deficiency, claim a refund, and then file a timely suit in a refund court (district court or claims court).

Leona can elect to have her case treated as a small tax case ("S" case) if the amount of the deficiency (including penalties but excluding interest) placed in dispute does not exceed $50,000. IRC § 7463.

A timely notice of deficiency is a legal prerequisite for assessment, and assessment is a legal prerequisite for collection. Here, once the IRS mails Leona a notice of deficiency, the IRS is prohibited from assessing tax during the 90 day period Leona has to file a Tax Court petition, and if Leona files a petition, until the decision of the Tax Court becomes final. IRC § 6213(a). The statute of limitations on assessment is tolled during this period (plus an additional 60 days). IRC § 6501.

(e) **Same as (d). Assume Leona has decided to litigate the issue. What are some factors she should consider in choosing whether to litigate in the Tax Court, District Court, or the Claims Court?**

Several factors are mentioned in the Overview above: (1) the prior precedential decisions of the three trial courts and their relevant appellate courts; (2) whether Leona wants a jury trial, which is available only in the district court; (3) the expertise of the Tax Court judges in deciding tax matters; and (4) the level of discovery required in each trial court, with discovery in Tax Court being much less extensive than in district court.

(f) **Same as (e). Assume that Leona litigated in Tax Court and lost (the decision became final on May 15, Year 7). Leona subsequently ignored the IRS notice and demand for payment. Can the IRS levy on Leona's wages to collect the tax due? Can the IRS barge into her house and take her clothing, jewelry, and other personal effects?**

The IRS may impose a levy on Leona's wages. IRC § 6331(a), (e), (h). A minimum amount of wages (based in part on the number of Leona's dependents) is exempt from levy. Wages that must be paid under a child support order are also exempt from levy. IRC § 6334(d). In sum, the employer must withhold the non-exempt portion of Leona's wages and remit the amount directly to the IRS until the liability is satisfied in full.

If Leona is in possession of property subject to levy, she must surrender the property to the IRS on demand. IRC § 6332(a). If she does not voluntarily surrender property subject to levy, the IRS can seize such property. *But see* IRC § 6335 (imposing certain restrictions on seizure of property); Form 2433 "Notice of Seizure." Note, however, that items exempt from levy include ordinary clothing and certain household and personal effects. Accordingly, the IRS cannot take these items. [Note also there are significant restrictions on the IRS's ability to seize Leona's personal residence. IRC § 6334(a) (requiring prior written approval by a federal district court); 6334(a)(13) (requiring the deficiency to be greater than $5,000).]

42.2. **You have been hired by Al Capone to provide an opinion letter—written tax advice about the tax treatment of a transaction. Al recently caught a record-breaking ball at a Major League Baseball game, and would like to take the tax return position that the value of the ball is not included in gross income in the year he caught it.**

(a) **Assuming you agree to provide the tax opinion letter, what level of assurance should you provide?**

Tax law has developed levels of confidence in reporting return positions. The percentages below project the chances for success if challenged by the IRS:

"non-frivolous" standard: approximately 10% chance of winning;

"reasonable basis" standard: significantly higher than the "non-frivolous" standard and lower than the "realistic probability of success" standard; approximately 20 to 25% or better chance of winning;

"realistic possibility of success" standard: approximately 33 1/3% or better chance of winning if challenged by the IRS;

"substantial authority" standard: greater than a "realistic possibility of success" standard and lower than a "more likely than not" standard; about 35 to 40% probability of success;

"more likely than not" standard: greater than 50% chance of success if challenged by the IRS; this is the highest level of accuracy required to avoid the accuracy related penalties;

"should" standard: 70 to 80% chance of success if challenged by the IRS; and

"will" standard: generally a 95% or greater chance of winning, the highest level of assurance.

The tax consequences of catching a record-breaking baseball are far from settled. While there are arguments for inclusion, there are also several arguments for exclusion: It could be argued for example, that Al's ball is a form of imputed income or a gift, both of which are excluded from gross income. It could also be argued that Al purchased the ball when he purchased the ticket, or that income has not been realized until the ball is sold for cash and value is established.

(b) **Might Al be subject to tax penalties if he excludes the ball from income, but the IRS later determines it was taxable? If so, should you inform Al of the potential penalties? Is there anything that Al can do to avoid such penalties?**

Yes, Al could be subject to penalties and should be informed of them. Your tax opinion letter may help Al get out of certain penalties if it sets forth a "reasonable basis" for your tax return position and the position is disclosed on the return. The highest level of penalty protection, however, would come if your opinion's position met the "more likely than not," or higher, standard.

APPENDIX — TAX TABLES

EXCERPT FROM REVENUE PROCEDURE 2015-53
TAX RATE TABLES FOR THE 2016 TAX YEAR

SECTION 3. 2016 ADJUSTED ITEMS

.01 Tax Rate Tables. For taxable years beginning in 2016, the tax rate tables under

§ 1 are as follows:

TABLE 1 - Section 1(a) - Married Individuals Filing Joint Returns and Surviving Spouses

If Taxable Income Is:	The Tax Is:
Not over $18,550	10% of the taxable income
Over $18,550 but not over $75,300	$1,855 plus 15% of the excess over $18,550
Over $75,300 but not over $151,900	$10,367.50 plus 25% of the excess over $75,300
Over $151,900 but not over $231,450	$29,517.50 plus 28% of the excess over $151,900
Over $231,450 but not over $413,350	$51,791.50 plus 33% of the excess over $231,450
Over $413,350 but not over $466,950	$111,818.50 plus 35% of the excess over $413,350
Over $466,950	$130,578.50 plus 39.6% of the excess over $466,950

TABLE 2 - Section 1(b) – Heads of Households

If Taxable Income Is:	The Tax Is:
Not over $13,250	10% of the taxable income
Over $13,250 but not over $50,400	$1,325 plus 15% of the excess over $13,250
Over $50,400 but not over $130,150	$6,897.50 plus 25% of the excess over $50,400
Over $130,150 but not over $210,800	$26,835 plus 28% of the excess over $130,150
Over $210,800 but not over $413,350	$49,417 plus 33% of the excess over $210,800
Over $413,350 not over $441,000	$116,258.50 plus 35% of the excess over $413,350
Over $441,000	$125,936 plus 39.6% of the excess over $441,000

TABLE 3 - Section 1(c) – Unmarried Individuals (other than Surviving Spouses and Heads of Households)

If Taxable Income Is:	The Tax Is:
Not over $9,275	10% of the taxable income
Over $9,275 but not over $37,650	$927.50 plus 15% of the excess over $9,275
Over $37,650 but not over $91,150	$5,183.75 plus 25% of the excess over $37,650
Over $91,150 but not over $190,150	$18,558.75 plus 28% of the excess over $91,150
Over $190,150 but not over $413,350	$46,278.75 plus 33% of the excess over $190,150
Over $413,350 not over $415,050	$119,934.75 plus 35% of the excess over $413,350
Over $415,050	$120,529.75 plus 39.6% of the excess over $415,050

TABLE 4 - Section 1(d) – Married Individuals Filing Separate Returns

If Taxable Income Is:	The Tax Is:
Not over $9,275	10% of the taxable income
Over $9,275 but not over $37,650	$927.50 plus 15% of the excess over $9,275
Over $37,650 but not over $75,950	$5,183.75 plus 25% of the excess over $37,650
Over $75,950 but not over $115,725	$14,758.75 plus 28% of the excess over $75,950
Over $115,725 but not over $206,675	$25,895.75 plus 33% of the excess over $115,725
Over $206,675 not over $233,475	$55,909.25 plus 35% of the excess over $206,675
Over $233,475	$65,289.25 plus 39.6% of the excess over $233,475

TABLE 5 - Section 1(e) – Estates and Trusts

If Taxable Income Is:	The Tax Is:
Not over $2,550	15% of the taxable income
Over $2,550 but not over $5,950	$382.50 plus 25% of the excess over $2,550
Over $5,950 but not over $9,050	$1,232.50 plus 28% of the excess over $5,950
Over $9,050 but not over $12,400	$2,100.50 plus 33% of the excess over $9,050
Over $12,400	$3,206 plus 39.6% of the excess over $12,400

TABLE OF INTERNAL REVENUE CODE SECTIONS

ALL REFERENCES ARE TO PROBLEMS IN THE BOOK

Legislative History

TABLE OF TREASURY REGULATIONS

ALL REFERENCES ARE TO PROBLEMS IN THE BOOK

TABLE OF CASES

ALL REFERENCES ARE TO PROBLEMS IN THE BOOK

TABLE OF ADMINISTRATIVE PRONOUNCEMENTS

ALL REFERENCES ARE TO PROBLEMS IN THE BOOK

Announcements/Notices
2002-18, 2.2, 6.3
2012-75, 2.1

Revenue Rulings
54-147, 7.2
55-109, 7.2
58-275, 30.2
60-226, 29.1
60-358, 28.4
64-56, 19.2, 38.1
64-237, 25.1, 25.2, 25.3
65-254, 2.3
66-7, 38.1, 39.1
67-136, 29.2
68-232, 9.2
69-484, 28.1
69-154, 34.3
69-357, 38.1
69-487, 19.1
70-498, 3.2
71-564, 19.2
73-20, 28.1
74-581, 30.1
75-271, 2.1
75-432, 7.2
76-391, 25.2
79-24, 2.1, 16.1
79-121, 30.1
79-285, 28.4
79-371, 26.1
80-248, 36.1
81-163, 20.1
84-176, 5.1
85-164, 38.1
85-186, 29.2

87-106, 11.3
87-98, 4.3
89-23, 8.1
92-80, 8.1, 28.1
2003-57, 11.4
2008-34, 33.2
2010-25, 11.1

Revenue Procedures
87-57, 9.3
97-35, 8.1, 28.1
99-7, 7.2
1013-15, 16.3
2000-50, 8.1
2002-9, 8.1, 28.1
2002-22, 32.1
2008-16, 24.1, 24.2
2015-53, 15.2, 16.3, 21.1

Private Letter Rulings
200041022, 34.1, 34.2
8143029, 21.3
8247062, 21.3

Technical Advice Memorandums/CCAs
200039037, 5.2
200125019, 28.1
200809001, 34.2
201045023, 34.2
9643003, 8.2

IRS Publications
I.R.S. Publication No. 17, 16.2
I.R.S. Publication No. 533, 37.1
I.R.S. Publication No. 556, 42.1

TOPIC INDEX